"I'm excited by this book because the way the many authors combine EMDR with IFS addresses [my concerns about EMDR being a protocol rather than a therapy] nicely and suggests ways that the combination can benefit IFS therapists as well—e.g., when they get stuck or want to access more Self."

Richard Schwartz, PhD, *founder of the Internal Family Systems model, and author of* No Bad Parts

"Several years ago, Richard Schwartz and Francine Shapiro each gave us paradigm-shifting approaches for helping people with desperate and complicated sources of dysfunction and unhappiness. This book shows clearly how these two powerful approaches are not only highly compatible, but in fact, can each add depth to the effectiveness of the other. I recommend it both for the new and experienced EMDR or IFS therapist."

Jim Knipe, PhD, *author of* EMDR Toolbox: Theory and Treatment of Complex PTSD and Dissociation

"An innovative and integrative guide for any EMDR therapist seeking to incorporate IFS therapy into the eight phases of treatment. Featuring insights from an array of talented thought leaders, this book is packed with practical interventions and invaluable knowledge. A must-read for clinicians looking to deepen their practice."

Rebecca Kase, LCSW, RYT, *author of* Polyvagal-Informed EMDR: A Neuro-Informed Approach to Healing

IFS-Informed EMDR

IFS-Informed EMDR makes the case that the integration of these two influential therapy models creates something greater than the sum of its parts. It's a book that can be used as a resource for therapeutic educational and training programs and as a supplement for people already familiar with at least one of these models.

Each chapter offers wisdom and practical guidance that will benefit anyone interested in learning the theoretical framework and practical applications of uniting EMDR and IFS for trauma healing.

David Polidi, LSCW, MEd, is the host of the *Empowered Through Compassion* podcast and has a private practice in Massachusetts with his wife Heather. He has been trained in the Syzygy Model of IFS-Informed EMDR (Level 3) and has been a guide for Syzygy trainings. He has also been trained in IFS (Level 2), has gone through the advanced training of IFIO (Intimacy from the Inside Out), and is an EMDR consultant in training through EMDRIA.

IFS-Informed EMDR

Creative and Collaborative
Approaches

Edited by David Polidi

R Routledge
Taylor & Francis Group

NEW YORK AND LONDON

Designed cover image: Cover image courtesy of Trevor D. Photography

First published 2026
by Routledge
605 Third Avenue, New York, NY 10158

and by Routledge
4 Park Square, Milton Park, Abingdon, Oxon, OX14 4RN

Routledge is an imprint of the Taylor & Francis Group, an informa business

ISBN: 978-1-032-89171-2 (hbk)
ISBN: 978-1-032-89167-5 (pbk)
ISBN: 978-1-003-54155-4 (ebk)

DOI: 10.4324/9781003541554

Typeset in Times New Roman
by SPi Technologies India Pvt Ltd (Straive)

David is very grateful for his loving family—his wife Heather, his daughter Kaeley, and his furry buddies Nala and Fozzy

Contents

Contributors

David Archer, PSW, MFT, MSW, is a Black Jamaican African-Canadian father and husband from Montreal, Canada (Tiohtià:ke). He is also a registered social worker, couple and family therapist, anti-racist psychotherapist, and EMDRIA-Certified Approved Consultant. With over 15 years of experience, he specializes in treating complex PTSD and complex racial trauma using Afrocentric principles and memory reconsolidation-based approaches. David is the recipient of the Emerging Leader Award from EMDRIA. He is the developer of Rhythm and Processing (RAP) Strategies, an integrative therapeutic approach for treating complex PTSD and racial trauma. David is the author of five books relating to anti-racist psychotherapy, mindfulness, complex trauma treatment, and revolutionary healing methods. He is a keynote speaker and regular conference presenter who offers workshops to help therapists integrate anti-racist principles into their practice and to teach people of all backgrounds to recognize their awesomeness. Learn more about David on his website: https://www.archertherapy.com.

Zandra Bamford, BSc, MSc, DClinPSY, works as a Consultant Clinical Psychologist with 20 years of specializing in the field of complex trauma. Zandra is an Approved IFS Clinical Consultant and a Certified IFS Therapist, trained in EMDR and a wealth of other psychological modalities. She has spent most of her career leading psychology services within the UK National Health Service and is a respected trainer, speaker, and program developer. Zandra founded Therapy North West to offer psychological services, IFS retreats, trainings, therapy programs, and consultation. Find out more about Therapy North West and the offerings here: www.therapynorthwest.org.

Bethany Barta, LCSW, CAS, ACS, is a Licensed Clinical Social Worker and Certified EMDR Consultant, and is certified in IFS and Level 2 trained in IFIO. She has been working in the mental health field specializing in trauma, addictive behaviors, and women's issues since 1999. She has extensive experience supervising, training, and consulting on topics related to trauma-informed care, trauma-specific treatment related to IFS and EMDR, psycho-spiritual integration and energetics, and nature-based interventions. She enjoys leading workshops and retreats in the Rocky Mountains and is the founder and director of Insight Counseling and Wellness Center and Insight Consultation and Training. Find out more about Bethany on her websites: www.insightconsultationandtraining. com and www.insightcounselingcenter.com.

Claire van den Bosch holds bachelor's and master's degrees from Oxford University in Psychology, Philosophy, and Physiology, as well as a postgraduate diploma in integrative psychotherapy with a transpersonal specialism. She went on to train in EMDR, Attachment-Informed EMDR, and then all three levels of IFS. Herself in addiction recovery, she specializes in treating addiction and the relational trauma driving most addictive processes. As well as working with her long-term clients, Claire teaches the second year of a postgraduate diploma program for trainee therapists, specializing in teaching Gestalt, Transactional Analysis, and theories of addiction. She also delivers introductory IFS training to EMDR therapists learning to integrate the two models. Claire is the cofounder of IFS Peers, an international online peer support addiction and trauma recovery community. Find out more about Claire on her website: www.atimetoheal.london

Bridger Falkenstien, PhD, MS, NCC, LPC, is the creative director and co-owner of Beyond Healing. He is an EMDR Consultant in Training through EMDRIA. Bridger is an Adjunct Professor and a published author. He also serves as a host, producer, and original music composer for multiple podcasts at Beyond Healing, including the popular EMDR podcast *Notice That*. Find out more about Beyond Healing on their website: https://connectbeyondhealing.com. You can also find out more about Bridger on his website: www.bridgerfalkenstien.com.

Janina Fisher, PhD, is a Licensed Clinical Psychologist and a former instructor at Harvard Medical School. An international expert on the treatment of trauma, she is an Executive Board member of the Trauma Research Foundation and a Patron of the John Bowlby Centre. Dr. Fisher is the author of *Healing the Fragmented Selves of Trauma Survivors: Overcoming Self-Alienation* (2017), *Transforming the Living Legacy of Trauma: A Workbook for Survivors and Therapists* (2021), and *The Living Legacy Instructional Flip Chart* (2022). She is best known for her work on integrating mindfulness-based and somatic interventions into trauma treatment. Her treatment model, Trauma-Informed Stabilization Treatment (TIST), is now being taught around the world. More information can be found on her website: www.janinafisher.com.

Bruce Hersey, LCSW, is perhaps one of the most recognized experts in teaching the integration of EMDR and IFS. Together with Michelle Richardson he created the Syzygy Institute, which offers IIE training and certification in IIE. Bruce is an Approved Consultant in EMDR and an IFS Approved Clinical Consultant offering individual and group IFS and IIE consultation. He has led numerous introductory and specialized IFS workshops and presented at the IFS International Conference. He has presented his approach to IFS-EMDR integration at the EMDRIA, EMDR UK Association, EMDR Australia Association (EMDRAA) conferences and before other international audiences. Find out more about his institute at: www.syzygyinstitute.com and more about Bruce on his websites: www. brucehersey.com and www.emdrifs.com.

Peggy Kolodny, MA, ATR-BC, LCPAT, is a licensed, board-certified and registered art psychotherapist trained in EMDR and in IFS (Level 2). Founder of the Art Therapy Collective of Owings Mills, Maryland, she has specialized in trauma treatment since 1982. Peggy is current adjunct faculty with the graduate Art Therapy departments of George Washington University and Florida State University, where she teaches in their specialized trauma tracks, as well as faculty for various professional training institutes. Recent past chair of the Creative Arts Therapies Special Interest Group of The International Society on the Study of Trauma and Dissociation, she is currently Co-Chair of the EMDR Special Interest Group (2025–2027). Recent publications include a chapter on "The Interweave of IFS, EMDR, and Art Therapy" coauthored with Salicia Mazero (Elizabeth Davis et al., eds., *EMDR and Creative Arts Therapies*, Routledge, 2023) (and several chapters on the neuroscience of trauma, addictions, and art therapy (in Patricia Quinn, ed., *Art Therapy in the Treatment of Addiction and Trauma*, Jessica Kingsley Publishers, 2021).

Laura Kosak, LMFT, is a Licensed Marriage and Family Therapist who weaves EMDR, IFS, energy-healing techniques, and spirituality into her professional practice. Her integrated approach is exemplified by her Crossliminal Passage Protocol™, as highlighted in her chapter contribution; the Protocol is available to therapists upon request. Both a therapist and a transformational coach, Laura specializes in a spiritually anchored, IFS-informed EMDR approach to intensive healing work and holistic retreats. Laura is certified in EMDR and formally trained in IFS. Learn more about Laura and her approach through her websites: www. TheCrossliminalWay.com and www.KnowThyselfCounseling.com.

Beau Laviolette, LCSW, is a Licensed Clinical Social Worker and a dedicated therapist specializing in the integration of IFS and EMDR. Based in Baton Rouge, Louisiana, Beau lives with his wife and their two boys.

As a U.S. Marine Veteran, he brings a unique perspective to his work, drawing on both his military background and extensive experience in mental health to help clients navigate trauma, grief, and emotional healing. In addition to his therapeutic practice, Beau is also a respected trainer, offering seminars and workshops to help other clinicians master the art of combining IFS and EMDR for transformative outcomes. Find out more about Beau on his website: www.therapyteacher.com and find recorded courses from Beau on this website: www.ifsemdr.com.

Annabel McGoldrick, PhD, MA, Diploma in Transpersonal Psychology, is a Certified EMDR Consultant in the UK and Australia and a Level 2-trained IFS practitioner. Annabel has developed a 16-week IFS-informed EMDR training course, as well as the shorter version she runs with the EMDR Learning Community. She frequently publishes articles on IFS-informed EMDR and is a regular podcast guest. With almost 25 years' psychotherapy experience, she has a background in addiction recovery and family therapy. Annabel sees private clients for IFS-Informed EMDR and supervision from her base in Australia. Her debut novel, *Mind Over Murder*, is published by Next Chapter. A former TV and radio reporter, Annabel won the Luxembourg Peace Prize in 2017 for her work in developing the theory and practice of peace journalism. Find out more on Annabel's website www.emdrinsight.com.

Jenn Pagone, LCPC, has a private practice, Pagone Psychological Services, PLLC, and is the Founder of Whispering White Horse Stables, a therapeutic horse ranch located in Marengo, IL. Jenn is the creator of Equid-Nexus®, an IFS-Informed EMDR with Equine Engagement Facilitation Model. She has been in the equine-assisted services field since 2012 and is dual advanced certified as a mental health and equine professional with the Natural Lifemanship Institute, where she served as a trainer from 2020 to 2025. Jenn is also a trainer for the IFS Institute and the Syzygy Institute and is an EMDRIA-approved consultant. For almost 20 years, she has specialized in treating women with complex relational trauma, somatic disorders, eating disorders, cancer, and infertility. Jenn has a background in teaching clinical psychology as an adjunct professor, is a conference presenter and clinical consultant, and offers professional workshops and training in the Equid-Nexus® model and Self-Led Horsemanship™ Clinics online and in person throughout the States and in Australia. She enjoys life with her husband, nine horses, two goats, three dogs, and many chickens and cats. Find more information and contact Jenn on her websites: http://www.equid-nexus.com

https://www.equidnexuslearningcommons.com/l/products https://www.pagonepsychologicalservices.com.

Athena Phillips, LCSW, is a certified EMDR therapist and trained in IFS. She is also certified in Critical Incident Stress Debriefing (CISD). Athena offers training and consultation for providers in dissociation and complex trauma. She has developed and presented the Multicultural Training (MCT) approach internationally. Athena is the founder of the Integrative Trauma Treatment Center, which is an outpatient mental health clinic that provides care for trauma and dissociative disorders. She is also the Founder of the Orenda Project, which works to expand informed support to survivors of trauma internationally. Find out more about the Integrative Trauma Treatment Center here: www.traumacenternw.com and more about the Orenda Project on its website: www.theorendaproject.org.

David Polidi, LICSW, Med, is a Licensed Independent Clinical Social Worker and a certified EMDR Consultant in Training, and has also been trained in IFS. He has been working with children and families since 2000. He has been in private practice for the past five years and has developed and facilitated the online couple's workshop, "Deepen the Conversation." David has the honor of speaking with innovators in the field of psychology on his podcast *Empowered Through Compassion*. This podcast seeks to integrate EMDR and IFS, and explores the natural convergence of these models with other trauma-healing modalities. Find out more about David on his website: www.empoweredthroughcompassion.com.

Michelle Richardson, LCSW, is an EMDRIA-approved consultant, IFS-certified therapist, and IFS-Informed EMDR trainer. Together with Bruce Hersey, she cofounded the Syzygy Institute, a continuing education company that provides training and certification in Hersey's IFS-Informed EMDR integration. Michelle is also the cofounder and CEO of an EMDR-focused group practice in southern New Jersey, Mindful Soul Center for Wellbeing. There, she specializes in the treatment of complex trauma, dissociation, and attachment wounding. As a seasoned clinical supervisor and consultant, Michelle has a passion for helping therapists wade through the murky and complex waters of psychotherapy toward clarity, confidence, and calm. Find out more about Michelle at www.mindfulsoulwellbeing.com and www.syzygyinstitute.com.

Nancy Simons, LMHC, is an EMDR trainer with EMDR Consulting and an IFS-Informed EMDR Lead Trainer with the Syzygy Institute. Nancy also offers her own trainings on self-compassion in healing trauma. Her Self-Compassion Container protocol appears in *EMDR and Sexual Health: A Clinician's Guide* (edited by Stephanie Baird, 2021) and *Advanced Sandtray Therapy: Digging Deeper into Clinical Practice* (edited by Linda E. Homeyer and Marshall N. Lyles, 2022). Nancy supervises a multilingual, multicultural staff of clinicians providing therapeutic services to the refugee community of Western MA, as well as maintaining a private practice in Amherst, MA. Nancy is available for individual and group consultation on EMDR and IFS-Informed EMDR and for trainings on integrating self-compassion with EMDR and IFS. For more information, please visit www.nancysimons.com.

Michelli Simpson, MS, LPC, NCC, CDVS-I, BC-TMH, is a Brazilian Black Latina mother, grandmother, educator, mental health therapist, certified EMDR-approved consultant, and IFS Level-3 therapist with IFIO training. She specializes in working with BIPOC individuals, couples, and groups, integrating the power of EMDR with the compassionate framework of IFS to help clients heal from trauma and navigate identity issues. As one of the first therapists to offer EMDR online, Michelli is passionate about creating a safe and inclusive space for healing. She encourages colleagues to critically examine their biases, broaden their understanding of diverse perspectives, and incorporate cultural and racial responsiveness practices into their therapeutic work to address systemic issues in our field and empower marginalized voices. Learn more about Michelli and her approach at www.spirosperopllc.com.

Tina Elleman Taylor, LCSW, LMFT, is a therapist practicing in Louisville, KY. She is a Licensed Clinical Social Worker and a Licensed Marriage and Family Therapist. She is an IFS (Level 3) certified therapist and consultant. She is also an IFS-Informed EMDR therapist and consultant. She is a lead trainer for IFS-Informed EMDR with the Syzygy Institute. Her specializations include chronic illness and chronic pain, dissociation, complex trauma, religious trauma, and more. You can check out her website at: www.newhopecounselingsite.com.

Patricia Bianca Torres, MA, LMFT, is an approved EMDRIA consultant specializing in Complex PTSD (CPTSD), preverbal trauma, insecure attachment, and dissociative disorders. She published her article, "Reducing the Cost of Trauma: Indirect Trauma Exposure on Mental Health Providers" (Torres et al., 2022) in the *Journal of EMDR Practice and Research* vol. 17, issue 1). As a proponent for parts work, she is Level-1 trained in IFS, and incorporates parts work and EMDR therapy in the intensive model. She enjoys providing EMDR resources in her EMDR therapy *Cheat Sheet Booklet*. More information on her upcoming groups and events can be found on her website: www.emdrempowered.com.

Joanne H. Twombly, LICSW, is a Licensed Independent Clinical Social Worker with over 30 years of experience working with Complex PTSD and dissociative disorders. She is a certified EMDR consultant and an IFS-certified therapist. Joanne is a Trauma and Recovery Humanitarian Assistance Program Facilitator and a clinical hypnosis consultant. Joanne is the past president of the New England Society for the Study of Trauma and Dissociation. She has been honored by the International Society for the Study of Trauma and Dissociation (ISSTD) with a Distinguished Achievement Award. She is also an ISSTD Fellow. Joanne has recently published an essential book titled *Trauma and Dissociation Informed Internal Family Systems: How to Successfully Treat Complex PTSD, and Dissociative Disorders*. Find out more about Joanne on her website: www.joannetwombly.net.

Elizabeth Venart, MEd, NCC, LPC, is a Licensed Professional Counselor, an IFSI-approved Clinical Consultant, an EMDRIA-approved EMDR Consultant, and an IFS-Informed EMDR Consultant and Trainer. Originally trained in EMDR Therapy in 2000, Elizabeth began integrating IFS into her work after attending Bruce Hersey's workshop on the "IFS Interweave" in 2012. She has been a Lead Trainer with the Syzygy Institute since 2022, training therapists in IFS–EMDR Integration. Her therapy practice focuses on IFS-Informed EMDR Intensives, supporting highly sensitive persons in transforming trauma and reclaiming self-trust. In 2008, she founded The Resiliency Center of Greater Philadelphia as a community where therapists could thrive together. She offers consultation groups, trainings, and retreats for therapists — and seeks to inspire resiliency, healing, and joy. Learn more about Elizabeth on her website at: https://elizabethvenart.com/.

Crystal Whitlow, LCSW, is a Licensed Clinical Social Worker in private practice in South Bend, Indiana. Crystal is an Approved Consultant and Trainer in EMDR with Roy Kiessling's EMDR Consulting. In 2017, she developed a two-day EMDR advanced training workshop titled "Dealing with Avoidance in EMDR Therapy: Blocking Beliefs, Defenses, and Getting Unstuck," based on Jim Knipe's EMDR Toolbox. Crystal is passionate about integrating IFS with EMDR and is an IFS-Certified Therapist through the IFS Institute. She teaches IFS-Informed EMDR with the Syzygy Institute, founded by Bruce Hersey and Michelle Richardson. You can find out more about Crystal on her website: www.crystalwhitlow.com.

Acknowledgments

This book has been a labor of love—I could not have accomplished it on my own. I am so grateful to my wife, Heather, and daughter Kaeley, who put up with all the late-night/early-morning hours of work. Thank you, Jane Gerhard, who has been with me through the beginning to set this project into the stratosphere. I am so grateful to Travor D. Photography, who gave me his lovely abstract photo of a rock under water to put on the cover of this book. Thank you for the support of my wise father-in-law, who picked this photo and said, "It's a perfect photo for a book on trauma!" I am so grateful for everyone who has been able to read this work and offer feedback. Thank you, to the Syzygy Institute—the founders and trainers who are all in this book, and all my fellow Guides who help teach the Syzygy model and bring it out into the world. Thank you to the incredible authors who have honored me, and collaborated with me throughout this process. Thank you, Gary Whited and Sabine Boots, for writing/helping choose the perfect poem to open this book with, and for all the poets who have graciously given permission to use their amazing work. Thank you, Francine Shapiro and Richard Schwartz, for the incredible models you both brought into the world. I have heard Dr. Schwartz say (and I can't agree more) that we learn the most from our clients. Thank you to all of my clients who have welcomed me on their sacred healing journeys. And a huge bow of gratitude to all of the people who have opened this book, and are curious to find out more about the quickly growing field of IFS-Informed EMDR. This book is for therapists and their clients (who want to take a deeper dive into the models), so that more healing and love can be brought into the world, one sacred healing moment at a time. I am so honored to be sharing this special collaboration with you.

In This Body

There are rooms
that close their doors.
Years pass

and a breeze moves through.
Maybe it was the look of that
man
with red hair and heavy hands,

or the woman crossing the street
with the soft fingers
and far away stare.

A door blows open slightly,
the hinges barely agree.
Behind that door

there's a small child
who wants you
to call him by name.
                    by Gary Whited

This Urge for Here

The sleeping dog by the stove,
the cardinal calling
in the maples out back,
that touch of wooden floor
on bare feet,
this taste of tea…

Oh urge grow deeper,
help me stay here.

So still now,
only the black tea steeping
into its darker self.
                    by Gary Whited

Introduction

David Polidi

Eye Movement Desensitization and Reprocessing (EMDR; Shapiro, 2017) and Internal Family Systems therapy (IFS; Schwartz & Sweezy, 2020) have been growing rapidly in the mental health world. As a Licensed Social Worker, I have found these two models to be game changers for my clients, and for myself as well. When combining these two models, the results have been profound. In the pages that follow, some incredible leaders from the EMDR and IFS community and I hope to share some of the underlying mechanisms behind the two models, and then to take you on a journey to show you how we combine the models and effectively use creative integrations with our clients.

You are invited to travel with us through the wonderful IFS-Informed EMDR[1] universe. I want to share with you the foundation of my understanding of IIE, which has grown out of my conversations with multiple people. I have a huge amount of appreciation for the authors in this book, each of whom have helped to shape my understanding of how these two models can be integrated.

Who This Book Is Intended For

This book is for people interested in EMDR and IFS, who seek to heal trauma within themselves or within their clients. We will present and demonstrate the alchemy of combining these two models, and we hope to inspire you on your journey. Please be advised that the invitations offered in this book are meant to be used by therapists with the proper training and supervision. In addition to being a licensed practitioner, therapists should have adequate EMDR training through an approved training program, and have attended at least an introductory workshop in IFS. If at all possible, attending a training offered by the IFS institute will be extremely worthwhile and valuable.

If you are a therapist, but not yet trained in EMDR and/or IFS, I hope this book can introduce you to some cutting-edge practices in our field right now, and might even inspire you to pursue training in one or more of these models. IIE has the very hopeful message: *Healing is possible. No matter how badly you (or the people you are working with) suffer from trauma, and no matter how hopeless your situation seems, you can heal. And the keys to unlock a meaningful and amazing life are already inside of you. This model, and therapy in general, can help you listen to your inner wisdom to find these keys and unlock this power.*

Each of these models provide us with more understanding of our inner worlds. In their own way, each model focuses on an often-overlooked cause of mental health diagnoses: trauma. Here is my working definition of trauma: *Trauma is an experience in time when you perceived your world to be unsafe, and you did not believe in your heart that you could be kept safe. You were alone and overwhelmed. Your body imprinted this feeling, and held onto it. Now, whenever you are reminded of this initial threat, your body travels back in time, and the original emotional memories are activated. This trauma is held in the cells of your body, keeping some element of this trauma's energy alive within you.*

A Map of the Book

IIE is a model that, similar to both EMDR and IFS, helps our clients reprocess and release their traumas, so that they are no longer holding onto this negative and stuck energy inside their bodies and minds (van der Kolk, 2014). The foundations of EMDR and IFS are provided in Chapters 1–3. Then, Chapter 4 recognizes ways that EMDR and IFS concepts benefit each other.

Chapters 5–8 share three innovative models: EDHI, the Syzygy Model, and TIST. Each one shows how EMDR can be integrated with IFS/parts work. I felt it was important to share different viewpoints, to illustrate some of the underlying truths that are consistent through different perspectives. These contributions help ground IIE into a theoretical context. As Bruce Hersey (personal communication, January 2, 2025) has said, "from the very beginning, I wanted to know why [IIE] works. All of IIE basically evolves from specific theoretical perspectives." Instead of moving back and forth between EMDR and IFS randomly during a therapy session, Bruce shared with me (and also shares in this book) how important and valuable it is to have a well-thought-through and organized way of integrating these two models.

As Judith Herman (1992) and Dan Siegel (2020) eloquently express, trauma is more than an individual experience. We are impacted by the larger cultural setting and the world we live in. Chapters 9–12 present frameworks that enhance the IIE model, and help illustrate how IIE can be understood within a larger social context. Chapter 9 explores how every interaction we have with our clients changes both us and them in profound, moment-to-moment ways. Chapter 10 eloquently speaks about the pervasiveness of systemic racism in our society, and how we can significantly increase the quality of our work by understanding the significant repercussions of this racism for everyone. Chapter 11 provides information on dissociation, a primary consideration when engaging in trauma work. We are then shown how Jungian roots and art can level up our work with our clients in Chapter 12. Chapter 13 brings us a meaningful and spiritual dimension we can weave into our practice.

Chapters 14–18 display ways that the authors have successfully implemented IIE with Complex PTSD (Chapter 14), physical pain (Chapter 15), and when working with military veterans (Chapter 16), Highly Sensitive People (Chapter 17), and those in female bodies (Chapter 18). Future work will hopefully show how many other populations of people can be successfully supported on their healing journeys with IIE.

The last chapters, Chapters 19–24, offer some extraordinary IIE tools and approaches that the authors have created and found extremely helpful in their work. Chapter 19 introduces some of Jim Knipe's wisdom into the IIE universe. A trailblazer in IIE, Joanne H. Twombly, is the author of Chapter 20. Together with the founder of IFS, Joanne (Twombly & Schwartz, 2008) wrote the first article connecting IFS and EMDR. In Chapter 20, Joanne shares an updated version of the "Fire Drill" (an IFS technique), and highlights the value of this popular intervention. Chapter 21 invites us to look deeper into therapists' parts that typically show up during therapy.

In Chapter 22 we are given a beautiful tool that externalizes parts and Self. Chapter 23 then shares a tool which brilliantly combines the EMDR container with the IFS concept of Self-energy. Chapter 24 introduces the Equid-Nexus ® Model, a pioneering way to bring equine therapy to IIE.

More to Explore

There is more to explore, and as future books on IIE become available, I hope that they will include the wisdom from diverse groups of people. If I had had more time and resources for this book, I would have loved to include the wisdom of how this model can be used with people from the LGBTQIA+ community, with neurodivergent clients, and with the elderly or children. Providing support to people with specific struggles (such as OCD, addictions, or concerns around food and body image) will be valuable to investigate through the lens of IIE.

Although there is so much more to explore in IIE, the ultimate message that will hopefully flow through the pages of this book is: *Everyone is able to heal. Though the answers are inside each one of us, the healing journey is not a solo journey and there are some profound ways to navigate it. This book shows one path, through many distinct and unique voices. The authors in this book have found IIE, EMDR, IFS, and parts work to be a profound map to use in navigating some of the uncharted places of our psyches. Parts of ourselves and our clients are desperately waiting to be healed, and we are thrilled and honored to be able to share with you some successful ways we have been able accomplished this.*

Note

1 There are different ways to refer to Internal Family Systems Informed EMDR (IFSiEMDR; IIE). For consistency, I will use IIE.

References

Herman, J. (1992). *Trauma and recovery: The aftermath of violence—from domestic abuse to political terror*. Basic Books.

Shapiro, F. (2017). *Eye movement desensitization and reprocessing (EMDR) therapy: Basic principles, protocols, and procedures* (3rd ed.). The Guilford Press.

Schwartz, R. C. (2021). *No bad parts: Healing trauma and restoring wholeness with the Internal Family Systems model*. Sounds True.

Schwartz, R. C., & Sweezy, M. (2020). *Internal family systems therapy* (2nd ed.). Guilford Press.

Siegel, D. J. (2020). *The developing mind*. The Guilford Press.

Twombly, J. H., & Schwartz, R. C. (2008). The integration of internal family systems model and EMDR. In C. Forgash & M. Copeley (Eds.), *Healing the heart of trauma and dissociation with EMDR and ego state therapy* (pp. 295–311). New York, NY: Springer Publishing.

Van der Kolk, B. A. (2014). *The body keeps the score: Brain, mind and body in the healing of trauma*. New York: Viking Press.

Part 1

Basics of EMDR and IFS

Two Transformative Healing Modalities

Chapter 1

Laying an EMDR Foundation

David Polidi

It all began with a walk in the park. Sometime back in 1987, Francine Shapiro was processing some disturbing thoughts and became aware that her eyes were moving back and forth. She found that disturbing memories were being processed, and the negative feelings associated with the thoughts were no longer upsetting. In her pivotal book, *Eye Movement Desensitization and Reprocessing (EMDR) Therapy: Basic Principles, Protocols, and Procedures*, Shapiro (2018) goes on to explain how she was able to replicate this phenomenon with friends and colleagues. This began her journey to prove through research and scientific data how this eye movement somehow held a key that could allow memory processing to take place.

At the time when Shapiro was constructing EMDR, there were other theories—and proven methods, such as exposure therapy—used to help alleviate some of the stress of trauma. While the other theories all claimed to *decrease* trauma activation, EMDR's claims were larger: It could completely eliminate the body's distress that had been caused by the trauma. In addition to this, the assertion was that *any* trauma could be healed, no matter the size, and *any* client could find this relief, no matter how long they had been suffering from it. This is based on a theory Shapiro created called Adaptive Information Processing (AIP). This AIP is a network that can be found inside everyone and is constantly processing incoming information. Any information that is crucial for survival is stored as memory, and all other information is released.

When trauma occurs, which is by its nature overwhelming and life-threatening, our bodies do not have the chance to pause and extract the unnecessary information. Instead, we hold on to the entire experience, which becomes trapped in our emotional memory. Our bodies hold on to these memories (van der Kolk, 2014). EMDR gives therapists a roadmap for how we can successfully heal these trauma memories. When therapists and clients agree that clients have enough internal stability to process their trauma, therapists help clients activate traumatic memories. When activated, these memories, which have been stuck in the body, can be moved to more adaptive

DOI: 10.4324/9781003541554-2

networks of the brain, so they can be processed (or reprocessed) by the AIP network. As this occurs, any unnecessary information is discarded (Shapiro, 2018).

A beautiful aspect of this model is its nonpathologizing feel: no one afflicted with trauma is broken or weak. Throughout existence, the human body has used the strategy of holding onto trauma memories as an effective and successful survival technique. In today's world, this can lead to distressing, even agonizing responses in our bodies, when we are reminded of the initial insult. Through three prongs and eight phases, EMDR is able to reverse these instincts in our bodies.

Three Prongs and Eight Phases

In a partnership with our clients, the three prongs of EMDR asks us to consider if our focus will be on (1) resolving past memories, (2) addressing current symptoms, or (3) increasing confidence and capabilities for the future. All of these three prongs are interrelated; however, we can use the prongs to establish where we will start, or what work is most important when there is a prescribed amount of time for therapy. After establishing which of the three prongs we are in, we then can use the eight phases to help guide our work (see Box 1.1 below).

Box 1.1 The Eight Phases of EMDR

- Phase 1: **History and treatment planning**. Assess the client's internal and external resources.
- Phase 2: **Preparation**. Build a therapeutic alliance. Explain EMDR and address any concerns. Prepare the client with specific coping techniques.
- Phase 3: **Assessment**. Identify events to focus on. Measure SUDS and VoC.
- Phase 4: **Desensitization**. Reprocess trauma memories with BLS.
- Phase 5: **Installation**. Focus on positive beliefs, continuing reprocessing of memories and transforming internal beliefs the client has learned to believe about themselves.
- Phase 6: **Body scan**. Have the client focus on any sensations in their body to see if there are any distressing feelings left in their body.

- Phase 7: **Closure**. Help the client return to the present moment and a state of calm and safety.
- Phase 8: **Reevaluation**. Before the following session, discuss recently processed memories and determine the future direction of treatment.

The Eight Phases of EMDR

As Rotem Brayer has explained in *The Art and Science of EMDR*, the eight phases of EMDR should not be seen as linear, but rather as a fluid guide where we can move in and out of different phases throughout our work (Brayer, 2023). Attunement and connection with our clients tell us where to go; the eight phases simply orient us to the landscape around us. As we move through these phases with our clients, it is beneficial to hold each phase lightly. When we know what phase we are in, the model helps guide our decisions. I will review each phase in a sequential way, as done in a typical EMDR training, below. As I describe the eight phases, I reflect how, in my understanding, these phases can have a nonlinear feel. While honoring EMDR's protocols, which are backed by a lot of research, I also respect Shapiro's guidance and encouragement to remain connected with our clients' needs. Shapiro also instructs therapists to rely on their judgment and training when employing EMDR with clients (Shapiro, 2018).[1]

Phase 1: History and Treatment Planning

The first phase of EMDR is history treatment and planning, and this makes sense to do at the beginning of treatment. This also needs to be an ongoing process. I find that throughout treatment with clients, as our relationships deepen, information is continuously disclosed and history-taking is an ongoing process. We also revisit treatment planning as new material comes to light, and so this also is ongoing in our work with clients.

I question why Phase 6 (body scanning) is not a part of Phase 1. After exploring clients' histories, and clarifying initial goals, I might say, "I want to invite you, if this feels OK, to notice what is happening in your body when we speak about some of the distress in your life. Are there any feelings or sensations that you are aware of?" This is a way for me to (a) access my clients' awareness of feelings and sensations, and (b) introduce how beneficial (perhaps necessary) becoming connected with feelings and body sensations when providing EMDR therapy. Throughout EMDR, we encourage clients to increase their understanding of how traumatic memories feel inside of their bodies, and so revisiting Phase 6 throughout therapy feels essential.[2]

Before moving to Phase 2, therapists should also assess whether there are any dangerous or destabilizing factors in the clients' external environment and present in their lives. If there are, our focus shifts to supporting clients and motivating them to address these concerns. When providing EMDR therapy, if our clients are confronted with dangerous situations around them, our focus must shift to supporting clients through these circumstances first, until there is some adequate level of safety in their environment. Therapists and clients work together to evaluate the stressful factors within clients' lives and determine whether intense trauma work should be recommended or not at this point in time, since EMDR therapy (particularly phases where past trauma memories are activated) could further destabilize the client.

Phase 2: Preparation

After we determine that the client has enough supportive factors and stability to continue to engage in EMDR therapy, we move into the preparation phase, or Phase 2. Understanding how long to remain in this phase can become a multifaceted decision. Through experience and guidance, we learn to make sure clients have enough resourcing before moving onto Phase 3 and activating their trauma memories.

On the other hand, we don't want to stay too long in this phase, or get stuck here so that no trauma processing occurs in the therapy. By looking at some of the essential components of Phase 2, outlined in Box 1.2,[3] we can, with the client, determine if they are ready to move onto Phase 3.

Box 1.2 Components of Phase 2

- Capacity to hold and feel a variety of emotions and sensations in the body.
- Ability to be inside their "window of tolerance" and in an emotionally regulated state.
- Multiple strategies to feel grounded or safe in the present moment ("Calm Safe Place" technique could be one of the many tools we can teach our clients).
- Strong connection and a secure attachment with the therapist, which can facilitate coregulation.
- A lived experience that contradicts the traumatic event and schema that was created at the time of the trauma. This creates a juxtaposition which is needed for reprocessing.

At the top of this list, we again see how important Phase 6 is, this time when we are assessing the client's capacity to hold and feel emotions/sensations. Rotem Brayer (2023) advocates bringing mindfulness into this phase as well. He shares how his clients have reported feeling more grounded and centered as he helps them focus on the present moment. Sometimes we can take a walk in nature or focus on our breath and feel an inner calm, and these practices can give us access to healing energies within us. Thich Nhat Hanh's book *Peace Is Every Step: The Path of Mindfulness in Everyday Life* (Hanh, 1992) teaches us that if we approach each activity with care and gentleness, we can reach a state of mindfulness in any moment, even while doing the most menial, everyday tasks.

We can also help clients understand their "window of tolerance" and how to maintain an emotionally regulated state. This concept was developed by Dan Siegel (2020) and refers to the optimal zones of arousal in which people can effectively process emotions and are able to engage in prosocial, interactive experiences with others. When stress becomes overwhelming, we move into one of two states: hyperarousal, where we could experience anxiety, agitation, and emotional reactivity, or hypo arousal, where we could feel numbness, lethargy, or dissociation. Many factors in a person's life, both internal and external, impact on this window and make it larger or smaller. Since clients must be inside of their window of tolerance for successful trauma healing to happen, we work with clients to help them expand their window of tolerance.

Another strategy that our EMDR trainings introduce us to is the "Calm, Safe Place." This tool is presented in Phase 2 as an example of a specific coping technique. When offering this tool to clients, we invite them to, "Recall a special place that you have been to in your life, or that you can imagine, which brings you a sense of calmness and peace. Imagine you are there in this moment." We can bring clients' awareness to their senses, "What do you see? What are the sounds around you? What is the temperature? What else can you feel? Are there any smells? Can you taste anything in your mouth?"

Even in this example of "Calm, Safe Place" we can notice how helpful it could be to include the "body scan" (Phase 6) and have clients notice any shifts in their bodies, or anything that they feel, while visualizing this peaceful scene. As we will explore in Chapter 12, we can even build on this tool by seeing if our clients would like to find some artistic expression for this "Calm, Safe Place" through painting or sculpting with clay.

Another strategy presented in Phase 2 is exploring secure attachments clients have (or have had) throughout their lives. We can invite clients to think about who offers them nurturance, who offers them protection, and who offers guidance. If clients do not have such people currently in their lives, did they ever have these people? Can they imagine someone based on books they have read, movies, or TV shows? Parnell (2013) suggests that these attachment figures, whether real or imagined, provide essential resources for clients.

If clients practice envisioning these figures during Phase 2, they could install the feelings that arise in their bodies. In later phases of EMDR, if clients feel overwhelmed or dysregulated, they can bring these figures to mind for comfort, safety, and clarity. Some clients might even find value in invoking non-human beings such as spirit animals, religious figures, and even special or magical objects to help them feel more grounded and regulated.

Throughout our work with clients, we should constantly be on the lookout to expand client's internal resources, and help our clients reflect on positive memories and relationships. These are the glimmers and heirlooms, the catalysts that will contribute to the transformation of the trauma memories in later phases of EMDR. These resources can also serve as anchors to help clients find their way back to safety. Therefore, similar to Phases 1 and 6, I will continually return to Phase 2 whenever the opportunity spontaneously arises. I will also return to Phase 2 whenever clients have so much dysregulation or distress that effective processing is not possible. Connection to these resources is a skill that comes with practice, guidance, and time.

Phase 3: Assessment Phase and Case Conceptualization

Although the model is primarily nonlinear, I believe there are some guidelines that should be adhered to. One of these requirements is that our clients have a critical amount of self-resourcing skills before progressing to Phase 3. When we feel that our clients have enough capacity to return to a balanced, safe inner state when needed, we can move to this assessment phase. Here we expose more precise information about our clients' traumas. Since this can be particularly activating for clients, it is highly recommended to consider the questions found in Box 1.3[4] as we make the determination to move to Phase 3.

Box 1.3 Can Client Safely Continue to Phase 3? Questions to Consider

- What is the client's diagnosis?
- Are there any medical or physical considerations? Is the client on any medication?
- Generally, how stable is the client's current life? Have we considered all of the stressors?
- Do we feel our client has enough internal and external resourcing?
- Are there any risk factors we should consider? Has there been past suicidal ideation that we should pay attention to?
- Does our client dissociate? If yes, to what degree?

If we feel comfortable that our clients are ready to proceed, we work with them to understand and conceptualize how they are currently impacted by past traumas. In our quest to find the initial traumatic event, also called a "touchstone" or "feeder" memory, we listen for how clients make sense of, and draw meaning from, traumatic and upsetting events in their lives.

This is a place in the model where a key decision must be made: What are our targets for trauma processing? With all of the information that we have collected so far, we can work with clients to identify which target events to work on, knowing that we can always come back and find more targets in the future if we need to. Some crucial factors that will inform our decision on which events and memories to target are: (a) which events have shifted clients' beliefs about themselves; (b) which traumatic memories are most distressing; and (c) looking back at Phase 2, which memories we determine clients are most prepared to reprocess. Holding all of these considerations in our mind, we select a target.

Phase 3 then proposes that we help our clients flesh out four elements of the target: (1) the most disturbing image of this target memory; (2) the meaning that clients made about themselves as a result of this event, and what they would rather think about themselves; (3) the emotion and level of distress of this emotion; and (4) where this is felt in the client's body. Each of these elements are elaborated below.

(1) The Image

Although not everyone is able to have a clear visual image of previous events, we invite our clients to, if possible, "imagine what image comes up in your mind when you think of the worst part of this event." If clients are not able to associate a picture with the memory, we might ask, "Is there a sound, or anything else, that is connected with this memory?"

(2) Meaning of the Event

We strive to help clients understand how they made meaning of the trauma by questioning, "what does this event make you believe about yourself?" We want to get a deeper appreciation for the negative views that the client has developed about themselves. Shapiro (2018) labels these thoughts negative cognitions (NCs). I have found that some of the more common NCs are: (1) I am unworthy or not enough and there is something wrong with me; (2) I am not able to keep myself safe, I am weak; or (3) The future is completely out of my control, and I have no autonomy, or there is no meaning in these events; (4) I am all alone. After clarifying the NC that developed from the traumatic experience, we help our clients identify a positive cognition (PC). The PCs are the thoughts and beliefs about themselves that the clients would rather extract from the traumatic event. Shapiro (2018) has clients rate their PCs on a rating scale known as the validity of cognition scale (VoC). This is a subjective scale from 1—7 where clients will rate how true the PC feels at this moment, with 1 being completely false and 7 being completely accurate.

(3) Emotional Experience

We identify this third element by asking our clients, "When you bring up the image of the worst part of the trauma, and you say this NC to yourself, what emotions come up for you?" The power of these emotions can then be assessed with a scale called the subjective units of distress scale (SUDS). We can ask clients, "how would you rate the intensity of your emotions right now on a scale from 0–10, where 0 represents no bad feelings at all, all the way to 10 being the highest level of distress?"

(4) Body Sensation

This is another moment where we are doing a body scan (Phase 6). We invite our clients to "recognize any body sensations. Where do you feel them? In what way do they show up?" As clients focus on all four of these elements simultaneously, we begin Phase 4.

Phase 4: Desensitization

The linear progression of Phase 2 into Phase 3 is also true for Phase 3 into Phase 4. At the same time, ironically, Phase 4 is particularly nonlinear. In this phase we are placing our trust in clients' minds to go wherever they need /want go, and trusting that healing will take place. As a result, Phase 4 and Phase 5 might be intertwined with each other. We also want to bring in resources from Phase 2 in this phase (and perhaps even create more) whenever we can. And of course, as we have seen in all of the other phases so far, Phase 6 is ever present.

Something that permeates Phases 4–6 and is fundamental to EMDR therapy is Bilateral Stimulation (BLS).[5] Originally, EMDR grew out of Shapiro's (2018) discovery of how eye movement metamorphoses trauma memories. Since the discovery of EMDR, almost 40 years ago, one of the updates to the model that have occurred was when it was found that eye movements were just one of many techniques that could transform memories. What Francine Shapiro had actually stumbled on when she created EMDR was BLS. This occurs when attention or focus alternates back and forth, at a relatively fast pace, for a short amount of time (usually less than a minute). One way to activate BLS is to have clients follow the therapist's finger, which the therapist moves quickly in front of the client's face from side to side. Other methods of BLS have emerged, such as electronic tappers,[6] the Butterfly Hug method,[7] and drumming.[8]

After clients choose the form of BLS they feel most comfortable with, therapists could bring up all of the elements of Phase 3—the image, NC, PC, SUDs, and VoC—and then say:

> Let the image, feeling, beliefs about yourself rest in your mind, and as we do BLS, just allow whatever happens to happen. You can stop this process at any time—you are in control of that. Your task is just to notice what is coming up for you. There are no wrong answers, we are going to trust that your mind is going to take you to the exact right spot that it needs to go. After around a minute, we are going to stop the BLS, and then I just want you to share whatever is coming up, if you would like to—without discarding anything as unimportant. When you are ready, let's start.

Shapiro also shares her way of introducing this to clients (Shapiro, 2018, p. 137).

We engage the client in BLS for a little under a minute, and then we pause and ask the client "What came up?" or perhaps, "What did you notice?" Throughout this process we also actively listen and watch for any changes communicated by the client's' behaviors. The conviction we are holding throughout this process is that if three factors are present—(1) activated traumatic memories, (2) BLS, and (3) an adequate amount of positive internal resources—then trauma healing will occur.

As therapists, our job is to encourage the client to notice the changes that are taking place. If there are no changes happening, and there is no distress when the client returns to the original trauma memory, Phase 4 is complete. Unfortunately, for most of our clients, who have experienced multiple layers of trauma throughout their lives, this desensitization/reprocessing of traumatic experiences is not always this smooth or straightforward.

In situations where something is blocking the client from processing the traumatic memory, Shapiro (2018) provides a variety of suggestions to help therapists successfully navigate this stuck processing. Some suggestions are included in Box 1.4. In addition to these suggestions, Shapiro also introduces the concept of interweaves. Although she says that interweaves should be used by therapists who already have experience with EMDR, Shapiro (2018) also points out that interweaves are often required.

The purpose of interweaves is to help stitch together painful material with present, adaptive information when this is not occurring independently for our clients. If clients are struggling with some of their NCs, interweaves can help clients place responsibility where it belongs, feel a sense of safety in

Box 1.4 Addressing Stuck Processing

- Can we change direction, length, or speed of BLS?
- We can invite the client to focus on any sensations in their body and explore what they notice. We can ask, "What are the strongest sensations? If your feelings could speak, what would they be saying?" Have your client move in any way they want to express the feelings inside.
- Ask your client if they can scan the image in their mind to see if there is anything particularly upsetting in the image. We might ask them if there are any sounds or dialogue they can hear or remember.
- Facilitating our client's active imagination, we could suggest that they make changes to some of the images on past trauma memories. This can include making the image brighter and clearer, smaller and further away, or black and white.
- We could reintroduce the positive or negative cognition and explore whether any negative beliefs are blocking progress, or if the positive thoughts still remain relevant.
- We could investigate whether there are any feeder memories or earlier memories that need to be addressed before the current memories can be processed.
- We could ask clients, "Do you have any fear of what could happen if there was progress?"

Source: Shapiro (2018, pp. 171–190)

the present, and ultimately embrace a sense of freedom and choice. We can do this by drawing from our therapeutic skills, listening closely to what clients are saying, and remaining highly attuned to the shifts that are occurring in clients' behaviors.

Phase 5: Installation

When clients are able to focus on the original image, and their SUDS remains steady at 0, we have officially moved into Phase 5. However, the processing that goes on in Phase 5 might also be happening concurrently with the desensitization in Phase 4. This is where we trust the process, and trust our clients' inner wisdom.

When we get to a point where there is a significant decrease in SUDS scores, a zero, or an ecological SUD of 1 or 2, we return to the cognition and ask our clients, "How true does the original PC sound? Does it still feel like the most applicable or appropriate thought?" Then we rate the VoC score. If this remains at a 7 for a couple of sets, Phase 5 has been accomplished. However, when there is no movement, and the VoC score is not a 7, we have some options. If the PC still feels like the most appropriate belief for the situation, we can go back to some of the interventions and interweaves we used in Phase 4, to see if these will help the processing.

Phase 6: Body Scan

As you have probably deduced from this chapter, I believe that Phase 6 is a nonlinear phase of EMDR and central to all the other phases. When I try to imagine why body scan is its own phase, I question whether this is because it can be particularly valuable to do a body scan and make sure there is no discomfort before assuming that the trauma is gone. The body can communicate very wise things to us, and will be able to let the client know if there is still something that they are holding onto. This phase makes sure that if there is any remaining negative energy in the body, or distressing body sensations, we do not move on before addressing this.

Phase 7: Closure

Phase 7 is another nonlinear phase, which I believe can be introduced in Phase 2, as part of resourcing. When the work is overwhelming and too distressing for progress, clients can be brought to a state of calm through inner resourcing (Phase 2) or through containment of the memory (Phase 7). Usually, therapists will also initiate Phase 7 in the last 10 minutes, when it is time to wrap up a session, regardless of what phase therapists and clients are currently working on. This is a way to help ensure that clients are grounded and calm before leaving an appointment. During a session, when activating information overpowers clients, Phase 7 can also serve as containment for the work.

One example of a containment method that is taught in EMDR training is aptly called "the container." We can say to clients, "I would like to invite you to imagine a container. How big would you like it to be? What material would it be constructed out of? When you have a sense of this container, see if you can imagine putting all of your distress into it. When you are ready, and all the suffering is out of your body, close this container and if it feels OK, place a lock on it. Imagine placing this container somewhere safe."

Some therapists have found ingenious ways to play with the creative imagery of containers, such as making them feeling-proof so disturbing feelings are unable to enter or exit these containers once they have been successfully closed (Twombly, 2022). There is also a brilliant upgrade to the container by Nancy Simons (see Chapter 23), who transforms the container into a vessel, and then fills it with Self-energy (an IFS concept introduced in Chapter 2).

Closure is also a way of reminding clients what they can expect to happen after a session, and before the next session. We could communicate the following:

> During this session there were a lot of things that were activated inside your body, and in your mind. Throughout the week, you might experience intense feelings, thoughts, or sensations. Sometimes we have new or strange dreams. Remember that nothing is broken inside of you, and there is nothing wrong with you—your mind and body are simply processing the new information. If it is helpful, you can record what is coming up through journaling or some other type of artwork. Feel free to reach out to me through email or the phone if you need to throughout the week.

Phase 8: Reevaluation

There is no Phase 8 on the first session. Then, on all ensuing sessions, Phase 8 comes first. In this phase we (re)evaluate all the progress clients have made. This completes a circle, and brings us back to Phase 1, where we might ask, "Has anything significant come up throughout the week? Have you noticed any changes?" The answers are all relevant to Phase 1, and can give us more information in regard to history and treatment planning.

When I spoke with Andrew Dobo,[9] he compared trauma work to jazz. Embracing this metaphor, I imagine we are all fellow musicians improvising with our clients. We study the music theory, the chords and rhythms, (the EMDR model), and just flow into whatever is coming up in the moment. As we get lost in the drumbeat (BLS), the music is found, and the client's inner wisdom is brought into consciousness.

Notes

1 In order to be trained and certified in EMDR, one needs to be a licensed practitioner. This also implies that when working with clients, we should implement all of the mandates of our training, and use therapeutic judgment over unilaterally following any protocol.

2 This has been spoken about on the *Notice That* podcast (see website: https://emdr-podcast.com/) and will also be addressed in Chapter 9.

3 This list is from the *Notice That* podcast (https://emdr-podcast.com/).

4 Found on the *Notice That* podcast (http://emdr-podcast.com/).

5 Some EMDR practitioners also refer to this as Dual Attention Stimulation (DAS). For consistency I have used BLS.

6 Some examples of the electronic "tappers" used for this method can be found at www.bi-tapp.com.
7 For information on this please see: https://emdrfoundation.org/toolkit/butterfly-hug.pdf.
8 For information on BLS Drum Therapy see: https://www.garybrotherscounseling.com/bls-drum-therapy.html.
9 Andrew Dobo, Personal communication, 12/9/2024.

References

Brayer, R. (2023). *The art and science of EMDR: Helping clinicians bridge the path from protocol to practice.* PESI.

Hanh, T. N. (1992). *Peace is every step: The path of mindfulness in everyday life.* Random House.

Parnell, L., Felder, E., Prichard, H., Milstein, P., & Ewing, N. (2013). *Attachment-focused EMDR: Healing relational trauma.* W. W. Norton & Company.

Shapiro, F. (2018). *Eye movement desensitization and reprocessing (EMDR) therapy: Basic principles, protocols, and procedures* (3rd ed.). The Guilford Press.

Siegel, D. J. (2020). *The developing mind: How relationships and the brain interact to shape who we are* (3rd ed.). The Guilford Press.

Twombly, J. (2022). *Trauma and dissociation informed Internal Family Systems: How to successfully treat C-PTSD, and dissociative disorders.* Self-Publishing.com.

Van der Kolk, B. A. (2014). *The body keeps the score: Brain, mind and body in the healing of trauma.* New York: Viking Press.

Chapter 2

Introducing Internal Family Systems Therapy

Zandra Bamford

The Most Important Thing (www.juliafehrenbacher.com/my-poetry)

I am making a home inside
myself. A shelter
Of kindness where everything
Is forgiven, everything
allowed—a quiet patch
Of sunlight to stretch out
without hurry,
Where all that has been banished
And buried is welcomed, spoken,
listened to—released

A fiercely friendly place I can
claim as my very own.

I am throwing arms open
To the whole of myself—
especially the fearful,
Fault-finding, falling apart,
unfinished parts, knowing
Every seen and weed, every drop
Of rain, has made the soil richer.

I will light a candle, pour a hot
cup of tea, gather
Around the warmth of my own
blazing fire. I will howl
If I want to, knowing this flame
can burn through
Any perceived problem, any
prescribed perfectionism,
Any lying limitation, every heavy
thing.

I am making a home inside
myself
Where grace blooms in grand
and glorious
Abundance, a shelter of kindness
that grows
All the truest things.

I whisper hallelujah to the
friendly
Sky. Watch now as I burst into
blossom.

By Julia Fehrenbacher

This concept of multiplicity of each person's inner world is at the heart of IFS. Subpersonalities, or parts, are regarded not as a product of trauma but rather as natural and universal, bringing us the colour and richness of our individuality, enabling us to both survive and thrive in life. Experiences of trauma can make these parts more extreme and internally conflicted in their

DOI: 10.4324/9781003541554-3

attempts to aid our survival and reduce the chances of further harm. Indeed, beyond trauma we have all experienced times in our lives whereby aspects of our being were perceived as unacceptable (for example, too loud, too active, too sensitive, asking too many questions). Usually, as children, we then had no choice but to exile these aspects of our personality in order to remain acceptable to others. This exiling of parts can be a result of experiences within the family, school, peers, the broader culture, or society. From the moment we are born, and even before we are born, we are all indoctrinated with messages of what aspects of ourselves are acceptable and what are not. Through this exiling of aspects of ourselves, we attempt to protect our inner vulnerabilities but begin to lose our sense of wholeness.

Schwartz also discovered that when parts were met with acceptance, understanding, respect for their good intentions, and care, they were able to release their grip or soften and create space for the emergence of a different state, which he called 'Self'. He found that no matter how trauma-saturated an individual's history was, this undamaged essence was present. Self holds the source of healing, and the secure attachment base for parts and is already within each person. Contrary to attachment theory (Ainsworth & Bowlby, 1991), an individual does not need to have experienced secure attachment in relation to another to then internalise it. A secure and compassionate Self is already there, although it can be well hidden by parts protecting many wounds. Self is able to tolerate and meet very high levels of emotion, has an infinite 'window of tolerance', and has the capacity to connect and relate to all parts with love, care, and compassion. Self sees the inherent goodness of all parts, moves towards inner and outer justice, and leads the process of healing.

The IFS therapy process results in powerful and lasting shifts in the emotions, beliefs, physical sensations, and behaviours held by parts. IFS often evolves into a way of being or way of living, and is more expansive and all-encompassing than a therapeutic model alone. As we begin to relate to our own inner parts from this place of Self—with love, care, and openness—our courage, confidence, and depth of love for others and the outside world also grows. Calmer, more harmonious, connected, and joyful relationships with others and the earth itself are the organic benefits of the creation of a more collaborative inner system. These are the explicit goals of IFS; to notice when a part has taken over or needs understanding, to free parts of their burdens and extreme roles, restore trust in the Self as the internal leader, achieve internal harmony and wholeness, and in turn to bring more Self-energy into the world for the benefit of others.

IFS is a *constraint release* rather than a *deficit* model of therapy and living, holding true to the assumption that everything a person requires for healing is already within them. Change is effortless and does not involve consciously applying a skill, technique, or tool. These are very hopeful and encouraging messages for clients to hear. Many of these fundamental principles of IFS create a way of approaching distress and a way of being and thinking that is deeply non-pathologising. The foundational principle of the presence of Self offers hope to all, regardless of the extent of the trauma or the absence of a secure attachment base in a person's early life. The language of words such as 'disorder', 'maladaptive' or 'dysregulation' does not make sense within this paradigm and the medicalisation of distress could be viewed as a broader cultural burden.

The Internal System

Within IFS, parts are broadly categorised into exiles and protector parts. Protectors are either 'managers' or 'firefighters'. Each of these will be described in turn.

Managers

Our manager parts develop protective practices in attempts to establish control, safety, and security for us. They invariably carry a lot of responsibility for keeping a person's life on track, managing day-to-day tasks, and pushing for progress, control, and success. These parts are often determined, highly diligent, and hard-working in their efforts to prove value and worth as well as avoid further pain or failure. Managers are proactive in their efforts to avoid vulnerability and the drive of these parts can show up in the body as holding, rigidity, and breath constriction, resulting in tension and pain. Their thoughts are often the thoughts we hear the most frequently, and these parts may consider themselves to be you. They may not know about the existence of Self.

Manager parts are concerned with helping us fit in and be liked, accepted, loved, and valued. They may fear that the pain held by exiled parts cannot be tolerated and could lead to overwhelm or triggering of a dangerous firefighter (see below subsection 'Firefighters'). Manager parts may believe that there are secrets in the system that the client cannot deal with, or that the client is too broken or damaged to ever heal. With these fears, it makes sense therefore that they are highly invested in maintaining control. Managers often hold other fears about the external consequences of the overwhelming feelings or the surfacing of exile (see below subsection 'Exiles'). My own career has been within psychiatric wards and crisis and community mental health services. The parts of clients in these contexts invested in keeping distress at bay often hold additional and valid fears of the consequences of sectioning and the use of community treatment orders or other coercive or restrictive measures. The concerns of internal and external consequences felt by these hard-working parts of us need to be explicitly addressed by the therapist, who is confident that Self never gets overwhelmed by any part.

Common traits of managers include the tendency to be intellectualising, appearance-focused, or food-restricting; they may be excessive caretakers, critics, pessimists, obsessional workers, people pleasers, or perfectionists, etc. An example from my own system is a hard-working manager who strove through learning and working relentlessly to prove my worth to others. This manager was determined in its efforts to get things just right, to shine, and keep me away from the pain of worthlessness and insignificance. These were the burdens held by some of my young exiles as a consequence of growing up with a parent figure who had critical raging parts protecting his own—most likely not dissimilar—wounds. This striving manager created consequences such as neglect of my relationships and less time for nourishing activities, as well as creating a successful career. During my own process I was guided to notice, appreciate, and love this part, her strengths, capabilities, and honourable good intentions, as well as her exhaustion. This part was young, felt alone in her quest, and had become very self-reliant, but yet longed for a trustworthy other to provide both care for herself and healing for the exiles being protected. She was too young to hold all of this responsibility and had sacrificed her childhood.

Protector parts of this nature are often young, trying to fill the shoes of an adult. Befriending this young protector in my own process allowed for the softening and releasing of physical constriction in my body. Unburdening exiles led to a change in motivation within my career (and career path), and the integration of gifts of connection and gentleness that were held by the exiled parts. In turn, this dear, exhausted, and hard-working part chose to no longer relentlessly work to prove worthiness. It now dedicates time to being outdoors, connected to the body, and likes to embrace its skills by productively spreading the gifts of IFS to others. This process of unburdening is outlined on p. 000.

Firefighters

Firefighter parts are also protective but in more reactive and impulsive ways. They often step in when the efforts of manager parts fail to keep us away from the wounds and pain of exiles, and operate as excellent 'plan B' parts in the system. Firefighters act rapidly to fight back the overwhelm or flooding of the system. They quickly step up to extinguish internal emotional flames, often at any cost, and without always considering the consequences of their chosen strategy. There is often a price to pay, and they may sacrifice their own popularity in the system in the service of protection. Firefighters are frequently judged, punished, or criticised externally by broader society and internally by other parts. They have one specific focus in sight in their heroic quest; that is, to do whatever it takes to get away from the pain of an exile and keep the system safe. For example, a hard-working perfectionist manager may develop in response to a family environment where a person is always corrected and punished for making mistakes. The manager seeks to ensure the criticism doesn't happen again, striving for straight As. This manager may be faced with failing a college assignment. A highly critical, angry, and denigrating firefighter may step in to blame, reject, and condemn a college tutor in a desperate attempt to keep the person away from the pain of feeling like a failure or not good enough, pain which was internalised by the younger child who was criticised and punished.

Firefighters provide relief in various and unlimited ways. They focus on behaviours which offer immediate distraction, relief, comfort, or distancing from emotional pain. These behaviours span a continuum of social unacceptability, ranging from over-shopping, mindlessly scrolling the internet, and gaming to gambling, smoking, drug or alcohol use, sexual addiction, self-harming, suicidality, violence, and abuse of others.

When we consider how we shift gears and how we switch off at the end of the day, we are likely in firefighter territory. Firefighters may develop early in life (consider how you may have got into trouble at school) or later in life (for example in retirement when a manager 'worker' part is forced to step down and a gambling or drinking behaviour develops). The energy of the firefighter often matches the energy of the manager; for example, a relentlessly hard-working, never-stopping manager may be matched by a firefighter who drinks heavily at the weekend, or even a part that takes a manager out and forces it to rest, with a bad back or other physical health complaint.

IFS makes it clear that there are 'no bad parts' (Schwartz, 2021); firefighters are never what they at first seem, and all have good intentions. Even perpetrator parts often adopt their strategy of violence or violation of others by witnessing their own experiences of trauma. Such parts observe 'who holds the power' in the room and who remains safe through not being victimised or harmed. Therefore they take on perpetrating energy as a form of protection to obtain safety, or even as a tragic form of obtaining connection, in a system wounded with aloneness and disconnection.

Exiles

Exiles are young parts that have experienced the trauma of rejection, neglect, misattunement, and marginalisation and hold the memories, emotions, beliefs, and sensations of these experiences. They are often children who make sense of their experience in the only way that children know how, which is to blame themselves rather than the adult. Exiles develop extreme beliefs such as 'I am bad, worthless, broken, unlovable.'

To reduce the chances of further harm or humiliation and to prevent the distress and memories from flooding the person, these young parts are shut away for their own protection and are often frozen or stuck in scenes of trauma.

In their natural state, young parts are not burdened in this way. They are relaxed inner children that love to unwind, play, enjoy life, and connect. They hold great gifts of sensitivity, innocence, curiosity, gentleness, openness, fearless love, and much more. These gifts are also shut away through the fears of protector parts, who often do not know that these exiles can now be witnessed, cared for, and 'brought home' by Self, ultimately releasing their pain, burdens, and finally their gifts. This unburdening in turn frees up the protector from its role, allowing more choices for how it functions within the system. For this process to take place, protectors need to trust the therapist, the therapeutic process, and the Self of the client.

Many 'deficit focused therapies' aim to develop skills, educate, or build up the muscles of a compassionate self. Within IFS, this would be skilling up a manager part. Often the exiles underneath remain unknown, burdened, and the gifts and precious qualities held by these parts are not integrated into the system.

Despite the shutting away of exiles for their own protection and benefit of the system, they often desire to be seen and cared for and to share their experiences. They may also attempt to be heard and seen through dreams and flashbacks.

Understandably, exiles may not trust the energy of Self, as they may never have been welcomed or accepted in their entire existence; as such, great patience, gentleness, and pacing is needed by both the therapist and client to develop a loving and trusting relationship between the Self and exiles.

Self

> And there is something within us that is never traumatised, something ever-present and trustworthy, something unbreakable, something that survives even the most intense sensations, that holds and releases trauma as the heart pumps[.]
> Jeff Foster (2013, n.p.)

Self is the very heart of IFS: It exists within everyone, can never be damaged, and represents a person's true core or soul. You may recognise this state within you when doing something that you truly love: Playing a sport, being outdoors, walking on the beach with the wind in your face, or being immersed in a creative activity, or any activity that takes you into a state of flow, ease, and open-hearted presence. Self can be felt as joyful moments of 'okay-ness' both within and outside. For many people the IFS journey is one of feeling and living with an ever-deepening sense of 'okay-ness' within. During Schwartz's early work, he discovered that when parts relaxed back—which means that, as they no longer have to protect, they can soften and step aside—Self emerged, consistently holding the qualities that he referred to as the eight C's (see Box 2.1).

Box 2.1 The Eight C's of Self-Energy

- **Curiosity**: Interest and desire to thoroughly understand, without any agenda to change.
- **Calmness**: A peaceful, still, and quiet physical and mental presence.
- **Compassion**: Open-heartedly connected to the suffering of others without overwhelm.
- **Courage**: Willingness to authentically connect to internal and external experiences, take action, and move towards justice.
- **Clarity**: Holding a clear view of a situation internally and externally without bias or judgement.
- **Connectedness**: In open relationship with others internally and externally.
- **Confidence**: Relating authentically and openly from a solid centre of goodness and worth.
- **Creativity**: Embodiment of a flow state with freedom of expression.

Despite this list of 'eight Cs', Self-energy within each person is as individual as a fingerprint and as expansive as the ocean. Ongoing inner work with IFS leads to an upward spiral of unburdening and Self-energy, as our exiles often hold qualities of Self to be reintegrated into the system.

Self-Energy in the IFS Therapist

IFS is primarily a model of therapy which supports the development of a Self-to-part relationship within the client. The Self of the client liberates parts from their extreme roles and burdens. The therapeutic or reparative relationship between therapist and client is secondary to this, but as in any other therapy, a relationship of safety and trust between client and therapist is essential. The importance of the IFS therapist doing their own personal work, connecting, understanding, and nurturing their own inner system cannot be underestimated. Self-energy that is expanded as a consequence of this work is both a particle and a wave (Schwartz & Sweezy, 2019); it can be felt, and acts as a magnet for another's Self-energy even across an online platform. A therapist embodying Self-energy brings their heart, their curiosity, and a deep sense of connection to the client and their parts, creating safety, calmness, and a true sense of partnership within the journey. In this way the

Box 2.2 Key Principles Held by the IFS Therapist

- Each client has a Self, which has all the qualities necessary for healing.
- The client's system knows how the journey needs to be paced. Parts will be excellent allies in the pacing of therapy.
- Each client's system is unique, and no two systems or parts can ever be the same; in this way formulations are redundant, replaced by curiosity and deep listening to the part's own truth.
- All parts are inherently good; all are deeply welcome in the therapy room, knowing that there was once a time when these parts were essential to survival.
- All parts hold some aspect of our true Self, waiting for us to reconnect to, expand, and grow with.
- Each system has an innate healing capacity to work through what it needs to, to find a state of flourishing and wholeness.

Self-led therapist respects and trusts the client's system, follows their lead and their pace, and holds the heartfelt belief that any amount of human suffering can be helped and met with love. This flow state of therapy can be deeply nourishing for the therapist themselves, no doubt greatly reducing their chances of burnout or compassion fatigue. See Box 2.2 for some key principles that IFS encourages the therapist to embrace.

It is essential that the IFS therapist has appropriate spaces to work with their own rescuing, judging, intellectualising, concerned, overwhelmed parts. This key aspect of clinical supervision or consultation can be summarised by this quote:

> Your task is not to seek for love, but merely to seek and find
> all the barriers within yourself that you have built against it.
> (Schucman, 1976, ch. 16)

Supervision often looks like working with the parts of the therapist rather than focusing on the client's own system. In addition to having the eight C's of Self, IFS also offers us five P's to help us focus on qualities of a Self-led therapist (see Box 2.3 for the five P's). These P's can be particularly helpful for therapists to nurture within themselves, to advance their therapy skills.

Box 2.3 The Five P's of Self-Leadership

- **Presence**: Being fully in the moment, engaged with one's internal and external space.
- **Patience**: Recognising the value of a pause and silence, and how this could foster trust and safety.
- **Perspective**: Seeing a situation from different angles and being able to appreciate a bigger picture.
- **Persistence**: Staying committed even when challenges arise.
- **Playfulness**: Approaching a situation with curiosity, lightness and humour.

The Uniqueness of IFS

IFS is unique in many ways, most noticeably in the presence of Self and its innate essence. In contrast to a therapy such as Compassion Focused Therapy, where the compassionate self is approached as requiring cultivation and practice, within IFS it is liberating and unique to know that Self is already there, waiting. As such, a phase-orientated approach to trauma, or the development of skills to self-regulate or develop an 'inner healthy adult', are not required. Box 2.4 demonstrates how to stay within the window of tolerance within an IFS session (see the discussion of the window of tolerance in the section on 'Phase 2: Preparation' in Chapter 1).

This paradigm shift of not being reliant on another person to bring healing to the system creates safety and reduces the possible threat of the therapeutic

---

Box 2.4 Staying Within the 'Window of Tolerance' Is Achieved By ...

- Hearing, respecting, and responding to the concerns of protector parts and enlisting them as allies in the healing journey.
- Ensuring there is enough Self-energy in the therapist and client to be with exiles.
- Agreeing with exiles not to overwhelm the system so that the client can stay with them: Agreeing, for example, to show one thing at a time.

---

endeavour. The main witnessing of trauma memories, feelings, beliefs, and physical sensations is done by the client themselves. If they wish to share all of what is shared with them by a part, then that is of course very welcome to the IFS therapist; however, the sharing with the therapist is not necessary for healing to take place. It is sufficient for the client to witness privately in their inner world. The very fact that healing is possible without external disclosure is often a huge relief to trauma survivors who hold deep shame about what happened to them. This shame can be unburdened without being witnessed outside of the Self.

The therapeutic endeavour is cushioned in safety in other ways unique to IFS. A full assessment and formulation are not necessary at the beginning of therapy. Many clients are greatly relieved by this, particularly people who have experienced multiple assessments within statutory mental health services. The system often holds shame. Exposing shameful experiences too soon will exacerbate fear, anxiety, and reduce safety. The IFS process trusts that the system will unfold as and when it is safe to do so. Therapy essentially begins exactly where it needs to through the client's focusing on what is present and what is safe to bring.

Despite the usefulness of formulation as an alternative to a medicalised view of emotional distress, it is usually a cerebral process and performed by a thinking, analytical, or intellectual part. This often reveals information that is accurate and useful. However, this may then determine the lens through which parts are seen and related to. Experiences held by parts are often not known to the person in the same depth that direct connection from Self can allow for. In IFS we gently invite the formulating or analysing parts to relax back and watch this process. This allows clarity to emerge through the intimate and direct relationship between the Self and the part that is holding the experiential memories.

Other therapies which embrace multiplicity may not always allow for the Self to engage in part befriending, or love of all parts of the client in the same way as IFS. There may be an explicit aim to reduce or banish certain parts; for example, a demanding inner critic part may be worked with by pointing out its unhelpful consequences or developing another 'kinder' part to keep the critic in check, setting limits on the critic, or even appraising the evidence for and against its validity. This may create inner conflict and pressure in the system, and may also lead to intellectual parts working extra hard to develop new skills in their attempts to create balance and ease. Within IFS, such a critic is approached directly with curiosity about its role and concerns, with care, compassion, and appreciation for its efforts to keep an individual safe and functioning. As the client learns of the dedication, commitment, and protective intent of the critic, the client naturally and authentically befriends the part. This in turn enlists its trust and releases it from its role once the core wounds it is protecting are unburdened.

Figure 2.1 The Infinity Sign: A Symbol of Inner Harmony and Integration.

Protector parts often experience great relief at being met in this way. They implicitly learn that 'someone else' is now available to help ensure safety for the client and thus they relax, allowing for space for Self to meet and be with more vulnerable exiled parts. Manager parts are not burdened anymore with having to work harder or learn new skills and techniques to keep firefighters in check. The critic eventually gets to choose how it wants to continue in the system. Often parts choose the very opposite of their original quest; an inner critic becomes an inner cheerleader or simply rests and releases more ease in the system.

This authentic warm befriending of all parts is deeply de-shaming for clients who have been or still are part of traditional psychiatric systems. Befriending and loving a self-harming, aggressive or heavy-drinking part is a radical move from the external messages an individual may have received about less socially acceptable ways of surviving experiences of trauma. This step in the IFS process often reverses the iatrogenic harm that some traditional systems can create in deepening a person's sense of themselves as flawed or unacceptable. In addition to external and cultural shaming or punishing, other internal parts often criticise or feel frustration towards these firefighters. The sweet medicine of truly honouring, acknowledging, and appreciating all parts for their efforts, intentions, dedication, and commitment creates the foundation for inner harmony, collaboration, softening, and Self-leadership. Just like any external conflict, a starting point of listening, understanding respective viewpoints, concerns, and good intentions is much more likely to lead to lasting resolution, harmony, and change as reflected by the infinity sign in Figure 2.1.

The Unburdened Internal System

The explicit goals of IFS are not to get rid of any parts, but to welcome them in, bring them home and unburden them from extreme roles or wounds. Parts are what provide an individual's uniqueness and colours around the light of Self. An unburdened system is one where once-rigid, inflexible managers become more creative, collaborative, and adaptive. Self takes on a more consistent inner and outer leadership role. Unburdened firefighters continue to add high energy into daily life through adventure, passion, and courageous action. Unburdened exiles free of hurt and pain offer play, tenderness, joy, warmth, and open connection. (See Chapter 3 to find the seven steps of unburdening.)

References

Ainsworth, M.S., & Bowlby, J. (1991). An ethological approach to personality development. *American Psychologist, 46*(4), 333–341.

Foster, J. (2013). *Falling in love with where you are.* Non-Duality.

Schucman, Helen. (1976). *A course in miracles.* Mill Valley, CA: Foundation for Inner Peace.

Schwartz, R. (2021). *No bad parts: Healing trauma and restoring wholeness with the Internal Family Systems model.* Sounds True.

Schwartz, R., & Sweezy, M. (2019). *Internal Family Systems therapy* (2nd ed.). The Guilford Press.

Chapter 3

Steps of the IFS Journey

Zandra Bamford[1]

The Appearing Act

Piece by piece I was stolen
My Disappearing Act
Wasn't an act of magic
Wasn't a trick, or a plan, or at all intended

Each piece, unacknowledged, unseen
Was thus taken away, vanished, forgotten
First by those with unseeing eyes, unhearing ears
Then by me, myself, mimicking the only thing I knew

I have been searching for those pieces
In an attempt to complete the puzzle
This is my Appearing Act
This is my lifetime work, in progress

I see and hear and witness
Those stolen pieces of myself
One by one
I acknowledge their invisibility
I gaze into their blank expressions
I witness their mistrust, their caution

You jolly well should be cautious, be mistrusting
I will wait here, until you are ready to come alive
Until you accept my embrace, and let me
paint you in glorious colours
Until you are ready to join hands and dance
No longer disappearing in a haze, vanishing
into a magic cabinet

DOI: 10.4324/9781003541554-4

Appearing, stretching to the light, still unsure, still hurting
But risking the exposure to the elements,
The warmth, the cool breeze
Even if just for a brief moment

Dear stolen pieces
I give you permission to retreat back into the dark,
Into the nothingness
But only if absolutely necessary

The thieves no longer have the power over you
Their script is no longer your story
Let's make a new story together—
A peculiar, unfamiliar sort of story

The one that doesn't shame and doesn't turn away
The one that is tasting life as if for the first time
The story of possibility of touching and being touched
The story of the Appearing Act and of what happens next

By Masha Bennet[2]

The Steps of the Journey

Getting Started: Introducing Parts Language

Rather than undergoing a full assessment or history taking, at this stage a person may be asked if there is anything that they want the therapist to know about them while the therapist listens and begins to track parts, their patterns, and their relationships to each other. For some clients, it may be important to begin with understanding the risky behaviours of firefighters within the system and work with these parts first. Here I will be offering some real-life examples to illustrate how therapists transition through the stages of the model, along with suggestions on the type of wording therapists might use to facilitate the process.

Once a client has outlined a dilemma or problem they are experiencing, these real-life examples of parts can be used to provide a brief overview of the model, for example:

What I'm hearing is that there is a part of you that works hard to be a good parent and another part that constantly criticises you as a mother ... Does that sound right?

A brief explanation of the IFS process can be provided using parts language, without a full outline of the model, as it is best learnt from the inside.

Clients can be signposted to many freely available resources for a comprehensive overview. The therapist might say, for example:

We can work to understand these parts, how they may be trying to help and then understand and heal the more vulnerable parts of you that may have been shut away over time. When we do this, we can begin to respond to situations in new and different ways, with a new sense of calmness and openness. Is this something that may be of interest to you?

Choose a Target Part

Staying with the above example, an IFS therapist may say:

Which of these parts would you like to know more about— the one that works really hard to get it right or the one that criticises you?

Using the 'Six F's' to Get to Know the Target Part

FIND, FOCUS, FEEL TOWARDS, FLESH OUT, beFRIEND, FEARS
   Once we have agreement on the target part, we can ask if the client has a sense of it with them now:

Do you feel the critical one with you now?

The first of the six F's in IFS is to FIND the part in or around the body and gain connection through focusing on how it shows up for the person. A commonly used question in IFS is:

Where do you find it, in or around your body?

Once this is known to the client, the connection with the part continues with FOCUSING on the part:

As you notice it in your head, how else are you experiencing it?

We may then ask how the person feels towards the part. Sometimes it can be helpful first to understand at least a little about the valid and honourable role the part plays, to elicit a deepening into compassion and understanding from the person. We can invite the client to learn more through FLESHING OUT the details and expression of the part. We may ask versions of the following:

Are there any other ways that you are sensing this part right now?

What else does it want you to know about it?

What does this part want for you by showing up in this way?

These questions are important for us to understand whether the part is a protector, with a role and protective function, or an exile. Sometimes exiles show up straight away; this is evident through emotional expression, a sense of the age of the part, and what the part is holding.

In order to establish how much Self-energy is present within the client, we can ask:

How do you feel towards the part?

This is a key question within IFS. If the client's response is anything other than one of the eight C's or another expression of feeling in line with Self (interest, a wish to know more, love), then we invite the client to acknowledge the part's reacting in this way and ask if it would be willing to step back to create space for Self:

It really makes sense that there is a part that is frustrated with the critic. Could you acknowledge it and see if it would be willing to step back for now, or is there anything that is important for us to hear from this one right now?

This 'unblending' is a key skill within IFS and will be elaborated on—within an IFS-informed EMDR framework—in Chapters 6 and 7. Some parts need much more time for us to understand them and their concerns about unblending.

Once the expression of Self-energy towards the part is clear (simple curiosity about the part is sufficient, and often a starting point), the client is invited to beFRIEND the part. Questions can be used to foster connection and closeness:

Does the part know that you are with it? Would you like to extend your curiosity .... care to this part? Can it sense or receive any of your care ... compassion? Is there anything else it would like you to know so you really understand it?

This BeFRIENDING phase of IFS is the foundation for inner harmony and trust. Once we fully understand a part's true intentions and efforts, we usually feel gratitude and appreciation. When the client extends this appreciation directly to the protectors, those protectors—just like anyone—rest into this. When the parts feel valued and known, perhaps for the first time in their existence, they often organically cooperate and collaborate.

The final step in the six 'F's' is to find out the FEARS of protector parts:

Can you ask the part, if it didn't show up in this way, what is it concerned would happen?

A part may respond that it fears the clients will be overwhelmed with pain; it will be never-ending; the person won't be able to cope, will fail; or that there will be nothing else there to protect the client. In this way, this question provides valuable information as to what burden(s) an exile is holding.

Gaining Protector Permission to Go to Exiles and Addressing Protectors' Concerns

This is an important step within the process that is often missed when EMDR is not combined with parts work. These inner parts are often children who have been working relentlessly for some time, often decades, to protect vulnerable parts. Bypassing them and moving directly into a trauma memory or feeling can lead to a backlash of more reactive and extreme firefighters, who jump in to keep the person from the pain, doing so in ways that can be risky or dangerous. They will do what they feel they need to in the service of survival and preservation. Establishing clear permission from a position of respect and valuing the protector part goes a long way towards ensuring the whole therapeutic endeavour is safe and paced in a way that is just right for the individual client.

There can often be a whole parade of protectors around a delicate exile; when one part steps back, another is there to protect. The therapist requires patience, persistence, and ongoing presence of Self, respecting and honouring these protector parts. An angry part may be replaced with a critic, followed by a minimising or dismissing part, followed by a disconnecting numb or 'spacey' part. Some parts may immediately step back once asked to do so; others may need more time to be named, understood, and met with Self. They may need time to get to know Self so as to feel able to hand over the reins of their protective role. Each part can be spoken to directly and explicitly reassured by the therapist when needed:

I get that you're really scared of what's in there; if you could let me know about your fear, I can help to address that. I want you to know that we are not going to go anywhere without your permission.

It is helpful to understand the sacrifices that the protector part has had to make in order to perform its role and what this has been like for it. Protectors are often tired and wish for support and care from someone else for themselves. We can ask to speak to a part directly (explicit direct access) to understand it more, particularly if there is not enough Self present in the system, or speak directly (implicit direct access) when the part is fully blended with the person:

What has it been like for you always trying to please people in this way? What is the price you have had to pay to do this job?

We can provide explicit assurance that meeting the exile will, in turn, help the protector to have more choice and to consider what it may like to do in the system instead:

When we unburden the part you're protecting from its pain and worthlessness, will you have to continue to work as hard?

When a part will not unblend, this is respected. We can offer a message of hope that this endeavour is designed to help it too, while acknowledging its fears. It is necessary to consider the safety of the person's external context and any relationships (for example domestic violence) within which protectors continue to be required. With persistence, patience, and care, and a safe enough external context, parts do in time make space for Self to emerge, so it can be the one that brings the exile home.

Occasionally parts will make space when they realise that do not have to be there to witness the work, and the part (which is usually holding fears) can be invited into a different space entirely. The client can be assured that 'when there is no fear, there is no power in parts'. This assurance can often be sufficient for fearful parts to rest and step back; it can also help for them to be invited into a waiting room or other space, and then we return to them towards the end of the session.

It is not uncommon for protectors to believe the client is still a young child, with the limited resources of a child. Most parts benefit from being updated, and often more than once. Here is an example of how I spoke directly to a part of one of my clients named Claire:

How old do you think Claire is?

Would it surprise you to learn that Claire is no longer 7, but she is 49 now with a much greater ability to cope with all sorts of things?

Could you take a good look at Claire and really take her in, her life now? What do you think about that?

For some protectors, these moments of *really* taking in the client as they are now are powerful realisations that the person has survived so long. This honours the role of the protector and acknowledges how necessary it was back then for it to aid the client's survival. This updating also helps protectors to learn they aren't required in quite the same way any more, allowing them to make space, even if just a little, to allow more Self. Parts also get to experience the energetic qualities of Self; how different it is to the energy they may feel within themselves. This energy is often very calming, soothing, and reassuring to parts.

At the core of protector parts is also a Self, and so once fully known and befriended, the protector can also be invited to be part of a healing circle around the exile. Rather than stepping back, protectors may also want to offer their own love and care while the exile is met, witnessed, and unburdened; in this way their own qualities and gifts can be harnessed to support the process. Loyal, hard-working, and prominent protectors often enjoy this role and wish to be involved in the healing of the young part they have lovingly been guarding. Explicit permission is sought prior to being with an exile:

Will the guard at the door give you permission to help the part in there that it protects? Does it trust that you can help too now?

Is the spacey one interested in you helping the part it has been protecting?

Polarised Parts

All systems have parts that are polarised, pulling in different directions, often unknown to them, with a similar goal or aim. You will recognise this in yourself: For, example a part that wants to go to the gym and get fit and a part that wants to spend the evening sitting in the garden. There can sometimes be more than one part at each end of the polarisation, in alliance, like mini teams competing against each other. Each side fears that the other one will take over and cause harm to the person. They present as an inner struggle or battle and represent an internal attempt to balance each other out; the more extreme one side becomes, the more extreme the other becomes, like a see-saw, a boat rocking at sea, or an internal game of tug of war.

When we notice that a person is describing two polarised protector parts within their system, they are best met together from a place of Self. This can be established as follows:

Is it possible to position yourself in the middle of these two parts, the perfectionist one and the one that wants to give up? So, you're in the middle, impartial and not siding with either, just with curiosity to get to know each. You can use a meeting room, campfire or whatever feels right. Let me know when you have that. … Ask each part to meet each other, reminding them that they will both get the chance to speak and neither will be taking over. See who would like to go first.

Each part is then invited to share its aims and intentions for the person as well as their fears and concerns of what will happen if they don't show up in the way they normally do. The parts can get to know each other and are invited to consider their similarities and shared intentions or fears. They are also asked to take in the client's Self and the Self's appreciation and care for them. This process of parts knowing each other's good intentions, their often similar aims of protecting the same exile or group of exiles, followed by awareness of Self being available to also help can lead to polarised parts spontaneously moving closer together, in collaboration, and offering a partnership as a solution to their polarity. We can move to asking their explicit permission to help the exile:

So would these two parts be interested in you being the one that helps the part that feels not good enough?

Unburdening Exiles

Prior to unburdening exiles using the steps below, safety can be further enhanced through explicitly gaining agreement from an exile not to over-whelm. Exiles are able to control and titrate the amount of emotion they reveal to the client. This is a delicate conversation, as exiles may never have been fully made welcome in the way they needed to be, and we want to acknowledge the pain of an exile, so the exile feels welcome and accepted. Some version of the following can be used. Let's return to Claire and some of her parts:

We're delighted to get to know you and want to know all that you're holding. Can you show us a little at a time so as to not overwhelm Claire and then she will be able to stay with you throughout and give you all the time you need and deserve?

We may need to return to the part again for more witnessing in another session. A particularly beautiful option for parts who have been alone or lonely, used by Michi Rose, is:

If it feels right for you, offer them a golden thread from your heart to hold onto and for you to find your way back to them to be with them some more next time. She doesn't have to take it, but see if she would like to.

Exiles, in their pain and desperation to be seen, welcome this and usually grab on tightly to the thread. This titration of the exile's feelings isn't always needed, as time progresses and trust in Self, encouraging exiles to blend to be witnessed and felt, can be more helpful. When titration is needed or indi-cated, it allows for Self to stay present without protector parts jumping in to manage the emotion. If at any point during the connection with the exile it appears too much for the client, we can gently ask:

Is it okay for you to feel this?

If the client suggests it is too much for them, then we ask the exile to pull back its energy a little to allow the client to stay with them fully, or unblend the part that is overwhelmed by what is being witnessed. Often as both the client and therapist become more familiar with each other, the model, and their own inner parts, the more comfort and allowing there is for exiles to blend and through this to be fully known, seen, and understood.

The unburdening of exiles can be summarised in seven steps:

1   Establishing a relationship with Self

We find and focus on an exile, and check how a client feels towards it, much in the same way as we do with a protector part, once protectors have given space and permission. Once we have established Self-energy and this has been extended to the exile in any way it can receive it, with words, energy, action, or any other way, it is helpful to check that the exile is aware of the Self and can feel its presence. We can ask how close the client is to the part and consider whether it is possible to get closer, without imposing any presence on the exile and always respecting and allowing it to lead.

This connection moves at a slow and gentle pace, with plenty of silences and feeling into the energy that is present, offering opportunities for attunement at the pace of the client's system and allowing the exile time to take in the presence of Self. The therapist can support the connection between the part and Self by explicitly stating to the client:

You can approach this part with great gentleness and warmth, she may never have been welcomed in this way before ... How is she responding to your presence?

2   Witnessing

Exiles often spontaneously begin to show their experiences, feelings, beliefs, and physical sensations once the relationship with Self is present. To foster this, we can invite the client to ask the part:

Is there anything you want me to know?

Is there anything else you want me to know about what this was like for you?

And, what else?

It is helpful to check whether the part feels understood:

Do you feel that I understand you or is there anything else you want me to know so I can really understand?

Exiles can present with or without words, instead showing emotions, scenes, images, sensations, or just a felt sense of their experience. We align with the way the part is communicating just as it is. Throughout the witnessing process, the therapist might ask the client how they feel towards that part. This strengthens the Self-to-part connection along with internal safety, allowing the exile to share and reveal more of their story.

3 Re-do

Asking the client where the part is and if it is in a particular place or time helps us to understand if a part is stuck in a particular experience in the past. If it is, the Self of the client is invited to enter the scene; the therapist can be there too if requested. In this scene, the client's Self reconnects with the stuck or frozen part by witnessing what it is holding. This moves to asking the part if it needs anything to happen within this scene. Some parts want to change the scene, and Self can do this, for example by talking to an angry parent to elicit a more caring and loving response, while the young child watches.

Self can directly provide the exile with what it needed at the time but didn't get (for example comfort, love, care, presence, understanding, allowing of feelings). The very presence of Self, witnessing and connected, is often the repair and re-do that was longed for and needed. Sometimes there are additional specific requests. This request for a corrective experience comes directly from the exile themselves, with Self responding to provide this, even if the experience needed is violence or an action that may not be acceptable in the outside world.

Is there anything that the part needs you to do for them back there?

4 Retrieval

The exile is invited to leave the scene and be with the client in the present—for example in their home, their heart, or any fantasy place, checking with it how it likes it there once it is retrieved. It is often helpful to explicitly let the part know that it will never have to go back to that scene or place again.

Ask the part if she would like to come and be with you in the present where you will take care of her now.

5 Unburdening

Once an exile feels fully witnessed and is in a safe place it is asked:

Is there anything you're carrying that you feel ready to let go of?

Are there any beliefs or feelings that this part took on back there, that she feels ready to let go of?

The part identifies where in the body the burden is being carried and if it is ready to let it go. The part is invited to release the burdens into the air, fire, water, earth, or any other way that it wishes. This release is supported by Self; once completed, the part usually reports feeling lighter or more spacious. With this unburdening, a client can release long-standing body tension, pain, constriction, or other physical sensations, emotions, and beliefs held by the part.

6 Inviting in new qualities

Following the release of the burden the part is invited to take in whatever qualities they would like or may now need. An example is a young two-year-old part who, after releasing into the sky a burden of feeling alone and not existing, invited in qualities of substance, solidness, existing, and connection. This is usually an effortless process of natural qualities returning into the part.

Exiles often contain many gifts for us, aspects of our true Self we have been disconnected from. Gifts of gentleness, openness, and playfulness can be named, allowing the part to see themselves through the eyes of Self. It can be a truly heartwarming and connecting experience for the part to be reflected back in this way. The exile's gifts can now be integrated into the system, releasing more joy, connection, and authenticity into the client's daily life. We can ask simply:

Can you see her for who she really is? What is it like for the part to hear about those gifts you sense?

Mike Elkin, an IFS Lead trainer, often guides a client to ask a part:

Would you like to see what you look like through my eyes?

Holding a mirror to the part in this way can also be done earlier in the process if there is enough Self-energy present to see the exile as they really are, rather than just their burdens.

It is helpful after an unburdening to check in with the part as to how it would like the client to connect with them going forward. A young part may need more of the same connection or may have a particular idea around an activity or time to spend time with the client.

7 Integration

Bringing back in protector parts

Once an exile has been unburdened, all the parts that helped the process by making space are invited back in to make sure they have witnessed the process and can see the healed part as it is now. Protectors are usually happy and relieved and often surprised by the transformation. Sometimes they need more time, even their own sessions, to unburden themselves of their roles. At times protectors spontaneously unburden at this point: Knowing their role is no longer needed they can immediately rest into a state of ease, putting down their tools and weapons, and choose a new role or simply take on a role of offering a loving presence to the exile they've been protecting. Occasionally, protectors may also be protecting another exile or even another protector; we may need to explore this before the protector can truly rest.

As the critic takes in the little girl with you playing, ask it if this has any implications for its role.

At the end of an IFS session parts are always thanked by the client for their sharings, presence, and cooperation; any parts that have been waiting patiently for their time to be known fully are noted and an internal commitment is made by the client to return to them.

Follow Up

After unburdening an exile, the client is encouraged to check in daily with the part for a period of 3 to 4 weeks afterwards to consolidate the process of change in the neural networks. A check-in can be a simple few minutes inside with the part. Parts can be met within a sitting silent practice or while out in daily life. This may involve bringing in a part to see how it is, if there is anything it wants the client's Self to know, or indeed any activity the part would like to spend time doing. This allows the part to be truly integrated, the unburdening process to last, and the trust in inner Self leadership to grow. The check-in itself can become a rich and enjoyable daily experience and a lifelong practice for many people, who find that connecting to their inner family can greatly enrich each day. This check-in may not always take place because of distracting, busy, or avoiding parts. Where this is the case, these parts become the priority to explore and work with to allow check-in outside of sessions to take place and ensure ongoing healing.

The Flow Of The Model

Although the full IFS process is presented here in a linear way for clarity and simplicity it can be much more dynamic and shifting. Protectors can step in at any point, leading to more unblending, or a shift in focus to spend more time with a protector part may be required. An unburdening, integrating gifts and allowing protector parts to release some of their load can be a lifelong process of ever-expanding Self-energy, wholeness, inner and outer harmony. As a clinical model alone IFS is a powerful healing modality. The IFS journey often also opens the door to a more spiritual journey or life, which may or may not be taken in by the client.

Notes

1 For a detailed and comprehensive deeper dive into guiding individuals through the IFS process see Internal Family Systems, 2nd edition (Schwartz and Sweezy, 2020).
2 From the collection *My Appearing Act: Healing Poems* (2023). Also see https://sandsoundcentre.co.uk/blog/f/my-appearing-act.

Reference

Schwartz, R. X., & Sweezy, M. (2020). *Internal Family Systems therapy* (2nd ed.) The Guilford Press.

Chapter 4

Integration and the Quest Towards an Ultimate Model

David Polidi

Why IFS and EMDR

Out of all the different evidenced-based practices that are available to clients, why am I committed to sharing the benefits of IFS-Informed EMDR (IIE)? There are many effective and advantageous therapy models in the psychological field today. In my search for an ultimate approach, I have found that there is no such thing as "the perfect paradigm." Truth can be found in many places and in many models. IIE appeals to me because it welcomes different points of view. In Bessel van der Kolk's (2014) popular book, *The Body Keeps the Score*, he was able to communicate in powerful ways how the scars of our past are held in our bodies. I have found that for my clients and me, IIE is a very effective remedy for these scars. When considering the benefits of combining IFS and EMDR, a crucial question emerges: "Does each model bring something substantial to the other one? And if so, what does each model contribute?" I believe the answer to the former question is "yes." This chapter is my answer to the second question.

What EMDR Offers IFS Practitioners

Within the IFS community, I have heard that IFS is a "Self-contained model." For this reason, IFS therapists might ask the valid question, "How is it beneficial to learn another model?" I have found through my experience that the majority of therapists practicing IIE have been exposed to EMDR first, and then incorporated IFS, or another ego state model, out of necessity. For an IFS therapist, the need of another model is not as evident.[1] I would like to explore some of the significant benefits that EMDR can bring to IFS therapy (see Box 4.1).

EMDR, with its eight phases of trauma healing, is a phase-based model. Judith Herman promoted and popularized this in the 1990s (Herman, 1992); however, this way of thinking had been around for over a century, and has been credited to Dr. Pierre Janet's work in the nineteenth century (*L'Automatisme*

DOI: 10.4324/9781003541554-5

Box 4.1 Contributions of EMDR to IFS

- The advantages of a phase-based model.
- Education on trauma and how it impacts our daily life.
- Significant scientific research that proves its efficacy.
- Bilateral stimulation as both a regulating practice and a way to activate parts of our clients' brains to desensitize/reprocess activated trauma memories.
- Containment exercises as well as other regulation tools.
- Resourcing figures, symbolic representations of qualities that can help clients feel safe and supported.
- Future templates to help envision and manifest desired outcomes.

Psychologique, 1889). Some of the noteworthy elements of a phase-based model which EMDR embraces include: (1) creating a safe and stable environment; (2) gradual processing, where there is gradual exposure to traumatic memories; (3) flexibility in the pacing of the work, which is dependent on client's readiness; and (4) generalizing the work so that the client can integrate it with their present and future life and functioning.

As we introduce EMDR to clients, we are providing psycho-education on trauma. We can help clients have a more comprehensive understanding of trauma, and clarify how traumatic memories are held in the body. As Bessel van der Kolk (2014) explains, when we are exposed to external or internal events that remind us (consciously or unconsciously) of past trauma, our bodies go into an automatic response mode. At this point, we are pulled into a timeless reality, where our bodies respond as if we are back in time, facing the original threat (van der Kolk, 2014). When building our case conceptualizations with clients, we help them better understand how past traumatic events might be impacting and causing overreaction within current situations (Herman, 1992; van der Kolk, 2014).

Another way that EMDR adds to IFS therapy is that EMDR has gone through rigorous research to prove its efficacy. With EMDR, we are able to inform clients with neurobiological language—this has been analyzed and scientifically substantiated much more than the concept of "parts" within our psyche. In EMDR, we teach clients about the important concept of neuroplasticity, and how this works in regard to the desensitization and reprocessing of traumatic memories.

EMDR can also invite clients to bring real people, fictional characters, or animals to their mind to serve as symbolic representations of qualities that can help clients feel safe and supported. Types of figures includes nurturing figures, protective figures, or wise figures (Parnell, 2013). This seems to bring an element of active imagination into the work. As Wikipedia describes it, "active imagination is a mediation technique wherein the contents of one's unconscious are translated into images, narratives, or personified as separate entities."[2]

Bilateral stimulation (see Chapter 1) is another gift that EMDR brings to the table that could help upgrade IFS work. Although there is no definitive answer on how or why BLS works, research has consistently shown that there are positive gains when BLS is added to help clients desensitize or reprocess trauma memories (Shapiro, 2017). The Syzygy Model of IIE demonstrations how BLS could also be used to increase and install Self-energy, as well as help protectors unblend as we use BLS to simultaneously appreciate their positive intention (see Chapters 6 and 7).

There are also containment strategies in EMDR which offer incredible value and safety to clients who feel overwhelmed by their parts in IFS therapy (for an example of this see the container method in Chapter 1, or the upgraded vessel imagery in Chapter 23). In EMDR, clients can be invited to imagine "containers" and then put some of their distressing memories and feelings into these spaces. Clients can place these boxes under mountains, at the bottom of the ocean, or any other secure place. These containers are also helpful to parts when we are doing IFS. We can invite parts to envision their own containers (which they have full control over), and then place some of their feelings and thoughts into them—giving parts a little reprieve or space from their distress. The parts can then return to these thoughts and feelings when they feel it is the right time. The vessel imagery (see Chapter 23) is particularly meaningful for IFS, as well as IIE, because it integrates Self-energy-into the concept, and so when parts step into the vessel, they are also remaining connected to Self-energy, and the healing relationship is maintained while they are inside the vessel.

Joanne Twombly writes that in addition to containment, coping skills in general (protective bubbles, safe spaces, affect dials) are beneficial, and at times necessary, for our clients (Twombly, 2023). In her book *Trauma and Dissociation Informed Internal Family Systems* she shares that "Coping skills can and have been used productively within a framework of IFS to provide extra support for weary managers, overactive firefighters, and overwhelmed exiles who carry extreme burdens" (Twombly, 2023, p. 42). By providing this support to our parts, we are able to "manage backlash and triggers during [clients'] daily lives, overwhelm during sessions, and to increase [clients'] level of competence, control and choices" (Twombly, 2023, p. 42).

Both EMDR and IFS work with past events that have occurred during clients' lives, and explore how this impacts current events. I feel that EMDR is more explicit when speaking about the future. EMDR has strategies to help clients construct future templates, which examine adaptive alternative responses to possible upcoming upsetting events. Through this process, clients are also invited to envision future hopes and wishes (Shapiro, 2017).

The Gifts of IFS

When we look to IFS, we can find a lot of remarkable enhancements that it brings to our EMDR practice. Some EMDR practitioners might ask the question: "We already have a deep appreciation for ego states; what does IFS brings to the table?" This is a valid question, and my response would be to share some of the unique elements that I have discovered with IFS (see Box 4.2).

IFS has a specific term that it uses for the religious/spiritual concept of divine inner light, buddha nature, higher self: Self-energy. This Self-energy is present when parts soften and relax back (see Chapters 2 and 3). IFS has explicit terms to understand this energy—the eight C's: Compassion, Courage, Calm, Clarity, Creativity, Calm, Connectedness, and Confidence. When we find any these qualities, we can use BLS (see Chapter 1) to install them (see Bruce Hersey's Syzygy Model, Chapter 6). Bruce Hersey also explains how a critical amount of Self-energy becomes the necessary ingredient to allow access to dual awareness for our clients (i.e., for EMDR to be effective).

In addition to opening a window to allow spirituality to come into the therapy room, IFS provides an insightful way to categorize our parts. As the

---

Box 4.2 Contributions of IFS to EMDR

- Spiritual/ religious concepts and terms are introduced into therapy: Specifically, the concept of Self-energy.
- The classification of parts into protectors (firefighters and managers) and exiles is an extremely effective way to understand our inner system.
- The 6 F's provide specific strategies to help clients unblend and regulate their emotions.
- IFS provides techniques for releasing burdens (traumas) through the use of imagery and natural elements.
- It offers a way to understand and process countertransference through a greater understanding of therapists' parts.
- It provides further understanding of legacy burdens, unattached burdens, and guides.

Syzygy Model explains, by noticing if we are interacting with a protector or exile, we gain a better sense of how to proceed with EMDR—do we focus on a positive intention of a part, or the negative cognition (see Chapter 6)? Also, by designating parts as protectors and exiles, we are cautioned to make sure we have the permission of protectors before rushing to expose an exiled part. This helps slow down the process, to make sure that we are not retraumatizing our clients.

IFS also offers us specific strategies on how to unblend from protectors, which further connects clients with their Self-energy (divine light, Buddha nature). This can be very helpful when a client feels stuck in Phase 2 of EMDR. The precise approaches are summarized by the 6 F's (see Chapter 3). Another original, amazing strategy that is introduced in this book is Claire van den Bosch's externalization of parts with her "Circle of Self-energy" (see Chapter 22). IFS offers practical steps to help parts release some of their burdens or traumas through an unburdening process (see Chapter 3); these steps can be used as interweaves in EMDR if processing stalls.

IFS provides new language for therapists to look inward and really explore the parts that are coming up for them (see Chapters 20 and 21), which can add a fascinating dimension to the discussion of inter- and intrasubjective space (see Chapter 9). As mentioned earlier in this chapter, IFS brings in language with which to honor and appreciate spiritual elements—which I have found to be minimal in, or even absent from, other therapeutic perspectives.

In Robert Falconer's incredible book *The Others Within Us* (2023), he explores how important this spiritual dimension has been for healers throughout time and space. In over 500 pages, he clearly documents and outlines ways that other cultures have been able to understand unfamiliar and misguided spirits. Throughout the ages, a majority of cultures and societies have held an understanding and appreciation of exorcism, and through his extraordinary work, Falconer (2023) demonstrates how we can relate to these misguided spirits in a Self-led way and compassionately exorcize them from our bodies. In addition to this, Falconer's work also describes another type of sublime being, called a guide in IFS (or a guardian angel in Christianity). As opposed to the misguided spirit (also referred to as an unattached burden), this guide is intentionally connecting with us to offer help and wisdom that will lead us towards our hopes and dreams (Falconer, 2023).

I feel Falconer's (2023) work aligns beautifully with Parnell's (2013) safe, wise, and protective figures, and invites us to envision how other beings might be all around us. Falconer then suggests how we can go about interacting with these beings in a Self-led way. All of this could be extremely valuable as we bring EMDR to clients and help them navigate their unconscious.

Parallels of EMDR and IFS

I have found that the connections between IFS and EMDR far outweigh the differences. Perhaps most importantly, both models see the relationship between the therapist and the client as foundational to proper treatment. Both models trust that the wisdom and healing are found inside of the client. As therapists, we are tasked with holding space for clients, and with helping them listen to their inner voices and truths. Whether we call the natural healing energy within us "Self-energy" or "Adaptive Information Processing" becomes more a matter of linguistics. The central skill that therapists must cultivate when applying both modalities is the ability to actively listen and connect with clients through words, tone, body language, and silence.

The two models both value and integrate practices such as yoga, mindfulness, and meditation (Brayer, 2023; De La Rosa, 2024; Schwartz, 2022). As shown by Bruce Ecker's (2024) and Bessel van der Kolk's (2014) work, transformation of trauma and memory reconsolidation occur in both EMDR and IFS. The journey that we take with our clients, whether in EMDR or IFS, is collaborative: We walk into the sacred space of a clients' inner worlds with acceptance and compassion. Both models also allow space for clients to conceptualize their traumas in whatever way feels right. Sometimes, clients might experience that their traumas have been inside of them for a long time, perhaps even before they were born. Both models also honor and value the intergenerational heirlooms and gifts that have been passed down to us.

The Ultimate Model

In the end, the "ultimate truth" is always evolving, and so is an ultimate model. IIE is an incredible map because of two wonderful models it brings together. A combination of models implies an inherent flexibility. I have found that the key questions, which are more important than any model, become: Who are our clients? What are their truths? What are the best ways for *them* to find healing?

Although I would not say IIE is "the ultimate model" (because I don't believe in any), I will say that I have found IIE to be extremely powerful in my work with clients. It has become an incredible resource for me in helping clients focus on their values and realize their full potential in their lives. When I first met Bruce Hersey, he said to me, "Truth is truth, it doesn't matter what model you are using or what you name it—none of these things make it more or less true. If something is going to be helpful to my client, I am going to use it!" These words were exciting to me as I first walked into the IIE universe. Ultimately, combining EMDR and IFS has helped me increase my hope, patience, and curiosity, and I am very grateful for this!

Notes

1 However, it is important to note that IFS draws heavily from other models such as the Family Systems Model and Hakomi therapy, as well as Shamanistic wisdom, to name a few.
2 Found at http://en.wikipedia.org/wiki/Active_imagination.

References

Brayer, R. (2023). *The art and science of EMDR: Helping clinicians bridge the path from protocol to practice.* PESI.

De La Rosa, R. (2024). *Outshining trauma: A new vision of radical self-compassion.* Shambhala.

Falconer, R. (2023). *The others within us: Internal family systems, porous mind, and spirit possession.* Great Mystery Press.

Herman, J. L. (1992). *Trauma and recovery.* New York: Basic Books.

Parnell, L. (2013). *Attachment-focused EMDR: Healing relational trauma.* W. W Norton.

Schwartz, A. (2022). *Therapeutic yoga for trauma recovery: applying the principles of polyvagal theory for self-discovery, embodied healing, and meaningful change.* PESI.

Shapiro, F. (2017). *Eye movement desensitization and reprocessing (EMDR) therapy: Basic principles, protocols, and procedures* (3rd ed.). The Guilford Press.

Twombly, J. (2023). *Trauma and dissociation informed Internal Family Systems: How to successfully treat C-PTSD, and dissociative disorders.* [Kindle Edition]. Self-Publishing.com.

Van der Kolk, B.A. (2014). *The body keeps the score: Brain, mind and body in the healing of trauma.* New York: Viking Press.

Part 2

Structured and Systematic Models that Combine EMDR with IFS and Parts Work

Chapter 5

Overview of IFS-Informed EMDR

Energy, Discovery, and Harmonious Integration

Annabel McGoldrick

> To see a World in a grain of sand,
> And a Heaven in a wild flower,
> Hold Infinity in the palm of your hand,
> And Eternity in an hour.
> > William Blake, *Auguries of Innocence*

Why these words, *Energy, Discovery, and Harmonious Integration*? These are the best words I've found so far that bring the essence of how IFS and EMDR enhance one another and express a way of conceiving of a new starting point for our therapeutic work. We could turn those words into the acronym EDHI and call it the spirit of IFSiEMDR, bringing a dynamism, a magic, an integration of macro whole into the micro of the session with the client.

Energy

This is an invitation for therapists to reflect on the energy in the room. Is it warm and welcoming or cold and clinical? With IFS we can go further: IFS brings the concept of Self-energy (see Chapters 2 and 3 for the basics of IFS) as the healing energy within both the therapist and the client, so we need to ask ourselves: How we can facilitate more of that? From an EMDR perspective, Self-energy can be seen as the fuel of the Adaptive Information Processing model. So as EMDR therapists we want as many tools and pointers as possible, to maximise this healing energy of openness, discovery, and integration.

Yes, Self-energy is all about the eight C's of compassion, curiosity, clarity, creativity, calm, confidence, courage, and connectedness, and the five P's of presence, patience, perspective, persistence, and playfulness. These words are primarily chosen because of the alliteration, which makes this an easy way to remember them. But there are some other extra words that are really important for good therapy, such as open-heartedness, attunement, nonduality, love, peace, and flexibility.

DOI: 10.4324/9781003541554-7

These are qualities necessary in both the therapist and client, because these words illustrate how well the therapy is going. If I'm feeling flexible, open-hearted, and attuned to the client, then the session unfolds quite magically in an easy flow and the client's mood shifts rapidly, no matter how disturbing the target we began with. IFS creator Richard Schwartz characterises it particularly well in his essay on being a Self-led therapist. Schwartz describes how he attunes with clients, and the work becomes 'effortless'. He shares how he finds the perfect words to say in the moment, 'as if something were speaking through me' (Schwartz, n.d.), which can bring him to a state of awe. I'm sure many EMDR therapists could echo this experience in many EMDR sessions too, yet IFS not only gives us language to describe this, but we are taught ways to enhance this energy in the room. Yes, we ground and give clients skills, but that's not the same as Self-energy; preparation skills can still be taught in a cold and clinical way.

The other words, 'nonduality, love and peace' come from Rupert Spira and his theory of nonduality (Spira, 2023, p. 76). He says that we are all one infinite consciousness having an individual experience. Basically, he argues that when you strip away our thoughts, beliefs and sensations, what is left inside is peace: and on the outside, love, often experienced through beauty, in nature, in art and in relationships. Our route to Self, according to Spira (2023), is through 'pure awareness'. We also know that EMDR invites people to be the observer, to witness, to be aware of their own distress when processing a target from a mindful place. So the more we can facilitate this place of awareness in a client, the easier the EMDR processing will be (Schubert et al., 2011, p. 2).

There are several other reasons for choosing the word awareness. Since awareness is truth seeking, it invites you, the therapist, to ask the following questions:

1 **What's really going on here?** You may play parts detective by enquiring into what parts of the client (and oneself the therapist) are showing up here. You could also play detective, anthropologist even, by delving into how the client got to be this way. As Mark Brayne (2022) puts it: 'What's this REALLY about?'
2 **What—where, how, with whom, and in what context—did they learn to do** (emotionally, behaviourally, cognitively) to manage their emotions and self-soothe?
3 **What, therefore, are the patterns that need to be repaired and rewired?** And in that context, 'What happened to them?' (Brayne, 2022 p. 6). We can observe the client's symptoms, and ask, 'What are they telling us about the client's attachment story?'; 'How did the client evolve to survive them?'; 'What maladaptive networks were created early in life?' and, 'What parts are burdened with carrying out those maladaptive networks?'

I've also chosen the word energy, because for some it might seem quicker or easier to ask: 'How is my energy: Is it warm, open, and attuned?' rather than having to check what parts are present, particularly for those not already IFS-trained. Really, emotions are simply energy in motion (split the word e-motion: e for energy in motion), so this is also another way of asking, 'How am I feeling?'; 'What energy am I (therapist) and client in?'; 'Do I feel bored, or curious?' and 'Do I feel compassionate or impatient?'

I include the word **permission** as an aspect of both energy and discovery, because it is polite to ask permission to go inside, to connect with part/s, for discovery and processing. As I mention later on in this chapter, EMDR can sometimes go too fast in accessing exile parts, thus triggering backlash from protectors. So, the energy of asking permission is very collaborative and respectful and is another reason why being IFS-informed with EMDR can be safer.

Finally, the term **Egoless** is an aspect of energy because Ego is the language used by many other disciplines and means the same as protectors, particularly the manager who wants to look good as a way of avoiding uncomfortable feelings. Deepak Chopra describes Ego as: 'your social mask', which lives in a constant state of fear (in Dent, 2024, p. 54). Continually searching for power, the Ego overanalyses, which leads to inauthenticity, suffering, and distress (Dent, 2024, p. 55). Also, if I'm coming from Ego as a therapist, I might be wanting to show the client how clever I am, what a great EMDR/IFS therapist I am, and in a subtle way believe that I'm better than the client. If a therapist is in such a 'better than' Ego-driven place, this will block an attuned connection with a client. Equally if the client is coming from the same 'better than' Ego-driven place, they'll find it hard to access their own feelings and exiles in order to process fully with IFSiEMDR.

Discovery

The word 'discovery' may be familiar to those who've trained with Bruce Hersey (see Chapter 6 and 7) or read Bruce Ecker et al. (2024). The intention here is to help therapists feel more positive about befriending those parts who can appear to be blocking processing. The other hope is to engender a sense of adventure in therapists about discovering which parts are here and why. IFS suggests therapists be curious (one of the eight C's) about protectors, to see them not as blocking the way, but guiding the way! Getting curious with protectors, by using Non-Violent Communication (NVC), healthy communication and appreciative inquiry can open the way to discovering so many helpful qualities of protectors. NVC was created by American psychologist Marshall Rosenberg as a form of compassionate communication to foster empathy, resolve conflict, and build peace. For more see Rosenberg's book *Nonviolent Communication: A Language of Life: Life-Changing Tools for Healthy Relationships* (2015). This is a lot about building trust between the client and the part. By building an internal relationship, rather than being in conflict, the parts can work together and ultimately increase the flow of energy (see Chapter 3). As the therapist maintains an attitude of discovery and curiosity, the energy of the session can remain light and the client can be given the message, 'As we move forward in this work, notice whatever comes up inside of you and remember: *You can't get this wrong!*'

Discovery Questions/Interweaves with Parts

These questions can be used in preparation and assessment phases of EMDR, and also as interweaves during Phase 4. If protectors (managers and firefighters) appear in any EMDR phase, ask the client:

- How is the part getting your attention in your body?
- If you could see the part, what would it look like?
- What does this part want for you?
- How do you (client) feel towards this part?
- How did it get this job? How effective is this job?
- If it didn't have this job, what would it rather do?
- How old is it? How old does it experience you as?
- What else does it want you to know?
- What does it fear will happen if it can't do its job?
- What if we could help the vulnerable part it's protecting?

Harmonious Integration

This is more about Phases 4–8 in EMDR, and refers to how the system might change during processing. Remember we're not just clearing targets, we're altering the whole balance of a delicate inner system that needs to integrate and harmonise with the changes made during EMDR. When this is ignored, it can be a reason why EMDR doesn't work. IFS brings the concept of unburdening parts, which can be helpful imagery to use towards the end of EMDR Phase 4. We might ask a client, 'Perhaps the part would like to release that shame and belief that I'm not worthy? Would they like to breathe it out, shout it out, wash it off in the ocean? Perhaps they want to throw it on the fire or bury it in the ground?' After unburdening, during EMDR Phase 5 the protector is consulted again, to see if it wants a new job: Maybe a critic now wants to become a cheerleader or early warning part? (see Chapter 2).

The goal in IFS is for the system to evolve to become Self-led, and resemble a choir or an orchestra playing their different parts in harmony. Imagine what it sounds like when a choir sings or an orchestra plays out of tune. Ouch! All the parts being in harmony is such a lovely metaphor for EMDR too, to not just clear the target but help the client's parts co-operate and function better in all aspects of their life. IFSiEMDR integrates IFS into each of the phases of EMDR that I have outlined below.

Phase 1: History Taking

Genogram

My preferred method of history taking is to draw a genogram of two generations of a client's external family system. Firstly, that gives me some clues about the factors forming their internal system, plus the genogram helps to contain the history taking —ensuring it will be brief. Several clients reported having left previous EMDR therapists because the history taking took too long and was too triggering. One client's firefighters went on a drinking binge after multiple sessions of history taking.

Mapping Parts

This can be done briefly by drawing ovals and writing words like 'worried part', 'anxious part', or 'controlling part'. Or it can be a longer process, using tools like the inner active cards (Holmes, 2007) or online sand tray to help the client get to know their internal system and begin to make sense of their inner world. Don't be afraid to map parts multiple times as the system changes during the course of treatment and according to the latest triggers.

History of Firefighters (Addiction)

In my first history-taking session, I always ask for a brief overview of the client's patterns of addiction and self-harm. I want to know what harm firefighters have done in the past and whether they might be triggered during our work.

History of Self-energy (Life Going Well)

In the same vein, I want to know what's worked, what's helped. That gives me some clues to their current access to Self-energy and what access they have to the AIP system. Sometimes I ask clients to name their best qualities. If they can't answer the question, we already have protectors present.

Self-care

Explore how they take care of themselves now. Do they do mindfulness? Journaling? Do they enjoy walking in nature? What are their hobbies? How about friends and family support? If they don't do any self-care then we need to spend some time helping to develop some.

Goal for Therapy

It is always important to make our EMDR treatment symptom focused, so I ask: 'What would you look like without your symptoms?' My discovery parts detector is really active here, noticing how they answer my questions and which parts want this goal.

Phase 2: Preparation

Explain how both EMDR and IFS work. I like to explain how both EMDR and IFS are memory reconsolidation therapies. EMDR is about processing maladaptive memories by using bilateral stimulation. IFS brings the useful concept of multiplicity of the mind. I show the client the IFS mandala to explain managers, firefighters, exiles, and Self-energy.[1]

I then install the EMDR Safe place as taught in basic training. Then I want to enhance safety in the client's system by installing a team of resources organised along the themes of nurturers, protectors, and wise beings (Brayne, 2022). Clients who can't easily access their own Self-energy often find it easier to visualise it externally in the form of these resource figures. Occasionally, clients can't even think of the figures, so I make suggestions. I make a note that protectors are blocking us, but try not to get bogged down here unless a protector makes a more overt move by saying something such as: 'She doesn't deserve nurture.' This is an ideal time to use the discovery questions with such a protector (see Chapter 7).

For more complex clients, such as those suffering from Dissociative Identity Disorder (DID), it may be that each part needs their own safe space; this place might be real or just somewhere the part, 'would like to feel safe' (Twombly, 2023, p. 63). I usually do this later in treatment when standard EMDR and IFS hasn't brought results—when therapy gets stuck. Then, it's helpful to return to Phase 2 and give each part their own safe space by suggesting: 'What about a room with a soft carpet, soft stuffed animals, with just the right kind of light and temperature? What does this feel like for the baby part?' (Twombly, 2023, p. 71).

The key is to ask the part—either directly or by asking the client to ask the part—where they would feel safe. A little child part might like a pink safe room filled with soft fluffy blankets and cushions; a self-hating part might like a tree house with a comfy sofa and books; a numb part might like a place up above the clouds in the sunshine.

There are lots of other ways to enhance Self-energy, the fuel for the AIP. I tend to go back to Phase 2 when therapy gets stuck, and to use tools such as a star chart. This is simply a chart with the Eight C's and Five P's of Self-energy, and ask the client to connect with a memory. When a memory is retrieved, I might suggest, 'Recall a moment where you felt compassion. Where do you feel it in your body?' and then I suggest, 'Add slow BLS to strengthen this feeling.' IFS and loving kindness meditations are lovely ways to access Self-energy in preparation for EMDR processing. The simplest IFS tool for giving access to more Self-energy is inviting the client to unblend from a part and suggesting 'Can you ask that part to step back and give you some space?'

Phase 3: Assessment

Many parts can pop up for therapists, particularly in the early days in finding an EMDR target: Image, negative cognition (NC), positive cognition (PC), validity of cognition (VoC), Subjective Units of Disturbance (SUDS), and body location of emotion. A therapist might have an 'Am I getting it right?' part, a worried part, a confused part. Therefore, using the discovery questions with the therapist's own parts can be helpful at this point (see Chapter 22). Another way of conceiving of an EMDR target, with its maladaptive information, is to see this as an IFS part holding disturbance in the body with an NC (see Chapter 6).

IFS always asks permission to connect with any part. This brings a really lovely energy of politeness and respect, which is particularly helpful when accessing a little wounded exile. Protectors may have guarded that exile for decades and so won't take kindly to someone gatecrashing the system. So, asking permission builds more trust in the system and between the client and therapist. This means there's less likely to be blocking, looping of parts, or backlash after the EMDR session.

In my own work, I find using the attachment-informed approach (Brayne, 2022) to be extremely valuable. In this approach, we establish a target in the present, with a symptom or issue, then 'bridge' from the present target into a memory of child or exile. You could invite the client to: 'drop back in time, go back as far as you can, very first place you land' (Brayne, 2022, n.p.). This becomes the new target, the child part's memory. This process is very similar to the floatback and affect bridge you might have learnt in basic EMDR training. An example of a childhood memory is captured in Rebecca Lazenby's wonderful artwork in Figure 5.1.

Figure 5.1 Blended with a Part.

Source: Image by Rebecca Lazenby.

Phase 4: Desensitisation

EMDR therapists are familiar with dual awareness—the concept that one foot is in the past and one is in the present. IFS has some useful imagery and language that can enhance dual awareness, making it feel more tangible and safer for the client when processing a childhood memory or the memory of an exile. Here is an example of desensitising from an IFS lens.

We can invite the adult client, with Self-energy, to step into a memory and be with the child part. We make sure Self-energy is present by asking the adult client: 'How do you *feel towards* the child part?' If the client says, 'I hate it, it is stupid' we gently ask that part if it can give us some space, so the client can connect directly to the inner child; see Figure 5.2.

Once the client has found enough Self-energy, the Self can offer connection to the child part/exiles so they are not alone any more. The wise adult client can then witness the child part/exile in memory. This usually makes it safer to feel those big feelings that have been squashed down, avoided, and exiled for so long, which can facilitate deep healing. When we bring in EMDR processing with this child part's memories, we've enabled the system to feel safer. Making sure we are speaking with the child part from Self-energy allows the part to feel held and heard; then, they're able to go deeper in healing.

Once the SUDS is close to zero there are a couple more steps that are common to both IFS and attachment-informed EMDR and that enhance the memory reconsolidation imagery. We can offer a repair and explore possible resources by asking the client: 'What did that child need then, that they didn't have?' Maybe they needed to have someone on their resource team challenge a parent, or to experience the parent apologising or just giving them a hug. This is when we might also ask the child, 'Would you like to leave this memory, and go to a safer or less stressful place?' (see Figure 5.3).

In EMDR, at this stage the trauma memories have already been desensitised and reprocessed with bilateral stimulation, but in IFS they are unburdened (e.g., parts let go of uncomfortable thoughts and feelings). In a shamanistic-type ceremony, we suggest, 'Perhaps the part would like to release

Figure 5.2 Connecting with Self-Energy.
Source: Image by Rebecca Lazenby.

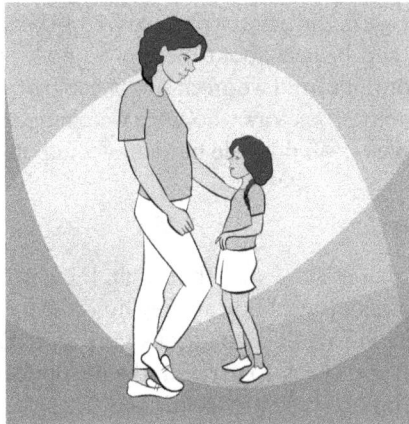

Figure 5.3 Self-Energy Forming Relationship with Part.
Source: Image by Rebecca Lazenby.

Figure 5.4 Self-Energy Comforting Part.

Source: Image by Rebecca Lazenby.

that shame and belief that they're not worthy. Would they like to breathe it out, shout it out, wash it off in the ocean, throw it on the fire, or bury it in the ground?' This is a way we desensitise the client's body to the memory.

Phase 5: Installation

During Phase 5 in EMDR, we install a positive cognition (PC), either by checking whether the PC named in Phase 3 still works or has changed, or, if you're using the simplified protocol, naming a PC for the first time at this stage. In IFSiEMDR we might ask the part we are working with, 'What would that part rather feel and believe about themselves now?' In EMDR we then check the VoC and continue until we are at a 7 (or ecological 7). In IFSiEMDR we also check back with protectors who were watching, and ask: 'Would any of them like a new role or job now the burden of the exile is released?'

Phase 6: Body Scan

To help the EMDR therapist be very thorough, the protocol asks therapists to invite the client to scan their body as they hold the memory (as it is now) along with the PC. IFSiEMDR also checks how unburdening has gone by asking the part, 'Can you check to see if all the uncomfortable thoughts and feelings have gone, and how you are feeling now?'

Sometimes in EMDR we do a future template to help the client enhance their PC, stepping into an imaginary day in the future where there might be some challenging or triggering events. In IFSiEMDR we can ask clients to step into this imaginative scenario and ask: 'If you imagine this challenging event, what parts might be present? How would you and your system feel if some of the younger, more worried parts stay at home during this future experience, so they feel safe?'

Phase 7: Closure

With an incomplete session of EMDR the child part/exile might be invited to leave the scene and be tucked up with the resource team or in their safe space. Perhaps the client would then like to put the memory in a drawer or a container to be kept safe until the next session? IFSiEMDR, with its relational approach, offers a little more support for a child part who is stuck in a traumatic memory—a commitment to be checked on by the adult client. As the therapist you might say: 'The session is about to end but the relationship continues; would any parts like you to check in after the session?' If the answer is yes, ask, 'How often, and when can you agree to check in?' There are also other ingenious ways to provide closure in IFSiEMDR that are written about in this book (see Chapter 23).

Phase 8: Re-evaluation

In EMDR it is important in the following appointment after a processing session to ask the client: 'When you think of that memory, what's there now?' In this way we can decide if we will pick up with an incomplete target or decide on some other direction to take in the session. In IFSiEMDR, this is a good time to check in with our parts and ask, 'How's the part been this week?' Many clients will have much to report if they've been checking in with their exile parts; but if they haven't, well, there's another opportunity for discovery. We might inquire, 'What part stopped you from checking in with your parts?'

EDHI

As EMDR is currently taught, the therapist is encouraged to just follow the standard protocol and all will be OK. But, as this book attests, our clients are very much more complicated than that, especially those with complex PTSD (see Chapter 14). This requires a more sophisticated, multi-dimensional approach—one that allows for and embraces our multiplicity. Using IFS therapy as preparation and interweaves within EMDR: IFSiEMDR becomes a safer, deeper, more respectful, healing therapy.

EDHI is intended as an overview of what all the authors here are bringing to each IFSiEMDR session. Another way of thinking about this integration of these two therapies is IFS's relational, big-picture approach is much like the right brain, to EMDR's focused left brain detail (McGilchrist, 2019). As we combine these two modalities, EDHI guides us and provides a foundation for this work: the underlying spirit of acceptance, compassion, and—ultimately—understanding, so each part feels seen and valued in the system.

Note

1 This is available for purchase at the IFS Institute's online store: https://ifs-institute.com/store/author/76.

References

Brayne, M. (2022). *Unleash your EMDR: Release the magic. A guidebook for attachment-Informed, integrative, transpersonal EMDR*. Mark Brayne.

Dent, A. (2024). Incorporating spirituality into EMDR using a BioPsychoSocial-Spiritual approach to treating trauma. Webinar presentation. April 26.

Ecker, B., Ticic, R., & Hulley, L. (2024). *Unlocking the emotional brain: Memory reconsolidation and the psychotherapy of transformational change* (2nd ed.). Routledge.

Holmes, T. (2007). *Parts work: An illustrated guide to your inner life*. Winged Heart Press.

McGilchrist, I. (2019). *The master and his emissary: The divided brain and the making of the western world* (2nd ed.). New Haven, NY: Yale University Press.

Rosenberg, M. B. (2015). *Nonviolent Communication: A language of life: Life-changing tools for healthy relationships* (3rd ed.). PuddleDancer Press.

Schubert, S. J., Lee, C. W., & Drummond, P. D. (2011). The efficacy and psychophysiological correlates of dual-attention tasks in eye movement desensitization and reprocessing (EMDR). *Journal of Anxiety Disorders*, 25 (1), 1–11.

Schwartz, R. (n.d.). The larger self. *IFS Institute* [Webpage]. https://ifs-institute.com/resources/articles/larger-self.

Spira, R. (2023). *An introduction to non-duality: Vol II. The recognition of the nature of reality*. Sahaja Publications.

Twombly, J. (2023). *Trauma and dissociation informed Internal Family Systems: How to successfully treat C-PTSD, and dissociative disorders* [Kindle Edition]. Self-Publishing.com.

Chapter 6

Syzygy
Alignment of EMDR, IFS, and Memory Reconsolidation

Bruce Hersey

IFS-Informed EMDR (IIE) is an integration of two powerful evidence-based therapies used in the treatment of PTSD, CPTSD, and other mental health concerns. Although many practitioners intersperse aspects of these modalities, such as by reverting to IFS if the EMDR procedure becomes stuck, or otherwise alternating between the two, a comprehensive integrated model is possible and ultimately advantageous. To attain proficiency in this comprehensive integrated approach requires separate mastery of each. A true integration is achieved by simultaneous application of both throughout the treatment process. This would not be possible if there were not significant alignment of the models in key respects. The alignment of EMDR, IFS, and (additionally) memory reconsolidation, as transposed to clinical applications of experiential therapy by Coherence Therapy (Ecker et al., 2024), is what I have named the Syzygy model of IIE. Syzygy is an astronomical term for the alignment of three or more celestial bodies within a gravitational field—a great metaphor for three perspectives sharing an underlying common trajectory and purpose. This chapter is devoted to identifying the theoretical roots of this alignment and tracing the path from these to the intertwining methods and refined clinical tools of this model. Focusing on the first four phases of EMDR will keep this account concise and establish an essential foundation for the unfolding of this combined model in the later phases.

An Inherent Natural Healing Process

EMDR and IFS share an assumption that there is an underlying natural healing process. If you can establish and maintain certain conditions, healing will result. In EMDR this is understood in the context of information processing (as Adaptive Information Processing), while IFS views it in a relational context as the healing relationship of Self-to-part. Coherence Therapy places this process on a foundation of neurobiology as a unique form of neuroplasticity called *memory reconsolidation* (Ecker et al., 2024)

DOI: 10.4324/9781003541554-8

and demonstrates how any experiential therapy process can be composed of a sequence of clinical experiences that triggers this transformative process. These three frames intersect within the EMDR construct of dual attention.

Functional Dual Attention

EMDR highlights the requirement of dual attention as a necessary condition for safe and effective trauma processing (Shapiro, 2018). The client has one foot in the present and one foot in the past. They are oriented in the here and now, while accessing a traumatic memory—simultaneously accessing the adaptive information network and a target network of dysfunctionally stored information. Coherence Therapy seeks to construct juxtaposition experiences where implicitly learned self-defeating schemas are precisely identified and activated alongside examples of mismatched adaptive knowing, known as disconfirming information, but without an intention to prove a point or challenge the implicit learning (Ecker et al., 2024). The juxtaposition unlocks a consolidated implicit memory and opens it to an adaptive rewriting: Memory Reconsolidation. But *who* is burdened with these self-defeating schemas, and *who* has access to adaptive and disconfirming information? *Who* is in the present, and *who* is stuck in the past? Is this entirely neuroscience and information processing? Could we be missing something in these formulations?

The body of literature on EMDR and Coherence Therapy inevitably introduces the language of ego states and parts, both in order for the therapist to understand defenses and other complications in the therapeutic process, and to enhance their communication with clients about the process. Multiplicity of consciousness in the human psyche appears to be a useful and universal language. It begins to answer the question of "who" when there are distinct or conflicting positions or perspectives within an individual. IFS asserts that, in addition to parts, there exists in the human psyche an extraordinary entity with the capability and desire to *heal* burdened parts. Securing Self-presence and facilitating a *relationship* between the Self and the burdened part is the crux of the healing process (Schwartz & Sweezy, 2020). In Syzygy IIE (SIIE), this positive internal attachment relationship provides additional dimensions which serve to broaden and refine our understanding of dual attention.

This more complete understanding of dual attention, which I have renamed Functional Dual Attention, specifies that there is *Self-presence in relationship to the targeted part*. The adaptive information network is an information network substrate of the Self, and the trauma memory network (whether narrative or implicit) is an information network substrate of a burdened part. These substrates include *disconfirming knowledge within the Self* and symptomatic *implicit learnings in the burdened part*. The overlay of consciousness and relationship are of critical importance to the healing process in SIIE.

Conscious Relational Entities

This new understanding of target networks *explicitly as parts* is a departure from conventional EMDR, which holds that the target is a specific narrative memory (EMDRIA, 2019; Shapiro, 2018). A specific memory means a traumatic episode, the memory of an *event*. However, an increasing awareness of the role of implicit memory has led to the expansion of EMDR targeting to include implicit memories as dysfunctional information networks (Paulsen, 2018; van der Hart et al., 2013). Implicit memory is better understood as the learning of schemas, unconscious ways of perceiving and strategies for adapting to life. Parts are the carriers of memories, whether episodic or implicit. Including implicit memory in our view of memory supports targeting of defenses, which are embodied as protector parts in IFS.

To the extent that these reactions, strategies, and perceptions are ultimately dysfunctional (self-defeating), they are understood by IFS as the *burdens* of parts: Burdens that can be unburdened. Seeing parts and burdens as distinct and separable is one of the beauties of IFS (Schwartz & Sweezy, 2020). Specifying those burdens is a key aspect of the witnessing and healing process. Separating and freeing parts from their burdens is a fundamentally different idea than that of dissolving target networks. Unburdened parts remain and find new adaptive roles in the internal system.

IFS views parts as distinct and separable from the Self (Schwartz & Sweezy, 2020). Parts blend or take over identity and consciousness, but can also unblend. A crucial component of IFS as an ego state model is that there is always an intact Self that can emerge when parts unblend. When we view a part as suffering from a burden, and there is a Self—unblended from not only that part, but any part which has reactivity to that part, the Self recognizes the suffering caused by the burden and has compassion.

Viewing parts as pre-existing systemic entities that take on burdens, rather than splitting off from an original whole Self, is another crucial distinguishing feature of IFS as an ego state model (Schwartz & Sweezy, 2020). The taking on of burdens preserves the intact Self, enabling eventual organic healing, which results from the unblending and witnessing of the part by a compassionate Self (see Chapters 2 and 3 for further elaboration and discussion of the Self). This witnessing process unfolds naturally and progresses to deep understanding followed by resolution through the final healing steps of redo, retrieval, and unburdening. These are steps that may be observed in *effective* EMDR therapy *even in the absence of IFS integration*. They are manifestations of the underlying healing process. The addition of IFS only optimizes conditions to ensure these outcomes in the face of so many possible complications posed by the myriad of parts in the protective system, each with their own stake, role, and identity.

Burden-Energy and Self-Organization of Parts

A central tenet of the Syzygy model is that *energy* binds parts and entire internal systems, in their burdened configurations. Energy operates like gravity, keeping individual parts and systems stuck. Stuck with their burdens, stuck in time.

To comprehend the healing processes of desensitization and unburdening, it is important to appreciate that in addition to being members of an organized internal family system, *parts themselves are organized systems*. Systems can spontaneously *self-organize*, arising from separate originally unrelated elements when they are exposed to a source of energy (Camazine, 2003). Thus, parts can self-organize in a burdened form, which has a ripple effect of causing the internal system of parts to self-organize in a burdened form. Beginning at the level of exiles, moving upward hierarchically through the internal system, layers of protectors become burdened as well. Energy causes organization and maintains it. That is what is called a self-organized system.

First, let's look at how this works at the level of individual parts. Images, emotions, body sensations, and cognitions are examples of originally unrelated elements of conscious experience. They do not necessarily have anything to do with one another. But they become charged by energy in the environment through exposure to a traumatic experience or some type of sustained stress. The original environmental energy sparks internal *affective* energy in the form of disturbance or distress. When this system is triggered and retriggered, the bond maintaining that system is strengthened. Traumatologists have referred to this process of strengthening the energetic bond as kindling (van der Kolk et al., 1996). The exact same images, emotions, body sensations, and cognitions reconstruct themselves in the traumatized person's experience with each retriggering.

This is precisely what Shapiro meant when she described neural networks as *organized by affect* (Shapiro, 2018). EMDR Phase 3 is structured to gather these elements and obtain a measurement of Subjective Units of Disturbance (SUDs). If we understand the disturbance that we are measuring to be the affect-energy that maintains the self-organization of a burdened part and keeps it stuck, we also realize that desensitization is a reduction of that energy. In IFS, unburdening would be a release of that energy. Disturbance is *burden-energy*, and our goal is to reduce and release burden-energy, creating increased possibility and freedom within parts and internal systems to enable flexible, adaptive responsiveness and behavior in a variety of environments. This adaptive responsiveness is equivalent to Self-presence and Self-leadership in IFS, which embody a different, positive energy called Self-energy.

Neural networks, ego states, and burdened parts are examples of self-organized systems that clinicians regularly encounter in the course of working with traumatized individuals. These entities are elements within a higher-order self-organized system known in IFS as the internal system. However, burden-energy takes a different form once the internal system organizes protectively to maintain exiling of the original traumatized part. Structural dissociation recognizes this when distinguishing between emotional parts (EPs) and apparently normal parts (ANPs) (van der Hart et al., 2006). The latter, viewed by IFS as protectors, possess intentions and strategies to prevent or suppress EPs or exiles from emerging into consciousness experience and executive control.

Exiles and protectors appear to be organized by different energies. Popky and Knipe were the first to recognize and make use of this difference within EMDR therapy (Knipe, 2019; Popky, 2005). They measured *urge-energy* with the Level of Urge to Use and Level of Urge to Avoid, respectively. Urges are protective. They have a purpose, which is always to prevent the person's experiencing something, actually or psychologically, which is perceived to be worse than any collateral damage that enacting the urge may cause. For example, substance abuse may be self-defeating in many ways, but it can obscure painful emotional states that a person believes they cannot tolerate.

Similar discrete elements of conscious experience (a visual image, physical sensation, or specific belief) become charged with urge-energy in the case of a protector part and are also kindled by repeated activation. This urge-energy could be measured by a Level of Urge to Protect (LUP) which subsumes the Popky and Knipe scales and would include any possible forms of protection which may not obviously fit into those scales. This would be obtained by asking, "How much do you need to [describe specific strategy, stance, behavior] from 0 to 10?"

Negative Cognition or Positive Intention?

Aside from the difference in organizing energy between exiles and protectors, their organizing cognitions are characteristically distinct. Exiles are burdened by truly *negative* cognitions, which are limiting beliefs about themselves, others, or the world. Examples would be:

- I am worthless.
- I am weak.
- I am a failure.
- Everyone is uncaring or mean.
- There is nowhere safe in the world.

Protectors, by comparison, believe that they must be, do, or think certain things to optimize survival. IFS maintains that all parts have a positive intention (Schwartz & Sweezy, 2020). For protectors, this means a *protective* intention. These are examples of a cognition that specify a protective purpose for a particular stance or behavior:

- If I am not wary and vigilant at all times, I will be destroyed by an unexpected danger.
- I must constantly do for others, so that they will value and need me—otherwise I will be abandoned and alone.
- I have to keep myself distracted with busyness or I will collapse into helplessness and despair.

Coherence Therapy informs the construction of a Protector Positive Intention (PPI) which corresponds to the protector's symptom-requiring schemas (Ecker et al., 2024), in that it contains (1) specific information about a strategy that solves a problem and (2) the problem it solves or situation it prevents. Similarly, IFS views the "problem" as what the protector fears, and what is being exiled. Taking the time to elicit these two components and make them explicit before attempting any processing will vastly improve the power and efficiency of subsequent processing.

These Protector Positive Intentions (PPIs) are a critical *organizing principle* (Watkins & Watkins, 1997) of protectors which distinguishes them from exiles, along with urge-energy (LUP). Compare these to the Negative Cognition (NC) and affect-energy (SUD) of exiles. This qualitative difference in typology of parts profoundly impacts the Syzygy approach to EMDR Phase 3. Substituting the PPI and LUP for NC and SUD, respectively, enables precise, focused targeting of protectors. This differential targeting arrangement facilitates targeting protectors earlier in the treatment process, when they are constitutionally blended (preventing dual attention from the outset), but also flexible, and rapidly pivoting to target the reactive protectors that emerge later in EMDR Phase 4.

A Revised Landscape

With this new understanding of information networks as conscious relational entities that can become burdened differentially as exiles or protectors, Phase 1 of EMDR takes on a whole new appearance (see Figure 6.1: Syzygy IFS-Informed EMDR Roadmap, which includes IFS upgrades and interweaves). Gathering each client's history and formulating a treatment plan is like visiting a foreign land, learning its language, customs, folklore, geography, and—most importantly—the people you will encounter on your journey, especially those who you will need to rely on to succeed. Exploring

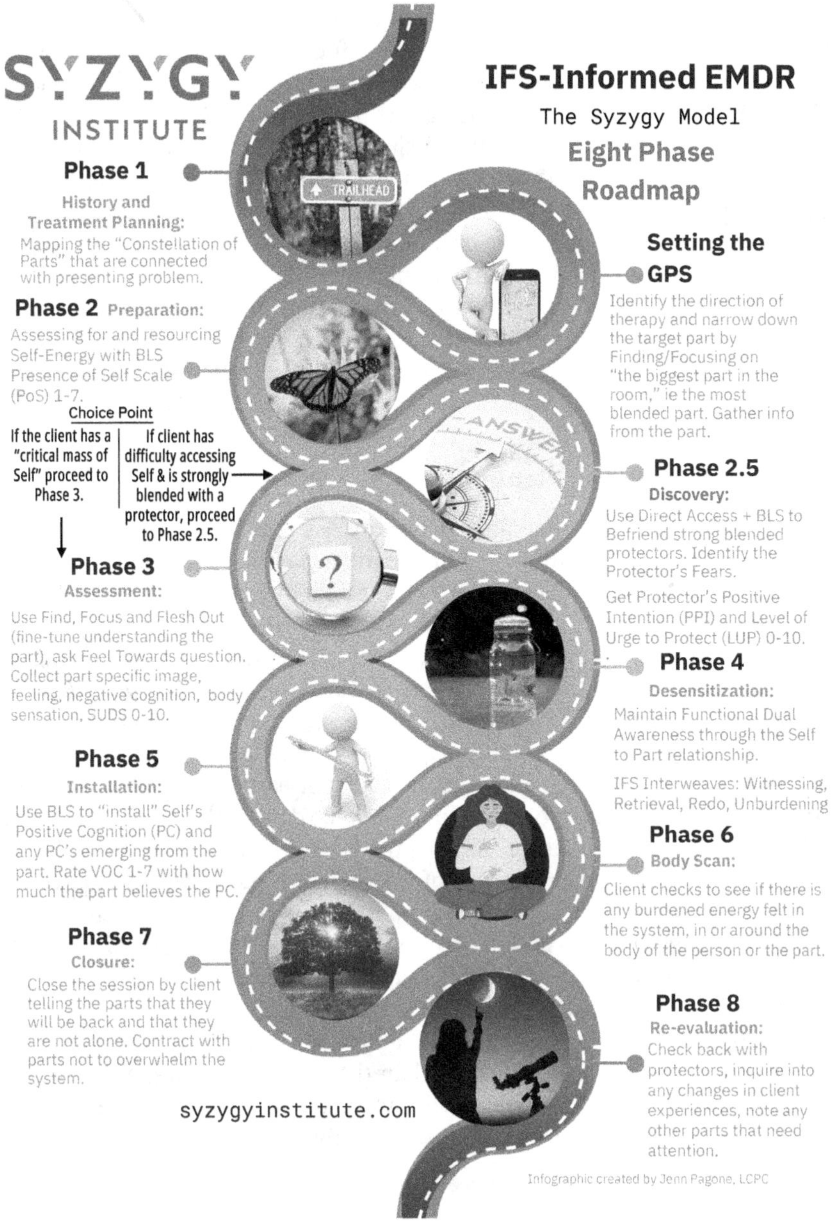

SYZYGY
INSTITUTE

IFS-Informed EMDR
The Syzygy Model
Eight Phase Roadmap

TRAILHEAD

Phase 1

History and Treatment Planning:
Mapping the "Constellation of Parts" that are connected with presenting problem.

Phase 2 Preparation:

Assessing for and resourcing Self-Energy with BLS Presence of Self Scale (PoS) 1-7.

Choice Point	
If the client has a "critical mass of Self" proceed to Phase 3.	If client has difficulty accessing Self & is strongly blended with a protector, proceed to Phase 2.5.

Phase 3

Assessment:

Use Find, Focus and Flesh Out (fine-tune understanding the part), ask Feel Towards question. Collect part specific image, feeling, negative cognition, body sensation, SUDS 0-10.

Phase 5

Installation:

Use BLS to "install" Self's Positive Cognition (PC) and any PC's emerging from the part. Rate VOC 1-7 with how much the part believes the PC.

Phase 7

Closure:

Close the session by client telling the parts that they will be back and that they are not alone. Contract with parts not to overwhelm the system.

syzygyinstitute.com

Setting the GPS

Identify the direction of therapy and narrow down the target part by Finding/Focusing on "the biggest part in the room," ie the most blended part. Gather info from the part.

ANSWER

Phase 2.5

Discovery:

Use Direct Access + BLS to Befriend strong blended protectors. Identify the Protector's Fears.

Get Protector's Positive Intention (PPI) and Level of Urge to Protect (LUP) 0-10.

Phase 4

Desensitization:

Maintain Functional Dual Awareness through the Self to Part relationship.

IFS Interweaves: Witnessing, Retrieval, Redo, Unburdening

Phase 6

Body Scan:

Client checks to see if there is any burdened energy felt in the system, in or around the body of the person or the part.

Phase 8

Re-evaluation:

Check back with protectors, inquire into any changes in client experiences, note any other parts that need attention.

Infographic created by Jenn Pagone, LCPC

Figure 6.1 Syzygy IFS-Informed EMDR Roadmap. Syzygy Institute.

issues and traumas for potential processing will identify exiles and protectors. Using the language of parts will be useful in making sense of the inner landscape collaboratively with the client. A client's rejection of this language is equally useful, since this reveals powerful blended protectors.

Access to exiles for trauma processing is only possible when protectors are not interfering, yet it is natural and expectable for blended protectors to be habitually engaged at the beginning of treatment. The more complex the trauma and attachment history, the more we can expect multiple intensely burdened protectors and internal conflict among parts. There is rarely a straight line to any trauma target for processing. It is usually a nonlinear circuitous path that begins with the most prominent protectors. We can think of this as *organic treatment planning*; the system will show you where you need to start.

Organic Treatment Planning

During the Phase 1 process summarized above, as issues and traumas are identified, protectors are naturally activated. Identifying a potential processing target among any of these possibilities and focusing on it by discussing it or labeling it as a target is what I call *setting the GPS*. Just like with a real GPS, when you enter a *destination, the system* calculates where you currently are and identifies the first road you must travel to reach the destination. *That first road is the protector that is presently most activated by naming the destination.* In this process you must use your IFS skills to identify what part that is, which is why training in IFS is essential. For example, a fearful avoidant part may blend at the prospect of initiating trauma processing, or a numbing dissociative part may appear. When this happens, you have discovered the *Biggest Part in the Room.*

Setting the GPS is a simple way of finding the Biggest Part in the Room, but in more complex and burdened systems, this process can be nuanced, perplexing, and time-consuming. However, a Self-led therapist will, through patience and persistence, ultimately detect this biggest part. Often it takes some trial and error. Doing this piece of work is necessary because powerful protectors exert influence directly and indirectly on any therapeutic process. Attempting to target any part other than the Biggest Part in the Room will result in various complications, which can be avoided by taking this organic approach. The Biggest Part in the Room will always be the Syzygy IIE choice for initial processing.

Assessing for Self-Presence: An IFS-Informed Phase 2

Phase 2 is clearly about determining the client's ability to sustain dual attention for trauma processing. This requires the ability to self-regulate during and between sessions, engage in proper self-care between sessions, and demonstrate the capacity for healthy relationships, especially with their own parts. These are all the things that are necessary to support dual attention. These capacities have in common that they all reflect access to Self-presence, the consummate resource according to Syzygy IIE.

The importance of Self-presence in the formulation of dual attention is immeasurable. Self-energy drives any healing process. For this reason, the therapist also must always embody and emanate the qualities of Self as they monitor the client system for the presence or absence of the same. The eight C's and five P's (see Chapter 2) are a handy IFS guide to identification of Self-energy. The presence of these qualities indicates Self-energy, and their absence reveals blockage of it by blended parts. Therapists must have awareness of their own parts becoming activated through the course of therapy and work with their parts to enable them to unblend to open the flow of Self-energy from the therapist into the treatment process (see Chapters 20 and 21). Finding support through their own IFS consultation or therapy is helpful for this.

IFS uses the *feel-toward question*, "How do you feel toward the part?" as the primary tool for assessing Self-presence. Client answers like "curious, connected, or compassionate" (three of the eight C's) connote Self-presence, whereas answers like "resentful, irritated, or uncaring" reveal blended parts. Syzygy IIE offers an additional tool, the Presence of Self (PoS) scale to supplement the feel-toward question. The PoS asks the client to self-rate their current level of any one of these qualities of Self from 1 to 7 (akin to the VoC), "How (patient, calm, curious, connected) do you feel from 1 to 7?"

The PoS can be used when the therapist senses that an apparent positive answer to the feel-toward question is not deep or authentic. The client may give the answer "compassionate," but asking the PoS for compassionate may reveal a self-rating of 4, indicating that compassion is compromised by a blended part. This offers an opportunity to ask what part may be around which keeps compassion from being a 7. Such a part may be willing to unblend after a brief interaction with it; or, if not, it can become the target of processing.

Another situation where the PoS is useful is when there is an obvious missing quality of Self needed to further the processing. An example of this would be when there is curiosity, connection, and compassion, but the therapist detects a lack of confidence or courage. The answer to "How confident do you feel from 1 to 7?" may be a 3, and similarly, a part can be identified for further attention. Often, clients may be somewhat audacious in their apparent readiness to tackle a trauma target, and asking, "How *patient* do you feel from 1 to 7?" can reveal an overanxious, impatient Self-like part.

Additionally, the PoS can be used in methodically assessing for each of the eight C's and five P's in order to identify and unblend numerous concerned and protective parts when there is a target part of immense magnitude that would require such careful and meticulous preparation. This is a Syzygy IIE strategy in Phase 2, the Preparation Phase of EMDR. Historically, EMDR clinicians have adopted a strategy of resource installation in this phase but, as the architects of the Progressive Approach have observed, in systems with entrenched protectors, resourcing can become interminable and processing forestalled indefinitely (Gonzalez & Mosquera, 2012). Paradoxically, because Self is the quintessential resource in IFS, resourcing is accomplished by identifying and unblending protectors, which results in freeing Self-energy for the healing process.

That said, in addition to using the PoS to identify blockage of aspects of Self and therefore uncover the parts responsible for that blockage, robust PoS scores denote facets of Self-energy which can be drawn out and strengthened as in resource installation. I am disinclined to use the word installation, though, since it implies putting something in that wasn't there before. Since the Self exists in everyone and is blocked by blended parts, Self-energy is not really installed. Finding these resources and fleshing them out with the additional associated elements of experience that we commonly use in the Assessment Phase (image, body sensation/location, cognition, etc.) can serve as a resourcing strategy during any EMDR phase by then adding BLS (Twombly & Schwartz, 2008).

An IFS-Informed Assessment Phase

If there is sufficient access to Self-presence in Syzygy IIE, we can advance to Phase 3. A target part is chosen in collaboration with the Self of the client, rather than by the therapist, because the Self is trusted by the client's internal system to lead. The therapist is an external resource available to the Self for guidance, but Syzygy IIE defers to the Self for its final decision. The relationship between the Self and chosen target part are assessed and established via the feel-toward question and PoS, and then part-specific EMDR Phase 3 information is collated. This would include items such as image, emotion, feeling in the body, Negative Cognition, and SUD, unless the target part is a protector. In that case, PPI and LUP would replace NC and SUD.

We are asking the Self to obtain these elements of part-specific information from the part through its internal connection and communication with the part (called in-sight in IFS). Then we ask the Self directly for a Positive Cognition, rather than the part. This is done by asking the feel-toward question again (after obtaining the part-specific information) to confirm that the therapist is communicating with the Self, repeating the NC/PPI obtained from the part ("The part believes ___"), and then asking the Self, "What do you know about this?" or "What would you want the part to know about that?" Such statements from the Self have established roots in the adaptive information network. They are believed by the Self, but not by the part. That is why we next direct the Self to ask the part how much it believes the PC just stated by the Self, on a scale from 1 to 7, and we obtain a part-specific VoC. It matters *who* we ask for which piece of information. This provides clarity and avoids confusion and other common pitfalls arising in the Assessment Phase.

A Neuroplastic Reset

Coherence Therapy aligns with this formulation of EMDR Phase 3 and provides additional depth and precision, since a PC known experientially by the Self is a mismatch experience in relationship to the target part's NC or PPI. The NC/PPI has been consolidated as an implicit memory which can only be *reconsolidated* or unlearned through experiencing a *juxtaposition* of this emotional learning with such *disconfirming knowledge* (Ecker et al., 2024). A Syzygy IFS-Informed EMDR Assessment Phase ensures that we are constructing a memory reconsolidation foundation and frame for the ensuing processing. The more precisely we can articulate the emotional learning within the NC or PPI, the more firmly we establish this unique form of neuroplasticity. It opens a window of roughly five hours in which additional juxtapositions echoing this initial construction will overwrite the encoded implicit memory (Ecker et al., 2024), which will inevitably occur during an IFS-Informed EMDR Phase 4.

IFS-Informed Desensitization

Syzygy IIE desensitization and reprocessing maintains the specific understanding that *the target is always a part*, rather than a memory, even if there is a memory in which the part is stuck or that the part is disturbed by. This is important because Functional Dual Attention requires the presence of Self in relationship to that part. Having this understanding throughout the course of the healing process primes the IFS-Informed EMDR therapist to detect loss of Self-presence, disconnection of relationship to the target part, or the emergence of an interfering part. As long as Functional Dual Attention conditions are met, the IFS-Informed EMDR therapist stays out of the way, just as in conventional EMDR. Trust the natural healing process.

Having these understandings suggests additional alternative cadence comments and interweaves. In addition to saying "Go with that" or "Notice that," we may say "What else does the part want you to know?" or "Let the part know you get that." Such comments and questions support the internal healing attachment relationship between the Self and target part and reinforce the process of compassionate witnessing that leads to further healing steps.

Asking "How do you feel toward the part?" confirms continuous presence of the Self or detects disconnection or interfering parts. Asking the Self for strategic disconfirming information along the way also reinforces unblending and infuses the process with juxtapositions. For example, when the target part demonstrates intense and difficult emotions, asking the Self "Is it OK to feel this right now?" functions very much like the *feel-toward question* in that it will always be OK for the Self (disconfirming knowledge), whereas for the part and certain protectors there has been an implicit knowing that these feelings are not OK or are intolerable and overwhelming. So, if the answer is "no" to that question, there is a blended part. Typically, when there has been robust Functional Dual Attention, Self will be present and provide a "yes" answer when we ask this question, thus generating a juxtaposition experience. Juxtapositions generated this way become interweaves, which are followed by a set of BLS.

Another way of creating healing juxtapositions is clarifying any new iterations of NCs/PPIs held by the part and *labeling these as burdens*, while asking the Self what it knows about that (a PC), just to compare, rather than challenge. This comparison and comprehending the NC/PPI *as a burden* reinforces compassion within the Self for the suffering caused by that belief.

Having patience and confidence in the process and utilizing this framework and these tools will support a natural process that results in various manifestations of deeper healing like redo, retrieval, unburdening, or corrective redoing, which are specifically named in IFS but are often seen in conventional EMDR when successful. Any well-timed and situationally appropriate IFS intervention can be used as an interweave to guide and support the process, especially if we understand that interweaves are aimed at restoring dual attention by resonating with adaptive information accessible through the Self.

Discovery: Processing Blended Protectors

Blended protectors may be so strong in the beginning of treatment that they preclude Functional Dual Attention. The client may not recognize that they are blended with a part. At other times a part blends and the client is aware of this, but is not able to unblend. The part could be unwilling to step aside. Conventional EMDR is not possible under those conditions. On the other hand, IFS-Informed EMDR treatment may have progressed into EMDR Phase 4, and somewhere during the processing, a protector has arisen and won't unblend.

These situations are remarkably common. Fortunately, Syzygy IIE has developed a systematic way of dealing with them. I have named this procedure Discovery, after a similar process outlined in Coherence Therapy (Ecker et al., 2024). Discovery may be utilized in either Phase 2, when there is insufficient Self-presence to move into a full EMDR Phase 3, or during desensitization, when the processing must temporarily pivot from targeting the traumatized exile toward targeting a protector that has blended during the trauma processing.

Discovery is a structured EMDR process that parallels IFS Direct Access. Similar to Direct Access, it can be applied implicitly or explicitly, depending on how self-aware the client is about being blended with a protector. When there is little or no self-awareness of being blended, implicit Direct Access or Discovery is the appropriate approach. This means speaking to the blended client without stating that you are talking to a part, even though you know you are. In explicit Direct Access or Discovery, the self-aware client acknowledges that you are speaking to their blended part. Either way, you obtain all the part-specific EMDR Phase 3 information for a protector described earlier in this chapter. This would begin with a PPI and LUP followed by an image and body sensation/location. But since this protector is blended (Self is not present), no PC or VoC are obtained. The PC and VoC in IFS-Informed EMDR are dependent on Self-presence. So this gives us a partial or modified EMDR Phase 3.

After compiling the modified EMDR Phase 3, we secure a Discovery Contract with the blended protector. This is an explicit verbal agreement to use bilateral stimulation to "deeply, completely, or thoroughly understand" the part. In implicit Direct Access or Discovery this would be phrased, "May we use bilateral stimulation to deeply, completely, or thoroughly understand 'you' (or 'this')?" This contract is genuine and requires that the therapist unblend from their own parts that wish to desensitize or unblend the part (what I call the unblend-agenda). This is one aspect where I differ from Knipe's clear desensitization objective and therefore do not continuously return to target and remeasure the urge (van der Kolk et al., 1996). This model is more aligned with befriending from IFS; clarifying underlying fears, witnessing, etc. (Schwartz & Sweezy, 2020). Additionally, this approach to processing meets two of the conditions van der Hart proposes for EMDR with C-PTSD; (1) restricted processing and (2) increased interweaves (van der Hart et al., 2013).

It is restricted processing, because it is not direct trauma processing. It is limited to the specific currently blended protector (the defense). Knipe views this targeting of defenses or protectors as indirect trauma processing; it results in reducing the overall negative charge of the underlying trauma before that trauma is directly processed (van der Kolk et al., 1996). The increased interweaves fall into two categories: (1) Self-Resourcing and (2) Informed Curiosity. The Discovery process is structured like desensitization, with contiguous sets of bilateral stimulation separated by reports from the client, followed by either cadence comments or interweaves. Conventional EMDR cadence comments like "notice that" or "go with that" may be used, but often Self-Resourcing or Informed Curiosity interweaves will be used instead.

Self-Resourcing interweaves are when the therapist notices and calls the client's attention to qualities of Self-presence which spontaneously emerge in the process and "taps them in." For example, the client-blended-with-protector reports a realization which surprises them, and they are curious.

The therapist says, "Isn't that interesting?" as a way to highlight curiosity and starts the next set of BLS. Or the client-blended-with-protector indicates increased calm or self-compassion, and the therapist verbally notes this and initiates the next set of BLS. This can be done for any of the eight C's or five P's, drawing out and resourcing qualities of Self.

Informed Curiosity is when the therapist simply asks a follow-up question, based on information in the client report, between sets. The therapist's question is informed by their knowledge of IFS and Coherence Therapy and has the effect of focusing the curiosity of the client-blended-with-protector and moving toward deeper self-understanding about: How it protects; when and where it learned its strategies and methods; what will happen if these don't work; what is being protected; and the hopes, fears, and frustrations of the protector. These questions are asked in a non-demanding manner and are followed by another set of BLS.

A Centrifugal Vessel of Self-Energy, Flipping the Part, and Shifting to Desensitization

The Discovery process is a carefully crafted vessel of Self-energy. Since all parts have positive intentions, these must arise from the part's own internal Self-energy. A PPI is the most compelling evidence of Self-energy within a protector. Beginning with a focus on this, opportunistically resourcing any additional spontaneously emerging Self-energy, and infusing the process with curiosity from an unblended Self-present therapist generates a massive flow of Self-energy.

This yields a centrifugal force which separates out all the blended ingredients as it gains momentum: Self, protector, and exile. Eventually the exile comes into clear view, the protector relaxes, and a critical mass of Self-energy is generated from within it. Self emerges from the inside out—what I call "flipping the part." At this point, recontracting with the emergent Self and now-evident exile (with permission of the unblended protector) to do healing work is possible. This healing work targeting an identified and willing exile can then be structured by compiling an IFS-Informed EMDR Phase 3 followed by IFS-Informed EMDR Phase 4 (both described earlier in this chapter).

Adhering to this alignment of EMDR, IFS, and Coherence Therapy, the Syzygy model produces reconsolidation of the foundational implicit memories held by burdened parts by generating repeated juxtapositions, with the knowledge of the Self, in the context of a Functional Dual Attention relationship. The reconsolidation happens in the form of desensitization and reprocessing (as seen in successful EMDR), as well as unblending, and deeper healing steps like redo, retrieval, and unburdening in IFS.

Discovery, a critical component of the Syzygy model, revolutionizes EMDR in two ways. It opens a door at any point to an alternative form of processing when dual attention is unavailable. It represents a third use of BLS besides resourcing and desensitization, which contains qualities of both, yet offers something additional. The following chapter (Chapter 7), by Syzygy Institute co-founder Michelle Richardson, provides further depth and case examples of Discovery.

References

Camazine, S. (2003). *Self-organization in biological systems.* Princeton Studies in Complexity (reprint ed.). Princeton University Press.

Ecker, B., Ticic, R., & Hulley L. (2024). *Unlocking the emotional brain: Eliminating symptoms at their roots using memory reconsolidation* (2nd ed.) Routledge.

EMDRIA. (2019). EMDRIA Definition of EMDR. https://www.emdria.org/wp-content/uploads/2020/03/EMDRIADefinitionofEMDR.pdf.

Gonzalez, A., & Mosquera, D. (2012). *EMDR and dissociation: The progressive approach* (1st ed., revised). A.I.

Knipe, J. (2019). *EMDR toolbox: Theory and treatment of complex PTSD and dissociation* (2nd ed.) [Kindle Edition]. Springer.

Paulsen, S. L. (2018). Neuroaffective Embodied Self Therapy (NEST): An integrative approach to case formulation and EMDR treatment planning for complex cases. *Frontiers in the Psychotherapy of Trauma and Dissociation, 1*(2), 125–148.

Popky, A. J. (2005). DeTUR, an Urge Reduction Protocol for Addictions and Dysfunctional Behaviors. In R. Shapiro (Ed.), *EMDR solutions: Pathways to healing* (pp. 167–188). W. W. Norton & Company.

Schwartz, R. C., & Sweezy, M. (2020). *Internal Family Systems therapy* (2nd ed.). Guilford Press.

Shapiro, F. (2018). *Eye movement desensitization and reprocessing: Basic principles, protocols and procedures* (3rd ed.). Guilford Press.

Twombly, J. H., & Schwartz, R. C. (2008). The integration of Internal Family Systems model and EMDR. In C. Forgash & M. Copeley (Eds.), *Healing the heart of trauma and dissociation with EMDR and ego state therapy* (pp. 295–311). Springer.

van der Hart, O., Groenendijk, M., Gonzalez, A. Mosquera, D., & Solomon, R. (2013). Dissociation of the personality and EMDR therapy in complex trauma-related disorders: Applications in the stabilization phase. *Journal of EMDR Practice and Research, 7*(2).

van der Hart, O., Nijenhuis, E. R. S., & Steele, K. (2006). *The haunted self: Structural dissociation and the treatment of chronic traumatization.* W. W. Norton & Co.

van der Kolk, B. A., McFarlane, A. C., & Weisaeth, L. (Eds.). (1996). *Traumatic stress: The effects of overwhelming experience on mind, body, and society.* The Guilford Press.

Watkins, J. G., & Watkins, H. (1997). *Ego states: Theory and therapy.* Norton.

Chapter 7

Phase 2.5 Discovery
Working with Blended Protectors

Michelle Richardson

Introduction: The Road of Discovery

If you've ever driven down a winding road in the fog, you understand the experience of working with blended protectors in EMDR. You have a map and a destination, and you know the general direction, but visibility is limited. Some roads look like the right way forward, only to dead-end in resistance, dissociation, or cognitive bypassing. IFS emphasizes that protectors, whether ours as the clinician or those of our clients, are often the primary source of disruption in the EMDR process. Clinicians who integrate these models will benefit from the IFS philosophy: "What's in the way is the way." Recognizing blocks in processing as opportunities for deeper insight and internal connection can transform these challenges into new awareness, growth, and Self-leadership.

EMDR, with its structured phases, promises to be an expressway to healing, until protectors throw down their roadblocks and detours. Conversely, IFS provides a more intuitive internal map, but its slower nature can sometimes feel like driving in circles in more complex systems. This is where Phase 2.5 of the Syzygy Model of IFS-Informed EMDR comes in, not as a detour, but as a crucial passageway forward that provides both effectiveness and safe travel.

Phase 2.5, named "Discovery," was developed by Bruce Hersey as an IFS-Informed bridge between EMDR phases, with added components from Coherence Therapy that contribute to memory reconsolidation. The travelers on this bridge are the blended protectors of the client's system, and Self-energy powers the vehicle required to carry our therapeutic work across to the other side. Discovery facilitates smoother movement between preparation and reprocessing, ensuring protectors are welcomed rather than bypassed. This chapter will explore how Discovery provides a systematic yet flexible approach to working with blended protectors by integrating the wisdom of IFS, the structure of EMDR, and the neuroscience of Coherence Therapy. This approach helps clients experience profound shifts in their relationships with some of their most prominent, or most hidden, protectors.

DOI: 10.4324/9781003541554-9

Achieving Functional Dual Attention Through Discovery

Bruce Hersey's earlier chapter (Chapter 6) provides a comprehensive discussion of Dual Attention, redefined by Hersey as *Functional Dual Attention*, or "Self-presence in relationship to the targeted part." Discovery directly addresses the challenge that arises when protector parts are too blended to allow for the necessary conditions of Functional Dual Attention. This approach aligns the relational depth of IFS with the structured, neurobiological activation of EMDR to welcome, engage, and understand blended protectors. Discovery promotes the Self-to-part connection by first befriending blended protector parts and addressing their concerns. This allows EMDR to unfold in a way that is both effective and compassionate.

Memory Reconsolidation and the Role of Discovery

Beyond establishing Functional Dual Attention, Discovery also paves the way for deeper transformation by facilitating memory reconsolidation. This is the brain's mechanism for updating and transforming implicit emotional learning. As described by Ecker, Ticic, and Hulley (2024), memory reconsolidation requires three essential conditions: reactivating the original emotional memory, introducing a mismatching experience, and allowing the brain to replace the outdated response with new learning.

One way to understand memory reconsolidation is to think of it as like updating old software on a computer. The protector has been running on outdated programming—an emotional learning formed in response to past trauma. It believes that its protective strategy is necessary for survival, even though the circumstances have changed. When we introduce a new, disconfirming experience from Self, it's like downloading a software update. The old program isn't simply erased; rather, the system integrates the new information and adapts, allowing the protector to develop trust in the therapy process and hope for the exile's healing.

Coherence therapy systematically facilitates these conditions for memory reconsolidation by helping clients identify their core emotional learnings and experience disconfirming knowledge (Ecker et al., 2024). While EMDR and IFS each support this process independently, Discovery enhances their effectiveness by combining elements of Coherence Therapy with IFS's relational depth and EMDR's structured neurobiological activation (Hersey, 2020).

In IFS, memory reconsolidation occurs when protectors unblend and witness new perspectives from the Self. EMDR facilitates a similar process in the Desensitization phase, where bilateral stimulation disrupts entrenched neural patterns, replacing them with more adaptive responses (Hersey, 2019). By integrating these principles, Discovery encourages blended protectors to become curious about the adaptive information from Self, allowing them to shift from rigid roles into more flexible and adaptive functioning (Ecker et al., 2024; Hersey, 2019). This process fosters trust in therapy, as protectors experience a tangible shift in their perceived necessity and recognize new possibilities for their role in the system.

Understanding the Emotional Learning of Protector Parts

Emotional learnings from Coherence Therapy are described as "recognizable expressions of non-conscious, learned emotional knowledge," such as attachment patterns, family of origin rules and roles, unresolved emotional themes, traumatic memory, and compulsive behaviors and reactions to internal or external triggers (Ecker et al., 2024, p. 15). Because these learnings are deeply ingrained, protectors often resist change, fearing that abandoning their roles could lead to harm.

Protectors who frequently become blended, who have led the system for a long time, or who feel an intense need to match their level of protection to the exile's burden often resist unblending. These blended protectors can be so subtle or deeply ingrained that they are not immediately recognized. When protectors are unaware of or distrustful of the Self, they cannot be guided into the conditions necessary for memory reconsolidation, advancing beyond the EMDR assessment phase, or allowing the unburdening of the exiled part they protect. As a result, they remain anchored in old emotional learnings, predicting and projecting outdated fears and beliefs onto present-day situations, blocking each therapeutic pathway.

The Steps of Phase 2.5 Discovery

With Discovery facilitating Functional Dual Attention and paving the way for memory reconsolidation, we now turn to the specific steps of this process, see Box 7.1.

Step 1: Uncovering a Blended Protector in Phases I and II of IFS-Informed EMDR

In the IFS-Informed EMDR preparation phase, the "feel towards" question—borrowed from IFS therapy and incorporated into the Syzygy Model's Presence of Self Scale—is designed to establish Self-presence and engage the Self-to-part relationship (Hersey, 2018). Additionally, the Presence of Self Scale helps identify protectors, allowing the therapist to explore unblending options and facilitate progress into the assessment phase. Although blended protectors can emerge at any phase of EMDR, a thorough history-taking and preparation phase often reveals these parts early, signaling the need to pivot to Discovery.

Box 7.1 Specific Steps of Discovery

Step 1:   Uncovering a Blended Protector in Phases I and II of IFS-Informed EMDR

Step 2:   Gathering the Elements of a Discovery Target in Phase 2.5
- Using Direct Access
- Protector Positive Intention
- Level of Urge to Protect

Step 3:   Establishing the Discovery Contract

Step 4:   Using Bilateral Stimulation in Discovery

Step 5:   Discovery Guideposts
- Self-energy Interweaves
- Disconfirming Knowledge and Juxtaposition

Therapists who are well versed in EMDR but are still developing their expertise in IFS often struggle to detect subtle signs of blending, polarization, and interfering protectors. Obvious indications, such as dislike, annoyance, or resentment toward a target part, clearly signal that a protector is blocking Self. However, responses like "I get it" or "I understand it" can be more ambiguous and require careful interpretation, for example:

1 Blending or Collusion: "I agree with it" suggests fusion with another part.
2 Polarization: "I get where it's coming from, but ..." indicates internal conflict with another part.
3 Intellectualizing: The client could have a logical, well-developed narrative about the part but remains emotionally disconnected, numb, or ambivalent.

Self-like managers might present an openness that is mistaken for Self-energy while secretly harboring a hidden agenda to control the process or other parts (Schwartz & Sweezy, 2020). A client might appear curious and engaged, but their *compassion* or *understanding* is more performative than authentic. Similarly, protectors whose behavior takes the form of caretaking, fawning, or compliance can be easily overlooked.

Case Example: Jenna's Blended Protector

To illustrate how subtle blending can obstruct therapeutic progress, consider the case of Jenna.

Jenna grew up in a household with a narcissistic mother prone to hysteria and catastrophizing. Without a co-regulating caregiver, her nervous

system adapted by remaining in a chronic state of hyperarousal. One of her most dominant protectors fixates obsessively on her health—constantly scanning, ruminating, and predicting worst-case scenarios. This part holds the belief: "I must stay vigilant to prevent disaster." Meanwhile, an exiled part of Jenna, who has never known safety in her body, remains locked away, consumed by fear.

Aware of her tendency to catastrophize, Jenna has another part that tries to counterbalance it with cognitive reframing, self-compassion, and mindfulness. Masking as Self, this part employs interventions that offer temporary relief but little lasting change.

In EMDR sessions, Jenna intellectualizes her experiences, maintaining a smooth narrative while her catastrophizing protector operates quietly in the background—much like an app running unseen on a phone. When this protector emerges, her Self-like manager skillfully steps in with understanding but ultimately prevents deeper engagement.

The Presence of Self Scale, guided by the "feel towards" question, might yield a lower-than-expected score, revealing an incongruence between Jenna's verbalized insights and her system's actual state. When asked "how much connection on a scale of 1–7 do you feel towards the catastrophizing part?" she said 3, an indication of the Self-like, blended manager creating a disconnect between the part and Self. Without the true presence of the Self, no Functional Dual Attention can occur, leaving the session ineffective. The ongoing interplay between Jenna's protectors—her catastrophizing part and her Self-like manager—creates a closed loop, keeping her exiled part suppressed, awaiting Self.

Jenna's case highlights how deeply embedded protectors can be challenging to detect, yet crucial to address. Therapists often sense that something isn't progressing but may struggle to identify the underlying block. Once a blended protector is recognized, standard IFS techniques can be used to facilitate unblending and invite parts into connection with Self. If these approaches prove insufficient, transitioning into Phase 2.5 and setting up the Discovery target becomes the next step.

Step 2: Gathering the Elements of a Discovery Target in Phase 2.5

Using Direct Access

Direct access is an IFS approach in which the therapist, speaking from Self, directly engages with the blended protector—either explicitly or implicitly.

This method, described by Schwartz and Sweezy (2020), offers several benefits, including fostering trust in the therapeutic relationship and improving the therapist's ability to work with a complex system of protectors that block the client's Self. Ideally, this process culminates in a transition to internal communication, or "in-sight," as Self emerges and the system becomes more open and trusting.

Protector Positive Intention

The Syzygy Model uniquely replaces EMDR's negative cognition target element with the Protector Positive Intention (PPI) (Hersey, 2019). This structured approach, influenced by Coherence Therapy's problem- and solution-defining constructs (Ecker et al., 2024), ensures that the PPI statement captures the implicit emotional learning of the protector.

In IFS-Informed EMDR, the PPI helps uncover why a protector remains committed to its role, shifting the focus to its underlying logic rather than pathologizing it. Protectors firmly believe their strategies are necessary for survival, adaptation, or safety, even if other parts of the system consciously wish to change the behavior. In Discovery, this belief can be explored by curiously examining what problem the blended protector is solving by remaining blended and executing its role to keep the system, from its perspective, safe.

A useful way to frame this is as follows:

- The problem is what the protector fears most—what it believes must be avoided at all costs.
- The solution is the protector's strategy—what it does to prevent the feared outcome.

The PPI reflects a "pick your poison" scenario—the protector's attempt to choose the lesser of two pains, opting for a familiar but necessary suffering to avoid something it perceives as far worse.

For example, consider the following protector strategies and the corresponding PPI statements:

- *I have to numb myself with drinking … so I don't feel the pain of past trauma.*
- *I have to obsess about what I'm wearing … so I don't feel defective.*
- *I have to be hypervigilant … so I don't get assaulted.*
- *I have to shut down … so I don't become overwhelmed.*

Though often maladaptive in the long run, these protector strategies are internally coherent solutions based on the part's emotional learning. In this way, the protector's urge energy is directed toward enacting its solution as a means of self-preservation. The problem the protector is trying to solve—what it perceives as the worst possible outcome—typically points toward an exile carrying unresolved trauma.

By articulating the PPI precisely, the therapist can uncover the deeper fears driving the protector's actions. Below are additional examples of Protector Positive Intention Statements containing both the problem and the solution:

- *I have to people-please (solution) … so I don't feel rejected and unloved (problem).*
- *I have to obsess about what I'm wearing (solution) … so I don't feel defective (problem).*
- *I have to be hypervigilant (solution) … so I don't get assaulted (problem).*
- *I have to restrict (solution) … so I don't feel out of control (problem).*
- *I have to distract myself (solution) … so I don't think about that bad thing and become overwhelmed (problem).*

In Discovery, this layered approach integrates EMDR's negative cognition target element, IFS's perspective on protector fears, and Coherence Therapy's focus on emotional learning. By clarifying the blended protector's logic, we create a more precise foundation for EMDR processing.

Measuring the Level of Urge to Protect (LUP)

Once the Protector Positive Intention has been identified through direct access, the therapist assesses the urgency with which the protector feels compelled to carry out its role. This urgency is measured using the Level of Urge to Protect (LUP), which parallels EMDR's Subjective Units of Disturbance (SUDs) scale (Hersey & Erhmann, 2013).

What About the Positive Cognition (PC)?

A Positive Cognition is not elicited here because, in the Syzygy Model, Positive Cognitions must originate from Self, which corresponds to EMDR's Adaptive Network. Since access to Self is currently blocked by the blended protector, any Positive Cognition at this stage would be artificially constructed rather than authentically emerging from Self.

Case Example of Gathering Discovery Target Elements: PPI and LUP

Diana had a protector that constantly isolated her, believing that staying alone was the only way to avoid the crippling pain of rejection and abandonment. She sought therapy to address this issue and to support her in becoming more social. However, all of her efforts were consistently undermined by this part, which harbored a fear so immense that Diana described it as "cataclysmic." After several attempts to connect with this isolating part, it became clear that another manager part was actually in the driver's seat—the part that wanted her to be more social. This part blended with and often masked as Self, fluctuating between waves of cheerleading energy—"Go to that event and meet people!"—and frustration—"What's the big deal?" This blended protector part is the Discovery target.

Once identified, the therapist asked Diana if they could speak directly to the protector (explicit direct access) and gathered information (find, focus, flesh out), such as Diana's described image of a social butterfly with perfectly manicured nails and the sensation of tension, anxiety, and a tightened jaw.

Therapist (using explicit direct access):	*So, you're the part in Diana's system that pushes her to be more social?*
Protector:	*Yes, I can't stand her being so alone—it feels like she's slipping away, like a hopeless loser.*
Therapist:	*I'd like to understand more about that, about your concern that she'll end up a hopeless loser.*
Protector:	*It's just ridiculous—she has people who want to hang out with her, but she never replies to their texts. Then they just move on! She sits at home and does nothing about it. I try to get her to put on makeup and do her hair like she used to in college, but she won't listen to me.*
Therapist:	*That sounds really frustrating. I can see how much you care about Diana and that you want her to have friends and be social. What are you afraid would happen if you stopped trying to convince her of this?*
Protector:	*If I didn't try? Well, she would never do anything.*
Therapist:	*And then what would happen?*

Protector:	*I know you're trying to tell me to let go, but that is not happening.*
Therapist:	*No, I'm not telling you to stop. I actually just want to understand this more. I see that you're trying to help her and that you care deeply about her.*
Protector:	*Yeah, I do care about her. If I stopped pushing, I'm afraid she would be so alone, and darkness would come.*
Therapist:	*And then?*
Protector:	*Well ... when she gets really dark, bad things can happen ...*
Therapist:	*Can you say more about that?*
Protector:	*Things like that time she had to go to the hospital, you know?*
Therapist:	*Yes, I see. That makes a lot of sense. That's an incredibly heavy burden to carry—trying to keep Diana safe from such intense pain.*
Protector:	*I just can't let her go back there.*
Therapist (PPI statement):	*Let me make sure I'm understanding this because it feels so important. You have to push Diana to be social because if you don't, she could isolate so much that darkness comes—and the risk of that darkness is dangerous, like the time she had to be hospitalized. Am I getting it?*
Protector (with a sigh):	*Yes, that's exactly it. I can't let that happen again.*
Therapist (Level of Urge to Protect):	*I really see how hard you're working to keep her safe. How strong is that need to keep pushing her to be social, to protect her from all of that, on a scale of 0–10?*
Protector:	*Like a 100!*
Therapist:	*That sounds pretty intense! Thank you for helping me understand better how massive this is for you.*

Diana's case illustrates how the Protector Positive Intention (PPI) statement captures the protector's solution to a perceived problem. In this case, the protector's problem was the fear that isolation would lead to a dangerous level of emotional darkness. Its solution was to push Diana into social situations, believing this would prevent her from slipping into despair. However, because this part operated with such urgency, it inadvertently created internal polarization, amplifying the very distress it sought to avoid. Through explicit direct access, the therapist helped the protector articulate its logic with greater precision, uncovering the deeper emotional learning behind its role—that without pushing Diana to be social, she would spiral into isolation, leading to emotional darkness and danger. This process not only validated the protector's efforts without trying to change it but also set the stage for the next step in Discovery.

Step 3: Establishing the Discovery Contract

A Discovery Contract is an explicitly stated agreement with a protector part to explore and understand it more deeply using bilateral stimulation. This agreement is typically introduced after gathering the initial Discovery target elements—image, body sensation, Protector Positive Intention (PPI), and Level of Urge to Protect (LUP)—but it can be revisited and expanded upon as needed. The blended protector, or other concerned protectors in the system, may require additional reassurance before engaging in this next step.

Continuation of Diana's Case Example

Therapist:	*Would it be okay if we get to know this more deeply by adding some bilateral tapping, like this? (demonstrates Butterfly Hug)*
Protector:	*OK, I guess.*
Therapist (reassuring, with a genuine invitation for understanding):	*You sound unsure, which makes sense given how much you care about Diana. I just want you to know that you are in the driver's seat, and this is simply an opportunity for us to understand this more clearly. How does that land for you?*
Protector:	*I feel less anxious about it with you saying that. I'm okay with keeping going.*
Therapist:	*That's good! Okay, so you identified the image of being social, the anxiety and tension in your jaw, and that really intense, 100/10 need to push Diana to be social—because if you didn't, she could isolate so much that darkness would come. And the risk of that darkness is dangerous, like the time she had to be hospitalized. As you notice these things, add a Butterfly Hug.*

Key Considerations for the Discovery Contract

The effectiveness of the Discovery Contract relies on the therapist's ability to engage with genuine Self-led curiosity and respect for the blended protector's role. Any subtle agenda of trying to get the protector to unblend can be counterproductive. In fact, while working with blended protectors, the therapist's own blended protectors can become the Achilles heel of the Discovery process—adding an unconscious pressure to "fix" rather than understand. Therefore, the therapist must also remain attuned to their own system, ensuring that their Self-energy, rather than their protector parts, is leading the process.

Step 4: Using Bilateral Stimulation in Discovery

If direct access in IFS is already effective on its own, why add bilateral stimulation? Imagine the therapeutic process as mining for gold. When working with a complex system, relying solely on direct access can be like sifting through layers of earth by hand—possible, but slow, with other parts surfacing and delaying progress. Bilateral stimulation, however, functions like a targeted excavation tool, accelerating the process and enhancing precision—an efficiency for which EMDR is known, though it is sometimes criticized for being too forceful or bypassing important protector dynamics.

However, when EMDR is powered by Self in the Syzygy approach, bilateral stimulation deepens engagement with the protector, fostering a richer understanding of its perspective. Rather than rushing the process, it fosters a deeper witnessing in which Self-energy can emerge organically. While traditional EMDR is often associated with its speed, Discovery harnesses bilateral stimulation not for rapid relief or quick unblending, but for greater clarity and connection.

Step 5: Discovery Guideposts

Discovery is a mission of deep, compassionate understanding rather than a targeted effort to unblend or desensitize. While unblending may naturally emerge from the process—and our therapist parts might hope for this—the intent must remain grounded in genuine, Self-led curiosity. The implicit emotional learning of blended protectors is embedded within their very being, shaped by lived experience. For this reason, the Syzygy Model emphasizes a "Be-Friend, Not Unblend" agenda (Hersey, 2020).

Once bilateral stimulation has been agreed upon, Discovery can begin. Here are key guideposts to keep the process on track:

1 Self-energy Interweaves

The therapist can model Self-energy by interweaving well-paced questions informed by their understanding of IFS and memory reconsolidation into the process and subtly resourcing Self-energy as it emerges in the client's system. As the protector is acknowledged and understood, early signs of unblending may appear—reflected in the client's statements between sets that embody the eight C's of Self (calmness, curiosity, clarity, compassion, confidence, creativity, courage, and connectedness). These shifts should be gently mirrored back by the therapist:

This sounds like a new perspective—does that feel true?

I'm hearing some curiosity that wasn't there before—are you noticing that too?

These reflections reinforce the client's growing capacity for Self-leadership.

2 Juxtaposition and Memory Reconsolidation

As the protector begins to unblend and a relationship develops between Self and the part, the therapist can pass the baton, allowing the client's Self to take the lead and transitioning from direct access to in-sight. As the Self-to-part connection deepens, an opportunity may arise to introduce juxtaposition, a concept from Coherence Therapy (Ecker et al., 2024). This process contrasts the protector's emotional truth—or old emotional learning—with new, disconfirming knowledge from Self.

A juxtaposition experience allows the protector to encounter a new reality—one that mismatches its previous experience. In Coherence Therapy, such mismatch experiences are essential for updating implicit emotional memories and dissolving outdated responses (Ecker et al., 2024). Previously, this disconfirming knowledge from Self was inaccessible due to the protector's blended state, preventing access to a Positive Cognition. Now, in an unblended state and connected with Self, this Coherence Therapy strategy serves as the catalyst for memory reconsolidation, allowing the protector to update its role, reorient within the system, and reacquaint itself with Self.

For a comprehensive discussion on the juxtaposition process and its role in memory reconsolidation, see *Unlocking the Emotional Brain: Eliminating Symptoms at Their Roots Using Memory Reconsolidation* (Ecker et al., 2024).

Determining the Next Step in the Healing Process

At this stage, the system may take different pathways. The therapist might transition from direct access to in-sight, proceed with Phase 4 IFS-Informed EMDR (Desensitization), shift focus to another protector that emerges, or receive permission to engage with an exile. The next step is always guided by the system's natural progression and readiness. The shifts that occur through Discovery foster Functional Dual Attention, ensuring that EMDR processing can continue in alignment with the entire system.

Therapist Protector Parts in IFS-Informed EMDR

In my experience as an IFS-Informed EMDR trainer and consultant, incorporating the IFS perspective tends to have a calming effect on the protective manager parts of the therapist. While IFS emphasizes an agenda-less Self and trusts in the organic unfolding of the internal system, EMDR therapists often carry protector-driven agendas—with parts that feel a strong need to know, help, and heal. These well-meaning manager parts frequently hold beliefs about our value, competence, and worth as therapists. When clients progress, these parts feel satisfied; when they don't, our own exiles—holding deeper fears of inadequacy or failure—threaten to surface.

For example, during a consultation, a therapist expressed distress over a client who was not "getting better" and voiced fears about the client's future. As we explored further, she uncovered a manager part carrying deep anxiety and an urgent need to fix the client. Initially, her focus remained on all the potential negative outcomes for the client. However, when she asked herself, "What does this part of me believe it means about ME if my client does not get better?," she connected with the deeper fear of her manager part. Beneath its efforts to control the therapy process lay an exile carrying a profound sense of inadequacy and shame.

The task of the IFS-Informed EMDR therapist, especially during the Discovery process, is to unblend from our own parts first. Schwartz and Sweezy (2020) describe a therapist's most challenging clients as our greatest "tormentors"—mentors in disguise who help us recognize the parts within ourselves that need healing (p. 90). Similarly, Twombly (2022), in *Trauma and Dissociation-Informed Internal Family Systems*, offers invaluable insights on countertransference and the *Fire Drill*—a framework for navigating therapist reactions during trauma work. These perspectives highlight that healing is not just for the client; it is an ongoing process for the therapist as well.

The Bridge of Discovery: Expanding Self-Energy and Healing Pathways

Discovery is a core component of IFS-Informed EMDR, one that is particularly beneficial for clients with complex trauma histories. Engaging with blended protector parts during the preparation phase not only fosters the expansion of positive and adaptive memory networks—manifested as increased Self-energy—but also naturally broadens the client's window of tolerance. As protectors are befriended and understood, Self-energy becomes more accessible, strengthening the Self-to-part relationship and facilitating internal relational repair.

Recognizing the challenges of applying standard EMDR protocols to complex trauma cases, leaders in the EMDR and IFS field have emphasized the need for modified approaches. These include implementing restricted protocols and increasing interweaves to ensure client stability and safety during processing (van der Hart et al., 2010). In alignment with these recommendations, Discovery serves as a modified assessment phase within IFS-Informed EMDR. Rather than directly targeting traumatic material, this approach focuses on protector parts, establishing a contract to understand and befriend them—keeping the process safely contained.

The Discovery approach is an alternative to Desensitization, functioning as a series of bridges or pivots between EMDR phases (Hersey, 2020). By narrowing the focus to blended protectors, therapists can restrict processing, gradually transitioning toward desensitization of traumatic material as Self-energy increases. In some cases, Discovery may serve as the primary phase of therapy, with clinicians taking time to understand complicated layers of blended protectors and tangled polarizations until sufficient Self-energy is present to engage in trauma processing effectively. Patience and persistence in this process, are of course, essential.

Conclusion: Arriving at a New Perspective

The journey through Discovery is not about bypassing obstacles—it is about understanding the road itself. Just as a winding path through the fog requires patience, curiosity, and trust in the process, working with blended protectors demands attunement to the system's natural progression. Discovery provides the necessary bridge between preparation and reprocessing, ensuring that protector parts are not pushed aside but actively engaged, allowing for the expansion of Self-energy and the establishment of Functional Dual Attention.

By integrating the structured efficiency of EMDR, the internal wisdom of IFS, and the memory reconsolidation principles of Coherence Therapy, Discovery offers a systematic yet adaptable approach to complex trauma treatment. This phase honors the protector's role, ensuring that therapy is not an expressway that forces healing without permission, nor a loop that keeps clients circling without progress. Instead, it is a thoughtfully constructed passageway that allows for meaningful shifts.

As clinicians, embracing this approach means shifting our perspective: *what appears to be resistance is often protection waiting to be understood.* When we recognize that *what's in the way is the way,* we step into a more compassionate, collaborative, and effective way of working. Through

Discovery, we help our clients build internal bridges—ones that lead not just to exiles, but to a profoundly different relationship with their own system, grounded in Self-leadership, trust, and healing.

References

Ecker, B., Ticic, R., & Hulley, L. (2024). *Unlocking the emotional brain: Eliminating symptoms at their roots using memory reconsolidation* (2nd ed.). Routledge.

Hersey, B. (2018). *IFS-Informed EMDR: The Internal Family Systems interweave.* [Online course]. EMDRIFS. https://emdrifs.com/p/ifs-informed-emdr-6-0-ce1

Hersey, B. (2019, January 26–27). *Through the looking glass* [Workshop]. https://secure.smore.com/n/bcedy-emdr-ego-states.

Hersey, B. (2020, April 20). *Discovery: IFS-Informed EMDR with blended protectors* [Online course]. EMDRIFS. http://emdrifs.com.

Hersey, B., & Erhmann, L. (2013, January 18–19). *EMDR & IFS: The Internal Family Systems Interweave* [Workshop]. Heartspace Wellness Alliance, Altoona, PA.

Schwartz, R. C., & Sweezy, M. (2020). *Internal Family Systems therapy* (2nd ed.). Guilford Press.

Twombly, J. H. (2022). *Trauma and dissociation-informed Internal Family Systems.* Pathways to Healing Publications.

van der Hart, O., Nijenhuis, E. R. S., & Solomon, R. (2010). Dissociation of the personality in complex trauma-related disorders and EMDR: Theoretical considerations. *Journal of EMDR Practice and Research, 4*(2), 76–79.

Chapter 8

Integrating Trauma-Informed Stabilization Treatment (TIST) into EMDR and Parts Work

Janina Fisher

The Legacy of Trauma: How We Become Fragmented

In the face of abuse and neglect, especially at the hands of those they love, children need enough psychological distance from what is happening to avoid overwhelm and survive psychologically intact. Preserving some modicum of self-esteem, attachment to family, and hope for the future requires victims to disconnect from what has happened, doubt or dis-remember their experience, and disown the "bad [victim] child" to whom it happened as "not me." By holding out some sense of themselves as "good" and disconnected from how they have been exploited, abused children capitalize on the human brain's innate capacity to split or compartmentalize. That "good child" might be precociously mature, sweet and helpful, perfectionistic, self-critical, or quiet and shy, but, most importantly, they have a way to be acceptable and safe-er in an unsafe world. Splitting or fragmenting in this way is an ingenious and adaptive survival strategy—but one with a steep price. To ensure that the rejected "not me" child is kept out of consciousness requires that, long after the traumatic events are over, individuals must continue to rely on dissociation, denial, and/or self-hatred to enforce the disconnection. In the end, they have survived the failure of safety, the abuse, and betrayal at the cost of disowning their most vulnerable and most wounded selves. Aware that their self-presentation and ability to function is only one piece of who they really are, they now feel fraudulent. Struggling to stay away from the "bad" side and identify with the good side, they have a felt sense of "faking it," "pretending," or of being what others want them to be. For some, this conviction of fraudulence engenders resentment; for some, shame and self-doubt.

As children of abuse continue to grow through latency into adolescence and subsequently adulthood, this splitting of the self supports another important aspect of surviving trauma: mastering normal developmental tasks, such as learning in school, developing peer relationships, and finding interests on which to focus and even enjoy. The "good" part of the child is free to develop normally, while that other part of the child bears the

DOI: 10.4324/9781003541554-10

emotional and physical imprint of the past, scans for signs of danger, and braces for the next set of threats and abandonments. To make the individual's situation more complicated, neither the "me" nor the "not me" self is likely to have well-developed memories of the traumatic events that could provide a context for self-understanding.

The "Living Legacy" of the Past

Without a clear chronological record of what happened but vulnerable to the uninvited activation of trauma-related feeling and body memories, individuals are left with a legacy of symptoms and reactions with no context that identifies them as memory. Survivors of trauma later present in therapy with descriptions of their anxiety, depression, shame, low self-esteem, loneliness and alienation, problems with anger, and impulsivity or acting out. They might be troubled by chronic expectations of danger: Intrusive fear and dread, hypervigilance ("eyes in the back of my head"), chronic shame and self-hatred, a conviction that the worst is about to happen, hopelessness and helplessness, fear of abandonment, numbing and disconnection from emotions. Or they may come to therapy as a last resort because they are fighting a losing battle against addiction, self-harming impulses, eating disorders, or a longing or even determination to die. Often, they can tell us very little about what evokes these self-destructive impulses that bring quick short-term relief at great risk to their safety: "I do it to punish myself," "I hate myself," "I don't deserve to live," "I'm disgusting—I wish I were dead." They sometimes struggle with how to connect these patterns to the past—but, more often, they prefer not to think about what happened then or minimize it: "It wasn't that bad."

I have long believed that trauma treatment must address the **effects** of the traumatic past, not its events. Being able to tolerate remembering a horrific experience is not as important a goal as feeling safe right here, right now—or being able to reassure oneself that the racing of the heart is just a triggered response, not a sign of danger—or being able to relate to shame, grief, and anger as feeling memories. EMDR is very effective in using the event to evoke an image, cognitions, feelings, and sensations—all unresolved effects of that event. In my view, however, full resolution cannot truly be achieved without reclaiming the lost children and disowned parts of ourselves, extending to them a helping hand, welcoming them "home" at long last, creating safety for them, and making them feel wanted, needed, and valued.

Parallel Lives: The Disowning of Dissociation

In the history of the trauma field, the concepts of dissociation and splitting have been repeatedly observed as complications of trauma, but consistently rejected as not valid or believable within the prevailing diagnostic systems and therefore to be avoided. One of the difficulties with gaining acceptance for the existence of dissociative splitting, and especially dissociative disorders, has been an absence of studies demonstrating a scientific basis for such dramatic, difficult-to-treat symptoms.

Theories of parts tend to be metaphorical rather than biologically or brain-based. In the dissociative disorders world, the explanatory hypothesis has historically been stress-related: When events are traumatic, the theory asserts, they exceed the brain's capacity to tolerate or process them as wholes. Therefore, they must be split or compartmentalized so that overwhelming event memories are shared by dissociated parts of the same age, each carrying some portion of the memory. Each part is viewed as a repository of memory, representing the history of the client at a specific time. In treatment, the parts are encouraged to "download" or disclose their memories so that the "host" can share their pain and accept their shared past. Although this hypothesis makes intuitive sense to many clinicians and clients, it lacks the scientific validity necessary to overcome the skepticism of dissociation by the mental health world.

Another theory is that multiplicity is normal, that all human beings have a multi-consciousness rather than a uni-consciousness. A mindfulness-based approach to understanding parts based on this hypothesis is Internal Family Systems, or IFS (Schwartz & Sweezy, 2020). Known for its compassionate tone and cultivation of mindful consciousness, IFS also depends upon a metaphorical theory, this one based on intrapsychic defenses: The disowned victim child is termed an "exile," hidden from conscious awareness by the activity of "managers." When the manager parts do not offer enough protection to keep exiles out of awareness, acting out by another set of parts, the "firefighters," creates distraction and crisis. Healing occurs in the IFS model when the exiled parts are reclaimed and can feel safe enough with "Self" (the higher self of the client) to share the disowned memories and be "unburdened" of the painful emotions and beliefs connected to the trauma (see Chapter 2 and 3).

Compartmentalization Under Stress

Attachment research has contributed to the literature supporting the concept of an innate tendency to compartmentalize under stress. In longitudinal studies of attachment behavior (Lyons-Ruth et al., 2006; Solomon & George, 1999; Solomon & Siegel, 2003), researchers have demonstrated that children with disorganized attachment status at age one are significantly more likely to exhibit dissociative symptoms by age 19 and/or to be diagnosed with Borderline Personality Disorder or Dissociative Identity Disorder in adulthood. When attachment figures are abusive, the child's only source of safety and protection becomes simultaneously the source of immediate danger, leaving the child caught between two conflicting sets of instincts. On the one hand, they are driven by the attachment instinct to seek proximity, comfort, and protection from attachment figures. On the other, they are driven by equally strong animal defense instincts to freeze, fight, flee, or submit or dissociate before they get too close to the frightening parent.

With attachment figures who may be withdrawn or neglectful at some times and violent at others, the ability to rapidly shift from state to state as needed to deal with different threats is essential: For example, in response to the sound of the abuser's voice or footsteps, panic or fear could alert the child to danger. Playfulness might lift the parent's irritable mood and facilitate a positive connection by making them laugh. At times, it might be helpful to capitalize on the submission response to become the precociously responsible child who tries to protect younger siblings in the face of the violent behavior, but at other times, it could be safer to rely on hypervigilance, staying "on guard," carefully observing the parent's mood, and reacting in whatever ways best defend against their "frightened or frightening" behavior. In such environments, it is safer to adapt using a system of Selves rather than becoming a fully integrated "self."

Extrapolating from the observations by Charles Myers of "shell-shocked" World War I veterans, Onno van der Hart et al. (2004) labeled these different drives or systems "part(s) of the personality." Van der Hart et al. (2006) borrowed the language of Myers (1915) in describing the part of the child driven by daily life priorities as the "Apparently Normal Part of the Personality" and parts driven by animal defense responses the "Emotional Parts of the Personality," or, individually, the Fight, Flight, Freeze, Submit, or Attach for Survival parts.

In this chapter, I will use terms more useful in clinical practice: The "Going on with Normal Life Part" and the "Trauma-Related Parts" of the personality. In avoiding the words "apparently normal," my goal is to challenge clients' tendencies to see their ability to function as a "false self" and their trauma-related responses as the "true self." Connecting different parts to the survival responses that drive them challenges clients' automatic interpretations of their behavior: Experiences of feeling rage make more sense when tied to a "fight part;" the inability to say "no" feels less shameful when connected to a submissive part whose sense of safety is tied to pleasing others or feeling "less than."

The concept that each part represents a way of surviving dangerous conditions, that each represents a different approach to self-protection, gives meaning and dignity to the fragmentation. The parts in this view are not repositories of memory; they were a means of surviving the "worst of the worst," not a means of remembering it. As carriers of instinctive survival responses, the parts remain poised for the next threat or trauma-related trigger for decades after "it" is over.

Recognizing the Signs of Structurally Dissociated Parts

Although each client's structurally dissociated personality system is unique, some characteristics of the parts are universal. The Going On with Normal Life part tries to carry on (functioning at a job, raising the children, organizing home life, even taking up meaningful personal and professional goals), while other parts serve the animal defense functions of fight, flight, freeze (or fear), submit, and "cling" or attach for survival. These defense-driven parts continue to be activated by trauma-related triggers, resulting in hypervigilance and mistrust, overwhelming emotions, incapacitating depression or anxiety, self-destructive behavior, and fear or hopelessness about the future, i.e., the difficulties that often lead clients to seek psychotherapy. Certain symptoms can alert us to the presence of underlying structural dissociation:

1 **Signs of internal splitting**: The client functions highly at work where there are "positive triggers" (work assignments, collaboration with peers, responsibilities), while regressing at home or in personal relationships. Or the client might report alternating fears of abandonment followed by pushing away those who try to get close, or describe a tendency to initially idealize others followed by disillusionment and anger when these individuals fail the client in some way.

2 **Treatment history**: The client reports a number of previous treatments that have resulted in little progress or clarity, or describes those treatments as rocky and tumultuous or having ended in some unusually dramatic way.

3 **Somatic symptoms**: Unusual pain sensitivity or uncharacteristically high pain tolerance, stress-related headaches, eye blinking or drooping, narcoleptic symptoms, and even physical symptoms with no diagnosable medical cause can often be trauma-related or a symptom of dissociative activity. One of the most common indicators of structural dissociation is atypical responses or non-responsiveness to medications.

4 **"Regressive" behavior or thinking**: Sometimes, the client's body language seems more typical of a young child than an adult of his or her chronological age: He or she might appear shy, collapsed, fearful, unable to tolerate being seen, unable to make eye contact. Verbal and cognitive style can also reveal the presence of younger parts of the self: Concrete or black/white thinking, words or style of expression more typical of a child than an adult.

5 **Patterns of indecision or self-sabotage**: Often misinterpreted as "ambivalence," a client's inability to make small everyday decisions or problems with carrying out his or her expressed intentions can reflect conflicts between parts with opposite aims. Often this phenomenon manifests in frequent changes of job, career, or relationship, or a history of success in

life alternating with self-sabotage or inexplicable failure, high functioning alternating with decompensation, hard work being suddenly undone by self-destructive actions.

6 **Memory symptoms**: While memory gaps and "time loss" are cardinal symptoms of dissociative disorders, more subtle memory problems can be indicative of structural dissociation. For example, all of the following memory issues are common manifestations of parts activity: Difficulty remembering how time was spent in a day, difficulty remembering conversations or the focus of therapy sessions, "blackouts," getting lost while driving somewhere familiar (such as going home from work), forgetting well-learned skills (such as how to drive), or engaging in behavior one does not recall.

7 **Patterns of self-destructive and addictive behavior**: Many studies have demonstrated correlations between suicidality and self-harm and addictive behavior with a history of trauma, so it should not be surprising that therapists encounter traumatized clients who struggle against their own self-destructive behavior. My assumption is that unsafe behavior consistently reflects the activation of fight- and flight-driven parts by trauma-related triggers. While the Going On with Normal Life Self of the client seeks therapy because he or she is committed to life, to wanting "all the things everyone wants," fight parts engage in high-risk behavior or attempt to harm or kill the body in the effort to get relief from implicit memories at any cost. Parts driven by the flight response tend to choose eating disorders or addictive behavior that alters consciousness, allowing distance from unbearable feelings and flashbacks. Fight-related parts are prone to more violent actions, whether aggression toward others or self-harm and suicidal behavior.

Helping Clients and Their Parts "Be Here" Now

Our first priority in treatment must be to challenge the subjective perception that client symptoms are indicative of current danger or proof of their defectiveness. Instead, therapists need to counteract the habitually triggered danger signals and trauma responses by calling attention to them as communications from parts. Stuckness, resistance, chronic depression, fear of change, entrenched fear and self-hatred, crisis and conflict, even suicidality all can be communications from parts that fear for their lives, unaware that the dangers they are bracing against are now in the past.

Disappointment, criticism, closeness or distance, or even authority figures may no longer be life-threatening, but each nonetheless evokes trauma-related implicit memories and the parts who hold them. Helping clients learn to become curious and interested in their symptoms and able to identify the voices who speak through their reactions can change their relationship to themselves and to the past from one of shame and dread to one of compassion. Understanding how each part has participated in the person's survival increases the sense of "we, together" and challenges the sense of being abandoned and alone. Feeling warmth and empathy for young, wounded selves becomes not only comforting but healing as well.

Trauma-Informed Stabilization Treatment or TIST

A trauma-informed parts approach offers some new possibilities for addressing the challenges our clients present. First and foremost, working with symptoms as manifestations of parts allows the therapist to incorporate mindfulness-based practices: Helping clients "notice" their experience rather than "get in touch with it." In traumatized clients, the heightened intensity (or numbing) caused by autonomic dysregulation makes "getting in touch with feelings" either overwhelming or deadening, either of which can evoke anxiety, depression, or impulsive behavior. "Noticing," as in mindful awareness, allows the client to achieve "dual awareness," the ability to stay connected to the emotional or somatic experience while also observing it from a very slight mindful distance. This is similar to the IFS conceptualization of "Self," the part in all of us that observes and notices the parts with curiosity and interest.

Secondly, a parts approach allows us to titrate emotions or memories: If one part is overwhelmed by emotional pain, other parts of the mind and body (or in IFS, the "Self-energy") can be calm, curious, or even empathic. If one part is remembering something alarming or devastating, the Going On with Normal Life part, connected to Self-energy, can offer support, validation, or comfort. As meditation practices, clinical hypnosis, and other uses of mindfulness attest, the human brain is capable of holding multiple states of consciousness "in mind" simultaneously, and this ability has important therapeutic uses. Using "dual awareness," we have the capacity to fully inhabit the present moment: To feel our feet on the ground through awareness of body sensation while our visual perception takes in details of the room in which we are sitting—while, in the same moment, we can evoke an image from an earlier time in our lives that takes us "back there" to a state-specific memory.

Describing these phenomena using the language of the brain, however, would not have the same result as does using the language of parts. To say, "I can sense my medial prefrontal cortex is curious about the negative mood state connected to the right subcortical areas of my brain" does not evoke interest, emotional connection, or self-compassion. However, when the therapist teaches clients to observe, "I can sense in myself some curiosity about the depressed part's sadness," they are more connected and attuned to their emotions and sensations—the first step toward achieving the ability to have compassion for themselves.

As the client is taught by the therapist to mindfully notice the child part's distress and understand it as this little child's pain, they are next encouraged to empathize with "the child part's feelings." This is not always an easy step for clients whose way of distancing the "not me" parts has been to loathe and despise their feelings. But the therapist whose compassion for the parts is genuine and spontaneous can create a contagion effect, evoking compassion even in the client who resists (see Chapter 9).

To evoke empathy for the child, the therapist has to ask the client to pause and be curious about this child part who is afraid, ashamed, or hurt and lonely. How old is he or she? Can the client see the part? What does s/he look like? What expression does the client see on that little face? Acknowledging the enormity of what this child part has experienced can also evoke compassion, as long as the therapist is clearly asking, "What kinds of things has *this child* experienced?" rather than "What happened to you at this age?" The latter is more likely to trigger implicit reliving, while the former helps the client "see" the child as a helpless, innocent victim.

Lastly, the client is taught to use the resources characteristic of the Normal Life self to "help" the child parts that are so frightened and in so much distress. In session after session, as clients present the issues or feelings most troubling on that day, the therapist continues to ask them to notice "which part" is upset today and what has triggered that part. The assumption that upset is always a communication from a part is not a scientific fact, of course—it represents a way of relating to triggered states or implicit memories in a mindful, compassionate, nonpathologizing way.

Underlying this assumption is a mindfulness-related bias that noticing our thoughts, feelings, and body experience with interest, curiosity, and compassion is likely to lead to positive change (Davis & Hayes, 2011; Ogden & Fisher, 2015;). If we as therapists consistently encourage the Normal Life self to take a mental step back, increase curiosity about the younger part(s) who are "having a hard time," notice the bodily and emotional signs that communicate "their" feelings, and then experiment with what might help the parts feel safer, better protected, and less ashamed, we will be "processing" post-traumatic memory. Simply by noticing spontaneously evoked implicit memories and assigning the feelings to younger selves, clients can learn to feel less afraid of their triggered responses and more connected to and protective of their parts, rather than ashamed and alienated.

With the help of a therapist who persistently reframes problematic emotions and issues as communications from parts, clients learn to identify the key features that indicate signs of a part's presence. They are taught to observe distressing or uncomfortable physical sensations, overwhelming or painful emotions, negative or self-punitive beliefs, internal struggles, procrastination, and ambivalence. Automatic reactions, the same thoughts repeatedly coming to mind, repetitive responses to triggers, negative reactions to positive events or stimuli, or "overreactions" should also be flagged as likely signs of parts activity.

For the first time, clients might notice that they can have a relationship to the feeling rather than **being** consumed by it or **identifying** with it as "mine." In addition, when individuals become curious and interested and focused on what they are observing, they intuitively slow their pace and increase concentration to heighten their observational capacity.

Even if available to the client, coping skills and problem-solving are less likely to work when parts are triggered because the "problem" to be solved is most often an implicit memory, not a current stress or challenge. And when "the problem" is the result of competing states engaging in a struggle for control, adult coping has little to no effect. However, when a client can access the Going On with Normal Life Self and its underlying Self-energy (see Chapter 2), the client can benefit significantly.

Fragmented Selves EMDR Protocol

The TIST or Fragmented Selves protocol was designed for clients presenting with Dissociative Identity Disorder (DID), Dissociative Disorder Not Otherwise Specified (DDNOS), Other Specified Dissociative Disorder (OSDD), and personality disorder diagnoses. Often, these clients are not ready for EMDR or risk either becoming destabilized or stuck. Some may tolerate the EMDR sessions but don't make progress in their day-to-day lives. Some may get flooded with memories and become more fragmented or even unsafe. For these clients, it is necessary to embark on an extensive preparation phase during which they are helped to notice, understand, and work with their parts. Success in EMDR treatment requires that they use a parts-focused protocol that ensures staying mindful and regulated throughout each session.

- First, the client must be provided with basic psychoeducation on the Structural Dissociation model derived from *Healing the Fragmented Selves of Trauma Survivors* (2017) or from *Transforming the Living Legacy of Trauma* (Fisher, 2021).
- As part of the psychoeducation, clients are invited to describe what parts they can recognize in themselves in that model.
- Next, clients must learn how to mindfully notice states of distress or trauma responses as communications from parts—but without connecting the parts to any particular single event.
- During this process, the focus should be on the parts' reactions, emotions, and beliefs now: "How old is this part now?" "Is s/he more afraid or more ashamed?" "Is s/he more angry or more sad?" "What triggers this part?"
- Learning to notice and to name distressing states as parts can be a prolonged process, especially for DID and DDNOS clients, but it is essential for the treatment. Without those abilities, EMDR will be either risky or unsuccessful

- Once clients have learned to mindfully notice thoughts, feelings, and body sensations as parts and can speak the language of parts, the therapist must help them learn to recognize when they are "blending" with parts: i.e., becoming flooded with a part's emotions or survival responses.
- The goal is to help clients increase their dual awareness: Awareness of the part and awareness of themselves as observers of the part. Since dual awareness is crucial to successful EMDR treatments, this is another piece of preparation that is essential.
- Once clients can unblend, they must learn to master the ability to conduct internal dialogue with parts regarding day-to-day problems and distressing experiences.
- Internal communication helps to build trust with their parts and can be used to help parts settle and calm when activated.
- Internal dialogue is also essential in managing impulsive and self-destructive parts and achieving some degree of stability.

Prior to the First EMDR Session

- The therapist must facilitate an internal dialogue between the client and parts about agreeing to the use of EMDR.
- Clients must offer the parts a meaningful reason for the work: "It will help us sleep better," "It will help us stand up to people or set boundaries," "It will help every part to get more of what it needs."
- But the client also needs to agree to supporting the parts: "We might remember things no one wants to remember," "There might be feelings that feel overwhelming, but I will help you if that happens."

Choosing a Target to Process

The best targets are not past events but moments when a part is triggered. That is because triggering tells us what implicit material is still "live" for this particular client and parts.

- Identify a moment in **recent time** when distressing thoughts, feelings, or physical reactions were triggered. Starting with a past memory could potentially stimulate a number of parts. The goal in this protocol is to stimulate one single distressed part.
- Help client mindfully notice the distress as a younger part: "Notice the shame as the child part's shame ... so you can feel his shame and also feel yourself noticing him ..."
- If necessary, facilitate unblending from the part so that the client feels the emotions of the part but can also feel some connection to some part of their body (i.e., feet, legs, spine).

- Initiate curiosity: "How old does this part feel?" "Can the client 'see' the part?" "Does the part more scared or more sad? More angry or more ashamed?"
- Ask the client to communicate to that part that they are there and that they understand the part's feelings.

Target Image

Because we are asking a child part for the image, the language has to be age-appropriate. I.e., "Would you show me a picture of what scares you about bedtime?"

"Would you show me a picture that would help me understand your feeling of shame?" Often, the "target image" emerges from a series of images: First, a more general visual picture, then more detailed, as clients ask the part to "show me a picture that represents the worst part of _____."

Negative Cognition

The NC must be the belief of the **part**, not the belief of the adult client, and how it is elicited must support the mindful separation between child part and the adult prefrontal self.

- "Ask this young girl what words go best to describe her belief about her-self now?"
- "What negative belief does this little boy carry now as a result of what happened?"
- "Notice what belief she learned about herself as a result of her experience ..."

Positive cognition: The PC too must be the wished-for belief of the part so that the client maintains dual awareness of him/herself and of the part.

- "Ask her what she would like to believe about herself now?"
- "If he could believe anything he wanted, what would he want to believe about himself?"

VoC: Is likely to be beyond the cognitive capacity of a small-child part. Another option is to use a multiple-choice approach: "Ask him: does he believe it a little, a lot or not at all?"

Emotions: Eliciting the *child part's emotions* is the key to the success of this protocol.

- "Ask him: When he sees the picture and hears the words [of the NC], what feelings come up?"
- "Ask her: When she hears those words [of the NC] and sees the picture, what feelings does she notice?"

SUDS Must Also Be Elicited From The Part

"Ask him on a scale of 0 to 10 (if 0 is settled and calm and 10 is the most intense feelings he can imagine), how strong are the feelings?" [Option: if the child part is very young, the SUDS may be beyond him/her cognitively. The other option is to use a 1–5 scale or ask the child part, "Are the feelings this big, that big, or THAT big?"]

Body

"Where does s/he feel the feelings in the body?"

Bilateral Stimulation

- "Ask **the part** to see the picture, hear the words [of the NC], notice the feelings in the body, and then [follow my hand/follow the lights] ..."
- When you pause, "Ask **the part**: what does **s/he** notice?" "Ask him: What does **s/he** get now?"
- Support dual awareness: **"Can you still feel your feet? [spine?] Can you still feel the little child? Great**—go with that ..." **"Tell her that you are right here with her**—you can keep her safe—it's OK—she is just remembering but nothing bad is happening now." (BLS)
- **Reprocessing always requires that the prefrontal cortex stay "online" so that past/present and child/adult experience be integrated.** With dissociative disorder clients, that means that we need the adult client to witness the child's experience and support the child part's processing. Because of the dissociative disconnection between parts of the personality (and therefore parts of the brain), the client cannot get the full benefit of desensitization and reprocessing without dual awareness. Worse yet, **BLS without dual awareness can stimulate increased autonomic dysregulation** and increased flooding of memory, risking exacerbation of the client's symptoms or even decompensation.

Remember that successful processing requires just the "right" amount of autonomic activation, not too much and not too little.

- **If the client loses dual awareness, pause the BLS** and help them regulate their autonomic arousal and reconnect to their Normal Life adult Self using somatic resources and interweaves.

- **Help them stay connected to the child**: "Tell her that you are going to stay with her—you just need a few minutes to feel your feet and your backbone. Ask her if it helps her when you feel your feet/spine?"
- **Facilitate the provision of a missing experience for the child part**: "Ask this little girl what she needs now to feel safer? To believe she won't be hurt again? To believe that someone cares now?"

  - **Facilitate attachment relationship between child and adult self**: "What is it like for **her** to feel **you** here with her?" "What is it like for **him** to hear **you** say that **you want** to protect **him**?" [Use short sets while building the relationship between adult and child Selves and longer sets for processing of memory.]
  - **"When you feel sad for her/protective of him, what's your impulse?"** Whatever the impulse, ask the client to "stay with the impulse [to reach out, to pick up the child, etc.], and notice what happens next." [BLS] Help clients to visualize the movements and feel them in the body: "When you take his hand in yours, how does that little hand feel in your big hand?" "As you lead him away, what feelings do you notice? Does he feel anxiety? Relief? Excitement?"
  - **Keep installing positive attachment experiences**: "When she says she's both excited and scared, can you understand that? Let her know that it's OK if she's a little scared—it's new to trust someone and have it be safe—of course, she's scared … Go with that."
  - **Future templates**: Especially when the child part is afraid to trust, it is important to rehearse how to stay in relationship with the child between sessions. "Imagine that you are leaving this session and notice what comes up: What are you walking into? Where do you go next?" "Now imagine that you are holding his hand as you walk into your home/office and notice what happens …"

Gauging Successful Reprocessing

Dissociative clients are less likely to get to a 0 SUDS than are clients with simple or complex trauma without dissociative symptoms. Often, the fight and flight parts are alarmed by a 0 SUDS or by pleasurable feelings. In addition, child parts may too young to use a numerical scale, leaving the therapist to estimate completion based on the client's body: Is the body calm? Is the spine straighter? Does the adult client report that the child is calm or feels warm and close? Does the client's skin have more color? Does the client's language reflect an adult cognitive capacity and vocabulary? Has there been a transformation in activation, perspective, emotions or body experience?

Going back to Target

In working with dissociation and fragmentation, **it is more important to check back with the part** than to go back to the target image itself. "Go back to the little girl/boy and see how s/he is doing now …" "What is it like for him/her to look at that picture again?" If the child part's SUDS is 0–2, it is appropriate to install the positive cognition. Keep in mind that with dissociative disorders, a SUDS of 0 is unlikely unless the client has dissociated.

Install Positive Cognition

"Ask this little girl does it feel more real now to believe that it wasn't her fault?" "Ask **him**: Does it feel more real now to believe he is safe?" Emphasize the relationship between part and adult self: "**When you feel me here with you,** does it feel more real to believe that everything is going to be OK?"

Make Sure to End Sessions by Installing a "Post-Hypnotic Suggestion" re the Attachment Bond Between Child Self and Adult

"Let her know that you will get better and better at taking care of her … at being there for her," "Let him know that you will never, ever, ever allow someone to hurt him like that again …" [use short sets to install].

Reprocessing From a TIST Perspective

In the TIST model and in TIST-informed EMDR treatment, the focus is not on traumatic events but on the "legacy of trauma" as it is carried by the parts and as it continues to intrude, even decades later, into the minds, bodies, and ongoing lives of survivors. "Processing the trauma" is equated in this model with "transforming" how the parts have encoded the effects of the traumatic events and transforming the client's relationship to the parts from one of alienation to one of unconditional acceptance and "earned secure attachment." Practically speaking, this requires that the therapist continue to emphasize how the parts are feeling and how able they are to allow the client to "go on with normal life."

The goal is not the elimination or "integration" of parts, but rather a transformed sense of safety and connection. Daniel Siegel (2010) emphasizes the importance of seeing integration as "differentiation and linkage" rather than homogenization. The ability to differentiate parts and attend to their needs for a safe, protective attachment figure is "integration" under this definition. Cognitions are more positive; the parts are less easily triggered; and the client feels compassionate toward rather than threatened by their feelings.

References

Davis, D. M., & Hayes, J. A. (2011). What are the benefits of mindfulness? A practice review of psychotherapy-related research. *Psychotherapy*, *48*(2), 198–208. https://doi.org/10.1037/a0022062.

Fisher, J. (2017). *Healing the Fragmented Selves of Trauma Survivors*. Routledge.

Fisher, J. (2021). *Transforming the living legacy of trauma: A workbook for survivors and therapists* (1st ed.). PESI.

Lyons-Ruth, K., Dutra, L., Schuder, M. R., & Bianchi, I. (2006). From infant attachment disorganization to adult dissociation: Relational adaptations or traumatic experiences? *Psychiatric Clinics of North America*, *29*(1), 63–86.

Myers, C. S. (1915). A contribution to the study of shell shock. *The Lancet*, *185*(4763), 316–320.

Ogden, P., & Fisher, J. (2015). *Sensorimotor psychotherapy: Interventions for trauma and attachment*. W. W. Norton & Company.

Schwartz, R., & Sweezy, M. (2020). *Internal Family Systems therapy* (2nd ed.). Guilford Press.

Siegel, D. J. (2010). The neurobiology of "we." Keynote address, Psychotherapy Networker Symposium, Washington, DC.

Solomon, J., & George, C. (1999). *Attachment disorganization.* Guilford Press.

Solomon, M. F., & Siegel, D. J. (Eds.). (2003). *Healing trauma: Attachment, mind, body and brain*. W. W. Norton.

Van der Hart, O., Nijenhuis, E. R. S., & Steele, K. (2006). *The haunted self: Structural dissociation and the treatment of chronic traumatization*. W. W. Norton.

Van der Hart, O., Nijenhuis, E. R. S., Steele, K., & Brown, D. (2004). Trauma-related dissociation: Conceptual clarity lost and found. *Australian and New Zealand Journal of Psychiatry*, *38*, 906–914.

Part 3

Conceptual Frameworks that Enhance IFS-Informed EMDR

Chapter 9

A Window and a Mirror

Somatic Integration and Processing for Case Conceptualization

Bridger Falkenstien

Somatic Integration and Processing (SIP) is a case conceptualization model, a foundation, that provides a window into how we can understand our clients and conceptualize their stories. At the same time, it also provides a mirror, as it reflects on our own role in the developing and active connection being formed with our clients. Constructed and refined at Beyond Healing—a counseling, personal growth, and wellness center—by Jennifer Savage, Melissa Sundwall, Caleb Boston, and myself, SIP represents the underlying core of our work. As Jennifer, Melissa, and I have discussed on our popular podcast *Notice That* and in multiple presentations, SIP informs and guides all of the therapeutic work that we do.

The multidimensional framework of SIP empowers clinicians to map and interpret complex clinical presentations through a bio/psycho/social/cultural lens while at the same time paying close attention to the connection between therapist and client. When we combine EMDR with IFS, we want to recognize and appreciate all the parts that are present in the room—both the therapist's parts and the client's parts (see Chapters 20 and 21). SIP invites us to witness another level of awareness—the intersubjective space between therapist and client, as well as the intersubjective spaces between all of the parts that are present and active in the room.

Through the therapist–client relationship, SIP activates this parallel process of the window and mirror, allowing both parties to see each other's inner worlds more deeply while continuously uncovering new dimensions of their own. This intersubjective process becomes a transformative element, where each person is shaped, understood, and invited to heal through the shared space of relational knowing.

Intersubjectivity in Therapy

As we tune into the intersubjective, the active and personal experience clients are having in the therapeutic relationship (Buirski et al., 2020; Stolorow & Atwood, 2002), we can help clients deepen their understanding of the

DOI: 10.4324/9781003541554-12

meanings they construct of their life story and the ongoing changes which are occurring during the therapeutic process. This perspective challenges the core of the medical model that many practitioners find themselves in. This framework defines the symptoms clients are struggling with not as disorders, but rather as instinctual survival strategies that have been engaged (sometimes consciously, sometimes unconsciously) to endure situations perceived to be unsafe.

In this space, we can strive to have an understanding of and collaboration in our shared space and mutual experience that is constantly evolving between therapist and client. It's the invisible mosaic connecting two embodied minds, allowing one person to sense, feel, and even intuitively grasp what another is experiencing. Unlike objective knowledge—facts that stand alone, independent of who observes them—intersubjective knowledge is co-created; it's born in the dynamic and reciprocal exchange between people as they actively seek to know and be known by one another. Opening a window into one another and the interactions of parts, intersubjectivity creates infinite connections and exchanges where the therapist and client become a part of a constant feedback loop. Intersubjectivity is what allows us to see and feel beyond ourselves, drawing us into the world of another person's emotions, thoughts, and inner reality.

In parallel, this shared space also reflects our own inner world back to us. When we open ourselves to another's experience, it brings our assumptions, responses, and hidden biases to light, offering us a clearer view of ourselves, if we're willing to see it. This process of witnessing both the other person and our own reactions is fundamental to growth and self-awareness.

From infancy onward, these intersubjective moments of being seen and seeing others construct our own self-concept and relational framework, informing how we experience connection, security, and identity (Hill & Schore, 2015; Schore, 2021). When we feel understood, we experience a sense of resonance and belonging, affirming that our feelings are both meaningful and shared. When this intersubjective bridge is disrupted or blocked— through misunderstanding, absence, or misattunement—both our sense of self and relational safety are compromised and disintegrated, leaving us to struggle against or away from one another.

This same process simultaneously occurs within our internal system as well. In the IFS paradigm, parts also have unique perceptions, assumptions, and experiences. In the context of the therapeutic relationship, we can help clients' parts explore their developing relationships and feel seen by each other. As parts increase their understanding of other parts, our clients' inner system is able to shift into greater harmony. Similar to the external relationship between people, when intersubjective internal bridges are not formed, precariously constructed, or completely destroyed, anxiety and dysregulation dominate the system.

The Valuable Map Which SIP Provides

Somatic Integration and Processing (SIP) emerged as a trauma-informed, nervous-system-focused framework intending to map the intricate influences of lived experience onto the embodied self, including the mind–body connection. Traumatic experiences, such as those that are "too much too soon, too much for too long, or too little for too long" (Duros & Crowley, 2014, p. 238), are conceptualized through SIP to have both immediate and developmental implications for the embodied self and its integration within the mind–body connection, including relationship patterns, self-concept, strategy formation (psychological, affective and emotional, and behavioral), and regulation limits (Fisher, 2017; Ogden et al., 2006).

Strategies for establishing security and safety are internal and external regulation attempts, uniquely emergent from the lived experience of an individual; these are necessary adaptations created by the nervous system in response to their environment (Cozolino, 2014). For instance, a client may have learned to shut down emotionally, stay vigilant, or avoid vulnerability to survive difficult relational or environmental conditions where vulnerability was complicated or dangerous. SIP conceptualizes these strategies not as "symptoms" to be eliminated but as wise, protective adaptations that were essential at the time of early emotional learning experiences (Ecker et al., 2024).

SIP functions through a Venn diagram that represents *attachment and neurodevelopment, somatic psychology*, and *adaptive information processing* (Figure 9.1). Used for history taking as well as in-session processing, the Venn diagram's domains are not isolated but intricately overlap, reflecting the reality that our minds, bodies, and relationships are in continuous and parallel interplay (see Figure 9.1).

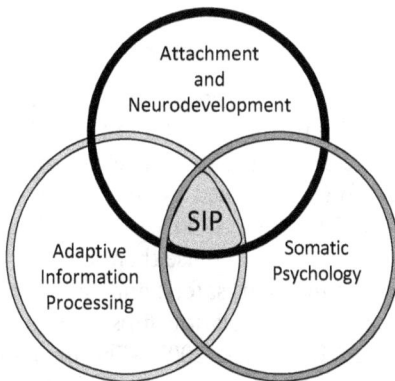

Figure 9.1 Somatic Integration and Processing Venn Diagram.

Through this SIP lens, "objective reality" disappears and we can grasp a more subjective appreciation of how a therapist's contextual framework contributes to how they perceive the client. Accepting this inevitability, our intention is to understand a client's unique history, attachment experiences, and nervous system responses, which are woven through these three domains. In this model, we have a sense of how adaptive strategies for survival and self-protection have developed in our clients over time. SIP's Venn diagram provides a visual map for therapists to understand not only the "what" of a client's experiences, but also how trauma and relationships have shaped the client's nervous system, coping strategies, and patterns of relating. Additionally, the Venn diagram reflects a conceptual organizing tool for existing and new research in the field specific to each lens, thus empowering therapists who use the model to integrate their perspectives and various training experiences to see the vivid picture of human nature and functioning that they can create when brought together.

Diversity and multiculturalism are foundational to SIP, as the model recognizes that trauma and healing are deeply shaped by cultural context, identity, and personal history. SIP understands that each client brings a unique constellation of cultural experiences, values, and beliefs that inform their perception of self, others, and the world. These cultural nuances shape not only how individuals interpret and respond to their experiences, but also how they construct strategies for survival, safety, and connection (see Chapter 10, which speaks about racial awareness in IIE).

SIP thus prioritizes an inclusive and culturally attuned lens in case conceptualization, ensuring that therapeutic interventions honor the client and therapist's individual background and worldview. Culture, from this perspective, is not viewed as a single layer to be "accounted for," but as an integral aspect of a person's identity that deeply influences all three domains.

Attachment and Neurodevelopment

Providing the fabric that holds SIP together, attachment serves as the bedrock of human development, forming the foundation of our self-concept and shaping the architecture of the mind itself. From infancy onward, the developing mind is profoundly shaped by the relational dance between the self and others (Schore, 2021; Siegel, 2020). Through early exchanges with caregivers, infants not only begin to sense themselves as individuals but also internalize patterns of attunement, safety, and validation that become templates for how they experience relationships and, ultimately, themselves (Trevarthen & Aitken, 2001; Tronick, 2007). This intersubjective process is a primary channel through which we learn to navigate the world, balancing our sense of self with the perspectives and responses of others.

As children, each moment of connection with an attuned caregiver provides a reflective space where emotions are not just felt but understood, validated, and named (Siegel, 2020). This reciprocal experience helps to establish a secure attachment framework, in which emotions become safe, and needs can be trusted as worthy of response. In the absence of this secure mirroring, parts of the self may become fragmented or underdeveloped, relying on adaptive strategies to protect against potential harm or rejection (Cassidy & Shaver, 2016). Thus, the quality of our earliest relationships fundamentally influences our internalized models of self and others, shaping how we perceive ourselves in relation to the word. Through SIP, we view this intersubjective dynamic as an ongoing developmental process, where each relational encounter continues to shape and refine the mind and its embodied expressions.

The self is therefore not a static entity but a constantly evolving intersubjective system, woven together through a myriad of relational experiences that connect, repair, and transform over time. The therapeutic space, when guided by SIP principles, reactivates this foundational process, offering clients a new opportunity to feel seen and known. Here, the therapist's awareness of hidden or neglected parts in the client's internal system and the simultaneous recognition of the therapist's own inner responses provide valuable data within the co-created healing process (see Chapters 20 and 21).

In SIP, then, the meaning that the client makes of their experience and their identity is not seen as a solitary construct but as a mosaic of intersubjective experiences, which are continuously shaped and reshaped through relational engagement. By embracing this dynamic, therapists can honor the diversity of each client's inner landscape, understanding that their self-concept and mind are deeply woven into an intricate web of past and present relationships.

Attachment and neurodevelopment are brought together in SIP as reciprocal agents of human development and relational functioning. Built and conditioned throughout the lifespan, this lens of the Venn diagram seeks to illuminate the relational and psychological foundation that each person develops based on early experiences of safety, trust, and connection. We also keep in mind the traumatic counterparts within this section. Our experiences and connections shape the architecture of our minds, and facilitate how we form relationships, respond to others, and experience ourselves in connection throughout the lifespan. SIP uses attachment (Crittenden, 2015) and affect regulation theory (Hill & Schore, 2015) principles to understand how these foundational patterns are expressed and recreated in the therapeutic space, offering an authentic invitation to heal and live an empowered life.

With such an encompassing purview, this lens of the Venn diagram makes space to further explore client strategies and clarify the connection quality and patterns of the therapeutic relationship to examine where these strategies may have come from. SIP views attachment patterns as more than just a set of strategies (insecure, secure, disorganized); they are the primary means through which individuals have learned to understand relationships and navigate relational dynamics (Tronick & Beeghly, 2011). Leaning on the well-established link between attachment patterns and neurodevelopment process (Schore, 2017; Siegel, 2020), this model recognizes that diversity in attachment experiences, influenced by factors of culture, family norms, and individual personality, results in a range of adaptive regulation strategies.

For example, if the attachment environment of a client's family of origin did not tolerate emotional engagement and attunement to intense affect, the client may internalize a series of beliefs and attunement conditions that make them feel shame for feeling something that might distress someone in the attachment environment.[1] In this example, the client would have to learn various strategies that protect them against the feelings of shame and rejection that the attachment environment may create should the client struggle and express too much of this distressing affect.[2]

Clients may come from a history of secure attachment experiences, where for the most part relationships felt safe and nurturing for a wide range of affective experiences, or they may come with strategies shaped by the fact that the vast majority of their attachment experiences were insecure and threatened. These strategies are not deficits, they are simply adaptations to the specific relational contexts they encountered, representing ways they learned to protect themselves, seek connection where available, and develop some sense of autonomy and stability, even in traumatic circumstances. This can be integrated well into an understanding of IFS, where clients' "parts" all hold positive intentions, centering around safety and survival (attachment being essential for this).

From an SIP perspective, the therapist's attunement to the client will activate the client's attachment strategies and provide the opportunity for a series of disconfirming experiences (Ecker et al., 2024).[3] For example, if a client appears emotionally guarded, SIP encourages the therapist to view this as a meaningful strategy that helped the client navigate past relationship dynamics and face present circumstances that may feel equally threatening. With active engagement and explicit acknowledgment of these strategies, the therapeutic relationship might be able to uncover the origin of these strategies and remodel their authentic expression toward empowerment, autonomy, and wellness. Additionally, SIP acknowledges that attachment and neurodevelopmental patterns influence not only the client, but also the therapist (see Chapter 21 for "parts" of the therapist). Both parties bring their relational histories and attachment styles into the therapeutic space, which can enhance and challenge therapeutic attunement and progress (Maroda, 2021).

Take, for instance, a therapeutic rupture in which a client mentioned they had "ghosted" a recent love interest by blocking their number without clearly communicating their uncertainty about the relationship and their fears of being rejected or abandoned. From the client's perspective, this is an expression of avoidant strategies, potentially long built by insecure attachments and fear of emotional vulnerability. However, if the therapist's own attachment history is filled with an anxious insecurity, they may be activated to the degree that they're pushed out of their own window of tolerance and are thus unable to see their client's strategies as an expression of insecurity and fear, and will likely be unable to thoroughly and authentically attune to the needs of their client. Both parties of the therapeutic alliance are bringing in the self-concept and attachment strategies they have built throughout their lifetime, whether we name these or not.

Somatic Psychology

In Western culture, a majority of psychotherapy approaches lean on conscious and spoken language as the primary access point to the healing process, subjugating other communication sources and embodied languages as insufficient (Damasio, 2005; Descartes, 1641/1996). SIP diverges immediately from these dualistic approaches by recognizing and honoring a holistic perspective of human beings in which equal attention is given to our bodies, affects and emotions, and cognitions. Each of these sources has a *native language* that we must learn to understand together as a therapeutic alliance, as well as how they integrate into spoken language. From this perspective, SIP recognizes that trauma is much more than a mental experience—it is deeply embodied, with stress and survival responses encoded within and throughout the extended nervous system and physical structures of the body (Ogden & Fisher, 2015; van der Kolk, 2015). In this way, the body provides a powerful, direct pathway to understanding and shifting adaptive patterns that words alone cannot reach. Through SIP's emphasis on embodied awareness, the therapist and client co-discover a somatic space that fosters mutual regulation, deepened connection, and a felt sense of safety. This, again, aligns beautifully with IIE. When we do "parts mapping" with clients (see Chapter 2), this process encourages clients to move out of their thoughts and minds and into their hearts, emotions, and body sensations, so that there can be space for them to notice any of their parts longing to be heard.

Mutual regulation then builds into co-regulation rhythms between the client and therapist, where they both influence one another and work together to build security and a greater tolerance for rupture and repair (Porges & Porges, 2023). For example, if a client becomes anxious, the therapist may intentionally slow their own breathing or soften their posture, intending to create a calming presence that supports the client in regulating their own body. This dynamic interplay of cues and responses establishes a shared somatic rhythm, inviting the client to feel safe and held, while the therapist remains attuned and present (Dana & Porges, 2018; Porges, 2021). This body-based awareness can foster a relational depth that spoken language cannot convey or capture, helping both the therapist and client experience a more embodied sense of connection and safety. This wisdom can be applied to IFS informed EMDR and it develops and clarifies how important it is for therapists to access their Self-energy, so this can lead the way until clients' Self-energy emerges in the clients' system (see Chapter 7).

Despite Western culture's objectification and domination of the body, SIP honors the diversity of somatic experience and expression intertwined in human nature, recognizing that each client's somatic experience and expression are shaped by their cultural background, personal history, and developmental environment (Galdos & Warren, 2022; Ma-Kellams, 2014). Different cultures, for example, have unique approaches to bodily expression, ranging from highly expressive to rigidly restrained. These cultural norms influence how trauma and stress are ingrained, embodied, and expressed. A client from a culture that teaches emotional restraint may internalize distress, resulting in hypertension or rigidity in their own somatic experience. Another client, perhaps from a culture that values and nurtures open expression, may embody their emotions more visibly, with expansive gestures and changes in vocal tone. From an SIP perspective, the therapist approaches these differences with humility and courage, honoring their client's unique experience and expression, seeking to explore these somatic experiences and expressions without pathologizing them, and understanding them as adaptive responses to the client's specific relational and cultural context.

The somatic psychology lens of SIP's Venn diagram deepens intersubjectivity into an embodied experience of subconscious interrelating in which the majority of regulated material is subverbal. While the therapist and their client are co-constructing their unique therapeutic space, their embodied minds (body, affects and emotions, cognitions) are beginning to dance with each other (Gendlin, 1998). As an equal participant in this choreography, SIP empowers therapists to monitor and lean in to their own physical sensations, posture, and breath as indicators of what may be arising within the intersubjective space. This awareness of embodied response allows therapists to notice when they are feeling tense, relaxed, open, or closed off, and to consider how these responses may relate to their process with the client. For instance, if a therapist notices their own extremities tightening during a session, they may take a moment to explore this sensation, considering whether it reflects a reaction to the client's material or their own history. Perhaps the therapist's body is responding to the client's unspoken tension, or it could be a mirror for their own challenges to presence in the session (Maroda, 2021). (See further discussion in Chapter 20.)

By recognizing these somatic cues, the therapist can make more conscious choices about how to respond, fostering a greater sensitivity to the client's needs and enhancing the safety and authenticity of the therapeutic relationship. Additionally, committed practice in cultivating this somatic awareness can support the therapist's own growth, inviting them to explore how their somatic responses reflect their unique attachment patterns, cultural background, and personal history (Geller & Greenberg, 2011). Through this process, the therapist honors their somatic experience and expression as a source for both reflection and connection, creating a therapeutic environment that is simultaneously attuned, present, and mutually regulated. From this perspective, the intersubjective space and the therapeutic relationship that resides in it become a fully embodied experience, where both client and therapist are invited to reconnect with themselves and each other in a space that respects the wisdom of the body. Through SIP, clients are supported in reclaiming their body as a source of safety, self-knowledge, and discovery, learning to experience their embodied responses as meaningful and adaptive. This somatic framework invites both client and therapist into a shared journey of exploration, regulation, and healing that is as diverse and unique as the individuals who come to participate.

AIP and Memory Reconsolidation

Francine Shapiro's Adaptive Information Processing (AIP) model and Bruce Ecker's work in Memory Reconsolidation (MR) are brought together in the third lens of the Venn diagram to explore the nature of embodied memory in presence and regulation. From this perspective, memory is understood as a fluid relational experience that shapes, and is reshaped by, the therapeutic process. SIP holds that memory is not a static record or a collection of newspaper clippings, but a dynamic narrative, influenced by present experiences and relationships. Experiences of trauma can fragment or rigidify memories, forcing the client to hold them in ways that can constrain their sense of agency, understanding, and self-worth (Ecker et al., 2024; Shapiro, 2017). By using AIP and MR together, SIP invites both therapist and client into a transformative process where these memories can be accessed, explored, and integrated within a safe, attuned relationship.

From an SIP perspective, memory is conceptualized as inherently relational and adaptive, constantly evolving with the interplay of interpersonal experiences. Our memories reflect not only past events but also the context of our attachments, interactions, and internalized beliefs about ourselves and others. Memory Reconsolidation (MR; Ecker et al., 2024) within the SIP framework seeks to uncover the relational roots of our embodied memory in a way that allows clients to access previously unavailable perspectives and emotional resources, empowering present authenticity and autonomy. Adaptive Information Processing (AIP; Shapiro, 2017) embeds the MR process in the context of a mind–body connection that organically and incessantly attempts to integrate and resolve experiences, especially within a supportive relational environment. Together, these concepts suggest that memories, even painful ones, have the potential to be reorganized into more adaptive, flexible self-narratives, where resources and autonomous resiliency abound. Within the safe, attuned relationship between client and therapist, memories that have been long-held and static are conceptually unlocked and thus open to reorganization and reprocessing, allowing the client to experience the memory as a part of a new and coherent self-narrative. SIP practitioners navigate within this relational space to support Memory Reconsolidation, where clients can process past experiences not only with insight but with felt shifts in the emotional and physical imprints of those memories. For instance, a client may hold a series of memories of abandonment that, over time, has hardened into a self-narrative of unworthiness.

Within the intersubjective space of the therapeutic alliance, this memory is brought into an empathic, accepting space where it can be re-experienced in a new context, inviting the client to feel witnessed and validated in a way that was missing from the original experience. This relational work does more than provide insight—it allows for corrective emotional experiences, new learning, that can shift the meaning of past events into a new and coherent self-narrative of autonomous resilience (Cozolino, 2024; Fonagy & Allison, 2014). By integrating AIP and MR, SIP empowers clients to evolve their once-isolating memories of abandonment and self-blame into an honest and self-compassionate narrative held within the context of relational safety.

Within the client, this AIP and MR lens gives therapists a window into the origin of their client's self-concept and their attachment and regulation strategies through implicit and explicit memory discovery and activation. This procedure, deepened throughout the therapeutic process, reveals glimpses of the adaptive ways clients have organized their past to make sense of and survive their experiences. Clients often arrive with memories that feel "stuck" or fragmented, causing them to relive the emotional and somatic weight of the past as though it were the present. SIP's approach offers a semi-structured, compassionate, and empowering space for clients to revisit these memories, while at the same time understanding them as key components of their survival strategies. For instance, a client may carry a fragmented memory of feeling powerless during a traumatic experience. SIP can help to facilitate an exploration that not only acknowledges the emotional reality of the experience but also reveals the adaptive strategies that arose from it, such as vigilance or avoidance, which once served to protect the client in surviving or adapting to their experience in context. By holding these memories in the Venn diagram, the therapist helps the client to contextualize these responses, viewing them as intelligent adaptations rather than sources of shame or confusion. This process, within the attunement of the intersubjective space, allows clients to access adaptive information that their nervous system may have stored as isolated fragments, moving toward a more coherent and empowered view of their story.

Additionally, the AIP and MR lens of the SIP Venn diagram serves as a mirror for therapist growth, encouraging therapists to reflect on their own relational histories, biases, and areas for growth. Witnessing clients' processes of memory integration often invites therapists to examine their assumptions about vulnerability, attachment, and resilience, using these reflections to deepen empathy and presence (Maroda, 2021). As therapists engage deeply with a client's therapeutic process, they may encounter moments that resonate with their own experiences or relational wounds. A therapist working with a client who revisits a memory of rejection may notice their own feelings of vulnerability arising. SIP encourages therapists to explore these responses, not as distractions but as mirrors that reveal their own growth areas. By maintaining this awareness, therapists can recognize and attend to their own adaptive strategies, which can enrich the therapeutic alliance by promoting authenticity and humility.

This reflective practice can benefit both therapist and client. Clients are supported in accessing, understanding, and transforming memories that have defined their lives, reclaiming these memories as part of an empowered narrative. Simultaneously, therapists engage in a parallel process of self-reflection, using their own responses to enhance empathy, authenticity, and attunement. This dynamic interplay allows the therapeutic relationship itself to become a transformative space, where past experiences are integrated and new possibilities are embraced.

A Final Encouragement

It's important to remember that healing is not a path walked alone, nor is it found solely in insight or technique. SIP invites both therapist and client into a dynamic, relational space—a space where past experiences can be revisited, reclaimed, and woven into a cohesive, resilient self-narrative. By viewing each lens of the SIP Venn diagram as an interconnected part of a larger whole, SIP honors the unique and complex ways that each individual adapts, survives, and ultimately thrives. Through the compassionate presence of the therapeutic alliance, clients can see themselves more clearly, discovering their own strength and agency within the context of authentic connection. For therapists, this journey is equally transformative, revealing that growth, empathy, and self-awareness deepen in tandem with the healing of those they serve. In SIP, the therapeutic relationship becomes both a mirror and a window, illuminating the power of human connection as a source of wisdom, resilience, and hope. Together, therapist and client share in a journey that transcends trauma, embracing a shared commitment to healing, empowerment, and the ongoing discovery of their fullest selves.

Notes

1 In IFS language, a client's part that has intense affect is exiled by another part who is holding shame, and does not want this part to negatively impact others in the environment.
2 In this case, this part appears to be a manager, wanting to remain connected to family members.
3 This is similar to therapists being in their own Self-energy (see Chapters 2, 6, and 20) and then holding space for parts in clients, until clients can access their own Self-energy.

References

Buirski, P., Haglund, P., & Markley, E. (2020). *Making sense together: The intersubjective approach to psychotherapy* (2nd ed.). Rowman & Littlefield Publishers.

Cassidy, J., & Shaver, P. R. (2016). *Handbook of attachment: Theory, research, and clinical applications* (3rd ed.). The Guilford Press.

Cozolino, L. (2014). *The neuroscience of human relationships: Attachment and the developing social brain* (2nd ed.). W. W. Norton & Company.

Cozolino, L. (2024). *The neuroscience of psychotherapy: Healing the social brain*. W. W. Norton & Company.

Crittenden, P. M. (2015). *Raising parents: Attachment, representations, and treatment* (2nd ed.). Routledge.

Damasio, A. (2005). *Descartes' error: Emotions, reason, and the human brain*. Penguin Books.

Dana, D., & Porges, S. W. (2018). *The polyvagal theory in therapy: Engaging the rhythm of regulation*. W. W. Norton & Company.

Descartes, R. (1641/1996). *Meditations on first philosophy*. Cambridge University Press.

Duros, P., & Crowley, D. (2014). The body comes to therapy too. *Clinical Social Work Journal, 42*(3), 237–246.

Ecker, B., Ticic, R., & Hulley, L. (2024). *Unlocking the emotional brain: Memory reconsolidation and the psychotherapy of transformational change* (2nd ed.). Routledge.

Fisher, J. (2017). *Healing the fragmented selves of trauma survivors: Overcoming internal self-alienation*. Routledge

Fonagy, P., & Allison, E. (2014). The role of mentalizing and epistemic trust in the therapeutic relationship. *Psychotherapy, 51*(3), 372–380.

Galdos, L. J., & Warren, M. (2022). The body as cultural home: Exploring, embodying, and navigating the complexities of multiple identities. *Body, Movement, and Dance in Psychotherapy, 17*(1), 81–97.

Geller, S., & Greenberg, L. S. (2011). *Therapeutic presence: A mindful approach to effective therapy*. American Psychological Association.

Gendlin, E. T. (1998). *Focusing-oriented psychotherapy: A manual of the experimental method*. The Guilford Press.

Hill, D., & Schore, A. N. (2015). *Affect regulation theory: A clinical model*. W. W. Norton & Company.

Ma-Kellams, C. (2014). Cross cultural differences in somatic awareness and interoceptive accuracy: A review of the literature and directions for future research. *Frontiers in Psychology, 5*(1379), 1–9.

Maroda, K. (2021). *The analyst's vulnerability: Impact on theory and practice.* Routledge.

Ogden, P., & Fisher, J. (2015). *Sensorimotor psychotherapy: Interventions for trauma and attachment.* W. W. Norton & Company.

Ogden, P., Minton, K., & Pain, C. (2006). *Trauma and the body: A sensorimotor approach to psychotherapy.* W. W. Norton & Company.

Porges, S. W. (2021). *Polyvagal safety: Attachment, communication, self-regulation.* W. W. Norton & Company.

Porges, S. W., & Porges, S. (2023). *Our polyvagal world: How safety and trauma change us.* W. W. Norton & Company.

Schore, A. N. (2017). Modern attachment theory. In S. N. Gold (Ed.), *APA handbook of trauma psychology: Foundations in knowledge* (pp. 389–406). American Psychological Association.

Schore, A. N. (2021). The interpersonal neurobiology of intersubjectivity. *Frontiers in Psychology, 12*(648616), 1–19.

Shapiro, F. (2017). *Eye movement desensitization and reprocessing (EMDR) therapy: Basic principles, protocols, and procedures* (3rd ed.). The Guilford Press.

Siegel, D. J. (2020). *The developing mind: How relationships and the brain interact to shape who we are* (3rd ed.). The Guilford Press.

Stolorow, R. D., & Atwood, G. E. (2002). *Contexts of being: The intersubjective foundations of psychological life.* Psychoanalytic Inquiries.

Trevarthen, C., & Aitken, K. J. (2001). Infant intersubjectivity: Research, theory, and clinical applications. *Journal of Child Psychology and Psychiatry, 42*(1), 3–48.

Tronick, E. (2007). *The neurobehavioral and social-emotional development of infants and children.* W. W. Norton & Company.

Tronick, E., & Beeghly, M. (2011). Infants' meaning-making and the development of mental health problems. *American Psychologist, 66*(2), 107–119.

Van der Kolk, B. (2015). *The body keeps the score: Brain, mind and body in the healing of trauma.* Penguin Books.

Chapter 10

Revolutionizing Therapy

IFS, EMDR, and the Anti-Racist Psychotherapy Perspective

David Archer and Michelli Simpson

Reviewed by Annabel McGoldrick and Laura Kosak

The West is in crisis. There is trouble at our borders. The creeping threat of fascism is ever-present and our racially diverse friends and colleagues need support, now more than ever. The purpose of this chapter is to highlight key considerations when working from an anti-racist perspective. We need approaches that are culturally responsive, humane, and able to respond to the needs of those who exist along the spectrum of marginalized identities due to the social categorizations of race, gender, or immigration status. We have written this chapter to raise racial consciousness, to tend to those who have been historically underserved, and to encourage therapists of all races and social identities to revolutionize their therapy. In consideration of the intersubjective space (see Chapter 9) that forms within any therapeutic relationship, this reflection and understanding is essential in IFS-informed EMDR (IIE) and is at the heart of the inclusive conceptualization that is being advanced in this book.

Double Consciousness, White Masks, and Racial Trauma

We are composed of parts. We exist as family members and as practitioners, and even our racial identities are facets of our ever-shifting selves. Unfortunately, certain identities are favored or pathologized by social structures, with Blackness, or being of African descent, being particularly targeted. The effects of systemic oppression can leave traumatic impacts, leading to a fracture in one's consciousness. In *The Souls of Black Folk*, Du Bois (1903) described how Black Americans experience a "Double Consciousness," torn between embracing Black culture and navigating the judgment of the white gaze. Similarly, Fanon (2007) highlighted the interpersonal challenges in the Antilles caused by the vicious grip of colonization, where identities were divided between the *colonized* and the *colonizers*. In both interracial and intraracial interactions, having Black skin often necessitates wearing "white masks" (Fanon, 1970, pp. 13–30)—not only as a

DOI: 10.4324/9781003541554-13

result of internalized oppression but also as a substitute for a unified sense of self, due to the crushing weight of white supremacy and insecurity.

Our parts seek harmony and reintegration, yet they often remain frozen in time, reenacting or reacting to the original context of traumatization. Dissociation is how we cope with traumatization, and it is integral to understanding the spectrum of trauma-based disorders. A systematic review and meta-analysis (White et al., 2022) found that nearly half (48.1%) of those diagnosed with PTSD experience significant dissociative symptoms. Beyond IFS, structural dissociation theory (van der Hart et al., 2006) is especially helpful in understanding complex trauma and dissociative parts. Behaviors that may seem irrational—such as bullying, self-harm, substance abuse, or suicidal ideation— are enacted due to conflicts between different parts of the personality. These substitute actions are driven by unmet physical and emotional needs originating from traumatic experiences, emotional neglect, and systemic injustices.

From an anti-racist psychotherapy lens, the struggle of double consciousness and internalized oppression necessitates that we confront negative cognitions rooted in introjects—internalized messages from the original oppressor, such as "I am bad," or those that reinforce oppression with thoughts like "If I am bad, then you are too." A similar process exists for those who subscribe to whiteness. Racists, whether consciously or unconsciously, often struggle with the scientific reality of Mitochondrial Eve—the concept that all humans share a common African ancestry (Archer, 2022). This denial of our shared origins, or the fear of being similar to what one despises, is central to the competition, division, and viciousness that sustain racial capitalism.

We argue that systemic oppression drives the internalization of self-deprecating beliefs, that horizontal violence among racial trauma survivors stems from vertical violence in social structures, and that it is in the best interest of people of all races to heal their internal family systems, so we can collectively heal, love, and protect our shared, collective, external family systems.

The Anti-Racist Psychotherapy Definition of Racial Trauma

Racial trauma is a psychological wounding caused by real or perceived experiences of racial discrimination (Comas-Díaz et al., 2019). These can include hate crimes, microaggressions (subtle, covert comments and behaviors that communicate prejudice and reinforce harmful stereotypes), and many other manifestations of race-based discrimination. Traumatization can also occur through witnessing racial injustice, sociopolitical stresses, and multigenerational harm. Racial trauma can manifest similarly to PTSD, affecting mental health, relationships, and overall wellbeing. Box 10.1 explores five important characteristics of racial trauma.

Box 10.1 Five Characteristics of Racial Trauma

- Systemic racism contributes to physical, emotional, and psychological harm.
- Racial trauma can be assessed and quantified both subjectively and through scientific and neurobiological data.
- We can inherit the suffering of our ancestors. The effects of racial trauma can be passed down through generations.
- Oppression can be reinforced in the present by chronic and repeated stresses of racial discrimination.
- Our society tolerates and thus accepts the suffering of some groups more than others.

Although race has no biological basis (Rutherford, 2020), it has serious consequences. Discrimination affects many aspects of life. National surveys indicate that 50 to 70% of Black, Hispanic, and Asian Americans in the US experience racial discrimination, and 70% of Black participants in Canada report everyday discrimination, with 53.1% experiencing major discrimination in healthcare settings (Cénat et al., 2022).

The holding of pseudoscientific (read: racist) beliefs about people of African descent leads to direct impacts on health outcomes, from pain assessment (Hoffman et al., 2016) to maternal mortality (Howell, 2018). LGBTQIA2S+ communities face increased risks of dissociative symptoms (Keating et al., 2021) and Black female veterans face increased trauma severity (McClendon et al., 2021) due to identity-based discrimination. Despite the fact that these groups generally report less suicidal ideation compared to white people, suicide attempts among Black and Hispanic individuals have seen recent increases, yet they still frequently face treatment delays (Bommersbach et al., 2023). Therefore, we must recognize that societal perceptions can influence trauma histories. Structural and systemic racism causes significant psychological, physical, and emotional injury to people. The range of experiences impacted by racism is vast, from the synergistic epidemics during the height of the COVID-19 pandemic (Gravlee, 2020) to the ongoing devastating climate crisis (Breakey et al., 2024). The harm caused by systemic racism is well established in the literature.

We also find that we can inherit ancestral trauma. Studies suggest that mental health vulnerabilities may be transmitted intergenerationally. Researchers have shown that trauma such as that experienced by Holocaust survivors and Tutsi genocide survivors can lead to epigenetic (Yehuda et al., 2016) and HPA-axis alterations in their offspring (Perroud et al., 2014), which affects stress regulation and emotion regulation. The mechanisms and duration across generations remain under study.

While the shadows of historical traumas linger, present-day oppression involves the chronic and repeated stress of racial discrimination. This repeated "wear and tear," due to a process called allostatic load, leads to an overactivation of the threat response system and health problems (Juster et al., 2010). Interpersonal microaggressions, perceived racial discrimination (Adam et al., 2015), and systemic barriers severely impact Black and Latino communities by concentrating poverty, reducing resources, and increasing risks for morbidity and mortality. Systemic oppression contributes to genetic vulnerabilities to physical health concerns such as hypertension, diabetes, cardiovascular disease, and emotional dysregulation (Massey, 2017).

What hurts worse than pain? Being gaslit about it. Society often normalizes or minimizes the suffering of certain groups, forcing trauma survivors to dissociate from their own experiences of suffering. Examples include genocide, marginalization of Indigenous voices, exploitation of Black lives, and the criminalization of migrants. Survivors of colonization, capitalism, and orientalism (Said, 1979) must find ways to adapt to a society that is unforgiving and actively attacks their existence.

An Anti-Racist and Culturally Responsive Approach

We aim to share approaches that acknowledge power dynamics in the therapist–client relationship, especially with global-majority communities labeled as minorities in Western countries. Applying anti-racist lenses to EMDR and IFS requires therapists to reflect on their own power, privilege, and culture. Training that privileges whiteness as well as potential defensiveness from non-marginalized therapists can hinder client progress, threaten rapport, and prevent the vulnerability needed for unburdening. This is consistent with the understanding that IIE therapists benefit and become more effective when they increase their awareness of their own parts (see Chapters 20 and 21).

Similar to IFS-informed EMDR, anti-racist psychotherapy views healing as residing within the client, positioning the therapist as a guide rather than an all-knowing expert (Archer, 2022; Schwartz, 1995; Shapiro, 2018). This client-centered approach resonates with those seeking treatments that prioritize Self-led healing and cultural adaptations for trauma treatment. Healing often involves trauma-informed therapy, community support, and culturally affirming practices that address both personal and collective experiences of racial stress.

EMDR's Eight-Phase Protocol from an Anti-Racist Perspective

The EMDR model has been shared throughout this book (see Chapter 1). This includes Shapiro's adaptive information processing (AIP) model, which underlies EMDR (Shapiro, 2018). A simplified explanation of this includes the tenets that: (1) All people have an innate capability for recovery; (2) when trauma exceeds what we can manage, it becomes dysfunctionally stored in the nervous system; and (3) EMDR therapy's structured protocol, which includes dual attention to the traumatic material and bilateral stimulation, helps to re-engage our adaptive capabilities (Archer, 2024).

EMDR therapy is a transdiagnostic and integrative approach (Wilson et al., 2018) which makes the AIP suitable for a range of different issues, including the treatment of racial trauma. From an IIE lens, the therapist's ability to cultivate a workable relationship with traumatized parts, operate from an adequate case conceptualization, and provide access to the Self-energy is essential for therapeutic progress. But there are times where certain kinds of stresses can stop progress in its tracks.

Interpersonal trauma that violates our established social and relational contracts can be highly destabilizing. Complex racial trauma (Cénat, 2023), cultural betrayal trauma (Gómez, 2023), and institutional betrayals in the context of gendered violence (Smith & Freyd, 2013) often result in severe dissociative symptoms. This necessitates the adoption of compassionate and intentional perspectives informed by parts-based interventions. Prior to engaging with phases that involve trauma reprocessing, therapists are expected to complete thorough trauma-history lists, which capture a range of events that therapists may not always think about asking and that clients may not always think about disclosing.

In addition to uncovering the identity-based stressors that are infrequently discussed, another culturally responsive, Self-led approach we propose is to modify specific terminology and concepts within the protocols.

Systemic Burdens vs. Cultural Burdens

When addressing legacy burdens, we propose replacing "cultural burden" with "systemic burden" to avoid implying that a culture is flawed. For example, hypersegregation (Massey, 2017) disproportionately impacts Black Americans more than any other racial group. The lack of resources placed in such communities contributes to poverty and lower access to safety, security, and wellbeing. This contributes to higher allostatic load and lower levels of mental and physical health in these areas. This is not the fault of those who live in these places but is instead the result of a history of redlining, job discrimination, and prevention of access to resources. Once more, the system contributes to the burden, but one's culture finds means of coping with it.

Exploring Intergenerational Trauma

For clients with intersectional identities, it's recommended to consider intergenerational trauma and increased risk of multiple traumas (Breslau et al.,

2008). Some traumas rarely occur on their own. For example, certain adverse childhood experiences can be categorized as polyadversity, where multiple adversities are experienced simultaneously or sequentially. Poverty, for example, leads to a clustering of additional adversities (Lacey et al., 2022) and is nearly inescapable once you're born into it. While wage slavery might be more of a present-day issue, it is impossible not to see the link with chattel slavery. The impact of centuries-long oppression, violence, and mistreatment necessitates transgenerational suffering and a society that accepts it. We can extend this understanding to recognize that intergenerational systemic burdens carry unintentionally inherited legacies that impact oppressed people in the present.

By incorporating these considerations into EMDR and IFS practices, we can create a more inclusive and culturally responsive approach to trauma treatment.

Before the First Meeting: Know Your Parts' Biases

Before proceeding through the eight-phase protocol, regardless of their approach, the vigilant therapist must acknowledge their own parts that might hold bias.[1] Because we all have trauma histories, sometimes we can express maladaptive countertransference responses to people we have been conditioned to see as an "other." Trying to pretend that we're not *that* racist does not work well with IIE, and trauma survivors are excellent at detecting insincerity due to their extensive histories of being betrayed. Rather than working out our own complexes in session, practices such as engaging in self-reflection and seeking consultation to manage our own maladaptive racial, gendered, or cultural countertransference reactions are especially helpful.

Phase 1: History Taking and Assessment Adaptations

We acknowledge that clients' parts may feel judged by their therapists, especially when talking about racial trauma.[2] To mitigate risks, we suggest integrating the Blind to Therapist (B2T) protocol (Blore et al., 2013). Doing so allows clients to nickname specific events, which hence empowers them to control their narrative. When using floatbacks to locate touchstone events, we must take heed and remember there is a chance that we could inadvertently and prematurely expose exiles; therefore, making a contract early on with the protectors can be a gentler way to approach traumatic experiences (see Chapter 5 for discussion on getting permission from protectors before interacting with exiles).

As Shapiro suggests, "The past is present," and this is especially true for racial-trauma survivors. Just by listing trauma histories we may activate parts, which can continue to be on high alert for the remainder of the session. Bringing up one event can often lead to a cluster of experiences that can rise to consciousness. Complex trauma survivors can benefit from having sufficient resources installed (covered later in this chapter) before even mentioning overwhelming targets. From an IFS lens, ensuring the client is in a Self-led state can facilitate communication between parts (see Chapter 6 on having a critical amount of Self for dual processing).

Conversational approaches to Phase 1 can be effective, especially with clients from collectivist cultures. Open-ended questions about relational systems like family or community can yield relevant information.[3]

Examples to Elicit Deeper Exploration

- "What are the main experiences that challenged what you believed about yourself or your family?"
- "What cultural or familial values were most challenged by your experiences?"
- "Which intergenerational patterns or beliefs do you most struggle with?"
- "What are the worst experiences that have shaped your relationships or your community?"
- "What was an unstated message about race that you internalized while growing up?"

We can also consider inherited legacies and posttraumatic growth from the experiences:

- "Which experiences were most important for defining your culture or personal values?"
- "What are the most unexpected gifts or insights that you have received from difficult situations?"
- "Who played an important role in providing insights?"

A large part of posttraumatic growth can be found within clients' connection to their ancestors or community values. This can assist during Phase 2 preparation and the cultivation of resources.

Assessing for Racialized Dissociation

Most therapists who assess for complex trauma do not assess for racial trauma. However, when we think about the intersection of both of these, we realize that the relationship between dissociation and psychological distress varies depending on the cultural context. Black participants and Asian American participants can in some cases report experiencing dissociation even during periods of lower psychological distress. This contrasts with findings for white participants, where dissociation did not appear to demonstrate the same degree of adaptive function (Douglas, 2009). A more recent study appeared to validate this in that while there is a greater degree of dissociation in Black individuals, Black people experience a higher level of nonpathological dissociation than white individuals (Kushnir, 2023). Dissociation can serve as a coping mechanism that helps reduce psychological distress in specific cultural contexts while navigating the chronic stress of systemic oppression.

When considering the role of dissociation in a client's system, IIE would recommend getting to know the parts involved, being respectful, and honoring their wisdom. It is not advisable to stop any part from using dissociation without fully understanding its role, its function in the system, or its "why." Assessments can help to bring insights to both clients and therapists on this topic.

Assessments are an instrumental part of conceptualization for EMDR and IFS therapists. Besides the standard DES-II (Dissociative Experiences Scale-II) recommended in EMDR therapy trainings (Carlson & Putnam, 1993), it is recommended that the therapist also use questionnaires such as the Somatoform Dissociation Questionnaire (SDQ-20) to assess for the presence of dissociative parts, which are most likely to be activated through the client's body. The MID-60 (Multidimensional Inventory of Dissociation-60), a shortened adaptation of the MID (Dell, 2006), is also a very helpful tool. It provides a concise screening option, illustrating different categories of dissociative symptoms and initiating conversations about the adaptive function of dissociative phenomena as well as potential motivations from different parts in bringing these symptoms to consciousness.

It goes without saying that some dissociative symptoms can be terrifying for the clients and highly disorienting to the untrained eye. When symptoms are too overwhelming, in some cases the cultivation of resources can restore stabilization and balance for those in need. Therapists are advised to seek supervision or consultation whenever they are in doubt.

Phase 2: Preparation

Beyond calm place and container visualizations (see Chapters 1 and 23), clients have infinite internal resources to draw upon, if we make space for them. Encourage clients to bring their unique skills, such as yoga, dancing, art, music, prayers, or rituals, into therapy to create a grounded base before initiating trauma processing. Although the preparation phase is the second phase in the EMDR standard protocol, the authors recommend these conversations happen early. When working in a North American context, we frequently hear that members of the global majority do not always hear that their cultural strengths are valid or welcome in therapy.

Archer has made adjustments to Resource Development and Installation (Korn & Leeds, 2002) based on feedback from his clients. This led to the development of Resource Integration, a technique helpful for those suffering from complex racial trauma. Being in a near-constant state of survival can lead us to feel distrust about our cues for safety and danger. Complex trauma survivors struggle with interoception: They either misread their internal cues or are cut off from feeling them (Archer, 2024). For this reason, cultivating resources that change what one feels can impact what one believes, and ultimately can lead to flexibility about one's beliefs. Cultural concepts, characteristics of Self-energy, ancestral role models, and forces of nature can be used to reduce the discomfort caused by the somatic expression of limiting beliefs, urges for self-sabotaging behavior, and fears of reprocessing certain targets, and can even assist in managing phobic responses (Archer, 2024). Because many of our clients are diverse and digital natives, it is also very possible to mobilize video and music streaming sites for healing. It is not unusual to use gospel music or video-game footage to help clients own their recovery process.

Being flexible yet intentional is especially essential when working with racial trauma survivors. Archer has written extensively on an approach to treating complex racial trauma called Rhythm and Processing (RAP) Strategies, based on Afrocentric principles and memory reconsolidation that emerged from his practice of EMDR therapy (Archer, 2022).

Rhythm and Processing (RAP) Technique

The RAP technique involves the use of BLS, eye blinking, and imagery that provides a disconfirmation for any present experience of distress. While it can be used to fully reconsolidate memories, the RAP technique ensures that at the end of a session, a client will be much less likely to experience overwhelming symptoms in between sessions. The client focuses on images, videos, or visualizations, while the therapist provides instructions which rapidly provides grounding even in the absence of the adaptive material that is often needed with the standard EMDR protocol. They are also provided with a self-care tool that they can use reliably and in between sessions, while customizing the specific imagery for their parts, to regain moments of clarity, autonomy, and inner peace.

We include this intervention under Phase 2 because in addition to its effectiveness for healing traumatic memories, the RAP technique can also be used to assist in cultivating resource states. In the same way that EMDR's phases have a nonlinear quality to them (see Chapter 1), the RAP technique can also be used throughout treatment.

In IIE, RAP could be introduced at any moment when the client feels that this could be beneficial for one or more of the parts that are present. Other parts might be asked to sit and observe, and if granted permission, RAP can also be customized to help parts connect with Self-energy. Whenever RAP is introduced to a part, any of the eight C's can increase within the system (courage, curiosity, compassion, creativity, connectedness, confidence, calmness, and clarity).

The COMEBACK Tool

The COMEBACK Tool, created by five women of color across four continents, integrates art and body movements to help clients during and between sessions, promoting self-regulation and a Self-led presence (Marchand & Simpson, 2022). This culturally diverse approach includes exercises that invite clients to bring awareness to their body, allow parts to rest, and create a safe space for observing internal parts, fostering a harmonious therapeutic environment. By using the tools above, clients can practice conjuring Self-led energy by teaching different parts of their internal system how to access useful resources, which reduces inner conflict between parts while reducing resistant dynamics.

Phases 3: Assessment

Culture-bound syndromes help to inform the rationale for anti-racist interventions. Psychosis, depression, and other mental health conditions can vary radically across cultures (American Psychological Association, 2017). Even the concept of emotion regulation, as understood in Western psychology, may not align with the lived experiences of individuals from diverse backgrounds. The stereotype of the "angry Black woman," for example, highlights the potential for the misinterpretation of emotional expression, especially when working interracially.

When exploring negative cognitions or using cognitive interweaves, therapists must be mindful of the potential harm caused by repeating the derogatory, historically offensive language used by the client to describe themselves. For instance, if a white or non-Black therapist is working with a Black client who uses a racially offensive word, there is never a need to repeat it. Instead, rephrasing the question to focus on the underlying meaning or emotion can be more helpful. For example,

When the part that holds this image is active, what negative belief or fear does it communicate to you? Now, from a place of Self-led energy and with the support of your spiritual guides or ancestors if you wish, what would you like this part to believe about you instead?

Phase 4: Desensitization

Therapists must demonstrate care not to shame abreaction or cast judgment when processing is blocked. Clinical observation and research literature have led us to believe that health professionals are susceptible to misreading and invalidating the pain of Black women (Howell, 2018). However, we are not saying that one must rush in as a savior prematurely; instead we are reaffirming the importance of attunement to the client and the cultural context, while encouraging the use of stop signs when necessary.

For bilateral stimulation, discussing with the client beforehand about their preferences promotes autonomy and strengthens the alliance. Through her clinical experience, Simpson has had great success with having clients play bongos or other musical instruments while simultaneously using visual BLS. Movement of one's entire body through yoga has also been used with success instead of eye movements, and as sessions progress and client parts develop trust for the process, the client gradually becomes comfortable with sitting still and using eye movements. Some clients need to rock their bodies side to side while doing eye movements. In these cases, we invite the part to borrow the eyes of the client and stare at the movement with them. Once more, being receptive to cultural differences is essential. Clinical experience has revealed that some clients may ask to have ancestors or spiritual guides tap with them while the part processes the memory.

Phase 5: Installation

Flexibility is essential. Remember, in some cases, using the word "positive" for a cognition may be unrealistic based on the specific trauma target. Some parts can even reject certain beliefs if they could be interpreted as being dismissive of identity-forming experiences. Additionally, we must be careful when using the Validity of Cognition (VoC) scale, as statements that are completely true and false can be triggering for protectors. Language is very powerful and what works best for English speakers may not work as well for others. For example, in some instances when working with Brazilian Portuguese speakers, qualifying the VoC, with 1 being "it doesn't make sense/doesn't fit" or 7 meaning "it makes much more sense now/that works now" can be very helpful. Always verify with the client's internal system to see if the statement can be received by parts before proceeding.

Phase 6: Body Scan

Noticing one's own internal state is essential for survival, but for some parts it can also be terrifying. Dysfunctions in our capacity for interoception are part and parcel with a variety of mental health conditions (Khalsa et al., 2018). Cutting oneself off from perceiving one's internal state, as previously discussed, can be adaptive when we have learned to distrust our internal cues due to betrayals or shame. For this reason, the body-scan phase can be especially significant. Even outside of this phase, clients can be instructed to use their hands, holding them above different body parts, to direct their attention and notice any areas of tension or sensation that deserve compassion.

Before a target is seen as resolved, checking in is essential. For multilingual clients whose parts may hold memories in a language other than English or the language of the therapy, it's important to create a space where they can express themselves authentically. This can be facilitated by adding the following invitation: "If any parts of you prefer to express themselves in a different language, please feel free to do so. You can use any language that feels most comfortable and true to your experience." Instructions such as these reinforce the client's felt sense of safety and ownership over the healing process.

Phase 7: Closure

After completing targets, it is important to help clients regain their footing. To end the session and help the client remain empowered, consider the following approach:

The work we've done today may continue to unfold within your inner system, even after our session. You or your parts might notice new insights, thoughts, memories, or even dreams emerging. If that happens, observe what's happening with curiosity and openness. Perhaps you or your parts can take a mental snapshot of the experience, noticing what you see, feel, think, and any triggers that may be present.

You can use the acronym for POWER below:

- **Pause**: Take a moment to breathe and ground yourself.
- **Observe**: Notice any thoughts, emotions, or memories that arise.
- **Welcome**: Acknowledge and accept whatever arises, knowing that these feelings will pass.
- **Expand**: Expand to the present moment. Engage your senses and notice what you can see, hear, smell, taste, and touch.
- **Respond**: Respond to your experience with self-compassion and kindness. What do you need in this moment to feel safe and supported?

Humanizing IIE with Anti-Racist Psychotherapy

Although diverse experiences lead to trauma, responses to it are equally diverse. We advocate for teaching revolutionary therapists, and IIE therapists are well positioned for this designation. We as revolutionary therapists challenge tradition, advocate for transformative change, and seek to empower all people regardless of their social identities.

We urge you to challenge the status quo in the following ways:

- Understand there are anti-racist frameworks that acknowledge the neurobiological, psychological, and social impacts of systemic racism, and ways to navigate them.
- Know that racial trauma is caused by real and perceived discrimination, but it also includes multigenerational legacies, present-day oppression, and our society's acceptance of suffering.
- Validate the experiences of complex racial trauma survivors and diverse service users, not just through our clinical experiences but even in the structure of our psychotherapy practice.
- Be responsive to the unique, expansive, intersectional identities of your client populations.
- Never stop learning, growing, and being who you are meant to be.

Welcoming the Revolutionary Anti-Racist Approach into IIE

Race is controversial. It's avoided in discussion, and underestimated by mental health professionals. Not only does this discourage marginalized people from seeking therapy, but it reduces the overall effectiveness of psychotherapy. Despite apologies from the American Psychiatric Association (2021) and American Psychological Association (2021) for systemic racism, most graduate programs fail to teach from anti-racist perspectives. This contributes to therapists preferring same-race clients, avoiding discussions of race, and leading to poorer outcomes for racially diverse clients (Williams et al., 2022). We seek to change this. We are here to give voices to the oppressed. We are advocating for revolutionary therapists who challenge assumptions and confront systemic racism.

By 2050, one out of every four people in the world will be African (Statista, 2023). Given this shift, the future will be multi-racial, intersectional, and international. Service provision must evolve accordingly. *Anti-racist psychotherapy*, initially conceived as an EMDR-informed approach to address anti-Black racial trauma (Archer, 2021), parallels IFS in recognizing different Self-states. Because we all exist as a constellation of our intersecting social identities, roles, and relationships, being an anti-racist practitioner is in alignment with the principles of IIE, while opening new possibilities of innovation to the IIE practitioner.

Anti-racism requires honest self-reflection because systemic oppression is a reality. As mental health professionals, we bear witness to the underbelly of our society. We hear the screams of gendered violence, see the gunshots of discrimination, and feel the crushing weight of poverty. Because we bear witness to the abyss of suffering, side by side with our clients, they deserve therapists who can be courageous. Anti-racism means taking hold of a mirror, looking at ourselves in that mirror, and being honest with what we see. Using IFS terminology, being anti-racist means ensuring we are connecting to our own Self-energy without "spiritually bypassing" (Welwood, 1984) by pretending for clients and colleagues that we are immune to racism or above microaggressions simply because we loudly proclaim, "I am in Self-energy!"

By embracing the principles of anti-racist psychotherapy, it is our hope that readers will find themselves inspired to embrace change. We have written this chapter in honor of the feedback we have received from our clients. Our goal is to inspire a new generation of therapists to not just read about anti-racism, but to **be about it**. All therapists have the potential to help people both inside and outside of therapy sessions. Let's endeavor to revolutionize how we look at therapy and make the world a more compassionate place for all.

Notes

1   As we explore what parts we bring (see Chapters 20 and 21), even if it can be hard to admit, we must know if any of our parts hold racist, ableist, or classist beliefs. This reduces the risk of projecting onto our clients or hindering processing due to unchecked countertransference responses.
2   For more on this see Archer (2022), *Racial Trauma Recovery: Healing Our Past Using Rhythm and Processing*.
3   If questions of this nature are prematurely asked, parts can become activated and defensive. As will be later discussed, when the authors use Rhythm and Processing (RAP) strategies, these questions become especially pertinent when developing a genogram or when already on the topic of exploring family patterns. Use clinical judgment, honor all parts, and cultivate rapport.

References

Adam, E. K., Heissel, J. A., Zeiders, K. H., Richeson, J. A., Ross, E. C., Ehrlich, K. B., Levy, D. J., Kemeny, M., Brodish, A.B., Malanchuk, O., & Peck, S. C. (2015). Developmental histories of perceived racial discrimination and diurnal cortisol profiles in adulthood: A 20-year prospective study. *Psychoneuroendocrinology, 62*, 279–291.

American Psychiatric Association. (2021, January 18). *APA apologizes for its support of racism in psychiatry* [press release].

American Psychological Association. (2017). *Guidelines for psychological practice with ethnic, racial, and cultural diversity.*

American Psychological Association. (2021, October 29). *Apology for systemic racism* [press release].

Archer, D. (2021). *Anti-racist psychotherapy: Confronting systemic racism and healing racial trauma.* Each One Teach One Publications.

Archer, D. (2022). *Racial trauma recovery: Healing our past using rhythm and processing*. Each One Teach One Publications.

Archer, D. (2024). *Transforming complex trauma: Reflections on anti-racist psychotherapy*. Duppy Konkara Publications.

Blore, D. C., Holmshaw, E. M., Swift, A., Standart, S., & Fish, D. M. (2013). The development and uses of the "Blind to Therapist" EMDR protocol. *Journal of EMDR Practice and Research, 7*(2), 95–105.

Bommersbach, T. J., Rosenheck, R. A., & Rhee, T. G. (2023). Racial and ethnic differences in suicidal behavior and mental health service use among US adults, 2009–2020. *Psychological Medicine, 53*(12), 5592–5602.

Breakey, S., Hovey, D., Sipe, M., & Nicholas, P. K. (2024). Health effects at the intersection of climate change and structural racism in the United States: A scoping review. *The Journal of Climate Change and Health*, 100339.

Breslau, N., Peterson, E. L., & Schultz, L. R. (2008). A second look at prior trauma and the posttraumatic stress disorder effects of subsequent trauma: A prospective epidemiological study. *Archives of General Psychiatry, 65*(4), 431–437.

Carlson, E. B., & Putnam, F. W. (1993). *Dissociative experiences scale-II (DES-II)*. https://traumadissociation.com/des [Webpage].

Cénat, J. M. (2023). Complex racial trauma: Evidence, theory, assessment, and treatment. *Perspectives on Psychological Science, 18*(3), 675–687.

Cénat, J. M., Hajizadeh, S., Dalexis, R. D., Ndengeyingoma, A., Guerrier, M., & Kogan, C. (2022). Prevalence and effects of daily and major experiences of racial discrimination and microaggressions among Black individuals in Canada. *Journal of Interpersonal Violence, 37*, 16750–16778.

Comas-Díaz, L., Hall, G. N., & Neville, H. A. (2019). Racial trauma: Theory, research, and healing: Introduction to the special issue. *American Psychologist, 74*(1), 1–5.

Dell, P. F. (2006). Multidimensional Inventory of Dissociation (MID): A comprehensive measure of pathological dissociation. *Journal of Trauma & Dissociation, 7*(2), 77–106.

Douglas A. N. (2009). Racial and ethnic differences in dissociation: An examination of the dissociative experiences scale in a nonclinical population. *Journal of Trauma & Dissociation: The Official Journal of the International Society for the Study of Dissociation (ISSD), 10*(1), 24–37.

Du Bois, W. E. (1903). *The souls of Black folk*. AC McClurg & Co.

Fanon, F. (1970). *Black skin, white masks*. Paladin.

Fanon, F. (2007). *The wretched of the earth*. Grove/Atlantic, Inc.

Gómez, J. M. (2023). *The cultural betrayal of Black women and girls: A Black feminist approach to healing from sexual abuse* (pp. 217–236). American Psychological Association.

Gravlee, C. C. (2020). Systemic racism, chronic health inequities, and COVID-19: A syndemic in the making? *American Journal of Human Biology, 32*(5), e23482.

Hoffman, K. M., Trawalter, S., Axt, J. R., & Oliver, M. N. (2016). Racial bias in pain assessment and treatment recommendations, and false beliefs about biological differences between blacks and whites. *Proceedings of the National Academy of Sciences, 113*(16), 4296–4301.

Howell, E. A. (2018). Reducing disparities in severe maternal morbidity and mortality. *Clinical Obstetrics and Gynecology*, *61*(2), 387–399.

Juster, R. P., McEwen, B. S., & Lupien, S. J. (2010). Allostatic load biomarkers of chronic stress and impact on health and cognition. *Neuroscience & Biobehavioral Reviews*, *35*(1), 2–16.

Keating, L., Muller, R. T., & Wyers, C. (2021). LGBTQ+ people's experiences of barriers and welcoming factors when accessing and attending intervention for psychological trauma. *Journal of LGBTQ Issues in Counseling*, *15*(1), 77–92.

Khalsa, S. S., Adolphs, R., Cameron, O. G., Critchley, H. D., Davenport, P. W., Feinstein, J. S., Feusner, J. D., Garfinkel, S. N., Lane, R. D., Mehling, W. E., Meuret, A. E., Nemeroff, C. B., Oppenheimer, S., Petzschner, F. H., Pollatos, O., Rhudy, J. L., Schramm, L. P., Simmons, W. K., Stein, M. B., Stephan, K. E., Van den Bergh, O., Van Dienst, I., von Leupoldt, A., & Paulus, M. P. (2018). Interoception and mental health: A roadmap. *Biological Psychiatry: Cognitive Neuroscience and Neuroimaging*, *3*(6), 501–513.

Korn, D. L., & Leeds, A. M. (2002). Preliminary evidence of efficacy for EMDR resource development and installation in the stabilization phase of treatment of complex posttraumatic stress disorder. *Journal of Clinical Psychology*, *58*(12), 1465–1487.

Kushnir, C. N. (2023). Racial differences in non-pathological dissociation. *Undergraduate Research and Creative Activities Journal*, *4*. Retrieved from https://escholarship.org/uc/item/2rg3862x

Lacey, R. E., Howe, L. D., Kelly-Irving, M., Bartley, M., & Kelly, Y. (2022). The clustering of adverse childhood experiences in the Avon Longitudinal Study of Parents and Children: Are gender and poverty important? *Journal of Interpersonal Violence*, *37*(5–6), 2218–2241.

Marchand, J., & Simpson, M. (2022). Inviting the body, movement, and the creative arts into telehealth: A culturally responsive model for online EMDR preparation. In E. Davis, J. Fitzgerald, S. Jacobs, & J. Marchand (Eds.), *EMDR and creative arts therapies*. Springer.

Massey, D. S. (2017). Segregation and stratification: A biosocial perspective. In K. M. Beaver & A. Walsh (Eds.), *Biosocial theories of crime* (pp. 49–67). Routledge.

McClendon, J., Kressin, N., Perkins, D., Copeland, L. A., Finley, E. P., & Vogt, D. (2021). The impact of discriminatory stress on changes in posttraumatic stress severity at the intersection of race/ethnicity and gender. *Journal of Trauma & Dissociation*, *22*(2), 170–187.

Perroud, N., Rutembesa, E., Paoloni-Giacobino, A., Mutabaruka, J., Mutesa, L., Stenz, L., Malafosse, A., & Karege, F. (2014). The Tutsi genocide and transgenerational transmission of maternal stress: Epigenetics and biology of the HPA axis. *The World Journal of Biological Psychiatry*, *15*(4), 334–345.

Rutherford, A. (2020). *How to argue with a racist: History, science, race and reality*. Hachette UK.

Said, E. W. (1979). *Orientalism*. Vintage.

Schwartz, R. C. (1995). *Internal family systems therapy*. Guilford Press.

Shapiro, F. (2018). *Eye movement desensitization and reprocessing (EMDR) therapy third edition: Basic principles, protocols, and procedures*. Guilford Press.

Smith, C. P., & Freyd, J. J. (2013). Dangerous safe havens: Institutional betrayal exacerbates sexual trauma. *Journal of Traumatic Stress*, *26*(1), 119–124.

Statista. (2023, April 28). *Forecast of the total population of Africa from 2020 to 2050*. Statista.com.

Van der Hart, O., Nijenhuis, E. R., & Steele, K. (2006). *The haunted self: Structural dissociation and the treatment of chronic traumatization*. Norton.

Welwood, J. (1984). Principles of inner work: Psychological and spiritual. *Journal of Transpersonal Psychology*, *16*(1), 63–73.

White, K. S. Lenz, A. S., & Hiraoka, R. (2022). The dissociative subtype of PTSD: A meta-analytic review. *Clinical Psychology Review*, *89*, 102085.

Williams, M. T., Faber, S. C., & Duniya, C. (2022). Being an anti-racist clinician. *The Cognitive Behaviour Therapist*, 15, Article e19.

Wilson, G., Farrell, D., Barron, I., Hutchins, J., Whybrow, D., & Kiernan, M. D. (2018). The use of eye-movement desensitization reprocessing (EMDR) therapy in treating post-traumatic stress disorder—a systematic narrative review. *Frontiers in Psychology*, *9*, 923.

Yehuda, R., Daskalakis, N. P., Bierer, L. M., Bader, H. N., Klengel, T., Holsboer, F., & Binder, E. B. (2016). Holocaust exposure induced intergenerational effects on FKBP5 methylation. *Biological Psychiatry*, *80*(5), 372–380.

Chapter 11

Exploring Structural Dissociation Through the Lens of EMDR and IFS

Athena Phillips

Dissociative disorders can be thought of as an orderly reaction to disorderly circumstances. Adult survivors of severe and chronic childhood trauma whose response was to create an internal world often bring unique and deeply personal gifts to therapy. The capacity for deep imaginative absorption enables the creation of a complex inner framework designed for psychological survival, which highlights an organic drive toward psychological preservation. The extent of suffering these survivors have been exposed to is often unimaginable, not only to the outside world, but also to survivors themselves. One of the primary therapeutic goals in this population includes the realization of what occurred, and recognition of the system as designed to protect against an unbearable truth. Internal family systems can create safety by working with protective parts to honor their concerns and gain permission to approach exiles while relying on them to monitor the therapeutic tempo. As skills are developed and exiles prepare to unburden the past, EMDR can be applied to enhance internal resources and to methodically work through trauma.

Like many other conditions, dissociation exists on a continuum. It is a multifaceted experience, commonly rooted in past trauma as an organic protection against the intolerable. It is described as a disruption in the continuity of consciousness that influences memory, perception, identity, and agency (Utomo et al., 2023). It can be a temporary or chronic occurrence that exists in nonclinical groups as well as in those with various mental health conditions such as panic disorder, major depressive disorder, borderline personality disorder, and posttraumatic stress disorder (American Psychological Association, 2022; Ducharme, 2017; Poli et al., 2023). This chapter will focus on the application of IFS and EMDR therapies to treat Other Specified Dissociative Disorder (OSDD) and Dissociative Identity Disorder (DID) (Ducharme, 2017; van der Hart et al., 2006). It will cover the standard of care for these conditions and outline how to safely implement their application, as well as the reasoning behind using these modalities in tandem for this population.

DOI: 10.4324/9781003541554-14

Dissociative disorders occur at a lifetime prevalence of 10% of the global populace, with DID occurring at 1.1–1.5% of the general population and OSDD (also referenced as partial DID), the most common of these conditions, occurring at up to 8.3% (American Psychological Association, 2022; Chien & Fung, 2022). Categories of symptoms of DID and OSDD can include depersonalization, derealization, identity alternation, amnesia, and identity confusion (ISST-D, 2011). Symptoms may include flashbacks, discontinuity in memory, identity confusion, and various somatoform symptoms (Poli et al., 2023). The internal experience is a systematic division between a minimum of two autonomous parts of self that often hold a first-person perspective, often referred to as the amnesic barrier (Lazarus & Rafaeli, 2023; van der Hart et al., 2014). Subsystems or subpersonalities are described as compartmentalized memories, cognitions, and somatic responses, all of which remain separate from other self-states (Lazarus & Rafaeli, 2023).

Structural dissociation is believed to be rooted in childhood trauma that occurs throughout development, often begins prior to age five, and may involve multiple perpetrators (Ducharme, 2017; ISST-D, 2011). Children in these circumstances are placed in the impossible position of retaining their affection for caregivers who are needed for survival while simultaneously being faced with the extreme circumstances of an abusive environment. Some children are predisposed to dissociate, which allows them to cope with an unbearable context through the strategic development of self-states that are experienced as "other than me" (Lazarus & Rafaeli, 2023; Robinson et al., 2024). Each emancipated self-state serves to distance children from the intolerable and the dissonance generated when a parent is also abusive. The schism between parts offers a solution to the intolerable problem of maintaining attachment to their caregivers, who implicitly or overtly partake in their abuse (Robinson et al., 2024). Those living with dissociative disorders could arguably be the most traumatized of the traumatized, with the reality being that insufferable experiences began before they had the opportunity for identity development.

Internal systems are built around protecting a pearl that resides deep within us and that shapes who we are fundamentally. Internal family systems conceptualize this as "Self," which is a defining feature that all other parts are organized around, and which is identifiable by its ability to hold compassion, curiosity, clarity, confidence, calm, creativity, courage, and connectedness (Schwartz, 2023). While those with classic PTSD may find themselves struggling to locate or trust in self, those with structural dissociation may believe this aspect of themselves has been annihilated or does not exist at all. Clients often assert that they "don't have a self" and that they are fundamentally broken, which is understandable considering that the onset of abuse begins early enough to interfere with identity development. Dissociative disorders such as OSDD and DID carry unique challenges surrounding self, identity, extreme phobia of and between parts (particularly exiles and firefighters), and consequential internal distrust (van der Hart et al., 2006).

Standard of Care for Dissociative Disorders: A Review

One of the primary goals of treatment in working with those with dissociative disorders is to cultivate the capacity to take ownership of the past as well as the associated post-trauma consequences (Robinson et al., 2024). The process of working through the past is a process that must be approached strategically with proper pacing, a solid therapeutic alliance, and clearly defined therapeutic parameters. The standard of care for working with OSDD and DID encompasses phase-based protocols that are applied to those with complex trauma and additional recommendations that are designed to help clients learn to connect with their internal system (Ducharme, 2017; ISST-D, 2011; Robinson et al., 2024).

Working within a stage-based framework is an established standard of care for working with dissociative disorders. The typical approach encompasses three levels, with the first focusing on skill-building and establishing the therapeutic alliance. The second stage[1] encompasses trauma processing, while the final stage aims to integrate the past with the present while updating core beliefs or schema (Ducharme, 2017; ISST-D, 2011; Robinson et al., 2024). Clinicians and clients will typically move between the first and second stages in an iterative fashion, allowing for organic titration of exposure while helping clients tolerate working through the past.

In addition to applying a stage-based approach, other recommendations include capitalizing on strengths, establishing healthy boundaries, addressing internal conflict, working toward collaboration between parts, challenging cognitive distortions, decreasing space between parts, and emphasizing personal responsibility in both client and therapist. Prior to engaging in trauma work, clients should have the capacity to remain within the affective window of tolerance (Siegel, 2020). Therapists should be skilled at minimizing flooding and dissociative responses to overwhelming emotional experiences, ensuring clients do not leave therapy compromised (Ducharme, 2017; ISST-D, 2011; Robinson et al., 2024).

Precautions

Approaching treatment in those living with structural dissociation rooted in complex trauma requires consideration of certain precautions. Many people with dissociative disorders enter therapy with deep attachment wounds, shame, and negative self-perceptions. They often carry unspoken fears of abandonment and betrayal, and may find the therapist's intentions suspect.

Safety, predictability, warmth, and structure should be prioritized as defining features of the relationship (Ducharme, 2017; ISST-D, 2011). Engaging directly with the internal family, or parts/ego states of the client, throughout the treatment trajectory is a crucial element in the treatment process for clients with dissociative disorders. Clinicians must also approach all parts with compassion and with the assumption that they are working on behalf of the system. Clinicians should maintain impartiality and avoid expressing favoritism or fear toward any specific part.

Memory work is a necessary component of care; however, therapists should approach it with skill and structure. Working through the past is arduous and comes with risks, thus therapists should be aware of when trauma work is contraindicated. Active substance abuse, unsafe or unstable life circumstances, significant external stressors, current contact with abusers, upcoming vacations for therapist or client, active self-harm, and suicidal or homicidal ideation are red flags that indicate poor timing for processing past trauma. Additionally, clients should have established self-soothing skills, and the therapeutic alliance should be well established before entering the second stage (Brand et al., 2012; Ducharme, 2017; ISST-D, 2011).

Proper pacing of trauma work is imperative, particularly when employing trauma processing, given the potential for decompensation and elevated risk for self-harm, suicide, or homicide. Utilization of EMDR in this population requires adaptations to the original protocols, and clinicians should expect to adapt their approaches to individual clients because of the heterogeneity that tends to exist within this population. Scrupulous preparation for trauma work should include psychoeducation on potential risks, developing a safety and recovery plan, and preparing a graduated exposure approach that limits the amount of time and subjection to memories (Ducharme, 2017; van der Hart et al., 2014).

IFS, EMDR, and Dissociative Disorders: A Rationale

The complexity and care required to safely work through developmental trauma honors the proportional pain being held by exiles. Working within an internal system through an IFS lens lends itself well to incorporating EMDR into the treatment trajectory, provided it is approached with caution. IFS inherently paces treatment by working with protectors to gain access to the system only after internal trust and permission to move forward have been granted. Firefighters or managers might block interventions such as EMDR processing if the right protections are not in place and if they are not well-timed. Internal collaboration and communication between parts should be established, alongside permission from protectors to address the identified memory.

Phobias of parts and memories they hold can prompt some firefighters or managers to interfere with processing. Clinicians and clients should conceptualize this intrusion as guidance for pacing the work. Prioritizing attending to these phobic parts, building internal trust, and expanding emotional regulation capacities is critical for successfully timed trauma processing (Ducharme, 2017; van der Hart et al., 2014).

Capitalizing on the client's capacity to compartmentalize can protect against unexpected softening of amnesic barriers and associated memory flooding when EMDR processing is employed. Assuming an internal structure has been established, clients and therapists can then invite nonparticipating parts to retreat to their internal safe spaces while memories are being processed (van der Hart et al., 2014). Traumatic memories should not be addressed if the following are not in place: coping strategies, a homelife conducive to rest, and a firmly established therapeutic relationship. Once trauma processing has begun, engagement of the system throughout the process can help facilitate healthy pacing, proper timing, containment skills, and erosion of phobias of the internal experience. The processing itself builds confidence and minimizes the risk of decompensation.

IFS and EMDR: The Three Stages of Trauma Work

Stage 1: Working from the Outside In

Internal Family Systems (IFS) theory is an approach that leverages a dissociative system to safely navigate trauma. It is relational, nonpathologizing, and focuses on addressing internal polarizations, which are a significant source of distress for dissociative clients (Hodgdon et al., 2021). Incorporating EMDR, and specifically BLS, to reinforce and "tap in" established foundational skills specific to this population can further enhance client capacities. These skills include: Affect regulation, *intra*personal communication, building *intra*structure, and establishing safety.

Clients with DID or OSDD are highly traumatized individuals who have survived their history by relying on their internal world as a means of psychological viability. While the interior experience was necessary in the past, it can become challenging to navigate two worlds once history is in the rearview mirror. Common sources of distress are polarizations, lost time, and when exiles are blended or flooding, which then compels the activation of firefighters and managers.

One of the functions of OSDD and DID is to hide the painful reality both from the person and from the world around them. Naming these conditions confirms the past, which can activate a variety of complex responses including shame, grief, and guilt. IFS has demonstrated success in cultivating self-compassion in traumatized people living with plurality, which can result in decreasing shame (Hodgdon et al., 2021). Helping clients work toward the acceptance of their diagnosis through a nonpathologizing lens is an important initial step. In this stage, clinicians can help clients understand the purpose behind the "problem" of plurality while working to identify associated cognitive distortions. For example, clients might believe they are permanently damaged or assume they cannot handle confronting their story. In this stage, the goal of the clinician, client, and their system is to use IFS and an awareness of parts to reframe multiplicity as protective while using EMDR to reinforce capacities.

A common polarization is a battle between parts who deny the reality of multiplicity and other parts who fight for it to be known. There are a variety of ways to help mapping be more palatable for those struggling with it, such as by allowing temporary acknowledgment of a part by using a whiteboard or other erasable medium. Titrated exposure to the internal system slowly decreases fear of it while increasing space for Self-leadership and gratitude for all their hard work. Whenever Self-leadership and Self-energy are present, we can augment these and expand them with BLS (see Chapter 6).

Another polarizing dynamic might be when external events result in internalization of perpetrator behaviors as a protective measure. Firefighters who abuse exiles have often aligned themselves with abusers to render them predictable or act as a protective shield against further harm (Okano, 2019). Providing a safe internal space for exiles is an important first step in creating a safe internal environment, which requires negotiation with perpetrator introjects, where we assume underlying positive intentions. The therapist can also model internal moderation, and soften polarizations by offering conflict resolution as a source of relief. The dissociative table technique can be introduced to facilitate a meeting place where parts can hold a conversation, and which they can even return to for future internal check-ins and to prevent the buildup of frustration when their needs are not met (Fraser, 2003).

Broken trust in self or parts of self is a common result of childhood trauma, particularly when children are put in the impossible position of having to choose between attachment to a necessary caregiver and surviving the abuse. Gradual exposure to the existence of distinctive subpersonalities can erode phobia of the internal experience, while IFS-guided inquiry can help build greater understanding of the impossible choices some parts had to make. Compassion for their plight and efforts to protect can develop over time as it becomes clearer that many were pigeonholed into roles they did not want and may not be able to see a way out of. Each moment of compassion toward subpersonalities that softens strife and builds cohesion benefits the system as a whole (see Chapter 7).

In Consideration of the Concept of "Self"

An important consideration is that the concept of Self-leadership can be complicated for those with DID or OSDD. Many will deny that they have any Self-energy at all, and describe their experience as being like a shattered plane of glass where all the pieces disperse with an absence of a central organizing feature. In this case, the therapist should not have an agenda of asserting the existence of Self-energy, but rather work within the client's existing paradigm. An alternative orientation would be to assume capacity for internal leadership in whatever form it exists and reinforcing it with BLS whenever it is revealed or practiced. Parts will often act autonomously in the absence of trusted leadership. Leaning into the connective tissue that holds the system together, while highlighting existing leadership capacities within a system, can yield comparable results.

Emotion regulation skills will organically grow through exposure to the internal experience; however, reinforcement of regulatory capacities (Phase 2 in an EMDR framework) should always be on our radars as therapists. Additional targets during Stage 1 should include emphasizing strides within the therapeutic relationship, building interpersonal skills, containment strategies, and helping clients set up their external life for the future of their internal work. As *intra*personal dynamics improve through the softening of polarizations alongside greater compassion between parts, movement toward the second stage of care can begin.

Stage 2: Titrating Trauma Work and Requesting Permission

The progression of cultivating internal cohesion alongside skill-building and reinforcement of existing strengths lays the groundwork for methodically working through the past. While the client and their system should have been well prepared for trauma processing prior to engaging in it, this stage of treatment remains risky and should be approached with caution. Chapters 2 and 3 contain IFS concepts and strategies (such as the six F's in Chapter 3) that support healthy pacing and gradual exposure to the story. Another approach aimed at minimizing systemic overwhelm is to limit exposure of other parts to the trauma by sequestering them to their internal safe spaces, which will have been established in Phase 1 (Paulsen, 2009).

Once an identified memory target has been identified, clinician, client, and their system should work collaboratively to time the work and develop a post-processing recovery plan. Memory targets can be broken into smaller, more manageable pieces and the client can then focus on a single aspect of the memory to begin with. As components of the memory are successfully targeted and processed utilizing EMDR, confidence and internal trust typically begin to expand. Breaking a singular trauma session down into three phases that mimic the overall triphasic approach assures ample time to request permission from the system, assess for Self-leadership, process the identified target, and ensure the client is regulated prior to their departure. The first 15–20 minutes should be characterized by assessing for Self-leadership and requesting permission to proceed. The second 15 minutes should be BLS, and the final 15–20 minutes should be focused on grounding in the present, containing the trauma memory, and planning for post-procedure recovery. It is highly recommended that the amount of time allocated to applying BLS is limited and that there is more than enough time to ensure the client leaves with an internal leader in charge.

Precautions

Clinicians should be prepared to end BLS if dissociative responses are activated, if their client seems "stuck" or nonresponsive to treatment, or if they are not tolerating the processing well. Even though assessment of potential contraindications to trauma processing occurred in Stage 1, there should be a reassessment of this each time the clinician plans to employ EMDR for trauma processing (Phases 4–7). Other protective approaches can include using slower BLS than what is typically recommended for nondissociative clients, planning for trauma sessions, pendulating between processing and planning sessions, ensuring the client can and will ask to stop if it is becoming overwhelming, and employing affect regulation strategies throughout the session.

Stage 3: Memory Consolidation and Planning for the Future

While the conclusion of care may have been long awaited, it can also activate old attachment wounds that exist alongside a new perspective on the past, present, and future. Many individuals with complex trauma and dissociation often find it disorienting to focus on the future, as they are accustomed to living in survival mode. Awareness of this shift can activate grief and loss surrounding what could have been possible had there been more opportunity for personal development. Clinicians and clients alike should be prepared to address the consequences of the past in addition to the activation of attachment wounding that may occur.

Structural dissociation is characterized by fragmentation in consciousness, memory, emotion, agency, and identity (Poli et al., 2023). Integration can thus be described as a stable sense of cohesion, perspective, memory, and for parts to develop greater a capacity to share a first-person perspective due to a softening of amnesic barriers between them (Steele et al., 2017). Some clients will want to work toward further integration of parts during this phase, whereas others may wish to focus on strengthening systemic collaboration. Some will have experienced some partial or full integration of subpersonalities organically because of trauma processing, whereas others may have little change to their internal life but are less distressed.

Memory consolidation and meaning-making are other important features of the final phase. Various detoxified traumas will already have been shared with the remainder of the system during the second phase, thus the focus here should be on making meaning and cultivating posttraumatic growth. The first and second phases of care are characterized by realization of the system and how it came to be, whereas the final stage addresses larger life questions that may be more philosophical in nature. Another important aspect of the final phase is planning, both in terms of life-design and of what to do in the inevitable exposure to future stress.

Case Example: Bridging the Space Between

The following is a composite case presentation, hence the material presented is not based on an actual person. However, the content is reflective of themes that have emerged in working with people living with DID and OSDD and is reflective of the overarching application of IFS and EMDR with this population. The case presentation is meant to highlight thematic ways we can integrate both modalities throughout the three stages of trauma work.

Client Composite

The client is a 29-year-old adult who works full time within the mental health care field. They were referred by another provider who specialized in addiction, self-harm, and disordered eating, due to the unexpected emergence of a highly dissociated traumatized part in session. This part of self was unaware of the therapist, confused, and fearful, and the client's shift in their overall presentation was stark. The client also had reported active self-harm behaviors and suicidal ideation, with two prior attempts within the past five years.

Their previous therapist indicated that the client affirmed that they had heard voices and lost time, and expressed confusion about their own behavior. They also reported nightmares and flashbacks of events that they did not recall, but these intrusions were accompanied by significant distress. The client struggled with emotion regulation, interpersonal challenges, and mood difficulties, and met criteria for chronic posttraumatic stress disorder.

They also reported awareness of several "parts" of them that were experienced as separate or distinctive, but they were simultaneously aware that these subpersonalities belonged to them. They completed a diagnostic test that revealed a diagnosis of OSDD and PTSD.

Stage 1: Relationship-Building, Stabilization, Preparation, History Taking

History Taking

Based on the client's diagnosis and evidence of dissociative symptoms, information gathering occurred over time, with the most necessary information being collected within the first three sessions. Demographic information, emergency contact, mental health history, and health concerns were gathered immediately, while information on family of origin or other historical data were collected in a titrated manner. An introduction to both EMDR and IFS was provided alongside psycho-education surrounding the etiology and treatment trajectory for their condition. Additionally, we spoke about how all parts of the client's system were welcomed, and we would be seeking permission from all of them, at each stage of our work together.

Relationship to Diagnosis

The client reported dissonance and distress surrounding the reality of their condition as well as the implications it carried, given its roots in developmental trauma. This internal dynamic emerged regularly throughout the first several years of therapy as part of the client's grieving and realization process. The denial of the diagnosis served to ensure the client remained within the window of tolerance, and that we did not approach the trauma narrative too quickly.

We focused on a part of the client that was reluctant to accept the reality of their experience and the associated trauma history. We explored its concerns, which revealed that they were fearful of the unknown and recognized that there would be a grieving process associated with learning about their history. There was also a fear of internal self-loathing toward exiles for their perceived complicity with sexual abuse.

The primary goal was to access Self-energy or internal leadership to offer validation of the client's concerns while developing a plan for safe exploration. Once leadership was available and this part felt understood, it was willing to step aside and allowed further inquiry.

Along the ways we also identified the client's internal resources and associated parts of the system that allowed this dynamic to unfold. They were able to identify other times when there had been enough certitude to allow for internal exploration and for leadership emergence.

Mapping the System

A task that began early on was to increase awareness of subpersonalities and what their roles were. Given that OSDD and DID are both conditions designed to protect against the painful knowledge of the past, there was hesitation in acknowledging parts. There was also a significant amount of shame and embarrassment related to their internal experience along with a fear of being "crazy."

The first step taken was to work with the part(s) who had concern about knowing or being known. We were able to hear the concerns the part had around mistrust of and resentment toward internal others. Once these concerns were validated and addressed and there was enough confidence to move forward, the client was able to acknowledge how this part had worked hard on behalf of the system. This allowed them to identify other memories of internal trust and safety, which we then reinforced with short, slow sets of BLS. The client was comfortable enough to temporarily put two parts on a whiteboard, employed the 6 F's, and then erased what they had written prior to the end of session. This process was repeated throughout our work until the system in its entirety was mapped out on paper. Acknowledging and externalizing the internal system can take time and a graduated approach; thus we began with a whiteboard and moved toward a more permanent representation on paper. We also occasionally utilized figurines or puppets to externalize subpersonalities, which was systematically reinforced with short, slow sets of BLS.

Building an Intrastructure

Another important task early on was to help this client create an *intra-structure* within their mind's eye. The purpose behind this task is to create order and compartmentalized spaces for parts to retreat to when they need rest, safety, and to create internal rooms of their own. This process often comes quite easily to dissociative people, given that imaginative absorption is a predisposition for these conditions (van der Hart et al., 2006). This task was difficult for some parts of the client, however, who believed that living with fragmentation meant that they were "crazy." They were inclined to "wish away" their reality with the hope that it would eventually resolve itself.

We targeted parts that were fearful and methodically explored each of their concerns. Reframing their system as an orderly response to a disorderly history was novel and supported a shift toward their internal organization.

The client's incredible imagination and dissociative capacity were highlighted as gifts this client had. We worked to characterize their dissociative capacity as both lifesaving and as a tool, which shifted the view of their experience from pathological to adaptive. As these themes emerged, we reinforced them with slow, short sets of BLS. The client was then able to identify other ways in which their mind protected them in impossible circumstances, which then elicited gratitude toward these parts for their efforts. We then reinforced internal gratitude using slow, short sets of BLS.

Stage 2: Permission, Planning, and Processing

Since processing past trauma with highly traumatized, dissociative clients requires planning and structure, we chose a section of a memory to address to titrate exposure to the past. Processing was limited to a pre-established maximum of 15 minutes of BLS, which consisted of a maximum of 20 passes at a slower pace than what is typically recommended. Tappers were the client's preferred method of processing. The first 15 minutes of the session was focused on revisiting the plan, requesting permission from protectors, and establishing agreement with the exile to proceed. The client and therapist also checked with the system to revisit the approved post-processing recovery plan. Protector parts were asked to help monitor the process for flooding and to alert internal leadership should there be hints of overwhelm. Helper parts were asked to remain on standby to provide nurturance and comfort to the exile during and after the process as well as to assist in containment and grounding at the end of session.

The protectors and helpers trusted by the unburdening exile were the only ones present while the remainder of the Ego states were to remain tucked in their spaces within the *intra*structure. Processing only began after the presence of internal leadership had been identified and collective safety had been confirmed by asking each part how they felt toward the exile. If there was anger, resentment, fear, or anything outside of the eight C's of IFS, we worked with the identified part to explore concerns before beginning the unburdening process.

Once the process was completed, the memory was contained by the client's placing the imagery and associated visceral content into an internal vault. After the memory was compartmentalized, the client was asked to ground into the present using each of their senses. The exile, protector, and helper parts were asked if they wanted to rest. Each agreed, and internal leadership facilitated walking them back to their internal safe spaces. Confirmation of Self-leadership as present while residual memory material was being contained was assessed by checking in for their presence.

Stage 3: Highlighting Dissociation

The final stage of work involves the dissemination of processed memories to the rest of the system, making meaning of the past, preparing to say goodbye, and planning for the future. Following a processing session with this client, it was important to assess their response to the work. They indicated they had been fatigued for approximately three days after our meeting and indicated they had had a lot of dreams without other adverse reactions. They reported minimal polarizations, a decrease in intrusions, and fewer incidents of lost time.

Given the function of a dissociative system is to concentrate memories and tasks to certain parts, it should be assumed that there will be some who remained unaware of certain aspects of the past. Sharing the processed memory content with the remainder of the internal team contextualized and expanded the narrative, transforming it from a past frozen in time into a more dynamic story with less emotionally laden content.

Parts who were prepared to hear the piece of the story that was processed were invited to listen as the exile shared their version of events with the support of leadership, protectors, and helpers. As the system witnessed the storytelling process, their positive cognitions were identified and reinforced using slow, short sets of BLS. The primary cognition was "I did the best I could," which was true considering the severity of abuse they were exposed to in the memory we targeted. The belief was held at a VoC of 6/7 at the end of session by most parts who were present. The client was stable and reported increased confidence in their internal system and their capacity to continue moving through other memories.

Conclusion

People living with DID and OSDD are often confronted with the fact their past continues to profoundly impact the present. The amount of time spent suffering and in treatment can become more for them to grieve, which is a quagmire given the importance of proper pacing. Combining IFS and EMDR to enhance skills and meticulously working through the past can expedite the work. By working with defenses designed to protect, we can help the therapy process move slowly and confidently, honor multiplicity, and provide hope. As some parts are recognized for the first time, and they are welcomed into the internal family system, they can finally find the love and healing that they have been waiting for.

Note

1 I will use the term "stages" as opposed to "phases" for this three-staged framework to differentiate it from the eight phases of EMDR.

References

American Psychiatric Association. (2022). *Diagnostic and statistical manual of mental disorders* (5th ed., text rev.). American Psychiatric Association.

Brand, B. L., Myrick, A. C., Loewenstein, R. J., Classen, C. C., Lanius, R., McNary, S. W., Pain, C., & Putnam, F. W. (2012). A survey of practices and recommended treatment interventions among expert therapists treating patients with dissociative identity disorder and dissociative disorder not otherwise specified. *Psychological Trauma: Theory, Research, Practice, and Policy, 4*(5), 490–500.

Chien, W. & Fung, H. (2022). The challenges in diagnosis and treatment of dissociative disorders. *Alpha Psychiatry*, March 1;*23* (2): 45–46. doi: 10.5152/alphapsychiatry.2022.0001. PMID: 36426292; PMCID: PMC9597071.

Ducharme, E. L. (2017). Best practices in working with complex trauma and dissociative identity disorder. *Practice Innovations, 2*(3), 150–161.

Fraser, G. A. (2003). Fraser's "Dissociative Table Technique" revisited, revised: A strategy for working with ego states in dissociative disorders and ego-state therapy. *Journal of Trauma & Dissociation, 4*(4), 5–28.

Hodgdon, H. B., Anderson, F. G., Southwell, E., Hrubec, W., & Schwartz, R. (2021). Internal family systems (IFS) therapy for posttraumatic stress disorder (PTSD) among survivors of multiple childhood trauma: A pilot effectiveness study. *Journal of Aggression, Maltreatment & Trauma, 31*(1), 22–43. https://doi.org/10.1080/1092 6771.2021.2013375.

(ISST-D) International Society for the Study of Trauma and Dissociation. (2011). Guidelines for treating dissociative identity disorder in adults, 3rd revision. *Journal of Trauma & Dissociation, 12*(2), 115–187.

Lazarus, G., & Rafaeli, E. (2023). Modes: Cohesive personality states and their interrelationships as organizing concepts in psychopathology. *Journal of Psychopathology and Clinical Science, 132*(3), 238–248.

Okano, K. (2019). The origin of so-called "shadowy personalities" in patients with Dissociative Identity Disorder. *European Journal of Trauma & Dissociation, 3*(2), 95–102.

Paulsen, S. (2009). *Looking through the eyes of trauma and dissociation: An illustrated guide for EMDR therapists and clients.* Booksurge Publishing.

Poli, A., Cappellini, F., Sala, J., & Miccoli, M. (2023). The integrative process promoted by EMDR in dissociative disorders: Neurobiological mechanisms, psychometric tools, and intervention efficacy on the psychological impact of the COVID-19 pandemic. *Frontiers in Psychology, 14*, 1164527.

Robinson, M. A., Purcell, J. B., Ward, L., Winternitz, S., Kaufman, M. L., Baranowski, K. A., Lived Experience Advisory Panel (LEAP). (2024, May 7). Advanced research on and treatment of dissociative identity disorder with people with lived experience. *American Journal of Psychotherapy, 77*(3), 141–145.

Schwartz, R. C. (2023). *Introduction to the internal family systems model.* Sounds True. (Original work published 2001.)

Siegel, D. (2020). *The developing mind: How relationships and the brain interact to shape who we are* (3rd ed.). The Guilford Press.

Steele, K., Boon, S., & van der Hart, O. (2017). *Treating trauma-related dissociation: A practical, integrative approach.* W. W. Norton & Co.

Utomo, Y. P., Adnan, M. L., & Susanti, E. A. P. (2023). Understanding Dissociative Identity Disorder: A literature review. *Archives of Psychiatry Research: An International Journal of Psychiatry and Related Sciences, 59*(2), 305–310.

van der Hart, O., Groenendijk, M., Gonzalez, A., Mosquera, D., & Solomon, R. (2014). Dissociation of the personality and EMDR therapy in complex trauma-related disorders: Applications in phases 2 and 3 treatment. *Journal of EMDR Practice & Research, 8*(1) 33–48.

van der Hart, O., Nijenhuis, E. R. S., & Steele, K. (2006). *The haunted self: Structural dissociation and the treatment of chronic traumatization.* W. W. Norton & Company.

Chapter 12

Active Imagination

Jungian Underpinnings in the Joining of Art Therapy, IFS, and EMDR

Peggy Kolodny

Reviewed by Bruce Hersey

The Creative Integration of Art Therapy with IFS and EMDR

Trauma treatment researchers' and authors' findings reveal that integrative approaches, along with phase models, are highly effective treatments for trauma (Cloitre, 2021; Fisher, 2017; Twombly, 2013). As evidenced by this book's topic, clinicians have been exploring integrating Eye Movement Desensitization and Reprocessing (EMDR) with Internal Family Systems (IFS) (Fatter, 2024; Fisher, 2022; Gomez & Krause, 2013; Hersey, 2022; O'Shea-Brown, 2020; Twombly & Schwartz, 2008). EMDR, IFS, and art therapy recognize that the client possesses the resources to self-heal, the emotions and body are central to the process, the therapist stance is neutral, compassionate, and nonjudgmental, and the relational aspect is held at the core, anchored by a neurobiological role in the healing process (Anderson, 2021; Fisher, 2022; Twombly, 2024; Warson & Warson, 2023). There is ample research on the efficacy of EMDR (O'Shea-Brown, 2020; Shapiro, 2018), IFS (Ally et al., 2025; Hodgdon et al., 2021), and art therapy (Schouten et al., 2015). Art therapy is a particularly flexible psychotherapy profession (not a modality), and is easily integrated with these two models (Kolodny & Mazero, 2022).

Ethical Considerations in the Use of Art in Therapy

It is ethically expected that, if the reader does not hold a master's degree in art therapy (or equivalent such as postgraduate certification) and plans to use these creative interventions into their EMDR/IFS practice, they do not utilize the term art therapy, as this term is a title-protected mental health profession in many areas. The creative prompts described in this chapter were specifically selected for use by the "non-art therapist," but please consider art therapy consultation as needed. Clinicians should practice each directive prior to use with clients. Familiarity with varied art media is also needed for skillful proficiency. Art therapists maintain a nonjudgmental stance and avoid direct, probing questions regarding the art product. Use

DOI: 10.4324/9781003541554-15

observational language: "I notice that you scribbled red, I wonder if you might say more about it?" Finally, art-making refers to drawing, painting, sculpting, collaging, sand tray, and creative activity with any media choice.

Art with EMDR and Bilateral Stimulation

When EMDR was launched as a trauma-focused therapy in 1990, it caught the attention of a small number of art therapists who began training in it. Publications on the "meeting" of art therapy and EMDR emerged in 1999 (Schmidt; Breed, 2013; Tobin, 2006; Tripp, 2007), along with articles on bilateral art-making (Cartwright, 1999; McNamee, 2003). Art therapists have recognized the benefits of bilateral art-making ever since art therapy was formalized as a profession (Cane, 1951; Capacchione, 1988). Beginning in 2013, art therapist Tally Tripp and I have developed workshops (Tripp & Kolodny, 2013, 2014, 2016) on integrating art, EMDR, bilateral movement, mindful practices, sensorimotor psychotherapy (Ogden & Fisher, 2015), and Kolodny's Neurosequential Art Approach (2021a, 2021b).

Clinical benefits of bilateral art have been studied, and protocols, typically trauma-focused, have been developed (Elbrecht, 2018; McNamee, 2003; Talwar, 2007; Tripp, 2016, 2022), with some focus on art-informed EMDR (Davis et al., 2022; Warson et al., 2024). Neurobiological responses to bilateral art have led to therapeutic gains, as exemplified by "cognitive restructuring and subsequent integration of trauma experiences" (Lusebrink & Hinz, 2016, p. 43) and Warson's observation that drawing figure 8's with both hands "creates a parasympathetic response with slow cadence" (Warson et al., 2024, p. 24). Rhythmic bilateral drawing has been found to be grounding, promoting affect regulation, attention span, and brain connectivity (Bolwerk et al., 2014), and engaging neural pathways (Warson et al., 2024). Chapman has noted that in post-kinesthetic activity "the brain instinctually shifts information processing to the affect/perceptual level of processing" (2014, p. 22). Perry, founder of the Neurosequential Model of Therapeutics, emphasizes the essential need for rhythmic and creative activities within trauma treatment (Gaskill & Perry, 2014). Art-making can take us into "flow" (Csikszentmihalyi, 2013), a state of concentrated attention associated with pleasure that can assist with trauma processing and integration.

The studied and observable benefits of bilateral art prompts, such as Chapman's sensory-motor scribble warm-up (2014), smoothly translate to integrative use with EMDR, and can include mirroring opportunities, attunement, and therapeutic alliance (Kolodny, 2021b). This joint warm-up exercise involves the therapist and client sitting or standing facing each other, a large sheet of paper between them, markers in both hands. The therapist directs the client to draw using both hands in a progression of random scribbles that evolve developmentally into intentional circles, while changing the pace and direction of bilateral and simultaneous gestures; they then change roles, with the client directing the therapist. Tripp and Kolodny (2014, Tripp, 2016) modified it so that client and therapist silently improvise the directions, mirroring each other's bilateral scribble movements in an attuned dance. Art therapy continues to reveal diverse benefits when integrated with EMDR, which has culminated in the book *EMDR and the Creative Arts Therapies* (Davis et al., 2022).

Examples of Art for Each Phase

I was introduced to formal EMDR training in the late 1990s, and as each phase of the EMDR protocol was taught, my mind responded with novel ideas of enhancing them with a creative experience. I have developed art exercises useful in each EMDR phase (as well as IFS).

Phase 1 (History Taking and Treatment Plan)

Creating timelines (on mural paper, creating a paper book) holds the potential to organize trauma memories, which are often fragmented and chaotic (van der Kolk, 2014). Creating a timeline can enhance both the client's historical memories and floatbacks, as art taps into limbic memory (Kolodny & Mazero, 2022). Timelines can offer a more paced approach, breaking memories into shorter periods, identifying IFS "trailheads," and increasing the Window of Tolerance (WOT) (Davis et al., 2022; Kolodny & Mazero, 2022).

Phase 2 (Preparation)

In Phase 2 of EMDR, there is development of resources and installation of these resources (Korn & Leeds, 2002). When I guide clients with creating their Safe/Soothing Place, my prompt is "Create an image of where you want to be, then place yourself in it," as clients may struggle with safe/soothing concepts (Kolodny & Mazero, 2022).

Phase 3 (Assessment)

Clients create a rating scale for subjective units of distress (SUDS) and validity of cognition (VoC), such as a selection of 10 images ranging from a calm sky to a tornado (Kolodny & Mazero, 2022).

Phase 4 (Desensitization)

If processing gets blocked, the novelty of drawing bilateral strokes for BLS may evoke a shift. The "Modeling Parts" art prompt uses clay to form three sculptures representing the target part, how the client feels toward this part, and any Self-energy noted (Kolodny & Mazero, 2022).

Phase 5 (Installation)

Draw a part with Self-energy and positive cognition in a new role with healthy traits, using bilateral drawing strokes to strengthen/install image (Kolodny & Mazero, 2022)

Phase 6 (Body Scan)

When asking the client to body scan in Phases 2 and 6, invite them to draw noticed sensations within a body template. This deepens an understanding of the senses felt and is often an initial step in identifying parts! See Figure 12.1.

Figure 12.1 Body Scan.

Phase 7 (Closure)

Revisit the "Place You Want to Be" image and add additional positive resources around it. The client can use the original body scan drawing and place it into this image.

Phase 8 (Re-evaluation)

Revisit the created VoC/SUDS scales and "Draw Future Self," so that this future self—or the client with insight from the future self—can share wisdom to the present Self (Husum, 2025).

A Deeper Dive into Phase 4

Full of creative ideas led by the concept of *bilateral drawing* as an alternate form of BLS, I continued to explore diverse ways to include bilateral drawing in Phase 4 and named this ArtMDR (Art Movement Desensitization and Reprocessing; Kolodny & Mazero, 2022). These bilateral strokes may be made over a drawing or photograph of a target memory or on a separate piece of paper. I find it helpful to have various sizes of the client's target

Figure 12.2 BLS Strokes over Artwork.

image available, which demonstrate the shrinkage of the image's impact as BLS sets advance. This is a form of assessing the subjective unit of distress (SUD).

In the following case example, as we progressed through sets, the client would glue an image down, and, with a pastel in each hand, draw bilateral strokes over the selected photo (finding a comfortable back-and-forth gesture), then replacing the image with a new smaller one as the memory's distressful impact decreased. As illustrated in Figure 12.2, the client provided various sizes of a photograph of the house where her childhood trauma occurred (I suggest using markers instead, as pastels break and create dust).

Integration of Art Therapy and Internal Family Systems

When completing Level 2 IFS training, my interest in integrative approaches fostered my immediate inclusion of this model into my arts-informed EMDR practice (Kolodny et al., 2016, 2022; Kolodny & Mazero, 2018, 2022). Davis and Kolodny (2024) developed multiple workshops on art therapy, IFS, and EMDR in working with the dissociative continuum. In response to this pioneering approach, other published works and dissertations by creative art therapists have evolved, and the evidential advantages of integrating creative arts with IFS continued to emerge (Lavergne, 2004; Pici-D'Ottavio, 2023; Sabados, 2024; Sorbara, 2024; Wood, 2015).

The intersection of IFS and art can be observed in framing how art possesses all the eight traits of Self-energy. Creative experiences invite Curiosity—what happens if I put this color here? It takes Courage—I will take the risk of trying clay! There's Confidence—whatever I create is ok. It's Calming—art can evoke a meditative state. Connection occurs with your internal system, as parts find their voice in art. Clarity is evident when art brings light to unexpressed thoughts, feelings, and insights. Compassion is intrinsic with nonjudgmental witnessing of art. Creativity is creative (Kolodny & Mazero, 2022)!

A central component of IFS (Schwartz & Sweezy, 2020) is to help clients identify and *unblend* from each part, via utilizing the six F's process (see Chapter 3). In Box 12.1, an effective interweave of art and IFS with the six F's is described (Kolodny & Mazero, 2022).

The witnessed narratives offered by exiles are expressed through memories, visual images, somatic sensations, thoughts, and emotions (Gomez & Krause, 2013). Art-making provides a visual graphic for these narratives, as trauma often inhibits verbal expression (van der Kolk, 2014). This opportune moment allows the Self to offer the part a corrective experience, referred to as a *do-over*, which can be expressed in art.

Box 12.1 Six F's with the Art Process

Find the part in and around the body → draw on body outline or create it.

Focus on the part that is visualized → create image of this part.

Flesh it out by asking "what does it want you to know?" → Add to creation.

Feel – Ask "how do you feel toward it?" → Add feeling to creation (shapes, colors, words).

Be**Friend** it and facilitate relationship → Sit with your creation, use metaphors, create being with it (draw, paint, sculpt).

Fears – what are its fears? → You can create what fear looks like.

If this is a Protective part – what is it afraid will happen? → Create what this might look like.

If Exile – what does it want you to know? → Create or write what this might look like.

When the Exile is "frozen in time" in a past distressing scene, the client or therapist will invite them to leave the past and enter the present in an act of *retrieval* to a safer imaginal place of that part's choosing (Anderson, 2021), again offering creative exploration. In *unloading*, the therapist/client suggests that the part releases its burdens to one of the five elements—fire, water, earth, air, or light; this provides numerous creative opportunities, such as painting the release or drawing burdens and throwing them away in a kinesthetic action that deepens the concept. Once the exile releases their burdens, they are invited to draw/paint/sculpt to internalize positive traits and strengths, restoring harmony within the internal system, led by Self-energy (aligning with Phase 2 and 5 of EMDR).

Unburdening and the do-over overlap with both recapitulating missed critical opportunities in childhood (Gaskill & Perry, 2014) and memory reconsolidation, concepts present in both EMDR and art therapy. Art therapy researchers such as Hass-Cohen and Findlay (2019) and Fatter (2024) support art therapy's contribution to memory reconsolidation. They have explored how art-making can foster the reorganizing of chaotic memory, cultivate cognitive restructuring, and promote integration of trauma memories, similar to the memory reconsolidation in EMDR's Adaptive Information Process (and the corrective experience of the IFS do-over). The last step in unburdening is *integration*, in which the part develops a new, healthier role in the system, promoting another imaginal opportunity.

Benefits of Combining Art into IFS and EMDR

Art therapy has demonstrated manifold advantages for clinical practice when it is used to augment EMDR and/or IFS with expressive interventions and prompts (Davis et al., 2022; Kolodny & Mazero, 2022; Marich, 2023; Schmidt, 1999), with evidence of benefits in trauma treatment (Schouten et al., 2015). There are multiple variations on the use of art prompts for containment: examples of such prompts can include decorated shoeboxes! Clients can color a mandala or a calm image, then be directed to draw a part of a distressing experience (titration), verbally process for a few minutes, and return to coloring the mandala while repeating a bilateral glancing back and forth between both images (pendulation), a regulatory process that can help calm parts (Tripp, 2016). Art organically provides pacing that can release emotions somatically, as in rapid scribbling or slow coloring.

Metaphor is the language of art therapy. Utilization of metaphor is encouraged both in EMDR–such as by imagining looking out a train window—and in IFS—as in the *invite and integration* phases, when the part is asked what affirmative qualities it would like to take in. Some clients' parts may find this concept challenging, and say they really aren't going anywhere or that this feels too spiritual. As they are often more acclimated to using art to represent something, the use of creative metaphor makes more sense. Creating an image such as that of sitting at the conference table with parts (Fraser, 2003) serves to support visualization, strengthening embodiment of therapeutic benefits.

Using art in EMDR and IFS exhibits efficacy in reducing the trauma responses that may interfere with these processes. Trauma can inhibit imagination, mentalization, and interoception (Davis, 2022; Schmitt & Schoen, 2022), resulting in clients with dissociation reporting an inability to "see" an internal image of a part in IFS, or having limited visual target memories in EMDR. Inviting these clients to notice a somatic sensation in their body scan, as described earlier in this chapter, and offering a body outline template through which they can use color, line, shape, texture, image, or even words to illustrate these sensations, will boost their ability to locate and witness a felt sense of parts and emotions. Having a concrete image, even if it's a scribbled red shape, will validate the existence of these parts and memories, and offer them an image with which to dialogue. Clients may add to the image in a literal "fleshing-out" process. Body scans often evolve into a body map of parts.

Art therapy shares numerous qualities with EMDR and IFS—foremost in its client-centered, nonjudgmental, paced approach. Leading trauma researchers (Levine, 1997; Ogden & Fisher, 2015; Rothschild, 2000; van der Kolk, 2014) express the imperative need for nonverbal and integrative trauma treatment methods including mindfulness, rhythmic activities, and the body-focused techniques found in somatic and sensorimotor approaches. They have recognized the value of imagery and creative expression. These same researchers conclude that we store sensory memories both implicitly (sensory, somatic, affective) and explicitly (conscious, declarative narrative). Art therapists McNiff (1998) and Capacchione (1988) reflect on art's ability to enhance the communication between internal parts of Self and the unconscious that allows for metaphoric, symbolic, somatic, affective, and tangible expression. It follows that the sensorimotor and somatic qualities found in art-making (consider the smell and feel of a crayon moving across paper), match how memories are stored in a sensory-somatic manner; in this way we can cultivate access to implicit memories, offering opportunities for recapitulation of disrupted developmental experiences (Gaskill & Perry, 2014; Kolodny, 2021a, 2021b). Art bridges these implicit and explicit memories and externalizes the internal image, offering shifts in perspectives and new meanings, allowing parts to experience new insights. Cohen et al. (1995) discuss the containment inherent in art; the canvas/ sculpture offers tangible boundaries, and the physical distance between artist and art creates emotional distancing. The art therapist may need to be Kramer's Third Hand (Henley, 2024) by guiding choice of media, offering directive and nondirective options, and inviting the client to create (a form of asking consent, aligning with the IFS process). Both art and IFS allow for agency, not agenda!

Jungian Active Imagination with Art Therapy, IFS, and EMDR

Jungian active imagination supports this implicit and explicit process in guiding internal and external healing dialogue that is also the core of IFS, EMDR, and art therapy. IFS and EMDR both recognize the significant need for internal imagery as a vehicle of healing, which helps the client to access resource strategies and distress tolerance skills, while inviting them to use creative and imaginal tools such as externalizing the internal target memory image. The six F's dialogue of IFS leads to an unburdening process, and this, alongside the practice of focusing inward that takes place during Phase 4 of EMDR reprocessing, encourages the client to directly dialogue with internal memories, sensations, or entities, all of which aligns with active imagination concepts (Kolodny & Mazero, 2022; Swan-Foster, 2018).

Swan-Foster (2018) defines Jung's concept of active imagination as intentionally engaging in dialogue with symbols, images, and themes, to deepen self-awareness and understanding of the subconscious mind. Influenced by Freud's free association, active imagination is centered on the healing energy of imagination, whereby art can be used to give form to our distress (McNiff, 1998). In Jung's letters (Adler, 1973), he described the active imagination process, suggesting that the artist should begin with any image in their artwork, focus on it, wait for it to change, and notice those shifts. He explains "… step into the picture yourself … if it is a speaking figure … say what you have to say to that figure and listen to what he or she might say …" (Chodorow, 1997, p. 164). Jung's words align with a lot of the six F's process (particularly Find, Focus, Flesh, and beFriend), and lead to unification with the system. Jung's wisdom also describes art therapy's role in IFS, as it provides the invitation to visualize a part as a figure, potentially fostering a deeper sense of compassion and attunement when one can "see" a part.

Jung's *Red Book* (2009) journaled in depth both his process writing and his art-making, especially that which focused on mandalas. Jung holds a foundational place in art therapy's evolution from Joan Kellogg's developmentally sequenced 13 Archetypal Stages of the Great Rounds of Mandala, based on Jungian archetypes (Quinn, 2021), to Swan-Foster's book *Jungian Art Therapy* (2018). Even as art therapy students, we studied Jung's *Man and His Symbols* (2023), practicing active imagination. Active Imagination describes one way in which art therapists intuitively guide clients in externalizing inner experiences, promoting a redo of traumatic situations (Swan-Foster, 2018, p. 209). Swan-Foster discusses Jung's observation that we build a relationship with our dreams, thus bringing them into consciousness. This process can occur during art-making, as active imagination dialogue softens the ego, allowing the unconscious to emerge. This overlaps with IFS when befriending managers allows the exiles to unburden and can assist in unblocking EMDR reprocessing (Twombly & Schwartz, 2008).

Dr. Andrew Dobo's 2023 book *The Hero's Journey: Integrating Jungian Psychology and EMDR Therapy* (Dobo, 2023) expands this theme of EMDR therapy and Jungian concepts. Dobo observes that EMDR brings clients to an "encounter" with their collective unconscious and, as healing progresses, core negative beliefs are "dismantled" as more adaptive beliefs replace them. Dobo posits that there is a window of chaos in this transformation when Jungian approaches become "essential." He notes that EMD moved to EMDR after Shapiro observed that reprocessing was a form of free association. Dobo emphasizes Shapiro's recognition that both EMDR and Jungian psychology tap into images and symbols to help clients resolve trauma memories, further validating the use of art therapy.

Jungian analysts such as Robert Johnson and Marie-Louise von Franz developed process steps in using active imagination in psychoanalysis. Johnson's book *Inner Work: Using Dreams and Active Imagination for Personal Growth* (Johnson, 1989) describes his four-step active imagination process, which is similar to IFS. Johnson clarifies that when active imagination is utilized, it brings more unity to our inner worlds, creating cooperation between the warring ego and the unconscious. He expressed that the art therapist must cultivate the sense of a third eye to harness insight and reveal wisdom in the artwork.

The Shadow Knows: Its Role in Art Therapy, IFS, and EMDR

Swan-Foster (2018) describes Jung's concept of Shadow as those aspects of ourselves deemed undesirable and thus rejected by the ego. (These may also encompass secret wishes that are potentially healthy but feel shameful.) While some cultures view the Shadow as our bad or even evil parts, Western culture often views it as the parts of us we denounce and project onto others. Jung named two types of Shadow, the Personal and the Collective. The Personal consists of parts we reject within ourselves, even those with "positive" traits. One can see the similarity with the IFS concepts of exiles, so-called as they are exiled by the protector parts whose role is to prevent them from overwhelming the system with their burdens of stressful memories; and perhaps even the firefighters, who take on protective but often maladaptive behaviors such as addictions in their efforts to calm the system.

These personal burdens can be considered the Personal Shadow. The Collective Shadow was perceived by Jung as disavowed archetypes within the collective unconscious, which are seen when an individual assumes cultural beliefs that can lead to cultural projections onto a different culture, as in the concept of "othering," leading to dynamics such as systemic racism (see Chapter 10). Here one could see the overlap with legacy, cultural, and generational traumas that may evolve as personal burdens/Shadows. These certainly could be processed through IFS concepts of legacy burdens (Sinko, 2017), art, and EMDR therapy.

Art therapist Charmaine Husum (2025) developed a two-picture art directive, centered on the Shadow, incorporating Dual Attention Stimuli (DAS), and integrating EMDR, IFS and art therapy principles. The first prompt is to draw a figure that represents your inner resources, your Self-energy. The second drawing, on black paper, is of your Shadow part. You then journal an IFS-informed dialogue with each of the figures. Husum suggests placing them side by side, glancing from the Resource image to the Shadow image to understand and enhance compassion for the Shadow part while decreasing distressful feelings by utilizing unblending, Self-energy, and active imagination. These concepts offer synchronicities with Hersey's Syzygy model of IFS-informed EMDR (see Chapter 6).

An Art-Informed IFS and EMDR Case Study: In the Presence of Shadow and the Goddess

The following case study illustrates the interplay of IFS, EMDR, art therapy, active imagination, and Personal Shadow work.

Connie (a pseudonym), is a divorced female in her early 70s, retired from a counseling career. She sought art therapy as her primary therapy to work with her own poor body image, which was exacerbated by aging and depression. During Phase 1 history taking, she traced the etiology of her poor body image to childhood, when she had several medical issues that impacted her appearance. Current impaired functioning included missing work at her current job, on days when she "collapsed crying" when getting ready, too distressed by how her clothing fit to be able to remain dressed.

Connie was familiar with EMDR and IFS, but had never used them in past therapy. She expressed that she was not comfortable with parts language but saw the validity of the IFS model. She often found her voice (and those of her parts) through creative writing and mixed-media collages outside of therapy, which had led her to seek art therapy. In her initial art therapy session, she created a self-portrait with a clay mask, etching in her facial creases and wrinkles with her fingers. Within minutes, she was gently caressing the mask, declaring in a compassionate tone (Self-energy) how these were evidence of her lived experiences and emotions, such as laugh lines. She expressed her internal conflict that, while she could appreciate what her aging skin represented (one part), she continued to dislike her appearance (another part). In a subsequent session, she did a body scan, like the one seen earlier in Figure 12.2.

In a few subsequent IFS sessions exploring this trailhead, she expressed some challenges with engaging in the somatic *Find and Focus* process and the internal dialoguing of *Fleshing-out* process with parts. Body outline templates enabled her to scan her body, *Finding and Focusing* on the somatic sensations of where she held emotions. Here is a place where Phase 3 Assessment/EMDR was briefly used. We completed a body scan and identified a negative cognition of feeling powerless. The positive cognition was "I have agency." SUDS score was 8, VoC was a 3. Client declined traditional BLS, preferring to begin bilateral drawing. We did several bilateral warm-up scribbles on paper. She announced that she hated her fat belly, yet wanted to understand it, indicating the emergence of curiosity, a trait of Self-energy. When invited to draw her belly, she drew a headless torso with a large round belly, sharp teeth, and scowling eyes, calling it a belly monster (Personal Shadow); see Figure 12.3.

She was able to witness and use active imagination by dialoguing with this scary image in a more regulated and grounded state, encouraging unblending from fearful and critical parts. As discussed earlier, the art product provides emotional distancing and containment by externalizing internal images onto paper, promoting the safety of dual awareness. When asked how she *felt* toward this image, she drew herself as a small stick figure "trapped" inside the belly.

Connie asked this belly monster what it needed her to know. It replied that it held all her pain and worked hard to protect her from greater pain. She softly cried, then drew herself as a stick figure

Figure 12.3 Connie's Belly Monster.

outside the body in an act of *unblending*. When asked how she *felt* toward the belly now, she drew her hands supporting this belly, in an imaginal act of compassion and connection, illustrating her access of *Self-energy*.

Sitting in internal dialogue with this protective part, *befriending* it, and building trust via listening and witnessing, she suddenly, with intense pressure of a black oil pastel, drew black lines bursting from the belly. See Figure 12.4.

Connie stated that "… the belly monster was releasing the pain …," in a spontaneous *unburdening*. Checking in with this part, she noted that the belly wasn't completely unburdened, as she felt the presence of an *exile* holding shame. She identified this small stick figure as the exile and continued to process a retrieval of this exile, writing that she was "negotiating a way out." See Figure 12.5.

Figure 12.4 Releasing Pain/Unburdening Belly Monster.

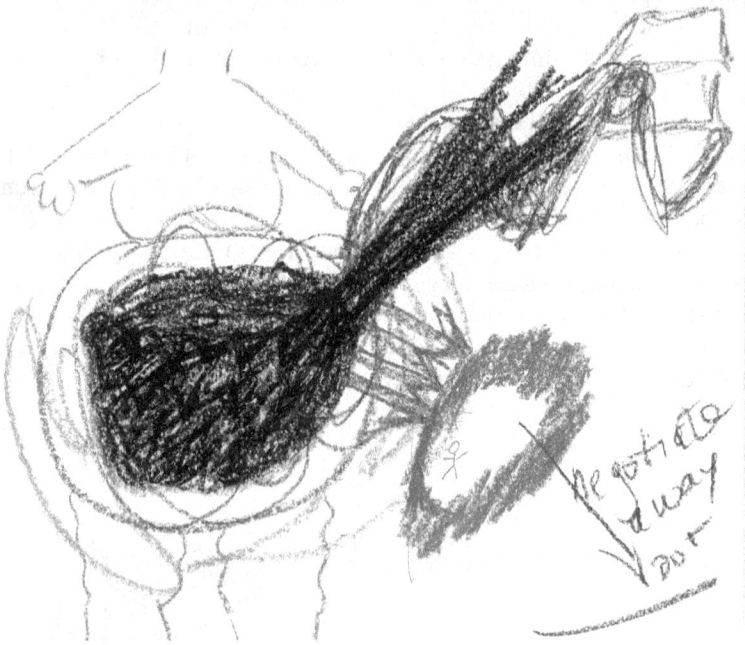

Figure 12.5 Negotiating a Way Out for an Exile.

The following week, Connie painted her manager part shaming the belly part (no longer calling it a monster.) This protective part disclosed feeling shame that the belly was fat, that people might be judgmental, and was protecting an exile hurt by her mother's critical stance toward her as a child. She began witnessing and unburdening these hurtful memories. She painted a torso with a smaller faceless belly and belly button, adding a pink V to represent her genitals. See Figure 12.6.

Connie expressed gratitude for her "life-giving womb" that had birthed several beloved children, represented by the small pink figures. She realized her "big belly" was a remnant of her pregnant belly, a joyful embodied lived experience. This awareness led her to name the image a Fertility Goddess, enhancing the Goddess traits of unconditional appreciation, feminine power, and fertility.

I happened to have a fertility goddess for my sand tray, hidden in a cupboard, and retrieved it to show her. Amazed by this ancient

Figure 12.6 Witnessing and Unburdening Manager Parts.

symbol, and the coincidental Jungian moment of the collective uncon-sciousness, Connie placed it on top of the drawing and used the bilat-eral butterfly tap, crossing the arms and alternating the tapping of each shoulder, to install this positive symbol, an act of do-over and resource development. See Figure 12.7.

Connie followed with several more IFS verbal sessions, checking in with parts, unburdening more memories of her relationships, explor-ing the fears of parts holding shame, and recognizing the family pat-terns of chaotic attachment and the exiles' fears of abandonment. She continued to notice more shame, this time from the exiles.

When she again felt ready to use art with IFS, I invited her to use clay in a fleshing-out IFS process–both metaphoric and literal!. Connie chose white modeling clay that air-hardened, as she wanted to keep the models she and her parts create, always a serious consideration. She opted to keep her eyes closed as she molded the clay, intentionally

Figure 12.7 Installing a Resource: Belly Representing a Fertility Goddess.

unguided by her vision, to tap into a more intuitive, Jungian internal process while I led her through the six F's.

Sculpturing clay involves using both hands, so there is a natural bilateral rhythm as a client creates, which contributes elements of BLS desensitization. In art-making, as in IFS and EMDR, clients shift their attention internally to notice what comes up. I asked permission to photograph the clay as it morphed, and invited her to pause and observe what she had created, with the option for dialoguing with the clay object. She agreed to this process and stated that she wanted to continue to check in on shame, in a more mindful manner, a no-agenda stance of "noticing what she noticed" rather than a pre-established target memory.

We began with a breathing meditation to enhance compassion, followed by a body scan. Her hands rapidly created a small shape that seemed to be a "something," so I asked if she felt this was a

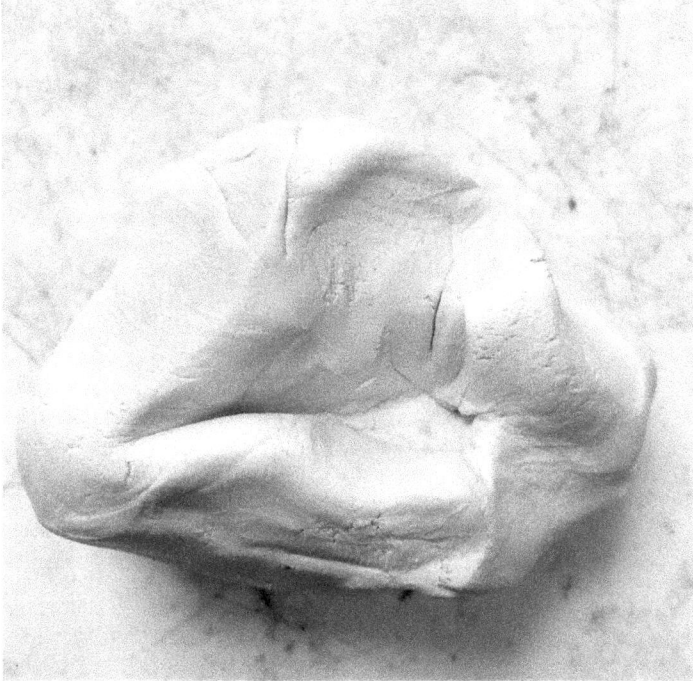

Figure 12.8 An Exile in the Form of a Mouth Expressing Shame.

good moment to pause and look. (It is always important to get consent from the client and all the parts that are present in a session.) She opened her eyes, gazed at the clay part, and sat with it. See Figure 12.8.

She noticed it appeared to be a mouth expressing shame (exile), and she asked it what it wanted her to understand. She closed her eyes, witnessing the exile's story, and continued moving both hands back and forth, molding the clay.

As the clay morphed into another shape, I again invited her to pause when she, and the parts involved, felt ready. Opening her eyes, she looked at the sculpture, asking it again what it wanted her to know.

Connie closed her eyes, her hands busy again, choosing not to share with me the details of her internal dialogue, then opened her eyes and let me know that the clay shape had transformed into a womb. See Figure 12.9.

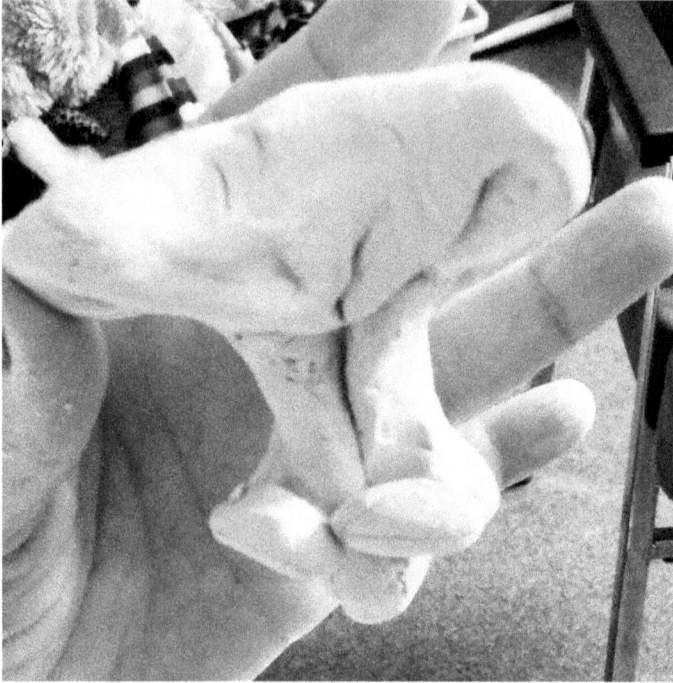

Figure 12.9 The Womb.

She expressed her gratitude to this part for her body and her "Womanhood," then told me her part was ready to *release* the shame into the earth, and closed her eyes as she witnessed this act. (It is interesting to note that clay is earth!) Her hands continued to work with the clay as she did this release. Opening her eyes of her own accord, she studied the clay, declaring that it was an elephant, an animal she admired for its positive traits of family devotion and strong memory. See Figure 12.10.

Continuing this process, she closed her eyes, her hands bilaterally transforming the clay into a new shape, then opened her eyes without my prompt (trusting her own somatic sense, enhancing in-sight, and Self-leadership). Examining the clay shape from different perspectives, she declared that, like her previous painting, her work once again looked like the Fertility Goddess (see Figure 12.11). She expressed that she was taking on more traits of a Goddess, including confidence and self-worth.

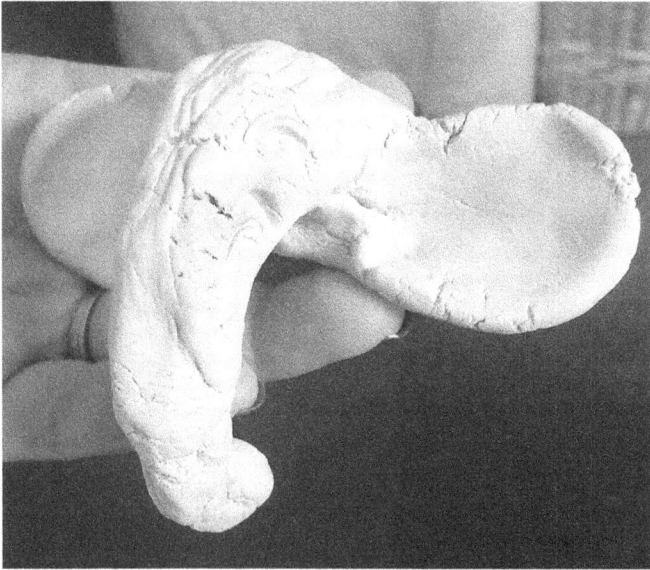

Figure 12.10 A Majestic Elephant.

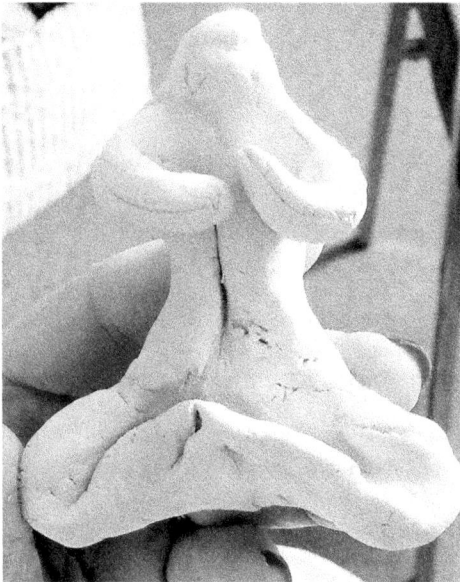

Figure 12.11 A Return to the Fertility Goddess.

In the following months, Connie continued to work with other parts that were holding their own shame and memories. She brought in a collage made at home, saying this felt like she had retrieved the Ancient Goddess, who chose to become the voluptuous full-bodied Wise Elder while the young Venus with her own rounded belly faded away into the past. This round-bellied part has continued to appear in her other art-therapy creations. These positive insights were reflected in Connie's exceedingly improved life functions.

Conclusion

Creative art therapists have collectively discovered the vast potential of bridging the arts with EMDR and/or IFS. I encourage both IFS and EMDR therapists to maintain curiosity regarding the inclusion and integration of creative interventions into these models to enhance their clinical work. Instead of actively analyzing or interpretating clients' art, we can observe and guide them in engaging with their creation, as they share their process with us. The client is the creator, and it is their voice (and parts), that guide that process. The Jungian underpinnings of all art therapy, IFS, and EMDR supports the nearly seamless connection between these approaches, offering more justification of this integration. Not only can the creative process enhance the alliance between therapist and client, but art-making can connect to the past, take on the energy of the parts, and provide pathways to ultimate healing.

References

Adler, G. (1973). *Jung letters 1906–1907*. Routledge.

Ally, D., Tobiasz-Veltz, L., Tu, K., Comeau, A., Bumpus, C., Blot, T., Rice, F., Orr, B., Rea, H., Sweezy, M., & Schuman-Olivier, Z. (2025). A pilot study of an online group-based IFS intervention for co-morbid PTSD and substance use. *Frontiers in Psychiatry, 16*, 1544435.

Anderson, F. G. (2021). *Transcending trauma: Healing complex trauma with IFS*. PESI.

Bolwerk, A., Mack-Andrick, J., Lang, F.R., Dorfler, A., & Maihofner, C. (2014). How art changes your brain: Differential effects of visual art production and cognitive art evaluation on functional brain productivity. *PLoS One 9*(7), e101035;.

Breed, H. E. (2013). *Integrating art therapy and eye movement, desensitization and reprocessing to treat PTSD*. (Master's thesis, Loyola Marymount University.) https://digitalcommons.lmu.edu/etd/15.

Cane, F. (1951). *The artist in each of us*. Art Therapy Publications.

Capacchione, L. (1988). *The power of your other hand: A course in channeling the inner wisdom of the brain*. Newcastle Publishing.

Cartwright, L. (1999). *SCtDTM meditations: Neurological approaches to dream and artwork*. Santa Fe, NM: Lee Cartwright.

Chapman, L. (2014). *Neurobiologically informed trauma therapy with children and adolescents: Understanding mechanisms of change*. W. W. Norton.

Chodorow, J. (1997). *Jung on active imagination*. Princeton University Press.

Cloitre, M. (2021). Complex PTSD: Assessment and treatment. *European Journal of Psychotraumatology, 216*(3), 129–131.

Cohen, B., Barnes, M., & Rankin, A. (1995). *Managing traumatic stress through art: Drawing from the center*. Sidran Press.

Csikszentmihalyi, M. (2013). *Creativity: The psychology of discovery and invention*. Harper.

Davis, E. (2022). A model for supporting complex trauma treatment integrating the power of creative arts therapies. In E. Davis, J. Fitzgerald, S. Jacobs, & J. Marchand (Eds.), *EMDR and creative arts therapies*, 7–63. Routledge.

Davis, E., Fitzgerald, J., Jacobs, S., & Marchand, J. (2022). *EMDR and creative arts therapies*. Routledge.

Davis, E., & Kolodny, P. (2024). *Integrating expressive arts and EMDR: Addressing dissociation and complex trauma*. Presentation for the *International Society on the Study of Trauma and Dissociation annual conference (ISSTD)*. March, Texas.

Dobo, A. (2023). *The hero's journey: Integrating Jungian psychology and EMDR therapy*. Soul Psych Publishers.

Elbrecht, C. (2018). *Trauma healing with guided drawing: A sensorimotor art therapy approach to bilateral body mapping*. North Atlantic Books.

Fatter, D. (2024). Integrating Internal Family Systems into EMDR 8 phases. *Go With That magazine. 29*(2). EMDRIA.org.

Fisher, J. (2017). *Healing the traumatic selves of trauma survivors: Overcoming internal self-alienation*. Routledge.

Fisher, J. (2022). *The living legacy of trauma flip chart*. PESI.

Fraser, G. (2003). "Dissociative table technique" revisited: A strategy for working with ego states in dissociative disorders and ego state therapy. *Journal of Trauma and Dissociation*, 4(4), 5–28.

Gaskill, R., & Perry, B. (2014). The neurobiological power of play: Using the Neurosequential Model of Therapeutics to guide play in the healing process. In C. Malchiodi & D. Crenshaw (Eds.), *Creative arts and play therapy for attachment problems* (pp. 178–194). Guilford.

Gomez, A., & Krause, P. (2013). EMDR therapy and the use of IFS strategies with children. In A. Gomez (Ed.), *EMDR and adjunct approaches with children* (pp. 135–154). Springer.

Hass-Cohen, N., & Findlay, J. (2019). The art therapy relational neuroscience and memory reconsolidation four drawing protocol. *The Arts in Psychotherapy, 63*, 51–59, https://doi.org/10.1016/j.aip.2019.03.002.

Henley, D. (2024). *The Kramer method of art therapy: Exploring the Third Hand*. Charles C. Thomas.

Hersey, B. (2022). *IFS-informed EMDR* [webinar]. www.emdrifs.com.

Hodgdon, H., Anderson, F., Southwell, E., Hrubec, W., & Schwartz, R. (2021). Internal Family Systems Therapy for PTSD among survivors of multiple childhood trauma: A pilot effectiveness study. *Journal of Aggression, Maltreatment, and Trauma, 31*(2), 22–43.

Husum, C. (2025). *Psychedelics and art therapy: A trauma-informed manual for somatic self-discovery*. Routledge.

Johnson, R. (1989). *Inner work: Using dreams and active imagination for personal growth*. Harper and Row.

Jung, C. G. (2009). *The Red Book*. W. W. Norton.

Kolodny, P. (2021a). The evolution of trauma theory and its relevance to art therapy. In P. Quinn (Ed.), *Art therapy in the treatment of addiction and trauma* (pp. 13–31). Jessica Kingsley Press.

Kolodny, P. (2021b). Healing addictions and trauma with expressive therapies continuum and a neurosequential art approach. In P. Quinn (Ed.), *Art therapy in the treatment of addiction and trauma* (pp. 59–73). Jessica Kingsley Press.

Kolodny, P., Bechtel, A., & Mazero, S. (2016). *Exploring our parts through Internal Family Systems and art therapy: Curiosity, courage and creativity*. Presentation for the *Expressive Therapies Summit*, November, New York.

Kolodny, P., Bechtel, A., & Mazero, S. (2022). *The ethical importance of promoting healing with clients from cultural/legacy burdens using art-Informed IFS*. Trauma certification/ethics class for the Ferentz Institute. September, Baltimore.

Kolodny, P., & Mazero, S. (2018). *IFS and art therapy: Clay and collage*. Master class presented at the *Internal Family Systems International conference*, November 2018. Rhode Island.

Kolodny, P., & Mazero, S. (2022). The interweave of IFS, EMDR and art therapy. In E. Davis, J. Fitzgerald, S. Jacobs, & J. Marchand (Eds)., *EMDR and creative arts therapies* (pp. 209–240). Routledge.

Korn, D. L., & Leeds, A.M. (2002). Preliminary evidence of efficacy for EMDR resource development and installation in the stabilization phase of treatment of PTSD. *Journal of Clinical Psychology, 58*(12), 1465–1487.

Lavergne, M. (2004). Art therapy and internal family systems therapy: an integrative model to treat trauma among adjudicated teenage girls. *Canadian Art Therapy Association Journal, 17*(1), 17–36.

Levine, P. (1997). *Waking the tiger: Healing trauma*. North Atlantic Books.

Lusebrink, V., & Hinz, L. (2016). The expressive therapies continuum as a framework in the treatment of trauma. In J. King (Ed.), *Art therapy, trauma and neuroscience: Theoretical and practical perspectives* (pp. 159–177). Routledge.

Marich, J. (2023). *Dissociation made simple: A stigma-free guide to embracing your dissociative mind and navigating daily life*. North Atlantic Books.

McNamee, C. M. (2003). Bilateral art: Facilitating systemic integration and balance. *The Arts in Psychotherapy, 30*(5), 283–292.

McNiff, S. (1998). Art therapy and trauma recovery: Theory and application. *Art Psychotherapy, 15*(4), 269–272.

O'Shea-Brown, G. (2020). Internal family systems-informed EMDR: An integrative technique for treatment of complex PTSD. *International Body Psychotherapy Journal, 19*(2), 112–122.

Ogden, P., & Fisher, J. (2015). *Sensorimotor psychotherapy: Interventions for trauma and attachment*. Routledge.

Pici-D'Ottavio, E. (2023). Art therapy and the Internal Family System for adolescents at a therapeutic school: A qualitative, arts-based study (MA thesis). Graduate School of Art and Sciences. Boston. *Lesley University Capstone Theses*.

Quinn, P. (2021). Jungian interventions to center, explore, and recover. In P. Quinn (Ed.), *Art therapy in the treatment of addiction and trauma* (pp. 135–154). Jessica Kingsley Press.

Rothschild, B. (2000). *The body remembers: The psychophysiology of trauma and trauma treatment*. W. W. Norton.

Sabados, D. (2024). A path toward healing: Integrating Internal Family Systems and art therapy. *Art Therapy, 41*(4), 1–9. https://doi.org/10.1080/07421656.2023.2292902.

Schmidt, S. J. (1999). Resource-focused EMDR: Integration of ego state therapy, alternating bilateral stimulation, and art therapy. *EMDRIA Newsletter, 4*(1), 8–26.

Schmitt, C., & Schoen, S. (2022). Interoception: A multi-sensory foundation of participation in daily life. *Frontiers of Neuroscience, 16*, 875200.

Schouten, K. A., de Niet, G. J., Knipscheer, J. W., Kleber, R. J., & Hutschemaekers, G. J. (2015). The effectiveness of art therapy in the treatment of traumatized adults: a systemic review of art therapy and trauma. *Trauma, Violence, and Abuse, 16*(20), 220–228. https://doi.org/10.1177/1524838014555032.

Schwartz, R., & Sweezy, M. (2020). *Internal family systems* (2nd ed.). Guilford Press.

Shapiro, F. (2018). *Eye movement desensitization and reprocessing (EMDR) therapy: Basic principles, protocols, and principles* (3rd ed.). Guilford Press.

Sinko, A. (2017). Legacy burdens. In M. Sweezy & E. Ziskind (Eds.), *IFS: innovations and elaborations in Internal Family Systems* (pp. 164–178). Taylor and Francis.

Sorbara, A. (2024). *An integrative somatic art therapy approach: EMDR & body-based practices for traumatic stress*. (PhD. Art Therapy Dissertation, Dominican University of California.) https://scholar.dominican.edu/cgi/viewcontent.cgi?article=1005&context=art-therapy-doctoral-dissertations.

Swan-Foster, N. (2018). *Jungian art therapy*. Routledge.

Talwar, S. (2007). Accessing traumatic memory through art making: An art therapy trauma protocol (ATTP). *The Arts in Psychotherapy, 34*, 22–35.

Tobin, B. (2006). Art therapy meets EMDR: Processing the paper-based image with eye movement. *Canadian Art Therapy Association Journal, 19*(2).

Tripp, T. (2007). A short-term therapy approach to processing trauma: Art therapy and bilateral stimulation. *Art Therapy, 24*(4), 176–183.

Tripp, T. (2016). A body-based bilateral art protocol for reprocessing trauma. In J. King (Ed.), *Art therapy, trauma and neuroscience: Theoretical and practical perspectives* (pp. 173–195). Routledge.

Tripp, T. (2022). Art therapy and EMDR: Integrating cognitive, somatic, and emotional processing for treating trauma. In E. Davis, J. Fitzgerald, S. Jacobs, & J. Marchand (Eds.), *EMDR and Creative Arts Therapies* (pp. 183–199). Routledge.

Tripp, T., & Kolodny, P. (2013). *Integrating EMDR and art therapy for bilateral transformation of trauma*. Workshop for the Expressive Therapies Summit, November. New York.

Tripp, T., & Kolodny, P. (2014). *Change the brain: Using bilateral methods to reduce anxiety and relieve traumatic stress*. Workshop for the Expressive Therapies Summit, November. New York.

Tripp, T., & Kolodny, P. (2016). "Wiggle, scribble, and squiggle": Bilateral approaches in art therapy for trauma treatment. Workshop for the *American Art Therapy Association Conference*, July. Baltimore.

Twombly, J. (2024). *Trauma and dissociation-informed Internal Family Systems*. Author.

Twombly, J. H. (2013). Integrating IFS with phase-oriented treatment of clients with Dissociative Disorders. In M. Sweezy & E. L. Ziskind (Eds.), *IFS Internal Family Systems: New dimensions* (pp. 205–228). Routledge.

Twombly, J. H., & Schwartz, R. C. (2008). The integration of the Internal Family Systems model and EMDR. In C. Forgash & M. Copeley (Eds.), Healing the heart of trauma and dissociation with EMDR and ego state therapy (pp. 295–311). Springer Publishing.

Van der Kolk, B. (2014). *The body keeps the score: Brain, mind, and body in the healing of trauma*. Viking.

Warson, E., Cowx, S., Curelo, J., Spier, E., & Sutrick, A. (2024). Arts-Informed EMDR: A continuum of resourcing practices from bilateral artmaking to visual journaling. *Go With That magazine. 29*(2), 22–35. EMDRIA.org.

Warson, E., & Warson, J. (2023). Bilateral movement and artmaking: Hemispheric integration across the midline. *Canadian Journal of Art Therapy*. doi: 10.1080/26907240.2023.2218727.

Wood, L. L. (2015). Eating disorder as protector: The use of IFS and drama therapy to help clients understand the protective function of their eating disorder. In A. Hershifelt (Ed.), *Creative arts therapies and clients with eating disorders* (pp. 293–325). Jessica Kingsley Publishers.

Chapter 13

Spiritually Anchored IFS-Informed EMDR

Deepening the Healing

Laura Kosak

Reviewed by Annabel McGoldrick and David Archer

As therapists, regardless of our approach, we all bear witness to deeply sacred moments in our clients' lives. Working from a spiritually anchored, IFS-informed EMDR framework can cultivate more profound and longer-lasting shifts, greater meaning in life, richer connection with others, and deeper overall contentment for our clients. This chapter offers specific tips and techniques throughout the eight phases and beyond. A case study is provided at the end.

What Is Spirituality?

As quantum physics shows us, the world is vaster than our five senses can experience or perceive. A spiritual experience connects us with that larger realm through a felt sense or deep knowing that we are both an individual person and an intricate part of the greater whole. Spirituality is beyond what is personally meaningful, beyond duality—there is mystery, awe, belonging, and expansion. There is connection to the universal and perhaps to the Divine, in whatever way we understand that. Note: There are various ideas for differentiating "spirituality" from "religious." This chapter only employs the word spirituality. However, religious beliefs, practices, and communities can also be deeply important to our clients, and we explore all of it using their language.

Why Talk About Spirituality in Therapy?

There are countless studies that show both physical and mental health are improved by spiritual meaning, connection, and practices. Spirituality is a protective factor and an essential aspect of resilience; spiritual beliefs can facilitate post-traumatic growth (Abdul-Hamid & Hacker Hughes, 2015). Additionally, the Pew Research Center reported in 2023 that: "Overall, 70% of US adults can be considered "spiritual" in some way, because they think of themselves as spiritual people or say spirituality is very important in their lives." Cultural competency requires that we consider spiritual influences, blockages, resources, and experiences for our clients.

DOI: 10.4324/9781003541554-16

As therapists, we do not need to maintain our own spiritual practice to facilitate healing and transformative experiences at a spiritual level for our clients. We do need to be Self-led, and to intentionally create the field for this type of healing to arise, as detailed below. It behooves us to tap into this powerful resource that is available to most of our clients.

A Mythic Journey

We in the West are most likely familiar with the hero's journey, Joseph Campbell's concept of a monomyth representing a rite of passage through the phases of separation, initiation, and return. George Lucas created an enduring example through Star Wars. An individual is called to leave their current life and community, faces ordeals with the help of a mentor or guide, and eventually returns home, reintegrating into the community and sharing their learning (Campbell, 2008). This myth can be a helpful framework for the therapeutic process. For some clients, mythic or archetypal language might be more accessible than spiritual language.

Dr. Andrew Dobo (2023) beautifully frames the process in partnership with EMDR. Many, if not all, of our clients can be seen as engaged in their own hero's journey. Viewing our individual life at a mythic level places our experience in the transpersonal and universal realms. Clients may have myths of initiation, journey, or spiritual transformation from their own cultures that can be used as a resource.

Special Considerations

When working with this approach we must be keenly aware of several important issues. Our clients may have experienced religious trauma, either directly or indirectly; tread lightly. There are numerous cultural and clinical considerations to evaluate, including where the line is drawn between spirituality and psychosis, or inner-world symbology and delusions. Seek the necessary training and consultation when appropriate. In some cases, consulting with cultural liaisons and, when appropriate, elders or community members, can help elucidate concerns. As always, do your own work and be aware of your own underlying assumptions. Remember, consent must be explicitly given throughout the therapeutic process, including when shifting into potentially unexpected transpersonal realms.

Building the Field, Therapist Preparation

The therapist's personal preparation sets the tone for each session as well as for the overall therapeutic journey. We begin with the intention to be Self-led, tending to our parts as needed. We have a moment of internal focus, aligning our inner world with the process of healing for our clients, before turning to their inner worlds (see Chapters 20 and 21).

We settle our nervous system through breath work, muscle relaxation, yoga, somatic shaking, or polyvagal exercises. We center in Self-energy and prepare to connect to the transpersonal field. We might use an opening and closing ritual to mark the time and space with intention: a candle, a prayer, a request for support from our guides or teachers, a bell, or singing bowl. We do these practices before sessions and throughout sessions, perhaps especially in the moments of silence that IFS and EMDR allow through going inside or Bilateral Stimulation (BLS)—moments of allowing space to hear the unconscious, where the spiritual unfolds.

Weaving Spirituality and IFS into EMDR's Eight Phases

The fundamental therapeutic steps of IFS and EMDR have been described in earlier chapters. Suggestions for integrating an awareness of spirituality into the combined therapeutic model are provided below. Each phase concludes with suggested interweaves, with the technical term "interweave" being used more broadly to mean therapist's guiding questions.

Phase 1: History and Treatment Planning (Parts Mapping, Contracting/Consent)

With this spiritually informed approach, we know that each therapy session is a kind of sacred time and space, and we hold that intention mindfully. We have our spiritually, or mythically, attuned ear listening. We notice how our client anchors meaning in their life. We are curious about what their main values are, and how those have been shaped. We normalize a transpersonal perspective by the language we use, allowing space for the client to bring forth their Self and parts that are connected to the realms beyond the personal/ego.

Jacobi (2009) suggests an explicit spiritual assessment using open-ended questions about the client's past and present practices and beliefs, as well as any familial or cultural forces at play for them. We want to know if clients have a spiritual belief system or community to lean on as a resource, or whether the absence of such is felt as an abandonment or lack, perhaps even an abandonment by the Divine.

Interweaves: Do you feel an interconnection, a common humanity at times? What have been the spiritual or value-driven teachings of your family, whether you identify with them now or not? What's your notion of what happens before or after this life?

Phase 2: Preparation/Resourcing (Increasing Access to Self, Connecting with Protectors, and Building Self-to-Part Relationships)

We add spiritual language to help clients create inner sacred spaces for their parts. A calm place can be built as an inner temple or refuge. Invite mythic and archetypal layers into the field of possibility and let the client's system take them far into the imaginal realm. Do this by adding simple prompts to the standard protocol: "Now imagine a place where you feel safe enough and comfortable, a place where you can feel peaceful and relaxed. Perhaps somewhere in nature, a type of sanctuary, a sacred space where you feel calm and relaxed." Note that we just add a few words that allow the client to feel that their spiritual resources are welcome.

As described by Parnell (1997) and others, encourage clients to invite in guidance, guides, ancestors, or any type of spiritual resource. Some clients will have mentioned spiritual resources in Phase 1 and we can directly reinforce connection to them throughout the process. We follow the client's lead while encouraging an expanded perspective of resources.

Interweaves: How much support are you feeling right now? What could make that a little more? Is there some guidance that comes to you here? Can you imagine some support from elsewhere arriving now? Do you have a relative or ancestor with whom you connect at times? Can you feel them here now?

Phase 3: Assessment/Target Prep (Connecting with a Specific Exile)

We identify the memory target, or the emotion or belief that needs to be released, and activate the accompanying neural networks. Activation can be understood as inviting forth an exile for support that includes witnessing and unburdening.

The burden of an exile can be viewed as the energetic pain of its core limiting belief, which frequently sprang forth from trauma. In standard EMDR, we commonly target specific experiences; in this approach, it is often more useful to work with foundational limiting beliefs and the exiles who hold them. Dobo (2023) refers to finding the client's mythic negative cognition—the principal belief that underlies their life struggle. Usually this is going to be: *I am not good enough; I'm unworthy; I don't matter; I'm unlovable; I do not belong*; or *I am alone*. Working with this foundational level of negative cognition can be much more transformative than focusing on specific experiences. These are universal, archetypal, and spiritual categories of human pain. The case study below follows the author's Crossliminal Passage Protocol™, and illuminates how the above interweaves can address core limiting beliefs.

Interweaves: At times we've been with the part of you that feels deeply unworthy. Do you sense her around now? We talked about supporting that part of you that feels like a burden, that shows up as a little one broken into pieces: Can you ask him if it's ok to sit with him now?

Phase 4: Desensitization (Witnessing and Unburdening)

We know that profound shifts happen for clients in this phase, and they often see their experience with greater self-compassion and with a widened perspective. When the self-hatred that took root in childhood has been released, clients are naturally filled with more self-love and can spontaneously have transpersonal, spiritual experiences (Parnell, 1997). The therapist steers toward certain pathways through interweaves, highlighting specific words of the client, turning toward or away from working with each part that arises. We can be spiritually informed when shepherding the client's process. The release of pain and shift to self-compassion is a fundamental aspect of the IFS unburdening process (see Chapter 3 of this book). That unburdening can happen spontaneously with standard EMDR. However, as we can see with the case study below, we can intentionally invite unburdening into Phase 4.

Dobo (2023) suggests listening for the language of the subconscious and not getting caught up in the ego (managers) and its content. He suggests not returning to target so frequently and instead being led by the client's unconscious into more mythical layers. Often it is helpful to allow silence, giving space for the more hidden realms to surface. Siegel (2017) suggests engaging with BLS led by the therapist's intuition, sensing into vibrational shifts, somatics, and breath, and noticing release in the subtle energy field rather than following a predetermined count.

Interweaves: Let's just rest/pause here a moment. This feels important to sit with quietly. As you hold all of this, feel yourself accompanied by your higher self/guide/resource and notice what comes up. Can you shift your perspective from the part to your guide/ancestor/Spirit's for a moment? What do you notice when you are considering this belief from their point of view?

Phase 5: Installation (New Role for Part, Positive Qualities)

Here we are anchoring in change and we must invite clients to rest for a while in the transformed belief and positive feeling state. We want the unburdened parts to settle more deeply into their new role or new positive qualities. If there has been a guide of any sort, invite that guide to delight in the unburdened part and witness the joy. The guide can implicitly provide the feeling of receiving ideal parenting.

Interweaves: How does the part feel knowing they are worthy just because they exist? How is the part experiencing the truth that they are a part of the universal whole and will forever belong? I notice this part soaking up the abundant love of the Divine, are you sensing that too?

Phase 6: Body Scan (Exploring Need for Further Unburdening)

We ask clients to intentionally tune in to their body to explore the need for further reprocessing or unburdening. The body is a clear connection to the universal experience of being a living creature. The "body" is much more than the physical senses, and this phase can bring awareness to the subtle energy body as well as the ancestral energy body (Siegel, 2017).

Interweaves: Take a moment to scan your energy field and notice the flow, or any remaining blockages. See yourself holding your ancestral line and scan it for any gifts or burdens that are flowing toward you. Accept the gifts and return burdens back up the line or to God.

Phase 7: Closure (Integration or Tucking In)

Closing an incomplete session is more than neatly containing emotions and distress until the next session. Rather than a locked vault, encourage imagery of gently and lovingly tucking in parts and the pain, alongside whatever or whomever they need. This is often connected to calm places in the inner world established in resourcing.

When a deep release of distress or unburdening has been completed during a session, closure is different and involves supporting integration. Invite reflection before ending the session, which allows the client to anchor in any shift. Since clients have been in a non-ordinary realm, stating key points aloud helps them to remember.

Invite the client to commit to a personal practice rather than "homework," as this highlights inner connection as a spiritual activity and engages Self more than people-pleaser or perfectionist parts. Invite clients to connect with parts through journaling, meditation, art, or movement and approach the therapeutic work as a spiritual practice that includes opening and closing rituals (e.g., lighting a candle).

Interweaves: It was such an honor to witness your journey today and I respect your parts and their sacred work. I invite you to intentionally set aside (sacred) time and space to connect with your parts. Before we close, I invite you to tuck in these little parts, in whatever way they need, so they feel tended to and safe until you're ready to connect with them again (see Chapter

23 for an example). Do they need a guardian with them? How will they be able to count on your heart-centered love while they are waiting for you?

Phase 8: Reevaluation (Check in with Parts)

In standard EMDR we check to see if the target is fully cleared; in IFS we wonder how the parts are doing and whether the client is building relationships within. With this approach, we can highlight growth and spiritual meaning through the language we use.

Interweaves: What have you noticed since that beautifully profound experience last week? Do you feel a growing connection with your inner wisdom/ Self? What would help to cultivate greater connection? Have you noticed any dreams or synchronicities? What has your sacred practice of internal connection been?

Legacy and Other Realms

Siegel (2017) suggests that the lasting impact of our personal and universal ancestral lines remains in the energy field around us. Bringing conscious awareness to this non-ordinary reality facilitates additional healing. There is a shared-family vibrational field, and circumstances can activate those patterns. Some of the forces involved are: epigenetics, archetypes, and explicit and implicit family traditions.

Opening into legacy realms, the gifts and burdens of our ancestors, helps clients move beyond the smallness and constriction of the personal into the universal. Sinko (2017) describes how burdens can be inherited through the family or cultural line. The parts are dealing with an energetic and physiological burden that came before them. It is possible to relieve, release, and heal the legacy burden, separate from a personal burden.[1]

Robert Falconer's important work *The Others Within Us* dives into the transpersonal realms in indigenous and Eastern cultures, as well as other worldviews differing from those of mainstream Western spirituality and psychology. Falconer (2023) asserts full healing cannot primarily be about the personal; it must include the others within, and the others beyond: ancestors, guides, spirits, etc. Profound and full healing must include a spiritual element. Falconer provides a protocol for working with patterns in the energy field that have come from outside the individual's system. Both Falconer's and Sinko's protocols can be enhanced through gentle BLS.

Interweaves: Can you notice the pride of your ancestors as they see you and your profound work at healing? As you sit with this pain, how much is yours and how much came from others or elsewhere? Can you see that pain being transformed into love/light for your sake and the benefit of all? Imagine your family tree as a living breathing force; where do you notice constriction, perhaps a disease present (family core limiting belief)?

Case Study: Leona[2]

The following is part of a session using the author's Crossliminal Passage Protocol™ with Leona, a client suffering from severe, chronic, childhood abuse and neglect. Leona has worked through numerous specific traumatic experiences with IFS-informed EMDR and has a practice of connecting with her parts. The parts holding core, mythic limiting beliefs have previously not been able to release those beliefs and their pain. The profound abuse endured has frequently been witnessed within the sacred space of therapy.

Therapist: I invite you to take a few deep breaths, centering your awareness in the heart, settling into our time together. Tap gently. Imagine a place in nature, some place tranquil, where there is a passage. It could be a bridge, perhaps over a creek, or from one meadow to another, a pathway, a portal, or anything else that represents to you a passageway. Whatever resonates with you is fine. Let me know when you see, sense, or know the place.

Leona: OK ... There's a bridge.

Therapist: Beautiful. Please invite your highest wisest you to be present here by this bridge. We all have available a type of protective, nurturing, wise support from beyond us. Please invite connection with that support, guidance or guide. It is here for you. I invite you to continue to gently tap and let me know when that support is also here with you.

Leona: My grandma is here. (Tears.) She's the only one I didn't burden.

Therapist: We recognize this part of you who so deeply feels that she is an unworthy burden. It seems like she's already here too. Is that right?

Leona: Yes, it's that darkness, that thick darkness. I feel constriction in my chest and it's harder to breathe.

Therapist: Welcome thick darkness. I invite all of you, the little one, your highest Self, and Grandma, to be by the bridge, and notice that on the other side of the bridge, even though they may not see it fully, understand, or even believe, on

	the other side there is acceptance, relief from pain, no more stuckness, just freedom and joy. Can everyone sense that possibility on the other side of the bridge?
Leona:	It's hard to believe it's possible. Grandma has her hand on my shoulder and ... I want to trust.
Therapist:	Please gently tap and see, sense, or know that all of you are taking a step toward crossing the bridge. (After BLS) What do you notice?
Leona:	(Crying.) I'm holding the little one, she doesn't want to go.
Therapist:	What keeps her from taking a step?
Leona:	She's afraid she'll be hit.
Therapist:	Aaah, that's the burden, this poor little exhausted one. She holds that it's her fault. Can you see or sense collecting up all the pain she feels, collecting it all up?
Leona:	It feels like it's the fabric of her being. It's dark, black. That's all there was: danger. It's all-consuming. (Sobbing.)
Therapist:	This blackness that's such a heavy weight, ask it, what is it that you want?
Leona:	To dominate, to drag down.
Therapist:	This darkness, how much of it is part of you?
Leona:	I don't know. It's her madness, Mom's! I don't know where my mind begins and where it's my mom. It feels like it's all her. The darkness is woven throughout.
Therapist:	How long has this been here?
Leona:	It was created with me, it's just always here. It hurts. It feels like it *is* me.
Therapist:	If it's ok, can you breathe this little one a bit bigger. From your heart-centered Self, begin to fill her with love, and feel her getting a little bigger. Continue tapping if it feels right. (Allowing silence.)
Leona:	She's getting bigger. That blackness that has been all around her, woven into her, it's a little separate now. It's like it's clay that's been around her. It's cracking some. I can feel the little one bigger now. Like the threads that are truly her are growing and the threads that are the darkness are staying small.
Therapist:	All that blackness, Mom's madness, is it around somewhere?
Leona:	It's become a small patch. We're on the bridge. We're ripping off the patch and throwing it off the bridge. It isn't mine; my mom's madness came to her. It didn't start with her, and it isn't mine. It's trash ... It's gone.

The session continues with noticing and staying with how good the little one feels now, knowing she's separate from Mom's madness, not the cause of it. She no longer feels responsible and can be her own person. Using BLS, we reinforce the presence and support of Grandma (who had not previously been available to the client as a resource). The little one can accept the help from Grandma that she was afraid to ask for before. Leona endorses a physical, energetic, and emotional release that she hasn't felt before: a hope that she can feel worthy and not be afraid to feel good. She holds a knowing that she is not the burden, and she is not alone. Leona agrees to check in with the parts and return to the scene in a way that feels supportive as part of her own personal practice.

Conclusion

Incorporating spirituality into an IFS-informed EMDR approach offers a powerful pathway for deep healing. By inviting forward the spiritual aspects of our clients' experiences, we create a space where profound transformations can occur, connecting them more fully to Self and the larger universal whole. As therapists, embracing this spiritually anchored framework enhances our ability to serve our clients and their personal growth in deeply meaningful ways.

Notes

1 Sinko (2017) offers a specific protocol for this type of unburdening.
2 Names and identifying information have all been changed, and the following is printed with permission.

References

Abdul-Hamid, W. K., & Hacker Hughes, J. (2015). Integration of religion and spirituality into trauma psychotherapy: An example in Sufism? *Journal of EMDR Practice and Research, 9*(3), pp. 150–156.

Campbell, J. (2008). *The hero with a thousand faces* (3rd ed.) New World Library.

Dobo, A. J. (2023). *The hero's journey: Integrating Jungian psychology and EMDR therapy*. Soul Psych Publishers.

Falconer, R. (2023). *The others within us: Internal family systems, porous mind, and spirit possession*. Great Mystery Press.

Jacobi, M. (2009). Using EMDR with religious and spiritually attuned clients. In R. Shapiro (Ed.), *EMDR solutions II: For depression, eating disorders, performance, and more* (pp. 472–494). Norton.

Parnell, L. (1997). Eye movement desensitization and reprocessing (EMDR) and spiritual unfolding. *Journal of Transpersonal Psychology, 28*(2), pp. 129–153.

Pew Research Center. (2023, December 7). Spirituality among Americans. Retrieved July 25, 2024. https://www.pewresearch.org/religion/2023/12/07/spirituality-among-americans/

Siegel, I. R. (2017). *The sacred path of the therapist: Modern healing, ancient wisdom, and client transformation.* W. W. Norton & Company.

Sinko, A. (2017). Legacy burdens. In M. Sweezy & E. L. Ziskind (Eds.), *IFS: Innovations and elaborations in Internal Family Systems therapy.* Taylor and Francis.

Part 4

IFS-Informed EMDR in Practice

Chapter 14

Mapping Complex PTSD and Attachment with EMDR and IFS

Patricia Bianca Torres

Understanding CPTSD versus PTSD

How does our field understand profound trauma? Judith Herman was one of the first scholars to advocate for survivors of prolonged, repeated trauma, referring to the *DSM-IV*, Disorders of Extreme Stress Not Otherwise Specified (DESNOS; Herman, 1992). She differentiated "simple" trauma from "complex" trauma by stating that "simple trauma" was represented by a single event. In contrast, "complex" trauma was not yet well understood by scholars in the early 1990s. More recently, there has been a marked interest in further understanding traumatic events that were interpersonal in nature and did not exactly fit the criteria of *The Diagnostic and Statistical Manual of Mental Disorders, Fifth Edition, Text Revision's* (DSM-5-TR) PTSD criterion A (exposure to a traumatic event directly or indirectly).

Since the addition of Complex PTSD (CPTSD) in the International Classification of Diseases, 11th Revision (ICD-11), researchers have aimed to advance the empirical evidence to support the most effective treatment. A diagnosis for CPTSD requires three elements of a PTSD diagnosis (i.e., re-experiencing, avoidance, sense of current threat) in DSM-5-TR (APA, 2022), as well as Disturbances in Self-Organization (DSO: affective dysregulation, negative self-concept, disturbances in relationships; Cloitre et al., 2018). Clinicians learning trauma treatment modalities have realized that "simple" trauma is a rarity, and that repetitive and chronic trauma is the norm. Many clinicians treating individuals with CPTSD may have observed intolerance to positive and negative affect and soma (e.g., positive and relaxing or negative and distressing emotional states and body sensations).

Theoretical Understandings of CPTSD

The Memory and Identity Theory of CPTSD (Hyland et al., 2023) posits that CPTSD differs from PTSD in that CPTSD involves the presence of negative identities, in addition to the intrusive re-experiencing of traumatic

DOI: 10.4324/9781003541554-18

memories. Hence, effective treatments for CPTSD include those that can accommodate both the targeting of traumatic experiences and addressing the negative identities, which may also be considered as the various "parts" of the client. Notably, inconsistent caregiving responses in early childhood (e.g., rejection, withdrawal, dismissiveness) may result in fragmented self-states. IFS conceptualizes protector parts as those that tend to distrust benefits of a positive self-concept or any ability in receiving help or relief. Examples of negative identities include *unsafe, powerless, worthless/inferior, betrayed/abandoned, alienated, fragmented, non-existent* (Hyland et al., 2024). These different identities, therefore, must be considered as part of the treatment to effectively treat clients with CPTSD.

Recent literature on underlying Early Maladaptive Schemas (EMSs) suggests that schemas of *abandonment/instability* and *social isolation/alienation* are significantly correlated with the DSO symptoms of CPTSD (Greenblatt-Kimron et al., 2023). These types of schemas may be understood as the various identities, or parts, holding these beliefs because of traumatic experiences. Moreover, as interpersonal trauma is associated with CPTSD (Maercker et al., 2022), these identities, or parts, may need to be targeted individually, e.g., understood in a manner that acknowledges the mechanism for their existence in the client's Self-system.

Assessing for CPTSD

The International Trauma Questionnaire (ITQ)[1] is a psychometrically valid instrument that assists clinicians in diagnosing CPTSD (Cloitre et al., 2018). Questions assess for symptoms of traditional PTSD, such as the presence of distressing dreams, re-experiencing trauma through intrusive images or memories, hypervigilance, and attempts to avoid triggers. Questions also assess for the presence of DSO symptoms through asking about feelings of worthlessness, low self-concept, numbness/dissociation, and emotional distance from others.

Attachment Theory and CPTSD

Interpersonal dysfunction, or the difficulty in maintaining relationships, is one of the three core features of the DSO clusters in CPTSD, and an attachment theory lens is essential for understanding these clients. As we know, developmental, or early childhood trauma impacts one's internal working models, or representations of expected relational interactions (Bowlby, 1982).

Due to prolonged periods of early childhood maltreatment (e.g., abuse, neglect), infants and children may grow into adults with internal working models that expect that others should not be trusted and, essentially, believe that *the world is not safe*. After all, the quality of attachment depends on how well the caregiver responds to the infant's attachment system when it is activated, or when they feel that their sense of safety and security are threatened (Benoit, 2004). In the latter of these examples, parts of selves may continue to hold feelings of desperation and longing, while other parts of selves may numb and dissociate due to feeling as if their caregivers want to get rid of them, e.g., in the case of annihilation terror (Paulsen, 2017). Additionally, other parts of Self may form to protect against any future abandonment, rejection, or disappointment (Forgash & Knipe, 2012; Hodgdon et al., 2021; Schwartz, 2013). For a further discussion on dissociation, and exploration into Other Specified Dissociative Disorder and Dissociative Identify Disorder, please see Chapter 11.

CPTSD and Considering Attachment Orientation in Practice

Most clinicians in the field have struggled with understanding the best form of treatments for individuals with CPTSD due to the presence of disorganized attachment interfering with clinical interventions (Ford & Courtois, 2021; Karatzias et al., 2022). Varied survival responses (e.g., submit, fight, flight, freeze, fawn) associated with traumatic experiences pose obstacles for successful treatment outcomes in standard PTSD care (van der Kolk & Fisler, 1995). Those with CPTSD tend to re-enact dysfunctional interpersonal dynamics in the therapeutic relationship, leading protector parts to utilize protective methods (e.g., avoidance, defensiveness, aggression, hostility) to avoid repetition of early attachment trauma, at the expense of unburdening exiles. Hence, novel clinical interventions for addressing the parts system are necessary to reduce internal conflicts, increase access to adaptive information, and enhance Self-energy.

Traditional clinical interventions may be unsatisfactory due to the presence of the various parts of selves, which, although they long for healing, may antagonize the clinician to avoid additional perceived pain. To appropriately assess for specific attachment styles, clinicians are urged to utilize proper psychometrically valid assessments to ensure tailored treatment such as: The Experiences in Close Relationships Scale—Revised (ECR-R; Fraley et al., 2000) and the Adult Attachment Interview (AAI; Main et al., 1985).[2]

Those with CPTSD may experience both symptoms of anxious and avoidant attachment and are known to express an intense need for validation and approval, deeply craving connection, while at the same time expressing an attitude of dismissing behavior in an effort to avoid real or perceived abandonment (Sandberg & Refrea, 2022). Clinicians may need to incorporate continued assessment of their clients' attachment security throughout treatment to assist in case conceptualization; an example of a bi-dimensional framework of attachment and CPTSD is provided (see Figure 14.1).

Anxious/ Preoccupied Attachment   Avoidant/ Dismissing Attachment

Craves intimacy   Values independence

Overt emotional   **CPTSD**   Covert emotional
dysregulation   dysregulation
                    Deep-rooted
                      shame,
People-pleasing   loneliness,   Thrives off admiration
tendencies   presence of   and adulation
                     compulsive
Higher rates of   behaviors   May exploit others
comorbid self-   and/or treat their
harm/ suicidal   relationships as
ideation   transactional

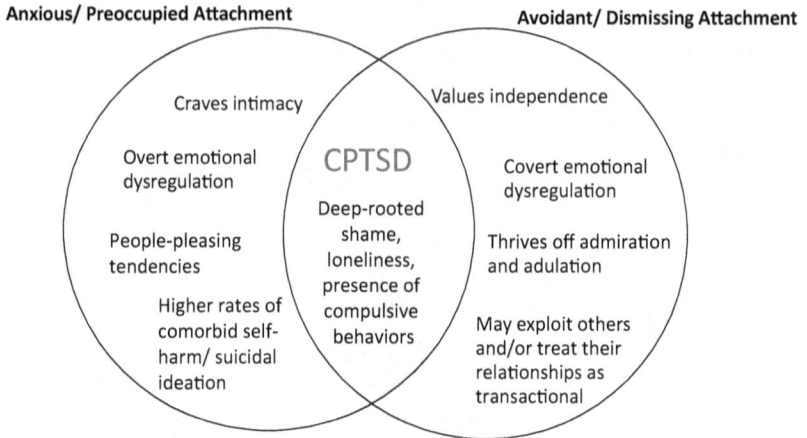

Figure 14.1 Bi-dimensional framework of attachment and CPTSD.

CPTSD and Dissociation

To avoid experiencing additional pain, individuals with CPTSD may engage in dissociation as a method of avoiding their internal suffering. Many trauma-treating clinicians may have noticed the tendency for individuals to dissociate, marked by forgetfulness, difficulties with remaining in the present, or avoidance of affect or soma (e.g., body sensations) to limit access to neural networks holding both explicit (i.e., declarative) and implicit (i.e., nondeclarative) trauma. Therefore, it is necessary for clinicians to understand the difference between dissociation (a symptom of CPTSD) and a dissociative disorder.

We can use verified assessments such as the Structured Clinical Interview for DSM Disorders for Dissociation (SCID-D) or the Multidimensional Inventory for Dissociation (MID). Understanding the "Dissociative Continuum" is also a helpful tool in ascertaining treatment. Those on the far left of the continuum can be seen as having PTSD and as benefiting from traditional PTSD approaches. Those in the middle of the continuum tend to be individuals with CPTSD and various personality disorders (PDs) and require the more informed care that is discussed in this chapter. Those on the far right of the continuum may be those with dissociative disorders, which require a very specialized treatment approach and are beyond the scope of this chapter; they are addressed in Chapter 11 (see Figure 14.2).

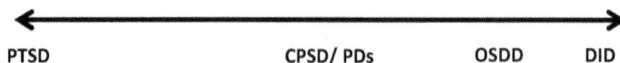

PTSD   CPSD/ PDs   OSDD   DID

Figure 14.2 Dissociative continuum.

Why EMDR and IFS for CPTSD?

The search for effective treatments for CPTSD has been a focus for many researchers and clinicians since its addition to the ICD-11. Individuals with CPTSD may have experienced a combination of developmental (e.g., attachment) trauma and adult-onset trauma. EMDR therapy is well known as one of the "gold-standard" methods for treating PTSD. The DSO components of CPTSD (e.g., affective dysregulation, negative self-concept, dysfunctional relationships) can be understood as the various parts of the Self-system acting in conflict with the more "resourced" parts of the client (e.g., hopeful, calm, trusting). As such, treatments for CPTSD should include both a mechanism to treat trauma and a way to target various identities, or "parts." IFS-informed EMDR is ideally suited to address the internal conflict among the client's different parts as well as the specific traumatic experiences.

Using IFS-Informed EMDR with CPTSD

When approaching EMDR therapy's phased approach, the following is a guide for integrating IFS in the treatment of CPTSD.

Phase 1: Case Conceptualization

A specialized case conceptualization may be necessary to clearly understand how the client's current symptoms, past history, and future goals all serve to map the internal system of parts: See Box 14.1.

Box 14.1 Case Conceptualization Figure

Assessment: DES-T, ITQ, ACEs, ECR-R

CPTSD diagnosis
Dissociation
Attachment

Client History

Abuse (physical, sexual, emotional)
Neglect (emotional, physical)
"Safe" attachment figures
Internalized caregivers as perpetrators

History of/Current Risk

Substance use, eating disorders, self-harm, suicidal ideation/ attempts

Mapping the System

Who holds the most power now?
  Which protectors?
  What is the level of cohesion, harmony, OR conflict within the system?
  Coalitions/Polarizations

Therapeutic Relationship

Re-enactments
Barriers to treatment
  People-pleasing
  Aggression
  Avoidance

Aip Model Using Three Prongs

Past, Present, Future

Often, individuals with CPTSD benefit from the targeting of early childhoodmemories that hold disturbance of attachment wounds, or memories at which strong protectors were "born." Attachment traumas can be understood as touchstone memories. Developmental reparative cognitive interweaves can be successful as long as protector parts have given permission to heal younger parts, e.g., exiles, who hold the attachment trauma memories.

It may be difficult to begin targeting more recent memories of abuse or traumatic stress, (e.g., adult relationships), or workplace trauma, due to the likelihood of feeder memories preventing SUDs from becoming zero. Parts of the system may not believe or agree with the cognitive interweaves that attempt to utilize "adult-held" adaptive memory networks. It is common for clients who have difficulties in reprocessing earlier memories to sometimes benefit from engaging in future templates as a starting point to increase the strength of their adaptive information networks. If this is the case, proceed with future templates first during the preparation phase.

Phase 2: Preparation

Clinicians can proceed with the various approaches of resourcing (e.g., container, peaceful place, light-stream, spiral technique) and proceed with EMDR therapy's standard protocol for slow BLS to enhance the identified chosen resource. It is important to note that for some clients, particularly those with CPTSD, it may be necessary to start with the installation of future templates (e.g., future scenario that can enhance current functioning). If the client experiences difficulties accessing positive feeling states, there could be a fear that experiencing a positive sensation or a felt sense of safety is dangerous, reminiscent of how it was during their past traumatic experiences.

If this is the case, permission may be needed from the protectors or the Self-system that perceives resourcing as somehow detrimental to their ability to fulfill their role in the client's life. The clinician should proceed with IFS's six F's (Find, Focus, Flesh out, Feel toward, beFriend, Fear) to identify protector parts (e.g., managers, firefighters), to engage with them, and to receive permission for proceeding with resourcing strategies. Though the process of unblending techniques can be beneficial, clinicians may need to be forewarned that those with CPTSD have grave difficulties in accessing the Self, and this process may need to be repeated throughout treatment. The use of direct access may also be a beneficial method for engaging directly with the part if the client is unable to access Self-energy to speak for the part.

Individuals with CPTSD tend to have lived their lives with protector parts in charge as a method of survival. If protector parts appear to be unwilling to "give space" during the process of unblending, the clinician must acknowledge that much of the healing work can be done with protectors, as opposed to merely seeking the healing of young exiles, or younger parts. Hence, clinicians must acknowledge the utility of aligning with protector parts and gaining fundamental clarity on their roles and the jobs that they have needed to take on to prevent future pain and suffering. We could also use some of the strategies outlined in Syzygy's Discovery phase, described in Chapter 7. To ensure this, clinicians must acknowledge their own Self-system and their parts' objectives, which could be perceived by the client's system as a threatening motive (see Chapters 20 and 21).

As a reminder, those with CPTSD may have difficulties staying in their Window of Tolerance due to heightened affective dysregulation. Such dysregulation may be exacerbated by comorbid neurodevelopmental concerns, psychiatric conditions posing functional impairments (e.g., OCD, characterological traits), medical conditions, and severe dissociative symptoms. Hence, a thorough assessment of confounding variables (e.g., neurodevelopmental concerns) must be made, including ruling out a dissociative disorder, to triage which condition must be targeted first.

Phase 3: Assessment

Clinicians can proceed with standard EMDR therapy protocol's assessment phase; however, it may be important to note that the SUD is retrieved from the part holding the memory. Therefore, receiving permission from protector parts through the process of unblending may be necessary to ensure that the components of the memory are properly activated (e.g., affect is adequately accessed), which is often held by the part who experienced the traumatic event that is being targeted in the therapy session.

Phases 4–8: Combining EMDR Therapy and IFS

When combining EMDR therapy and IFS in the reprocessing phases and beyond (4–8), there are several considerations. Firstly, as mentioned earlier, targeting attachment trauma is a helpful place to begin. In this process, the standard protocol of EMDR therapy is combined with IFS through accessing the young, exiled parts. When given permission from the protectors, memories of attachment wounds, held by exiles, are the target memories to be reprocessed. The combination of bilateral stimulation and the expression of the attachment trauma narrative (e.g., memories under 10 years old) can be viable approaches to treatment with CPTSD. However, clinicians may need to plan for affective dysregulation as a result of internal conflict within the system. Parts seeking to "attach" to seek a sense of safety, e.g., subconscious loyalty to the caregiver, may be opposed to the protector-held beliefs of distrust and fear of certainty. Hence, when referring to those with CPTSD who may have higher rates of attachment anxiety or avoidance, it is helpful to consider the potential cognitive interweaves that can be used during reprocessing of target memories and the inclusion of the parts involved.

Healing attachment trauma for those with CPTSD requires the client to experience that not only is the trauma no longer occurring, which usually allows for SUDs to drop to zero for those with PTSD, but also that they are no longer alone and instead that they are comforted, soothed, and understood. Therefore, cognitive interweaves may need to include a reference to building an adaptive relationship with the part with Self-energy, similar to the steps in the *unburdening* in IFS. The challenge in those with CPTSD is their difficulty in accessing Self-energy due to their chronic and repeated experiences connoting distrust of others, in addition to themselves. Protector parts may disavow the unburdening of exiles due to the necessary inclusion of their own unburdening. Hence, repeated permission may be needed from protector parts during the reprocessing phases. Shifting to target the trauma of the protector part may be necessary if the protector part feels that this would be important to them. The clinician can then proceed with the rest of the reprocessing phases until the target is complete.

It is important to consider that clients with CPTSD have memory networks that store traumatic memories in a disorganized fashion (similar to that of a "ball of yarn"). Therefore, it is common for SUDs to not drop all the way to zero if the early attachment trauma (touchstone memories) cannot be targeted first. For this reason, clinicians are encouraged to continue through the target sequence plan as agreed with the client. However, when treating those with CPTSD, clinicians should be aware of additional interventions to assist in stabilizing the therapeutic relationship as various parts may appear threatened. Even for the best-trained clinician who has years of experience, it is humbling to know that our clients with CPTSD often question our trust and sincerity as a reflection and mirror of their traumatic experiences.

Dealing with Treatment Impasses and the "Challenging Client" with CPTSD

Working with those with CPTSD and significant attachment trauma necessitates addressing special concerns. The following methods may be necessary to assist in navigating the various parts of the Self-system to assist in the development of harmony and co-regulation among the Self-system: (1) Targeting re-enactment attachment wounding; (2) targeting therapeutic relationship ruptures; and (3) Resourcing therapeutic relationship repairs.

Targeting Re-enactment Attachment Wounding with EMDR and IFS

Re-enactments, or the projection of dysfunctional interpersonal interactions, may occur as an unconscious mechanism for the client to have a sense of "mastery" of their trauma, significant affective dysregulation, and ego deficit (Levy, 1998). Clinicians are encouraged to facilitate the verbalization of, and acknowledgment that this process is occurring to assist in the emotional and somatic expression of dissociated or repressed trauma sequela. Targeting the re-enactment requires an understanding of the various parts involved (e.g., protector parts), which are essentially making efforts to change their encoding of the traumatic memory. Clinicians should take note that these moments demonstrate that the Self-system may be willing to address this subconsciously, but the clinician's Self-energy is needed, as protector parts may be highly sensitive to expecting a similar maladaptive response that the abuser/protector had made in the associated neural networks.

Once the clinician has explicitly acknowledged the re-enactment, they must facilitate, either through the client's "Self" (if present) or by direct access, a dialogue indicating that this protector part has been wounded. It is not uncommon for clinicians to recognize how their own system has subconsciously engaged in the re-enactment and apologize. The protector part is looking for ways in which the clinician is growing "tired of," or discouraged by the difficulties in working with the client to substantiate that the negative core belief, "I am unlovable," is true.

The clinician can facilitate the dialogue through questions such as, "How has it been for you to feel like you did in the past?," or "What is it like for you to expect that people will treat you like they used to?"

Once the protector part feels that they have truly been acknowledged and witnessed for the burden they carry, they may allow the process of Targeting the Re-enactment. Additional questions for the clinician might be: "Could it be true that someone would not want to treat you like they (abusers/perpetrators) did in the past? Would that be something that you would want?"

Through back-and-forth dialogue with bilateral stimulation, the protector part may allow for the associated trauma target to be accessed. If they do, the clinician may encourage that the "movie of the incident (e.g., associated memory of re-enactment)" be played.

Through direct access with the clinician's Self-energy, or via Self-to-part relationship, it is important to proceed through the Witnessing and Unburdening phases of traditional IFS along with bilateral stimulation throughout each set of responses.

Targeting Therapeutic Relationship Ruptures via EMDR and IFS

If the client is unwilling, or not ready, to target the memory associated with the re-enactment with the clinician, it is beneficial to identify and target any therapeutic relationship ruptures that might have occurred. For the client's Self-system, the re-enactment may be due to a subconscious pattern of interacting with others that they have now felt safe in the therapeutic office to undergo. This may be the point at which the clinician has now been flagged as the abuser/perpetrator, which often occurs with individuals with CPTSD, similar to Karpman's Drama Triangle of perpetrator-victim-savior (Karpman, 1968). If this is the case, the clinician may engage in interviewing the protector part(s) of the system that express discontent with the clinician and offer the option of targeting the moment or experience of disappointment that occurred.

According to the AIP model (Shapiro, 2018), the client may benefit from titrating the EMDR model to desensitization of a component of the trauma (EMD), or titrating to the trauma memory only (EMDr), or traditional EMDR to access the trauma memory and associated memory networks. If the system refuses and chooses to stay in the moment or experience (e.g., disappointment with the clinician), you can proceed with the traditional EMD or EMDr protocol of reprocessing along with distancing maneuvers of watching the event like a movie. You might wish to express any gratitude from Self-energy, and maintain the eight C's and five P's of IFS, to assist the client in re-engaging and experiencing a corrective emotional experience.

Resourcing Therapeutic Relationship Repairs

After the re-enactment/therapeutic rupture has been reprocessed, whether through targeting the original memory or through targeting the moment or experience of disappointment with clinician, Phase 5 of EMDR therapy may be utilized as an effort to resource the memory into the client's adaptive neural networks. At this point, it is beneficial to ascertain or collect a positive cognition, with the system's consent, and the seemingly small, but effectively significant moment at which an attachment rupture was repaired. It has long been held that the therapeutic relationship is a relevant environment for encoding a felt-sense secure base. As taught in EMDR therapy basic training, be mindful of utilizing slow bilateral stimulation during resourcing and fast bilateral stimulation during reprocessing.

Conclusion

Adding a formal CPTSD diagnosis has provided the field with the fervor needed to identify and assess the efficacy of tailored treatments for this population. With the knowledge that attachment insecurity is often at the basis of the mechanisms underlying diagnostic criteria and behavioral symptom presentation, clinicians can utilize the EMDR and IFS therapy modalities to facilitate healing and thriving. Clinicians must ensure proper assessment of both CPTSD and attachment styles to better ascertain what types of protectors may be present. Though still *without an agenda*, clinicians may acknowledge the potential treatment impasses and pitfalls that occur due to the re-enactments that take place in therapy. With a thorough case conceptualization and tools to target therapeutic attachment ruptures, clinicians can leverage EMDR therapy's AIP model to integrate adaptive information that is experientially processed, with the maladaptive neural networks holding the cognitions of distrust and disappointment. It is especially important that clinicians acknowledge their own system of parts and how their need to help the client find relief may reflect danger to the client's system. Thus, further knowledge in order to anticipate these treatment impasses and therapeutic ruptures, as nodes to the target memories associated with delicate and complex neural networks, can help those with CPTSD finally incorporate the felt sense of the attunement they have always deserved and craved.

Notes

1 This assessment tool is available in multiple languages and for various ages, and can be found at the International Trauma Consortium: http://www.trauma measuresglobal.com.
2 For more information on assessments and training opportunities, visit: https://center-for-attachment.com.

References

APA (American Psychiatric Association). (2022). *Diagnostic and statistical manual of mental disorders* (5th ed., text rev.). American Psychiatric Association. https://doi.org/10.1176/appi.books.9780890425787

Benoit, D. (2004). Infant–parent attachment: Definition, types, antecedents, measurement and outcome. *Paediatrics & Child Health, 9*(8), 541–545. https://doi.org/10.1093/pch/9.8.541

Bowlby, J. (1982). Attachment and loss: Retrospect and prospect. *American Journal of Orthopsychiatry, 52*(4), 664–678. https://doi.org/10.1111/j.1939-0025.1982.tb01456.x

Cloitre, M., Shevlin M., Brewin, C. R., Bisson, J. I., Roberts, N. P., Maercker, A., Karatzias, T., & Hyland, P. (2018). The International Trauma Questionnaire: Development of a self-report measure of ICD-11 PTSD and Complex PTSD. *Acta Psychiatrica Scandinavica, 138*(6), 536–546. https://doi.org/10.1111/acps.12956

Ford, J. D., & Courtois, C. A. (2021). Complex PTSD and borderline personality disorder. *Borderline Personality Disorder and Emotion Dysregulation, 8*(1), 16.

Forgash, C., & Knipe, J. (2012). Integrating EMDR and ego state treatment for clients with trauma disorders. *Journal of EMDR Practice and Research, 6*(3), 120–128. https://doi.org/10.1891/1933-3196.6.3.120

Fraley, R. C., Waller, N. G., & Brennan, K. A. (2000). An item response theory analysis of self-report measures of adult attachment. *Journal of Personality and Social Psychology, 78*(2), 350–365. https://doi.org/10.1037/0022-3514.78.2.350

Greenblatt-Kimron, L., Karatzias, T., Yonatan, M., Shoham, A., Hyland, P., Ben-Ezra, M., & Shevlin, M. (2023). Early maladaptive schemas and ICD-11 CPTSD symptoms: Treatment considerations. *Psychology and Psychotherapy, 96*(1), 117–128. https://doi.org/10.1111/papt.12429

Herman, J. L. (1992). Complex PTSD: A syndrome in survivors of prolonged and repeated trauma. *Journal of Traumatic Stress, 5*(3), 377–391.

Hodgdon, H. B., Anderson, F. G., Southwell, E., Hrubec, W., & Schwartz, R. (2021). Internal Family Systems (IFS) therapy for Posttraumatic Stress Disorder (PTSD) among survivors of multiple childhood trauma: A pilot effectiveness study. *Journal of Aggression, Maltreatment & Trauma, 31*(1), 22–43. https://doi.org/10.1080/10926771.2021.2013375

Hyland, P., Shevlin, M., & Brewin, C. R. (2023). The memory and identity theory of ICD-11 complex posttraumatic stress disorder. *Psychological Review, 130*(4), 1044–1065. https://doi.org/10.1037/rev0000418

Hyland, P., Shevlin, M., Martsenkovskyi, D., Ben-Ezra, M., & Brewin, C. R. (2024). Testing predictions from the memory and identity theory of ICD-11 complex posttraumatic stress disorder: Measurement development and initial findings. *Journal of Anxiety Disorders, 105*, 102898. https://doi.org/10.1016/j.janxdis.2024.102898

Karatzias, T., Shevlin, M., Ford, J. D., Fyvie, C., Grandison, G., Hyland, P., & Cloitre, M. (2022). Childhood trauma, attachment orientation, and complex PTSD (CPTSD) symptoms in a clinical sample: Implications for treatment. *Development and Psychopathology, 34*(3), 1192–1197. https://doi.org/10.1017/S0954579420001509

Karpman, S. (1968). Fairy tales and script drama analysis. *Transactional Analysis Bulletin, 26*(7): 39–43.

Levy, M. S. (1998). A helpful way to conceptualize and understand reenactments. *The Journal of Psychotherapy Practice and Research, 7*(3), 227–235.

Maercker, A., Bernays, F., Rohner, S. L., & Thoma, M. V. (2022). A cascade model of complex posttraumatic stress disorder centered on childhood trauma and maltreatment, attachment, and socio-interpersonal factors. *Journal of Traumatic Stress, 35*(2), 446–460. https://doi.org/10.1002/jts.22756

Main, M., Kaplan, N., & Cassidy, J. (1985). Security in infancy, childhood, and adulthood: A move to the level of representation. *Monographs of the Society for Research in Child Development, 50*(1–2, Serial No. 209), 66–104. https://doi.org/10.2307/3333827

Paulsen, S. L. (2017). *When there are no words*. Bainbridge Institute for Integrative Psychology Publishing.

Sandberg, D. A., & Refrea, V. (2022). Adult attachment as a mediator of the link between interpersonal trauma and International Classification of Diseases (ICD)-11 Complex Posttraumatic Stress Disorder symptoms among college men and women. *Journal of Interpersonal Violence, 37*(23–24), NP22528–NP22548. https://doi.org/10.1177/08862605211072168

Schwartz, R. C. (2013). Moving from acceptance toward transformation with Internal Family Systems Therapy (IFS). *Journal of Clinical Psychology, 69*(8), 805–816. https://doi.org/10.1002/jclp.22016

Shapiro, F. (2018). *Eye movement desensitization and reprocessing (EMDR) therapy: Basic principles, protocols, and procedures* (3rd ed.). The Guilford Press.

Unger, J. A. M., & De Luca, R. V. (2014). The relationship between childhood physical abuse and adult attachment styles. *Journal of Family Violence, 29*(3), 223–234. https://doi.org/10.1007/s10896-014-9588-3

van der Kolk, B. A., & Fisler, R. (1995). Dissociation and the fragmentary nature of traumatic memories: Overview and exploratory study. *Journal of Traumatic Stress, 8*(4), 505–525.

Chapter 15

Healing Pain with EMDR and IFS

Tina Elleman Taylor

Reviewed by Beau Laviolette, Athena Phillips, and Claire van den Bosch

I've learned more from pain than I could've ever learned from pleasure.

(Unknown)

We all experience physical pain, yet it comes in so many forms and manifestations, and is a source of suffering for many. Pain impacts people's functioning by removing them from the workplace, family involvement, and leisure activities. It often leads to the misuse of prescription medications, alcohol, and other drugs. Pain could contribute to depression, anxiety, and feelings of isolation. Therefore, by helping our clients deal with and even decrease their experiences of pain, we impact their lives in profound ways.

There are three types of pain: Nociceptive, neuropathic, and nociplastic. Nociceptive pain is caused by tissue damage through injury, infection, or inflammation. Neuropathic pain is caused by nerve damage. Finally, nociplastic pain results from altered processing of pain in the central nervous system.

Chronic Pain

Chronic pain can include all three types of pain (nociceptive, neuropathic, and/or nociplastic) and any configuration of these three. Conditions such as arthritis, migraines, and fibromyalgia are examples of pain that sometimes combine all of these, significantly impacting an individual's quality of life. Unlike acute pain, which is typically a sudden and short-term response to injury and serves as a warning signal to protect the body, chronic pain persists for three months or longer and can continue even after the initial cause has been addressed. As the frequency and severity of pain increases, so does the likelihood that chronic pain will develop (Bonezzi et al., 2020).

DOI: 10.4324/9781003541554-19

How Does Chronic Pain Develop?

If acute pain persists, it can alter brain chemistry, making the brain more sensitized to pain and increasing the risk of developing chronic pain. Recurring acute pain flares can also lead to more chronic pain, particularly as seen in arthritis, neuropathies, and spinal issues.

In addition to these more physical types of pain, we also experience sensory and emotional pain. Interestingly, the place in the brain that registers pain, the anterior cingulate cortex (ACC), is activated by both physical pain and by emotional distress (i.e., the pain of rejection). We can view both physical and emotional pain as protective mechanisms, warning systems for danger and potential harm. If pain persists, the brain intensifies sensitivity to pain. In this process, called central sensitization, our brains rewire to anticipate pain, and this can remain even after the original injury is healed. Some examples of this include fibromyalgia and phantom limb pain.

Ongoing emotional pain also increases the chances that chronic pain will develop. We have found that there are connections between Adverse Childhood Experiences (ACEs) and chronic pain, and that the impact of trauma on the brain can lead to increased sensitivity to pain (Giordano et al., 2022).

If you work with individuals suffering from pain, it is important to rule out medical diagnoses that could cause or contribute to that pain, understand the type of pain that is experienced and how it might impact the individual's life. Not only can therapy help improve the ability to manage and cope with pain, it can also reduce the experience of pain itself.

EMDR and Chronic Pain

In contrast to Cognitive Behavioral Therapy (CBT), which decreases anxiety and depression around pain, research has shown that EMDR also leads to direct improvements in pain intensity. It is suggested that this is because EMDR directly impacts the corticolimbic levels involved in pain processing, altering the perception of nociceptive information rather than merely affecting higher brain functions like cognition or coping behavior. Essentially, EMDR engages different brain regions compared to therapies that remain on a cognitive level (such as CBT), which could explain the differing outcomes (Grant, 2014; Grant & Threlfo, 2002; Mazzola et al., 2009).

This aligns with the adaptive information processing (AIP) model, which posits that past traumatic experiences contribute to current psychological and physical symptoms in the body (see Chapter 1), including pain. It is hypothesized that EMDR desensitizes the limbically augmented portion of the pain experience (Grant, 2014; Grant & Threlfo, 2002; Mazzola et al., 2009). Traumatic or painful memories heighten the pain response to current stimuli even if the stimuli is not inherently painful. As we desensitize and reprocess emotionally traumatizing memories, this pain response will be desensitized also.

Moreover, EMDR may be effective in treating pain because it specifically targets the affective aspects of pain, which interact with the client's overall pain experience. Affective distress can be both a component and a consequence of pain, and it can also coexist with pain as a comorbid condition. Originally developed to address distress from traumatic memories, EMDR likely alleviates pain by addressing both the affective distress and the painful memories associated with the pain. Mark Grant's Pain Protocol (Grant, 2010; Grant, 2014) and Robin Shapiro's adaptations for Multiple Chemical Sensitivities (Shapiro, 2009) are examples of how EMDR can be used to treat pain and inflammatory processes.

IFS and Chronic Pain

The IFS approach is particularly hopeful for those who have struggled with chronic pain for many years. By recognizing that parts may use pain as a protective mechanism, therapists can help clients explore and understand underlying reasons for their pain. As individuals become more aware of the parts of them that feel and hold onto the pain or even create pain, we can support these parts, understand their role, and unburden from these roles. There has been research which shows how this can be effective in treating rheumatoid arthritis (Shadick et al., 2013).

Adding IFS to an EMDR protocol (see the Syzygy Model, Chapter 6) can help separate the many competing internal reactions to pain, helping a client process it faster and more completely. This IFS upgrade to EMDR helps titrate the processing in a way that feels less overwhelming to clients with complex trauma or multiple blocking reactions (see the TIST model, Chapter 8).

Parts Connected to the Pain

We all have parts that are related to pain. Some parts increase our perception and experience of pain in order to protect us (Shadick et al., 2013). Using an IFS-Informed EMDR model (IIE), we get to know the parts that hold and feel the pain and their roles in the system. We also learn about which parts are polarized with them (i.e., which parts want to get rid of the parts holding the pain). This might include stoic parts, numbing parts, or even self-care parts, who all work to keep the client active, engaged, and moving forward in their life. Understanding and appreciating the positive intent of all parts, increasing insight and self-compassion, and creating more harmony among parts can all lead to softening and relaxing of the parts holding the pain.

When a person experiences chronic pain, the world often judges them, minimizes their pain, or even condemns them, which often leads to parts internalizing these messages of shame and worthlessness. Parts might even question their own experience. In order to offer support to the individual and these parts inside of them, it is vitally important to look at our own parts (see Chapters 20 and 21). We can ask ourselves, "How do we feel about pain and those who suffer from chronic pain?" and observe what parts come up within us. We could also identify any parts within clients, who hold this same energy and shame toward pain. We can also be on the lookout for parts that are anxious, depressed, or hold trauma, since these parts are usually intimately involved in the internal reactions that lead to a heightened experience of pain.

The concept of an unharmed, resilient center that all humans have, also known as the Self (see Chapter 2), is central to working with chronic pain. Although typically, we respond to our pain with other parts that may hold emotional responses or meanings around our pain, when we are able to have more access to our Self-energy (compassion, connection, creativity, curiosity, courage, clarity, confidence, and calm) we work through our pain more effectively. As we help clients have more access to Self-energy, we help them change their relationship with pain, regardless of whether pain is coming directly from other parts or from their body. As there is more self-compassion and wisdom, there is also more freedom to make balanced decisions on how to move through the world, even when the pain is present. This empowers clients to have more access to their inner wisdom, so they can make the best choices for themselves, and make lifestyle changes to support their health and protect their bodies.

There is a typical pattern of experiencing pain and moving away from it, shutting it down, or even numbing it. IFS helps individuals move toward the pain with curiosity and calm so they can better understand it. If we can explore the pain with this openness, pain will communicate what it is doing for the body. Pain is just communication. It may be coming from a part or from the body but it is communication. We can even ask this pain: *What important message is it wanting or needing to communicate with us?*

Applying IIE For Clients with Pain

To begin a parts exploration around pain, I will use the following steps:

- Parts Map.
- Identify and Work with Polarizations.
- Identify Ongoing Trauma.
- Identify Legacy Burdens.
- Work with Our Own Parts.
- Move Toward Exiles When the System Allows.

Parts Map

I begin by constructing a parts map with clients. Using a blank sheet of paper, I have them write "Pain" in the center. They are free to use color with pencils/markers, or they can keep it simple with a pen. I ask them to just notice what comes up when they look at the pain on the page. I then invite them to write down a word to represent whatever is coming up. After this, I might say, "Let's refocus on the pain, and see what else comes up." I continue in this manner until all their reactions to the pain are on the page. These can include emotions, beliefs about pain, thoughts, behaviors and more. Once this is complete, we explore how these different reactions or parts feel about and respond to one another. This helps to identify the polarizations around the pain that are likely to be present. The exercise itself can begin to help the client to understand and unblend from the parts they are able to identify. As their work continues and they discover more parts connected to pain, they can add additional parts to the map. This creates a roadmap for which parts will need focus.

Identify and Work with Polarizations

Polarizations are parts that have very opposite functions. As one part does its job for the system, other parts respond with opposite reactions. An example of a polarization might be: A client has a stoic part that wants to ignore the pain and another part that increases the pain, wanting the client to rest and have more self-care. The more the stoic part pushes to achieve its goals, the more the "I want more rest" part increases pain in the client's body. They become locked in a power struggle, and the part that they are both trying to protect gets further exiled. Unfortunately, it is very common for this dynamic to play out and exacerbate the pain. We might be able to help the stoic part see how, ironically, the more work it does to suppress, control, or push through the pain, the more the pain increases, only leading to more endless work.

As we look to healing pain with IIE, and specifically to reprocessing or reconsolidating the memories and reactions associated with the pain (see Chapter 6), we see how important it is to help work with these polarizations, and help clients to unblend from their parts.[1] In order to access positive neural networks so there can be dual awareness (see Chapter 1) or a critical amount of Self to reconsolidate memories (see Chapter 6), I utilize the Discovery Phase of the Syzygy Model (see Chapter 7) to help clients unblend from parts and increase their connection with Self.

Identify Ongoing Trauma

In many cases chronic illness will create recurrent acute pain or persistent nerve pain. This recurrent or persistent pain will create an ongoing stressor for parts and might be experienced as an ongoing trauma. IFS-Informed EMDR will still increase the presence of Self, increase the ability to cope with pain, increase self-care, reduce anxiety and depression, and create a stronger sense of stability in the system. It may even decrease the perception of pain that could be turned on by parts that are attempting to prevent more pain. It is important to recognize, however, that this approach will not end all pain particularly when acute pain or nerve pain exists. It can be validating to normalize reactions to this ongoing trauma or stressor.

Identify Legacy Burdens

Legacy burdens are burdened beliefs that our parts take on from our family, culture, or society. These legacy beliefs about pain include how the individual is supposed to respond to pain, how the family responds to others in pain, or beliefs about the cause of pain. These beliefs must be explored and updated with beliefs that make sense in the present day. Families can often respond from beliefs about stoicism and pushing through pain, or on the other extreme might respond with high levels of fear and concern about pain. By examining these beliefs passed on through parents or other family members' parts, parts are able to re-evaluate if these are beliefs that are beneficial, and if not, if they want to let go of these beliefs.

Work With Our Own Parts

Working with individuals with chronic pain, it is imperative that the therapist explore their own parts around pain. As therapists, we come in with predetermined ideas about pain and what can be possible in therapy. This will impair our ability to explore the client's systems with openness. It is important to sit with the discomfort of a client in pain without trying to "fix" it. If we cannot maintain open-hearted exploration, how can we expect our clients to do the same?

An important feature of IFS is learning to track our own system. We can do this by noticing what thoughts, feelings, body sensations, or other reactions we have toward clients with pain. This gives us the opportunity to ask those parts to give us space during session and spend time with those parts outside of session. Clients provide incredible access to our own trailheads to work through our own personal growth.

Move Toward Exiles When the System Allows

Often my clients with chronic pain have specific memories of early pain that was overwhelming. Their protective parts keep us from being able to access those exiled parts, because the experience of pain was too much for the age it was experienced. Often there is a fear that exploring these parts will lead to overwhelm. To address the fear of these parts, I have used a container exercise to help the parts titrate the pain. This helps to show the part that the Self can be present with the pain without overwhelm. The exiled part puts the pain in a container and is held or present with Self. The part is able to look in the container with control and in the arms of the Self. These ideas are based on the Constant Installation of Presence of Orientation and Safety (CIPOS), with an IFS adaptation of using Self as the present orientation and safety (Knipe, 2019).

Case Example: Elizabeth[2]

Elizabeth is a young adult who came to see me to work through her trauma. Much of her trauma was related to the misuse of religion in her family. Her family and church sent her messages that pain and illness were the result of sin. The family frequently used painful abuse to punish behaviors that were deemed inappropriate or bad. As an adult my client was diagnosed with Ehlers–Danlos, a genetic condition resulting in the inability to produce collagen correctly. This condition results in many symptoms, including hypermobility and joint pain. My client was very distraught at this diagnosis. She would have dislocations and subluxations of her joints, which led to being triggered to have somatic flashback experiences of her previous abuse. Our work together began with her becoming very overwhelmed when discussing her painful memories. Many of the EMDR sessions using standard protocol led to overwhelm and shutdown. When I introduced IFS-Informed EMDR to her, we began to make progress.

She began to identify parts of her that push her to achieve, parts that hold grief around not having a life which is pain-free, and parts that want to shut down so that they can avoid any pain. She identified the family messages that were held in her body as legacy burdens. Though she rationally rejected that it was her fault she had Ehlers–Danlos, there was an internalized belief that she was being punished for a sin, that she was flawed, and that feeling such intense pain was a weakness of hers. Mapping these parts allowed her to see how they polarized and impacted how she showed up in her life. We used direct access and eventually insight work to understand and accept these parts fully.

As we worked with these parts, we moved closer to a particular exile that held the trauma of a particularly painful abusive memory. We got permission to work with this part; however there was concern that the part would overwhelm her as soon as we accessed it as it had in multiple EMDR sessions. In typical IFS fashion, I had the client ask the part not to overwhelm, to prove to the protector that she can be with the part. The part expressed that it did not know how, since that was how the pain had been experienced. It also expressed an inability to allow just a small portion of the experience through.

Using my EMDR knowledge to help decrease the overwhelm. I asked the client to invite the part to put any pain in a container. The part quickly became upset, feeling that we were asking the part to be in the container, so I clarified for the part to stay with the client, in her arms, and to continue experiencing her love, while putting the pain in the container. The part was relieved to stay with the client. Then, I suggested that the part could look at the memory from the client's arms for a few seconds, before closing the container.

The part was able to tolerate the memory for a short period of time. We continued this process of staying in the client's arms and looking at the memory a few seconds at a time. After a period of time, the part was able to look at the memory without overwhelm. The part still rated the distress level (SUDS) at 10, but the part was now able to begin the IFS-Informed EMDR process of allowing the part to share the memory while adding BLS. This was a turning point in her therapy; we were finally able to process the earliest memory of pain—triggered when her disorder created pain.

I now often use this technique with many clients if they feel overwhelmed at any point in treatment. This combines many ideas of EMDR and IFS, including the container exercise, using presence of Self as the resource, and Jim Knipe's Constant Installation of Present Orientation and Safety (CIPOS: Knipe, 2019) in a new, creative way.

When I interviewed this client as to what had been most helpful in our treatment together, she told me that two things had been the most helpful: (1) the IFS work of learning to be with her parts even in their most distressed moments, and (2) my own use of Self in session (see Chapter 9). My disclosure that I suffer with Marfan Disorder added to a shared emotional space where she felt recognized and understood. She was also able to feel the hope I held—that her capacity to heal and ability to find relief were both realistic and well-founded. My personal work with my own parts made this possible.

Some Final Considerations

On a final note, when nerve pain or recurrent acute pain (such as the pain that occurs with chronic illnesses) exists, this will not be completely removed by the implementation of IIE. IIE works with clients to increase the presence of Self, the ability to cope with pain, and the effectiveness of self-care. IIE has been successful with reducing anxiety and depression, which is connected to pain, and creating a stronger sense of stability in the system. It may even decrease the perception of pain that could be turned on by parts that are attempting to prevent more pain. Ultimately, chronic pain is a constant stressor, perhaps even a trauma for the system; however, through IIE there is hope that we can successfully walk through this pain, soften it, and allow it to pass through our system more quickly. We stop fighting our pain, and instead turn toward it and recognize the incredible internal system we have. And when this system is working in harmony, the size of the pain is decreased and, at times, processed right through our bodies.

Notes

1 See Chapter 19 for more insightful and helpful ways to work with polarizations in clients.
2 Name and identifying information has been changed to protect client confidentiality.

References

Bonezzi, C., Fornasari, D., Cricelli, C., Magni, A., & Ventriglia, G. (2020). Not all pain is created equal: Basic definitions and diagnostic work-up. *Pain and Therapy*, Dec; *9*(Suppl 1), 1–15. doi: 10.1007/s40122-020-00217-w. Epub 2020 Dec 14. PMID: 33315206; PMCID: PMC7736598.

Giordano, R., Kjær-Staal Petersen K., & Arendt-Nielsen L. (2022). The link between epigenetics, pain sensitivity and chronic pain. *Scandinavian Journal of Pain* (Sep. 26); *22*(4), 664–666. doi: 10.1515/sjpain-2022-0086. PMID: 36149940.

Grant, M. (2010). Pain control with EMDR. In M. Luber (Ed.), *Eye movement desensitization and reprocessing (EMDR)* (pp. 517–536). Springer Publishing Co.

Grant, M., & Threlfo, C. (2002). EMDR in the treatment of chronic pain. *Journal of Clinical Psychology*, *58*(12) 1505–1520 (www.interscience.wiley.com). doi: 10.1002/jclp.1010.

Grant, M. D. (2014). Eye movement desensitization and reprocessing treatment of chronic pain. *OA Musculoskeletal Medicine* Aug. 17;*2*(2): 17.

Knipe, J. (2019). *EMDR toolbox: Theory and treatment of complex PTSD and dissociation*. Springer Publishing Co.

Mazzola, A., Calcagno, M. L., Goicochea, M. T., Pueyrredòn, H., Leston, J., & Salvat, F. (2009). EMDR in the treatment of chronic pain. *Journal of EMDR Practice and Research*, *3*, 66–79.

Shadick, N. A., Sowell, N. F., Frits, M. L., Hoffman, S. M., Hartz, S. A., Booth, F. D., Sweezy, M., Rogers, P. R., Dubin, R. L., Atkinson, J. C., Friedman, A. L., Augusto, F., Iannaccone, C. K., Fossel, A. H., Quinn, G., Cui, J., Losina, E., & Schwartz, R. C. (2013). A randomized controlled trial of an internal family systems-based psychotherapeutic intervention on outcomes in rheumatoid arthritis: A proof-of-concept study. *The Journal of Rheumatology*, *40*(11) 1831–1841.

Shapiro, R. (2009). Treating multiple chemical sensitivities with EMDR. In R. Shapiro (Ed.), *EMDR Solutions II: For depression, eating disorders, performance, and more* (1st ed.) (pp. 448–455). W. W. Norton & Co.

Chapter 16

Military Veterans and Nature Retreats with IFS and EMDR

Beau Laviolette

On March 27, 2001, at 3 a.m., I found myself standing on a set of yellow footprints. My heart raced, and a voice deep within questioned my decision. The young men around me were silent; the only sounds were the harsh drill instructors yelling commands, attempting to break us. These yellow footprints symbolized the countless men and women who had stood there before me, earning the title of United States Marine. I wondered, would I be one of them? Did I possess what it took to earn the right to be called a US Marine? At that moment, I had no idea that my life was about to change in ways I had never imagined, challenging me mentally, physically, and spiritually.

Since then, a lot has changed. As I sit down to write this chapter, I am filled with gratitude. It is 2024, and life is very different now. I am much older, have a family, and have found something in life that keeps me fulfilled. Professionally, I have found that IFS and EMDR are among the best gifts. These two models, and the combination of them, have added a lot of value to my professional and personal life. Thank you for reading this chapter and I hope it adds value to your life as well.

To truly understand a veteran, we must acknowledge the complexity of their experiences. Veterans have many parts of the internal psyches that have been shaped by layers of life—childhood, military service, and the transition back to civilian life. Whether due to cultural norms, survival instincts, or physical safety, some parts were simply not safe to reveal and so they were suppressed. When we work with veterans, we must strive to see the whole picture. Every part of their story, no matter how conflicting or complicated, is essential. All parts are welcome. This comprehensive view is vital as we explore the transitions veterans navigate, and consider how we can be most supportive to them. Box 16.1 illustrates five crucial elements that must be present in order to have a meaningful therapeutic relationship with veterans.

The most crucial element when working with veterans is authenticity. They have a strong ability to detect insincerity or when someone is "blended" with a part, so it's essential to show up as your genuine self (see Chapters 20 and 21). If you're unsure about something, curiosity is always welcome—veterans

DOI: 10.4324/9781003541554-20

Box 16.1 Five Crucial Elements When Connecting with Veterans

- Authenticity—we need to be genuine.
- Trust—there needs to be honesty and transparency to build this.
- Safety—using language that will help veterans feel comfortable and safe.
- Understanding—really respecting what a veteran has gone through in their life.
- Empathy—Veterans need to feel like you "have their back" and you care about them.

appreciate honesty and transparency far more than a façade of knowledge. Building trust starts here and grows through consistency, respect, and a genuine willingness to understand their experiences.

Using language that aligns with veteran's lived experiences helps foster a sense of safety, another critical element. Thoughtful communication, combined with deep understanding of their perspective, creates the foundation for a strong therapeutic relationship. When veterans feel truly seen and understood, they are more likely to engage fully in the process.

It's important to recognize that many veterans have had challenging experiences with healthcare providers, particularly during transitions from military to civilian life. These experiences may have left them feeling unseen or reduced to just another number. Countering this requires treating them with genuine care and respect, and showing that you "have their back." This fifth critical element, a sense of empathy, reassures veterans that you are committed to their well-being.

Understanding the Roots of Trauma

When working with veterans, it is essential to recognize that their internal struggles often stem from experiences long before their military service. Research has consistently shown a strong link between early-life trauma and the mental health challenges faced by military personnel (Blosnich et al., 2014; Vest et al., 2018). Understanding this connection is vital to providing effective support and interventions. One in five veterans in the United States has experienced childhood physical or sexual abuse, significantly contributing to depressive symptoms, PTSD and suicidality—even after accounting for combat exposure.[1] In my work with veterans, I have also found that many veterans are impacted by having been given subtle, and not so subtle, messages that they needed to suppress some of their emotions, as children and then again in their military careers.

One study found that 80% of war veterans seeking treatment for PTSD also met the criteria for complex PTSD (CPTSD) (Letica-Crepulja et al., 2020). This distinction is crucial, as CPTSD involves deeper relational wounds and pervasive issues with self-worth and emotional regulation—often rooted in childhood trauma (see Chapter 14).

In the military, service members often face additional barriers to seeking help, which include:

- **Stigma**: There is a pervasive belief that seeking help for mental health struggles signals weakness, which clashes with the military's emphasis on toughness and resilience.
- **Pressure from higher-ups**: Service members are often urged to "get back to work" quickly, prioritizing mission-readiness over personal well-being.
- **Fit-for-duty concerns**: Seeking treatment can raise questions about a service member's fitness for duty, creating fears about career repercussions.
- **Guilt about burdening others**: With the demands of ongoing conflicts, service members may feel that prioritizing their mental health adds to the burden on their peers.

Long after a veteran has transitioned home and military service has ended, these external pressures could cause hurt and resentment within parts of the veteran. By addressing these parts with compassion and curiosity, we create an opportunity for healing and integration, empowering veterans to reconnect with their sense of self and move forward with greater wholeness and harmony in their internal systems.

Transitioning to Civilian Life

The military teaches you how to put the uniform on, but it doesn't teach you how to take it off. The transition from military to civilian life is a profound and often overwhelming experience for veterans. Leaving the structured, mission-driven environment of the military can bring up a host of emotions. Along with relief, veterans also report feeling uncertainty, loss, and even guilt. Despite years of service, many veterans find themselves facing significant challenges during this period, often compounded by a lack of adequate support systems to guide them through the process. Many veterans feel abandoned by the very institution they dedicated their lives to, and don't feel that they were given adequate (or sometimes any) preparation for reentering civilian life. Mental health services are often insufficient or delayed, leaving many veterans to struggle with unresolved traumas—whether from childhood or their time in service—without the resources they need to heal.

The process of securing benefits, such as healthcare, education assistance, or disability compensation, can be intimidating and filled with bureaucratic hurdles. For many veterans, this system feels cold and impersonal. Even worse, there's often a sense of guilt associated with applying for benefits, as though they don't deserve them or maybe it should go to someone else who has endured more than them. This guilt, coupled with the stigma of asking for help, leaves many veterans struggling in silence.

Nature Retreats

My friend and colleague, Ray Mount, led the first retreat, conducting a pilot IFS Nature program in Boston with a group of therapists. Each therapist brought a special "gift" to share—some brought art and shamanic drumming. I brought EMDR. One of the exercises we conducted was called a trail hike with your part. Essentially, this involved going for a walk with one of your parts and then finding a place to sit with it and witness it. I did that, but when I got to my spot, I decided to add some BLS. My part, the one I was walking with, showed me a memory.

I had just left the Marine Corps. It was a time in my life when I was struggling. I was 25 years old and had gone home to my parents' house. It was late at night, and I was scared. I went to the side of my mom's bed and asked her to put her hand on my back. She used to do that when I was a young boy. As I re-experienced this memory, a warm feeling washed over me. I realized that my part had been missing a secure touch from a mother. But then, a wave of sadness hit me because I no longer had that. At that moment, as the clouds cleared, the brightest moon I had ever seen revealed herself. The thought came into my mind: I have Mother Nature, and I could connect to her warmth and safety. My takeaways were twofold: first, something significant happened when I started the BLS, and second, I don't think this could have happened in my office. There was something about the experience as a whole (the night-life, nature's energy, the moon) that facilitated this profound feeling.

There are numerous studies and educational initiatives that underscore the profound impact of nature on mental, physical, and emotional well-being. Richard Luv has written about it in his book, *Last Child in the Woods: Saving Our Children from Nature-Deficit Disorder* (Luv, 2005). In Theodore Roszak's *The Voice of the Earth* he coined the term "ecotherapy" (Roszak, 2001). The field of ecotherapy, or nature-based therapy, continues to grow as researchers and practitioners explore how natural environments can enhance healing processes.

Nature's Benefits

When we compare nature to an urban environment, we find multiple ways that nature can benefit our health, reduce our stress, decrease anxiety and depression, and even improve some cognitive functions, such as attention. When we think of the sounds of rain falling, waterfalls, and birds chirping, a lot of times we enter into a more relaxed state of being. This activates our feeling of safety and connection, also known as the parasympathetic nervous system (or the "rest and digest" branch). This creates observable and measurable changes in our body, which include changes in blood pressure, pulse rate, heart rate variability, and salivary cortisol and hemoglobin levels (Williams, 2018).

Modern urban life triggers the sympathetic nervous system, associated with fight-or-flight responses. Chronic activation of this can lead to elevated cortisol levels and high blood pressure, which increases the risk of heart disease, metabolic disorders, dementia, and depression (Williams, 2018). Lower stress is extremely beneficial for our mental health, and nature exposure has been linked to decreases in depression and anxiety. There are significant statistic differences in rumination and emotional well-being when comparing a walk in nature to a walk in a more urban environment. Nature is seen to cultivate more mindfulness and decrease sensory overload (Bratman et al., 2021).

As nature helps us increase our attention, we can also see improvements in memory and problem-solving skills (McDonnell & Strayer, 2024). There is an "attention restoration" effect which occurs as the brain recovers from overstimulation common in urban settings. In fact, Rachel and Stephen Kaplan created Attention Restoration Theory (ART) to explain how natural environments help restore depleted attention and improve cognitive functioning (Kaplan & Kaplan, 1989). "Attention fatigue" happens when we are overwhelmed by stimuli requiring directed attention such as screens, conversations, and multitasking, which reduces our focus, increases irritability, and diminishes problem-solving abilities. Natural environments, according to ART, provide restorative experiences that rejuvenate our cognitive resources by engaging a different kind of attention: effortless attention, also known as "soft fascination." This form of attention allows the mind to rest and recover, replenishing depleted cognitive resources.

Soft fascination is a cornerstone of ART and describes the way natural environments gently and effortlessly capture attention. Unlike activities requiring intense focus, such as problem-solving or reading, soft fascination allows the mind to rest and recover without becoming overstimulated. Soft fascination occurs when we encounter stimuli that are inherently interesting but do not demand directed attention. These stimuli, such as the ripple of water in a stream, the swaying of trees in the wind, clouds drifting across the sky, or the sound of birds chirping, provide enough engagement to hold our interest but not so much that they overwhelm or exhaust the mind. Being in nature is a very different experience than being in the center of an urban environment, where traffic noises, phone alerts, and crowded streets demand our attention and overstimulate our minds. By providing this sense of calm, nature becomes an ideal place to complement structured therapeutic interventions.

Adding the Gifts of EMDR to a Nature Retreat

If nature is so healing, why do we need to add anything? There are two very important elements that IFS-informed EMDR (IIE) adds and that are beneficial to veterans: Structure and relationship. Veterans deeply appreciate structure, and it is a core part of their life. For their protector parts to trust the healing process and feel safe, an external and internal structure provides a lot of comfort. EMDR, with its eight phases, brings this much-needed structure to the work.

When I conducted my first veteran nature retreat, there wasn't much structure, and instead we dove into a conversation about IFS: The Self and parts. While this was valuable, when more teaching and structure was added to this, the veterans reported feeling more grounded and reassured. Anxious parts relaxed, because veterans had greater clarity about their objectives and expectations. They communicated that they felt more confident in the process, and had more of a framework in which to anchor their experiences.

When teaching IFS and EMDR concepts of IFS and EMDR, I found it incredibly helpful to use language that the veterans were already familiar with—terms like "about-face" or "checking your gig line" resonated with them. Due to the incorporation of language and concepts they were comfortable with, they needed less mental energy to try to figure out what was happening and were able to engage with the process. This helped build a bridge between their military training and the healing process, which made it feel more accessible and relatable (see Appendix 16.A for a full list of specific military language and terms).

In addition to incorporating structure into the retreat, IIE also introduces bilateral stimulation (BLS), a beautiful gift from EMDR (see Chapter 1). BLS is helpful for veterans and can be used in several ways during a nature retreat. In addition to adding a depth to reflection walks, BLS can be used by veterans to assist them with resourcing and processing information. When combined with IFS, the BLS can become pivotal in unblending and accessing quieter parts (see Chapter 6). In my experience, it's crucial that BLS is used on the veterans' own terms, allowing their parts to guide the process in the way that feels most comfortable and safe for them.

While we have explored various forms of BLS (walking/marching, tapping with sticks, on the chest, and on the knees), one particularly powerful method in our retreats has been drumming, which provides a rhythmic and grounding form of stimulation. Through trial and feedback, we found that the intensity of the drumming plays a significant role in its effectiveness.

Loud taps or hits on the drum were often too intense, triggering anxiety and discomfort for the veterans. On the other hand, soft, rhythmic tapping on the drum created a much more calming and soothing effect. This subtle variation allowed the veterans to experience the benefits of BLS without feeling overwhelmed, offering a gentle, grounding rhythm that helped them process emotions in a safe and contained way. Tailoring the experience to the needs of the individual parts ensures that the BLS enhances the healing process without inadvertently retraumatizing the veterans.

What was really happening during these sessions was an increase in Self-energy, the core healing quality in IFS. We used the Presence of Self scale (POS) (see Chapters 6 and 7), developed by Bruce Hersey, to gauge how much Self-energy the veterans noticed in the moment. One veteran remarked that while he was drumming (and noticing his Self-energy), he had an experience that was like nothing he had ever experienced before. While the veterans drummed, I might guide the group through an IFS meditation, focusing on observing and connecting with their parts, and finding ways to access and resource Self-energy. At the end of the experience, the veterans consistently indicated that they felt a noticeable increase in Self-energy. This integration of rhythmic drumming with IFS practices creates a profoundly grounding and healing environment, allowing the veterans to connect more deeply with their core sense of Self.

Adding the Contributions of IFS to a Nature Retreat

When combining IFS with the inherently grounding, nonjudgmental presence of nature, a veteran's connection with the natural world is amplified. This helps them foster a deep, relational engagement with their inner system. IFS offers a framework that encourages individuals to interact with their internal parts in a compassionate and understanding way. The experience of being in nature can also become a mirror for the self: With its diversity and balance, nature reflects the multiplicity and balance of our inner worlds. Whether it's the strong, towering presence of an old tree or the fragile beauty of a delicate flower, nature exemplifies how every part—no matter its strength or vulnerability—plays a vital role. Similarly, every part of us, no matter how resilient or tender, has an important function and purpose for our system.

Since CPTSD is common in veterans who have been exposed to prolonged or chronic trauma, typically involving relational wounds, IFS can also be extremely helpful and effective in understanding and healing a fragmented sense of self (see Chapter 8). In these instances, recognizing and having a compassionate stance toward young parts, which are often stuck in survival mode, can become transformational. Whether these parts are protector parts that defend against emotional pain, or exiled parts that hold the trauma and need to be nurtured, we invite veterans to honor all of their parts. As these parts are welcomed back into the "internal family" which comprises all the other parts in the system, emotional healing and a greater sense of wholeness is realized.

When immersed in nature, with an IFS lens, a veteran might sit beneath a powerful tree, and feel connected to internal protective parts—those aspects of themselves that represent strength, resilience, and safeguarding. Conversely, a veteran might turn to a fragile flower, and this might evoke a more tender, vulnerable part— an exile that needs nurturing and care. Nature and IFS can offers a safe space to acknowledge, name, and connect with these parts, allowing individuals to process and integrate their feelings within the present moment.

Furthermore, IFS enables a profound connection with one's Self-energy— qualities like calmness, compassion, curiosity, and nonjudgment—which align closely with the healing and non-agenda nature of the outdoors. Nature provides the space for this Self-energy to thrive. The natural world becomes not only a source of external support but a sanctuary for cultivating self-compassion and insight. In this way, nature transforms from a soothing environment into a dynamic, healing space.

Unplug, Connect, Let Go: The Structure of an IFS-EMDR Nature Retreat Program

The intention behind sharing these concepts and exercises is to provide a clear understanding of the main components of the nature retreat and how they can be applied when working with clients. By incorporating IIE into the nature retreat, these activities are designed to help veterans navigate their emotional landscapes, release burdens, and build healthier relationships with themselves.

Arrival Process

Veterans familiarize themselves with their new environment, and are invited to find a secluded spot that "feels right to you." This is where they will set up their tent. The intention of this is to help veterans feel a sense of freedom and comfort as they adjust to their new surroundings.

Self-Energy Cards Exercise

We reflect on the eight C's of Self such as Calmness, Compassion, and Courage (see Chapter 2), and each of the eight C words are written on index cards. Each veteran is invited to select a card that resonates with them, and recall a time in their life when they felt that quality. Each veteran is given a chance to share their thoughts with the group. We focus on how these qualities manifest in their bodies and emotions.

Self-Energy Hike

This individual hike encourages veterans to be mindful of both their internal and external experiences. While walking, they observe their surroundings and notice any sensations or feelings that arise within them. This exercise helps veterans deepen their connection with the Self and enhances awareness of the interplay between their environment and their internal world.

Identification of Parts

This exercise introduces veterans to the concept of "parts." Cards are laid out, representing a common part (such as the Inner Critic, a Stoic part, or a part who holds a lot of anger), and each veteran chooses a card that resonates with them. Each veteran has an opportunity to share the card they picked and how it resonates with one of their parts. Afterward, they go on an individual hike to find a token in nature that represents that part. This helps them externalize and symbolize the part, reinforcing the idea that parts are distinct from the Self. When they return, each veteran speaks *for* their part, not *from* it. This means they express what the part might say or feel, rather than being blended with the part, and being overtaken and controlled by it. This practice allows them to begin seeing the part as separate, fostering a sense of self-awareness and emotional distance from the part.

Creating a Self-to-Part Relationship

This exercise focuses on building a connection between the Self and the various parts of the veteran's system, shifting from a critical or reactive perspective to one of curiosity or compassion. The goal is to help the veteran approach their parts as if they were getting to know a new friend, from a place of understanding rather than judgment.

Veterans go on another walk, this time with the intention of connecting with the part they have been getting to know in a more compassionate and curious way. They allow themselves to explore and understand this part, rather than trying to change or fix it. There is the invitation for veterans to deepen this process by incorporating bilateral stimulation (BLS) to strengthen the growing connection between their Self and the part.

During the walk, we invite the veterans to pause whenever they feel it is right to do so. When pausing, veterans are asked reflect on what they notice, allowing the experience to unfold naturally. At each pause, each member sets an intention for the next phase of the walk, which could involve continuing relating with the part they have been connecting with, or getting to know a different one that has emerged. The intention is to create a deeper understanding and strengthen the relationship between the Self and the part, ultimately fostering integration and healing.

Identification of Burdens

This exercise involves helping veterans separate their parts from the burdens they carry. A key realization in this phase is that many people mistakenly believe their parts are inherently burdensome. In reality, parts often take on burdens in response to past experiences, such as negative emotions, beliefs, or sensations.

A central focus during the retreat is on protectors—the parts that act to shield the individual from harm. A significant shift occurs when veterans begin to understand that protectors are trying to help by preventing further hurt. Through a process called Discovery (see Chapter 7), we look for the protector's positive intention (PPI). When the PPI is identified, this reinforces the understanding that protectors are not inherently "bad" or disruptive, but rather are motivated by a desire to safeguard the system as a whole.

Sometimes an exile (a part that holds painful memories or emotions) may emerge during this process. If that happens, the group checks in with the veteran to ensure that it's okay to proceed with that part. The level of Self-energy the veteran has access to will guide our decision on how to move forward. Through the entire experience, it is critical that our decisions are based on helping all the veterans remains in a grounded and compassionate place as they work with their systems.

Letting Go

The "Letting Go" ritual is a deeply meaningful and transformative part of the retreat. In the evening, we gather around a beautiful fire by the river, sitting in a circle. Earlier in the day, each participant is encouraged to write a letter or journal entry about something a part of them is ready to release. This could be a burden, an emotion, or a belief that no longer serves them. It's important to note that not all parts may be ready to let go of everything. Often, just a small release—like 1, 2, or 3%—can create a significant shift. The process doesn't need to be overwhelming; even a small step toward letting go can bring a sense of relief and clarity.

During the fire ritual, we create a quiet and respectful space where each person has the time they need to reflect, connect with their intentions, and symbolically release what they're ready to let go of into the fire. This powerful experience allows veterans to move toward healing and transformation, with the fire serving as a sacred space for releasing and creating new possibilities.

Time with a Trail Guide

Throughout the retreat, veterans have opportunities to spend time with a Trail Guide—a fellow veteran who has already gone through the program. This time provides a more intimate and personal setting for the veterans to explore any issues or experiences that arise for them during the retreat. When not on an individual walk or participating in group debriefings and check-ins, veterans are paired with a Trail Guide, usually in small groups of two to three people, including the guide. This setup allows veterans to dive deeper into their personal journeys, ask questions, and process feelings in a sup-portive and peer-driven environment. The Trail Guide's role is to offer guid-ance and share their own experiences, creating an opportunity for mutual learning and growth. This also serves as a way for those who have already gone through the program to give back, supporting newcomers with their unique insights and encouragement.

The Graduation Ceremony

Finally, the retreat comes to a close with a graduation ceremony on the morning of Day 3, after breakfast (chow). Each person in the circle says something positive or affirming to another participant. This can be a deeply emotional part of the retreat, as it's often difficult for people to receive posi-tive feedback. Yet there are parts of us that need and long to hear these affirmations. This ceremony honors the work we've done together while also acknowledging the end of "boot camp."

Ongoing Support

The next phase of this program focuses on fostering long-term connections among participants, recognizing that sustained support is vital for veterans' well-being. As the participants meet regularly or through virtual Zoom calls, this phase provides a platform for ongoing interaction, accountability, and mutual encouragement. As a Marine Corps veteran, I recall the profound bonds formed during boot camp, which were often lost over time—a fear shared by many veterans who struggle with transient relationships. This important phase aims to counteract that fear by creating a structured, reli-able network of peers. By maintaining these meaningful connections, par-ticipants can continue to support each other in their personal growth, resilience, and in the integration of lessons that they would like to take from the retreat, and bring into their daily life.

Compassion Connections with Our Parts

With IFS-EMDR Nature Retreats, we are not just addressing trauma; we also are giving a voice to those parts of the Self that feel misused, misunder-stood, or silenced. These parts are often burdened with feelings of resent-ment, guilt, or invisibility. For many veterans, this is about more than healing—it's about reclaiming their humanity in a system that has often overlooked that humanity and their sacrifice.

I have found that veterans carry a strong desire to continue serving others, especially their fellow veterans. This sense of purpose can be a source of strength, but it can also add pressure, especially when veterans feel they are struggling themselves. Balancing the need to help others with their own healing journey is a delicate process that requires support, understanding, and community.

Transitioning to civilian life is not just about leaving the military; it's about navigating an entirely new identity. Whether through simplifying the Department of Veterans Affairs (VA) benefits process, reducing the stigma of seeking help, or creating more supportive environments in education and employment, we need to ensure that veterans have the tools and resources to thrive in civilian life. The pain and hurt that veterans are holding could be addressed as we help them navigate through the emotional, logistical, and societal challenges of integrating back into society. The IFS-EMDR Nature Retreat is just one of the ways that veterans can be given hope that healing is possible, and the belief that their voices and all of their internal parts matter.

Note

1 See Davis (n.d.).

References

Blosnich, J. R., Dichter, M. E., Cerulli, C., Batten, S. V., & Bossarte, R. M. (2014). Disparities in adverse childhood experiences among individuals with a history of military service. *JAMA Psychiatry*, *71*(9), 1041–1048.

Bratman, G. N., Young, G., Mehta, A., Lee Babineaux, I., Daily, G. C., & Gross, J. J. (2021). Affective benefits of nature contact: The role of rumination. *Frontiers in Psychology*, *12*. https://doi.org/10.3389/fpsyg.2021.643866

Davis, J. O. (n.d.). Military matters: Childhood trauma among veterans: Impact and implications. International Society for Traumatic Stress Studies (website). https://istss.org/military-matters-childhood-trauma-among-veterans-impact-and-implications-jacqueline-o-davis-wright-phd/

Kaplan, R. & Kaplan, S. (1989). *The experience of nature: A psychological perspective*. Cambridge University Press.

Letica-Crepulja, M., Stevanović, A., Protuđer, M., Grahovac Juretić, T., Rebić, J., & Frančišković, T. (2020). Complex PTSD among treatment-seeking veterans with PTSD. *European Journal of Psychotraumatology*, *11*(1), 1716593.

Luv, R. (2005). *Last child in the woods: Saving our children from nature-deficit disorder*. Algonquin Books.

McDonnell, A. S., & Strayer, D. L. (2024). Immersion in nature enhances neural indices of executive attention. *Scientific Reports*, *14*(1), Article 52205.

Roszak, T. (2001). *Voices of the Earth: An exploration of ecopsychology*. Phanes Press.

Vest, B. M., Hoopsick, R. A., Homish, D. L., Daws, R. C., & Homish, G. G. (2018). Childhood trauma, combat trauma, and substance use in National Guard and reserve soldiers. *Substance Abuse*, *39*(4), 452–460.

Williams, F. (2018). *The nature fix: Why nature makes us happier, healthier, and more creative*. W. W. Norton & Company.

APPENDIX 16.A: MILITARY ACRONYMS AND THEIR RELEVANCE IN IFS-EMDR THERAPY

The Military Mind

Here are some military acronyms that I have found very helpful. If you're interested in engaging with veterans in your practice, I hope these acronyms provide you with language and concepts that are helpful for both you and the veteran you are working with. Understanding the unique military mindset and communication can bridge the gap between civilian life and military experience, allowing for more effective therapy and connection. These short-hand terms are more than just a means of efficient communication; they could fosters a sense of belonging among service members. In therapy, understanding and even using these terms can help veterans feel seen and understood. I have been using these acronyms to help explain IFS and EMDR concepts to veterans and in this way construct a language to connect therapy and military.

About-Face (U-Turn)

An "about-face" is a 180-degree turn from a position of attention. It symbolizes a sudden and complete change in direction. In IFS, this can be seen as the moment when, instead of reacting impulsively when triggered, we pause and turn inward. This "about-face" allows us to identify the parts of ourselves that are activated and understand what they need, facilitating healing rather than conflict.

Checking Your Gig Line

The "gig line" refers to the alignment of a service member's uniform, from the shirt buttons to the belt buckle. Just as a buddy in the military might check your gig line before inspection, in therapy, others can help us see things about our parts that we might not be able to see on our own. This highlights the importance of community and support in the therapeutic process.

Roll Call (Parts Map)

"Roll call" is done at the beginning of the day during formation, to account for who is present. Similarly, in therapy, veterans can use a "roll-call" technique to check in with their parts, noting which ones are present and how they're showing up in the session. This process helps identify the various parts of the veteran's internal system, providing insight into which aspects of themselves are active at the moment.

In Phase I of EMDR (History Taking and Treatment Planning), we are essentially trying to get a lay of the land. Just like in roll call, we assess which parts are present and how they are influencing the veteran's emotional state. This initial check-in provides valuable information for the treatment process, allowing the therapist to map out the parts and experiences that need attention and to tailor the therapy accordingly. By integrating IFS and EMDR, veterans can better understand their internal system, leading to a more targeted and effective approach to healing.

Stand To (Parts on Alert)

"Stand to" is a command given to troops to be alert and ready for action. From a parts perspective, this can represent parts that have blended with the Self because they feel the need to protect in response to a perceived threat. Recognizing this can help in understanding the triggers and responses within the system.

Stand Down vs. Step Back

To "stand down" means the threat level has decreased. In IFS, this can be likened to asking a part to unblend. "Step back" signals that it's safe to relax; in IFS this might mean that Self-energy is present, and the part is no longer alone.

SOP (Standard Operating Procedure)

A "Standard Operating Procedure" (SOP) is a set of step-by-step instructions for carrying out a mission. In therapy, an SOP could be seen as a treatment plan—a structured approach to achieving therapeutic goals. We also have standard operating procedures for EMDR (i.e., the eight phases) as well as IFS (i.e., the six F's for getting to know a part, and the Syzygy Model's "Discovery" phase).

Doc

"Doc" is the term used in the military for a medical professional. Veterans might refer to their therapist as "Doc," regardless of the therapist's credentials, as a sign of respect and trust. This nickname reflects the role you play in their healing journey, similar to the role a medic would play in a military context.

Outside the Wire

"Outside the wire" means being beyond the safety of a secure area or base, where the risk of encountering the enemy is higher. In therapy, "outside the wire" could represent any place where a veteran feels unsafe or triggered—potentially even the therapist's office at first. Over time, as trust builds, the therapeutic space can become a safe haven, much like the group setting in my nature retreat.

MIA (Missing in Action)

"MIA" refers to someone who is missing and unaccounted for. In therapy, parts of the Self can feel MIA—disconnected or lost—especially when trauma has fragmented the sense of identity. Recognizing these MIA parts is the first step in bringing them back into the fold.

AWOL (Absent Without Leave)

"AWOL" means leaving one's post without permission. In therapy, this can symbolize parts that feel abandoned by the Self, leading to feelings of desertion and neglect. Understanding this dynamic can be crucial in addressing feelings of abandonment and betrayal within the internal system.

POW (Prisoner of War)

A "POW" is someone who has been captured and held in a prison camp. In IFS, our exiles can be seen as prisoners of war—trapped in painful memories and unable to function fully until they are rescued and reintegrated into the system.

Drafted

Parts can be "drafted" into roles they never asked for, much like how soldiers are conscripted into service. This often applies to firefighter parts, who step in to protect but might later be criticized or misunderstood. Acknowledging their sacrifices and the burdens they carry is a vital part of the healing process.

MST (Military Sexual Trauma)

"MST" stands for Military Sexual Trauma, a profound and often hidden issue that many veterans face. Recognizing the impact of MST and addressing it with sensitivity and care is essential in therapy.

Who's Got My Six?

This phrase means, "Who's got my back?" In therapy, this could mean identifying supportive parts or external allies who are there to help protect and guide the individual through their healing journey.

Chapter 17

Highly Sensitive People and the Healing Presence of Self

IFS–EMDR Integration in Practice

Elizabeth Venart

Reviewed by Nancy Simons, Crystal Whitlow, and Jane Gerhard

What Is High Sensitivity?

Psychologist and researcher Elaine Aron is largely credited with first identifying the trait of high sensitivity. Her book *The Highly Sensitive Person* (1996) illuminated an internal experience previously overlooked, mislabeled, and misunderstood. She confirmed that having a highly sensitive nervous system is normal, an innate biological trait, and is found in approximately 20% of the population (Aron & Aron, 1997; Pluess et al., 2023). High sensitivity is **not** a clinical diagnosis or deficit; rather, it exists in humans as well as hundreds of other species. Researchers believe the trait's abundant persistence is fundamental for herd survival.

Aron (2010) has identified four core attributes that comprise high sensitivity in the acronym DOES: *Depth of processing, over-arousability, emotional intensity, and sensory sensitivity* (p. 24). In *Sensitive* (2023), Jenn Granneman and Andrew Solo conclude that, at its core, high sensitivity is about environmental sensitivity and responsiveness. Highly sensitive people pick up more sensory information and process it more deeply. As a result, they are more likely to notice and react to environmental stimuli (such as bright lights, loud noises and music, strong fragrances or odors, and large crowds). They also feel deeply, pick up more emotional cues from the people around them, and are naturally empathic.

High sensitivity is different from introversion (with 30% of highly sensitive people being extroverts) and is equally common among women and men. High sensitivity is also distinguished from forms of neurodiversity like autism and ADHD; instead, a "spectrum of sensitivity" exists across all neurotypes (Nerenberg, 2020, p. 48). There is some debate about whether high sensitivity is considered neurodivergence. There is immense variability in our human population for how minds and sensory systems process information and experience the world. Historically, researchers have incorrectly concluded that traits found in the center of a given bell curve were "normal,"

DOI: 10.4324/9781003541554-21

while less common traits must be pathological. We have a responsibility to challenge that erroneous paradigm. Only then can we bring greater compassion and curiosity to our clients, learning directly from them how *they* experience the world.

In *Psychotherapy and the Highly Sensitive Person* (2010), Aron notes that while highly sensitive people comprise roughly 20% of the population, they comprise nearly 50% of all clients in therapy. She attributes this to several factors. First, sensitive children are impacted more negatively by toxic environments, leaving them more vulnerable to consequent anxiety, depression, and post-traumatic stress. Secondly, sensitive clients are likely to stay in therapy longer. Third, sensitive clients are deep thinkers often fascinated by psychology and curious to understand themselves well.

It is important to identify and highlight the **strengths** of high sensitivity, as many highly sensitive clients have internalized decades of derisive commentary about their way of being in the world. In addition to empathy, depth, and sensory intelligence, sensitive people are creative. They notice more nuances and details, make more connections, and are skilled at seeing multiple perspectives simultaneously. Their creativity can be demonstrated in their personal aesthetics, art and writing, flexible and innovative thinking, and creative problem-solving. They excel in careers that require emotional sensitivity, complex thinking, and the ability to notice and respond to subtleties. Unsurprisingly, a significant number of therapists are highly sensitive.

While clients may arrive in your office already knowing they are highly sensitive, many will not be familiar with the term. Discussing the trait, inquiring whether they feel it applies to them, and re-examining their lives through this lens can provide tremendous clarity and relief.

Identifying High Sensitivity in Clients

Sensitivity is an essential aspect of how people *experience* the world, but other variables impact how they *move* through it. These include the context of early and current lives, individual strengths, and necessary protections. No two highly sensitive people will present the same way.

Highly sensitive people benefit from emotionally intimate relationships, including therapy, where they feel safe to share their inner world and express themselves honestly. They feel deeply. In session, they may cry easily, react strongly, and find their emotions overwhelming. They may protectively avoid experiences likely to trigger big feelings, including violent movies, the news, and certain therapy topics. Alternatively, they may have strong protector parts that guard against emotion, presenting as overly intellectual or dissociative.

Acutely attuned to sensory stimuli, sensitives notice details others miss. This can create frustration in relationships and in work and home environments when others are less perceptive. Skilled at reading group dynamics and knowing how to increase the comfort in an environment, they can also become vigilant and drained in environments where they are unable to exert influence. They often describe feeling overstimulated—at work, socially, in crowds, in public—by environments that are loud, busy, and demanding. They are particularly distressed in situations where they feel pressured by deadlines, high levels of scrutiny, or being observed. To cope, they may need sensory breaks and downtime, take frequent naps, or yearn for quiet time alone at the end of the day. A busy day, even a fun one, often feels like too much.

They tend to be highly attuned to somatic cues from their bodies, sensitive to problems before medical testing even registers an issue. This can be mistaken by physicians as hypochondriasis. Instead, the sensitive person simply notices more. They are likely to experience subtle sensations others don't notice (for example, during scans using contrast dye) and report higher levels of pain. Similarly, they are often sensitive to the effects of caffeine, alcohol, drugs, and medications (including side effects).

Many are intuitive, insightful, and often spiritual, interested in existential questions around meaning. Consequently, they may struggle with small talk or doing routine tasks they find tedious and boring. They are also future-oriented and analytical—seeing ten steps ahead, asking why questions, and noticing trends. As a result, they are apt to worry about the future in its broadest terms, such as climate change, international politics, and patterns of oppression and injustice. They can become preoccupied by news of natural and man-made disasters—and stunned by others' apathy.

Many are conscientious researchers known for cautious, thorough decision-making. They may painstakingly weigh every choice, taking longer than most people to initiate change. Sensitives are often quite perfectionistic in their expectations of themselves and sensitive to criticism. Their thoughts may get stuck on replay, analyzing situations that ended poorly or resulted in negative feedback.

They sense the emotion and energy of those around them; as a result, they are easily impacted by others' moods. They often experience anxiety in the presence of conflict and actively work to avoid it, even when that means neglecting their own needs. They may also assume responsibility for helping those in pain—motivated by altruism as well as a desire to reduce the vicarious distress they feel.

The complete inventory and further descriptions can be found on Elaine Aron's website at https://hsperson.com/ and in the book *Sensitive* (2023).

The Clarifying Lens of IFS

Internal Family Systems provides a blueprint for understanding the highly sensitive clients that enter our offices and helping them to understand themselves.

While sensitivity itself is an inborn trait and not a part, a constellation of parts develop *in response to* the challenges of being highly sensitive. Sensitive children may describe feeling like a turtle without a shell or a radio antenna tuned into every station at once. They feel more intensely, react more strongly, and are more prone to overwhelm than their peers. They *need* protection. They need *protectors*. In supportive home and school environments, they may find some of that protection. They may learn skills and adaptations to navigate the world well. However, not all settings or people will be supportive. Since the majority of the world is not highly sensitive, they will invariably experience dissonance between their inner and outer worlds. *Why aren't other kids reacting to sirens and alarm bells? Why am I the only one crying?* Invariably, some inner protection will be necessary.

Reviewing Aron's sensitivity checklist with an eye toward parts, you may notice a commingling of inborn biological responses, patterns of protection, and positive qualities of Self-energy. Early discussions with clients about the trait and whether it describes their experience should keep this in mind. Clients who struggle with confidence may have difficulty giving themselves credit for their positive qualities. Those with highly developed intellectual and numbing parts may be so skilled at thwarting emotional reactivity that they are quick to reject the idea of sensitivity. However, when clients affirm the presence of the trait's four core qualities (sensory sensitivity, deep processing, deep feelings, and overarousal), stay curious. Not every sensitive person will respond in the same ways to their sensitivity. What they learned in their early environment about being sensitive will have a big impact on the jobs their protectors assumed to keep them safe.

While the internal family of each client is unique and the interrelationships among parts will vary, sensitive clients usually share the need for certain kinds of protection. This may include protection against big feelings, sensory overwhelm, confusion and powerlessness, and the empathic weight of others' emotions.

Common Reasons Sensitive People Seek Therapy—and Specifically EMDR Therapy

Because the trait of high sensitivity is not a clinical condition or mental health diagnosis, it is important to note that the focus of therapy should *not be* on solving the "problem" of sensitivity. This would be akin to responding to a tall person's complaints about their height by suggesting strategies to make themselves shorter.

Even so, sensitive people may seek therapy with an expressed desire to reduce their reactivity and overwhelm in the world. When they do, get curious about the specific problems described and *who* is holding that agenda to change. Is there a part that wishes they could be busier and push harder, without rest or consequence? Or a part that longs to fit in and hates the attention their sensitivity draws? They may embrace some aspects of their sensitivity, such as empathy, depth, and intellectual curiosity, but reject other aspects of the trait. Getting to know protector parts and the burdened beliefs they hold is where therapy begins.

While research shows that sensitive children actually excel more than their nonsensitive peers in nurturing families where their needs are met, they also suffer more significantly in misattuned or toxic environments (Belsky et al., 2007). Highly sensitive people rarely feel seen, heard, or helped by standard cognitive-behavioral techniques. They often seek EMDR therapy specifically for its promise of deep, transformative change. They want to get to the root of current struggles and process unresolved trauma; EMDR effectively does both (Shapiro, 2017).

IFS and the Therapeutic Alliance

In *Internal Family Systems Therapy*, Richard Schwartz (1995) revolutionized the way we conceptualize healing. He introduced a paradigm shift whereby the most essential relationship for therapeutic healing was no longer between therapist and client but rather between the client's Self and their parts. In *Internal Family Systems: New Dimensions*, Richard Schwartz (2013) clarified that the therapeutic relationship is actually foundational for the deep healing in IFS to occur. A therapist's ability to embody the eight C's and five P's of Self-energy creates the safety necessary for clients' protectors to trust it will be okay to unblend (see Chapter 2 for discussion on the eight C's and five P's). Further, when therapists genuinely convey acceptance for *all* parts, they model compassion even for those a client's system has labeled as "bad," "shameful," or "dangerous." The therapist's compassionate Self-energy can "seep through the cracks into all levels of the [client's] internal system" (Schwartz, 2013, p. 5).

Building a strong therapeutic alliance with highly sensitive clients requires honoring the needs of their sensory systems. Accustomed to environments where they feel overstimulated, they may or may not express their needs directly. Therapists can inquire about their responses to the physical setting and anything they might need. Examples may include a mug of tea, a soft blanket, dimmer lighting, and a space free of strong fragrances or loud noises. Vigilant protectors within the system are likely to relax when they receive this consideration.

Sensitive clients process deeply. In therapy, they may process in silence for long periods. Silences can offer a productive time for processing, but they may also indicate distress, overwhelm, and an attempt to self-soothe. Seventy percent of highly sensitive people are also introverts, so prolonged silence may stem from their difficulty putting internal experiences into words (Aron,

1996). Some sensitive clients are external processors who may speak at length and in detail to share their reflections, connections, and concerns. Interrupting sensitive clients when they are deep in silent thought or in the midst of an impassioned monologue can prove fraught. They may feel the interruption thwarts their ability to process or inhibits their full expression. Check in with your own parts to make sure your intervention is Self-led. When it is, be mindful that your offering is an invitation, not a requirement. Welcome feedback from their parts and Self about how you can best support them.

Sensitive clients are like tuning forks for others' emotions. As such, they are skilled at discerning incongruence between words, actions, and emotions. This includes an ability to read their therapists. They thrive in therapeutic relationships where they can speak candidly about what they are "picking up" in therapists' nonverbal behavior and trust therapists will respond authentically.

Sensitive clients may have learned to make themselves likable as a primary form of protection against anticipated rejection and abandonment. This can impact their willingness to give constructive feedback in therapy. Before any significant pivot points or transitions in the therapy work, it is important to invite forward any parts that may have concerns. When the client is routinely agreeable, get curious about whether any of your own parts may have taken the lead. *Who* in you are they deferring to? *Who* in them feels they must? Parts concerned about offending or alienating you will be important early targets in the work.

Using IFS-Informed EMDR with Highly Sensitive People

The Syzygy Model of IFS-Informed EMDR (see Chapter 6) provides a full integration of IFS and EMDR. Respecting the complexity of highly sensitive clients' protective systems, its gentle pacing is an ideal fit for highly sensitive clients.

Phase 1: Welcoming Parts, History Taking, and Establishing the Frame

The Phase 1 tasks of identifying goals and gathering history will automatically bring forward parts. Getting to know parts and helping them feel welcome is our primary focus.

When sensitive clients have an attitude of acceptance and appreciation for their trait, they are more likely to make requests that honor their needs and nervous system. This could include asking for silence, pausing to drink tea, and taking any necessary breaks to regulate. However, when parts carry burdened beliefs about sensitivity, they may neither be aware of their needs nor willing to express them. Polarizations are common. You may sense the eagerness of a growth-oriented protector wanting to start trauma work quickly and then encounter a part who slams the brakes, because it is intensely focused on understanding the mechanics of EMDR. Spend time connecting with each protector in the polarizations that surface. What is its positive intent? We can trust that the protectors coming forward are not an obstacle but the path.

Also consider the frame of therapy that will best support healing. It is important that the container for the work be spacious enough for the emergence of Self-energy. Sensitive people often have parts that get activated by any sense of feeling rushed, so the standard 45–50-minute session may be too short. Longer sessions provide more time for deep processing, and for pausing, reflecting, being curious, and integrating learning. Longer sessions can also include creative activities to support processing (art, journaling, use of miniatures, meditation, drumming, etc.). Sensitive clients also benefit from focused attention on transitions—how the session starts and ends, and ways to buffer the session with additional time for reflection. Working in an intensive format (3–6 hours in a day) can provide a powerful corrective experience for sensitive clients: *With adequate space and support, I can be present with my pain and heal.*

Phase 2: IFS-Informed EMDR Tools for Resourcing Self-Energy

The core focus in Phase 2 is strengthening access to Self-energy. Highly sensitive people are deep, empathic, and insightful, and, as a consequence, they usually arrive to therapy with an eagerness to learn, process, and grow. Their natural strengths include many qualities of Self (such as perspective, clarity, and compassion), and this is a tremendous resource for their EMDR therapy work.

As clients demonstrate qualities of Self (the eight C's and five P's) in session, therapists can name and focus on them. This simple act of drawing attention to the organic emerging of Self helps amplify it. Historically, sensitive clients' qualities of compassion and patience may have been used in service of supporting others. As they discover that they can access these qualities to support their own healing, it can be transformative.

For some clients, it can be helpful to spend time identifying explicit memories of embodied Self-energy. Invite them to remember times when they experienced one or more of the eight C's, especially courage, confidence, creativity, or calm. These memories may provide a useful shortcut to anchor Self-energy during processing, if needed.

Sensitive clients have often been seekers from a young age. They may be avid readers of self-help and philosophy books, practice yoga and meditation, and have robust spiritual practices. Their parts may already possess a plethora of strategies that calm and contain their distress. As a result, a traditional EMDR Phase 2—with its focus on a safe place, container, and allies—may come very easily. While Self-energy is present, it may also be mixed with the healing agenda of parts that seek to soothe and comfort. Often blended, they are unaware that there is a healing presence beyond them. Working with these parts, through the *Discovery process*, facilitates their connection with the innate, boundless presence of the client's Self (see Chapter 7). This connection is often a pivotal turning point. These helpers may continue to stay close, but once they trust the existence of Self, they become a strong ally for healing.

Phase 3: Selecting Assessment Targets and Identifying Target Parts

The EMDR target will always be a part, and the assessment phase helps us determine if it is an exile or protector. It may have a specific memory as its focus, or it may share a collage of experiences central to its burdened feelings and beliefs. While therapists may be used to targeting vulnerable child parts at the center of a burdened system, this is not always possible or advisable. Gathering elements for the assessment phase requires clarity on who the biggest part is *at this moment* and having access to enough Self-energy to insure functional dual attention (see Chapter 6).

As you ask questions in assessment, listen for *who* is giving the answers. Keep in mind that sensitive clients likely have a strong team of helper parts skilled at advocating on behalf of younger ones. They may also have perfectionist parts determined to answer *correctly*. Self already knows the positive belief and that it is true. When it is difficult for clients to imagine believing anything positive, Self-presence is not yet strong enough. It is important to move through the assessment phase slowly enough to allow time for protector concerns to be addressed and to pivot to a different target part when necessary. When curious, patient, and Self-led, therapists create enough safety for the organic direction of the client's system to become evident.

Gathering sensory data in the assessment phase may unintentionally trigger protectors unrelated to the initial target. Because their sensitive nervous systems were prone to overwhelm from birth, many sensitive clients have protectors that instinctively disconnect them from their bodies. They may also have cognitive protectors that learned to minimize their pain. Noticing their feelings and body sensations may feel intrinsically fraught. When protectors arise in response to these assessment questions, they become the focus. If their concerns aren't addressed and burdened beliefs remain, future processing work will likely stall.

Phase 4: Interweaves to Maintain Connection Between Self and Part

The focus in Phase 4 is to facilitate the client's deepening relationship between Self and target part. All interweaves stem from that awareness.

If there is already a strong connection between Self and part, processing may flow easily, and there may be little need for therapist interweaves. For sensitive clients who may have difficulty attuning to themselves in the presence of another person (in this case, the therapist), silence may be preferred. It may provide the space necessary to listen deeply to their parts.

Therapists' primary role during processing is to attend to their own parts so they can remain Self-led. Be mindful of any parts in your own system that may feel a sense of pressure or panic when you are unsure what is happening in the client's system. It is okay to check in periodically with clients to ensure the connection between part and Self is still strong; however, if this is too frequent, it may disrupt the work. Sensitive clients are emotionally responsive and may shift their attention to you.

Processing is effective to the extent that the client is able to stay in their Window of Tolerance (see Chapter 1). When we have functional dual attention (part and Self present and in connection), clients remain within their window. When the target part is an exile, protectors are often nearby, closely monitoring the system for signs of overwhelm. Consider the "interference" of protectors as a flashing red light that arousal may be increasing. It provides an opportunity to hear any concerns, check for Self-presence, and suggest practices to help mitigate emotional overwhelm as necessary.

When emotions become too strong and threaten to overwhelm the system, it is helpful to shift the focus to body sensations as a natural way to regulate emotions (McConnell, 2020). The practice of *noticing* physical sensations can support the client in unblending enough for the curiosity and compassion of Self to re-emerge. Therapists can invite dual awareness to help clients navigate emotional overwhelm by suggesting:

Continue to stay connected to this part with its distress. Simultaneously, notice your physical presence in the room at this moment: the natural rhythm of breath in and out, feet on the floor, sitting bones on the surface beneath you.

This can invite a sense of calm that makes it possible for clients to continue witnessing the part's story in whatever way it wishes to express itself. To encourage connection, therapists may ask clients to notice the size, depth, color, movement, energy, and direction of sensations. McConnell emphasizes that "the answers are less important than whether or not they help the client stay engaged with the sensation" (2020, p. 67).

For some sensitive clients, empathy for others can create a block to processing. They may feel unable to leave or resolve a situation without first attending to the hurt of others. Empathic since birth, their pull to help can be strong. The urge may belong to the target part or a nearby helper. Either way, therapists can invite the possibility of imaginal resources to support the other person (such as an ally, protector, or nurturing figure). Once addressed, parts typically relax and can shift their attention back to their own experience.

Sometimes concerns arise that Self will not be able to handle the intensity of what the part might share. When this happens, get curious about *who* is voicing the concern and also about *who* they see when they look at Self. Are they seeing the client as they are today? Or are they looking at a younger part? While sometimes parts need updating, sometimes their caution indicates that another, undetected part is present. Protectors often travel in pairs. As the cautious part shares what it fears would happen if it loosened its grip on the wheel, you may discover that its gaze is fixed on a part that it *believes* is Self. Its caution is often warranted, as that part may be blocking full access to Self. As clients get to know both parts in the polarization and parts feel seen, it invariably welcomes new perspective and ease. As the flow of Self-energy strengthens, processing can continue.

Sensitive children's natural empathy may make them especially vulnerable to legacy burdens. They absorb pain, both from stories told and the ways ancestors still carry burdens of terror, mistrust, rage, shame, and helplessness. During processing, listen to the perspectives offered by parts as they share family, ancestral, and cultural stories. Consider the possibility that, in addition to the pain directly experienced, they may be carrying some burdens that don't actually belong to them.

Phases 5 Through 8: Slow, Steady, and Centered

Throughout the process, the therapist's mindful attunement to Self-presence creates an experience of spaciousness and flow. This gentle pacing is an excellent fit for sensitive clients. When clients maintain connection with Self throughout the first four phases, the final phases in EMDR (installation of the positive cognition, body scan, closure) and IFS (witnessing, retrieval, unburdening) occur organically. Before closing the session, be sure to check with other parts that surfaced and to provide clients with enough time to discuss their experience or sit in silence to digest it. Clients may appreciate an opportunity to write down notes about the work, so that they remember to circle back and connect with parts between sessions. Sensitive clients often report vivid dreams and significant processing between sessions. Re-evaluation provides an opportunity to honor this work and continue building upon part-to-Self connections made.

For highly sensitive people I have found IFS-Informed EMDR (particularly the Syzygy Model, see Chapter 6) to bring significant clarity and advantages to therapy. When targets shift or processing loops, we know parts likely have stepped forward. This approach honors the complexity of the sensitive person's internal family as adaptive. It emphasizes that connection with Self-energy is foundational for trauma healing. It also provides an informed, compassionate way to befriend protectors through the process of Discovery (see Chapter 7). Perhaps most importantly, it is a respectful approach that trusts the system of parts to guide the path to healing. It also paces the work in a way that promotes safety, ensuring clients can more easily stay within their Window of Tolerance. Overwhelm is a large concern for sensitive clients, so the Syzygy mantra "slower is faster" brings welcome relief that big feelings will not take over. The core message to clients is "I trust the innate wisdom of your system." Our calm and compassionate confidence in the Self-energy of sensitive clients creates the necessary foundation for healing.

References

Aron, E. (1996). *The highly sensitive person.* Birch Lane Press.

Aron, E. (2010). *Psychotherapy and the highly sensitive person: Improving outcomes for that minority of people who are the majority of clients.* Routledge.

Aron, E., & Aron, A. (1997). Sensory-processing sensitivity and its relation to introversion and emotionality. *Journal of Personality and Social Psychology, 73*, 345–368.

Belsky, J., Bakermans-Kranenburg, M. J., & van IJzendoorn, M. H. (2007). For better and for worse: Differential susceptibility to environmental influences. *Current Directions in Psychological Science, 16*(6), 300–304.

Granneman, J., & Solo, A. (2023). *Sensitive: The hidden power of the highly sensitive person in a loud, fast, too-much world.* Harmony Books.

McConnell, S. (2020). *Somatic Internal Family Systems Therapy: Awareness, breath, resonance, movement, and touch in practice.* North Atlantic Books.

Nerenberg, J. (2020). *Divergent mind: Thriving in a world that wasn't designed for you.* Harper One.

Pluess, M., Lionetti, F., Aron, E., & Aron, A. (2023). People differ in their sensitivity to the environment: An integrated theory, measurement, and empirical evidence. *Journal of Research in Personality, 104*, 1–12.

Schwartz, R. C. (2013). The therapist-client relationship and the transformative power of self. In M. Sweezy & E. Ziskind (Eds.), *Internal family systems therapy: New dimensions.* Routledge.

Schwartz, Richard C. (1995). *Internal family systems therapy.* The Guilford Press.

Shapiro, F. (2017). *Eye movement desensitization and reprocessing (EMDR) Therapy: Basic principles, protocols, and procedures* (3rd ed.). Guilford.

Chapter 18

An Integrated Approach to Healing

How Blending Warrior Goddess Empowerment with IFS and EMDR Facilitates Deep Healing for Women

Bethany Barta

As a woman of European descent with ancestral roots in the British Isles, Germany, and Czech lands, I want to acknowledge the deep well of indigenous wisdom that informs many of the practices I draw from. My intention is never to appropriate the sacred traditions of cultures that are not my own, but rather to honor them with deep respect and reverence.

I recognize the historical and ongoing harm caused by colonization, including the suppression, commodification, and misrepresentation of indigenous spiritual practices. I make every effort to approach these teachings with humility, to credit the origins of the traditions I reference, and to continue learning about the cultural, historical, and spiritual contexts from which they come.

In honoring the wisdom of other cultures, I also continue to explore and reclaim the earth-based and ancestral spiritual traditions of my own lineage, seeking to reconnect with the indigenous roots of Europe that have often been forgotten or erased.

Burdens Women Carry

Many women[1] show up in our therapy offices expressing a sense of disconnect from themselves. We hear them say some version of "I don't know who I am anymore" or "I've lost myself in my relationship." Being disconnected from a sense of self can lead to emotional numbness, loss of identity, inner conflict, feeling directionless, and a profound disconnection from one's body. Women experiencing this disconnection often struggle to identify their emotions and connect to their felt sense, which can lead to confusion about who they are, what they want, and what their life purpose is. This detachment can result in pervasive self-doubt, harsh self-criticism, and low self-esteem, making decision-making challenging and leaving them feeling helpless and confused, worried, and sick from chronic health problems. Mental health struggles such as depression, anxiety, and dissociative disorders are common in women who

DOI: 10.4324/9781003541554-22

feel disconnected from themselves. This is especially true for our clients who have experienced severe attachment wounding leading to Complex Post-Traumatic Stress Disorder (CPTSD) (see Chapter 14). I am passionate about helping women find healing and resolution, and I have found that the most effective practices often integrate elements of nature. In my work, I integrate awareness of women's minds, bodies, and emotions, as well as their spiritual and energetic being.

We are all connected and part of a greater energy field that moves through us and links us to the natural world. To me, Western psychology alone cannot fully address the depth of human experience without embracing the spiritual realm, which includes our energetic body and an awareness of something greater than ourselves. Almaas (2000) suggests that while Western psychology focuses on healing and personality integration, Eastern spirituality emphasizes transcending the ego and realizing a deeper state of being. By combining Western with Eastern spirituality, we can find a more holistic path to well-being, emotional regulation, and resilience (Miller, 2021).

Warrior Goddess Empowerment[2]

Warrior Goddess Training: Become the Woman You Are Meant to Be is a book and program based on earth-based spirituality, ancient yogic philosophy, and Toltec philosophy. I have integrated this model with IFS and EMDR to help women feel more connected, whole, and empowered in their lives. Many women present in therapy feeling disconnected because they've been primarily focused on meeting the expectations of partners, caregivers, children, coworkers, and bosses, along with pursuing societal developmental goals. This intense focus on external demands can cause them to lose sight of their own desires, needs, and preferences.

In the workshops, retreats, and group therapy I facilitate, we discuss how "domestication" leads to a painful disconnection from a woman's sense of self. We can view this domestication as cultural and familial burdens that keep negative cognitions—disparaging beliefs women have about themselves—wrapped in shame, and often the heavy energy of shame gets trapped inside women's bodies. Across cultures, women have carried deep-rooted burdens shaped by traditions, societal roles, and patriarchy. In many places, they've been treated as property, denied choices, and expected to shrink themselves to fit expectations. While Western cultures often push people-pleasing, fawning, and self-silencing as survival strategies, other cultures enforce strict rules around modesty, obedience, or putting family and community above all else. These patterns get passed down through generations, shaping how women see themselves and their power.

Carrying these cultural burdens can lead to chronic stress, anxiety, and a disconnection from one's true self, as survival patterns override authentic expression. When women are weighed down by these inherited expectations, it can be difficult to access Self-energy (see Chapter 2), the inner wisdom, clarity, and confidence that allows for true healing and empowerment. Recognizing and releasing these burdens creates space for greater mental well-being, self-trust, and the ability to lead life from a place of strength rather than fear.

Preparing Women for Deeper Trauma Healing

In the beginning of my group, I guide everyone through a type of history-taking, exploring the agreements and cognitive beliefs they have adopted that have resulted in losing connection with their true selves. Additionally, we create space for other struggles the women might be dealing with, which might include: Feelings of loneliness, a sense of inadequacy from being spread too thin, and the experience of shame and embarrassment related to not knowing their true selves. The participants frequently share that they are trapped in comparison, which has led to a sense of failure, and the thought, "Everyone else has it figured out while I am merely floundering." This might result in the development of unhealthy self-soothing strategies (in IFS we call them firefighters) such as abusing alcohol, drugs, food, sex, or other compulsive behaviors.

Establishing a container of safety and trust, within oneself and among the group, is a focus throughout the group process. Every session begins with grounding participants in the natural and unseen world of allies and guides. We stand together, turning to face each of the cardinal directions, consciously connecting with the four elements—air, fire, water, and earth—inviting in the animals, guides, and Self-energy qualities each represents.

Additionally, incorporating breath and sound fosters a sense of safety, connection, and regulation (Dana & Porges, 2021). This might include chanting, singing, and breathwork, as direct pathways to self-regulation and Self-energy. This not only soothes the nervous system but also deepens cohesion among participants, uniting them through shared rhythm and voice. In addition to connecting with one another, the group members are also cultivating a mind-body-spirit connection, as they attune to their own internal experience. During group sharing and discussion, I help participants turn inward by asking questions like, "What am I feeling?" and "Where do I sense this in my body?" This supports the practice of unblending by helping participants step back from parts that want to caretake, fix, or give advice, and instead turn their attention inward toward their emotional responses and bodily sensations. To support deeper self-connection, we use bilateral stimulation (BLS) (see Chapter 1) to help anchor positive emotions and new insights in the body.

I invite participants to deepen integration by incorporating creative expression through crafts and art-making, a practice women have shared for generations. Together, we create vision boards and art to reinforce connection, self-expression, and healing. One of our practices involves co-creating a collaborative art piece on a large sheet of paper, allowing each participant to contribute their unique expression to a shared visual experience. As we connect with our root chakra (see reference to energy work below), we sit in a circle and draw images and symbols that represent inner safety, security, and a grounded sense of connection to the earth. Throughout this process, participants are invited to connect with ancestors as guides to help provide inspiration and insight.

An Awareness of Goddess Warrior/Self-Energy

Early on, we speak about the IFS concept of Self-energy (see Chapter 2), with the intention of relating to ourselves from a place of curiosity, calmness, confidence, and compassion. We explore protector parts that might be present, who prioritize approval and belonging over authenticity. I share with the women:

The drive for acceptance and belonging is a natural part of human development, deeply rooted in evolutionary psychology. Historically, survival depended on being part of a social group—those who were excluded or rejected faced significant risks, much like being thrown out of the cave, which could result in significant danger or even death. Over time, this survival mechanism became ingrained in human behavior, conditioning us to prioritize external approval over our own needs and desires. This process is further reinforced by historical and intergenerational trauma, where cultural expectations, gender roles, and survival-based adaptations are passed down through generations, shaping how we relate to ourselves and the world.

We discuss how protective parts emerge with extreme strategies, such as the inner critic and the perfectionist, among others, to keep us safe. These protective adaptations are often reinforced by intergenerational wounds, such as patriarchal conditioning, racial oppression (see Chapter 10), and systemic traumas that have shaped survival strategies for centuries. By recognizing these patterns not just as individual responses but as part of a larger collective and ancestral inheritance, we create a deeper foundation for understanding where to begin our healing, opening space for more self-compassion, more self-leadership, and reclaiming our true essence.

This all provides a context for how growing up in a chaotic, stressful home—marked by inconsistency, emotional or physical neglect, and abuse—layered with intergenerational and historical trauma might contribute to extreme strategies of protection and survival. It also offers participants a powerful reframe for their experiences: These patterns were adaptive survival responses shaped by many factors (see Chapter 9).

With this awareness, participants are invited to explore some of their "parts" such as "the perfect mother," "the ideal employee," or "the devoted partner"—roles that often overshadow their true desires and personal aspirations. Reconnecting with their authentic selves requires identifying these roles and understanding the protective strategies and positive intentions behind them. The goal is to compassionately connect with these parts, while accessing a deeper sense of Self. From this place, women can find a more balanced relationship between connection with others and staying true to themselves, shifting from seeking external validation to living in alignment with their inner truth.

The Warrior Goddess/Self is a sacred, whole, and untarnished inner guide that holds the power to provide healing. This vision offers group members a clear and embodied sense of something within them that they will connect with during this experience. We explore warrior energy of developing clear intentions, holding courage and confidence to take the next right step, and perseverance in the face of obstacles (which align with the eight C's in IFS). When this energy is unbalanced, extreme managerial strategies show up, such as perfectionism, overachievement, hyper-independence, and a drive for control. When reclaimed and integrated, healthy warrior energy fuels clarity, courage, and aligned action in the world.

Unbalanced goddess energy can lead to enmeshment, poor boundaries, and toxic empathy. Toxic empathy, or hyper-empathy syndrome, is particularly relevant here, as it leads individuals to prioritize others' needs over their own, often feeling responsible for fixing or saving others. While the instinct to support and nurture is natural, we find this excessive overextension diminishes self-care and personal well-being—and in addition to being incredibly draining, it is almost always ineffective as well. Balanced goddess energy, in its Self-led form, is expressed through qualities like compassion, connectedness, creativity, and curiosity. It offers a deep well of presence, receptivity, and intuition which is grounded in inner knowing rather than self-sacrifice. When we invite this energy into the system consciously, it helps soothe overburdened parts and restores a sense of internal balance, making space for the wholeness we are seeking.

Resource Development and Installation[3]

Nurturing and protective allies are a powerful resource tool that we can offer women, who often express frustration and grief over the absence of strong nurturing role models or guides in their lives. Participants are invited to identify a figure that embodies the qualities they would like to access in themselves. When this is not available in their life, they can choose someone from their past, whether living or deceased, or they could select a character from a book or movie, a historical or spiritual figure, or even an animal that embodies the energy they wish to cultivate.

We can also cultivate the positive qualities we observe in the natural world. As we align more fully with nature and deepen our connection to something greater than ourselves, we begin to attune to the steady power of the ocean's vastness and the quiet harmony found in a grove of trees. In this process, participants will begin to reclaim a felt sense of belonging—to themselves, to the earth, and the larger rhythms of life.

This sense of disconnection from nature didn't happen all at once. It's likely the result of many cultural shifts layered over time. One early thread may come from the biblical story of Adam and Eve, in which humanity is cast out of the garden and must work to tame the earth and their own desires to regain divine favor (Kimmerer, 2015). This narrative casts nature as something separate, even dangerous, and something to be conquered rather than communed with.

The transition from nomadic, hunter-gatherer communities to agrarian societies also played a role (Harari, 2014). As humans began settling and cultivating land, we grew more dependent on controlling environmental conditions. Droughts, floods, and other natural forces became threats to survival, which likely deepened a mindset of fear and control toward the natural world.

Added to this is the cultural emphasis on extreme expressions of "masculine" qualities—rationality, productivity, dominance—while emotional attunement, embodiment, and relational wisdom were devalued. In many ways, wisdom became equated with detachment: From our bodies, our emotions, and the earth itself.

And yet, nature continues to invite us back. Through the language of wind, water, trees, and honoring cyclical living, we're reminded of our place within, not outside of, the living world. By "reclaiming" our sacred feminine energy, honoring our bodies and emotions, and living in harmony with the natural world, our bodies and the natural environment can be experienced as sacred guides and allies for us on our journey.

The Tree Meditation

The Tree Meditation is a great example of how nature can be brought into the work to support women.

We start by entering into a communal space, where there is multisensory input present, such as the steady rhythm of a drum or the grounding scent of incense. We can say to the group:

As we experience this meditation together, allow your intuitive imagination and energy to lead you wherever it wants to go. If it feels right, just notice any of your body sensations, emotions, words, or thoughts.

To start, I invite you to take three long, deep breaths. Visualize or feel yourself standing somewhere in nature; it can be real or imagined. Notice the colors and textures your eyes take in. Take in the sounds around you. Are there bird sounds, leaves rustling? Notice what you are feeling, such as the ground beneath you, or the wind, or the sun's warmth. What smells are around you? Notice what you taste in your mouth.

Now that we are here in nature, let's imagine that you see a beautiful tree in front of you. Walk toward this tree, and allow it to get bigger and bigger. Notice its bark, the branches, the leaves. As you approach the tree, you can reach out and touch it—see how it feels on your skin. You make out a door in the trunk of the tree, and as you touch this, it turns into a large opening. You can step into the tree. Feel yourself entering the tree.

As you enter fully into the tree, notice how you can feel your body expanding and becoming the tree. Your legs and feet start to grow, going deeply down into the earth as your roots. Your chest and abdomen, and all of your organs, are the long trunk of the tree. Your arms, hands, fingers, and head reach up and out in all directions toward the sky, and become the branches and leaves.

As you breathe, feel your breath coming in through the leaves and branches, and going all the way down the trunk and into the roots of the tree. Have your breath connect with all of the earth's qualities: The feminine, the sacred mother, compassion, love, abundance, creation/creativity, grounded presence, compassion, nurturing. Check inside to see if any other qualities are showing up for you. Breathe in all of these wonderful qualities through your entire being.

Reach your branches and leaves out just a little more, and expand into the open sky above, where you can feel the light and warmth of the sun. Feel the sky and sun's qualities of: Compassion, clarity, expansion and openness, spaciousness, persistence, courage, or confidence. Check if any other qualities are showing up and resonating within you. Breathe in all of these qualities through your entire being, and feel this energy flowing into every cell of your body. Allow yourself to become a vessel, as all of these qualities move through you.

Notice what is happening inside your body. Is there a word that describes what you are experiencing? Do 10 slow butterfly taps back and forth, focusing on the word and positive sensations you are experiencing. Allow the feeling to grow as you tap.

Allow the participants to sit with their experience. When they are ready, they can write down what words came up for them and whatever else they would like to take with them from this experience. After the meditation, we move into partner-sharing to reflect on and integrate the experience further.

Elemental Visualization

Another way that the natural world could provide powerful resources for women is in the "Elemental visualization" where we facilitate connection with the four basic elements—Air, Fire, Water, and Earth. Below, I explore some of my thoughts on how each of these elements can represent different qualities of Self/Warrior Goddess energy with the group:

- **Earth** is connected to the physical body, representing: Groundedness, Strength, and Abundance.
- **Air** is connected to the mind, representing: Clarity, Insight, and Perspective.
- **Water** is connected to emotions, representing: Flow, Release, and Adaptability.
- **Fire** is connected to the energetic spirit, representing: Passion, Motivation, Creativity, and Transformation.

Then, participants are guided through the following elemental visualization by saying:

I invite you to take a moment to consider each of the elements and connect with them on a deep level. You may invite your observing Self to notice whatever is coming up inside in this present moment. Your imagination can be your guide on this journey.

We repeat the following paragraph four times, each time exploring a different element: Air, Fire, Water, and Earth.

We will begin with the element of _____. How does this element show up for you? Can you feel it, touch it, sense its power around you? See if it takes on any form. Does it arrive as an animal or any other being? Allow a symbol or image to come to you. Listen closely and see what you notice. Welcome this element to share any wisdom it has with you at this moment. Let it feel your curiosity, and see how it reacts to this. Notice if there is anything that it wants to communicate. How does it feel toward you? If it feels right, you can ask it for guidance, especially with something specific you may be dealing with. Notice how it responds. Notice what happens in your body, and how your body reacts to the connection with this element. Invite it to become an ally for you, and see how it responds to this request. Notice any changes that might be happening inside you as you continue to connect with this element. Ask the element anything that you would like, and notice the response. When you feel ready, send appreciation to this element. If you are experiencing any new positive sensations or awarenesses, tap in (with BLS) any of the positive feelings that you had during this experience. Take time to write down any words, feelings, thoughts, or symbols that came to you.

After repeating this with each of the elements, we return to the group and share whatever came up for the participants.

As we help women deepen their connection with nature and their authentic Self, through different experiences such as the Tree Meditation and the Elemental Visualization, we help them connect to something greater than themselves. They are able to anchor into positive feeling states and rewire a new way of being in relationship with themselves and nature.

The Energy Inside of Us

True energetic purification means tending to all parts of ourselves—body, heart, mind, and spirit—so we can reclaim our full vitality and power. It invites women to come home to their energy, to notice where it flows and where it feels stuck, and to gently begin clearing what no longer serves. We use the map of the chakra system, developed in India, as a guide to connect to the energy flowing in and around the body.

They can reclaim this energy and power by looking at their life's challenges with curiosity. These challenges are doorways to healing, or as we say in IFS, "trailheads." When we become aware of the thoughts, feelings, sensations, and images that arise when we are activated, we are becoming more aware of "parts" that are protecting us, and the exiles they are focused on. These parts have noble intentions, which usually center around survival of the system; however, they sometimes also have roles in the system that take up a great amount of energy.

Some parts of us—like the inner judge, the victim, or the blamer—can hold a lot of our energy hostage, keeping it tangled in patterns of shame, fear, or blame. When participants acknowledge these parts as protective mechanisms guarding the pain of past hurts, they can offer loving witnessing, unblend from them and start befriending these parts. Through building this relationship with the parts, we can move into an ancient healing practice known as recapitulation.

Recapitulation

Recapitulation is rooted in the spiritual and shamanic concept that every interaction we've had with others and each memory we hold onto, has a piece of our personal energy. Every time we replay a memory, we invest energy to keep it alive, maintaining the emotions tied to that encounter. Recapitulation involves revisiting past experiences and reclaiming the energy that may have been lost or fragmented during those events. By consciously recalling and reprocessing these memories, we can retrieve and reintegrate our energy, leading to greater personal power and wholeness. As we revisit these earlier life experiences, we can also integrate new understandings and relationships with those experiences (in EMDR terms, we are desensitizing them and then installing new beliefs about them). To bring this to a group we could say:

In this next exercise, we will go back to a previous event in our lives as a witness, with love and forgiveness. We want to pick an event that is still "charged" without picking something too painful. We want to avoid moments that still cause powerful emotions, because then we might just relive the moment or start judging or reanalyzing the situation. Once we have an appropriate event, we can move to the first step.

1   ***Set your intent on why you want to create more energy in your life.*** *You might want to have more energy to create more connections with others in your life, be less angry, or increase your ability to remain calm when you are feeling activated in relationship with your children/partner/ parents.*

2   ***Connect your will to a higher energy source.*** *Identify your higher energy source, such as the sun, earth or God as you know it, and then imagine a cord connecting your solar plexus with this higher power.*

3   ***Sitting or lying comfortably, let your mind go back to this event.*** *See the circumstances, people, and places as clearly as possible, without getting attached to the emotional aspects of each scene. Breathe back your energy from this scene by either visualizing your energy returning to you or feeling the energy coming into your body—or both. Make your breath audible. You can imagine yourself as a vacuum cleaner, inhaling your energy out of the scene. Pay attention to which part of your body you are feeling the energy coming back into. Do not get caught in analyzing. Simply breathe in your energy.*

4   ***Breathe out any energy you took from someone else.*** *If you feel judgmental or angry, shift to another memory. When you are in a memory and you feel connected to your Warrior Goddess energy enough (or your Higher power) that you are feeling compassionate and forgiving, imagine breathing in your energy and breathing back out any energy you may have taken in that does not belong to you. If you feel that you sent out some negative energy in the past, you can practice breathing this in and then breathing it down into the earth beneath you and letting the earth transform this old energy.*

5   ***When you feel complete, take three deep breaths and visualize that you are using light to clear out anything that does not belong to you in this moment.*** *Release your connection to your Higher power, and if it feels right for you, offer appreciation to your Higher power for any support it provided during this experience.*

Shields

Similar to EMDR strategies, there are also containment tools, in the form of energetic shields. These tools are effective for self-regulation and developing energetic boundaries. Energetic shielding is especially beneficial for women who are sensitive to energy and easily absorb other people's emotions. By learning to create a protective boundary between their energy and the energy of others, participants can prevent feeling overwhelmed or emotionally drained. This is vital for those in caregiving or therapeutic roles, where absorbing others' emotional burdens can lead to confusion about which feelings are truly their own.

Establishing an energetic shield allows women to maintain emotional clarity, distinguishing their own feelings from those of others, reducing empathic distress, and preserving their well-being. When women consistently protect their energy, they gain more control over their emotional state and build greater confidence in setting both energetic and relational boundaries.

A powerful shield is the "invisible cloak." By using their imagination, women can visualize a cloak around them, protecting them from absorbing others' thoughts, feelings, and emotions. This practice supports the development of differentiation, leading to a stronger sense of self. Other examples might include wetsuits or an iridescent bubble that offers protection. When we shield ourselves from taking on others' energy, we can also stay attuned to our own energy.

Deep Healing

Through this group experience, women become ready to embark on the next phase of their trauma journey. If we are using the map of EMDR, this group focuses primarily on resourcing (Phase 2). If we are using the IFS map, this group aligns with IFS unblending steps. Different "parts" of participants are recognized, appreciated, and connected with Self-energy—or, in the words of this group, with their "warrior goddess energy." Guides and allies, particularly ones found in nature, are invited into this healing space. Through these guides' assistance and love, women are able to reclaim and protect their own inner energy.

Deep awareness and alignment of our energy body is often ignored or left out of the Western, traditional therapy room. In this group, participants are supported to notice blocks, heaviness, and emotional activations, which can all become trailheads for ways that energy has been absorbed by something else. As participants deepen their understanding of the experiences and relationships that have impacted their energy system, they also begin to recognize the internal patterns and beliefs that allow these dynamics to persist. They might uncover blended parts carrying old burdens (as we explore in IFS), or notice trauma memories surfacing—offering potential targets for deeper healing work with EMDR. As these layers are acknowledged and cleared—whether through therapy or through the recapitulation process described in this chapter—energy that was once bound up begins to return to the system and allow for more internal harmony and peace.

When this group is completed, a community is established and participants are encouraged to continue to meet as a group and continue the healing journey together. It has been amazing to see how transformational these groups have been, and then to witness women starting brand-new businesses, returning to school, ending toxic relationships, healing wounds from the past, and opening themselves up to living from a whole new paradigm. This sometimes even leads the women to seek out IFS-Informed EMDR therapy to continue the journey that they have started here.

Notes

1 When I refer to "women" in this chapter, I am referring to anyone who is female identified or gender-fluid—however, it is important to note the false simplicity of masculine vs. feminine, and limited binary definitions of each.
2 This group draws heavily on concepts from IFS, EMDR, and Warrior Goddess Training: Becoming the Woman You Are Meant to Be (Amara, 2014).
3 This is an EMDR term (see Chapter 1).

References

Almaas, A. H. (2000). *The void: Inner spaciousness and ego structure* (2nd ed.). Shambhala. (Original work published 1986).

Amara, H. (2014). *Warrior goddess training: Become the woman you are meant to be.* Hierophant Publishing.

Dana, D., & Porges, S. W. (2021). *Anchored: How to befriend your nervous system using polyvagal theory.* Sounds True.

Harari, Y. N. (2014). *Sapiens: A brief history of humankind.* Harper Perennial.

Kimmerer, R. W. (2015). *Braiding sweetgrass: Indigenous wisdom, scientific knowledge and the teachings of plants.* Milkweed Editions.

Miller, L. (2021). *The awakened brain: The new science of spirituality and our quest for an inspired life.* Random House.

Part 5

Treasured Strategies and Tools for IFS-Informed EMDR

Chapter 19

Integrating Knipe's *EMDR Toolbox* Skills to Enrich Your IFS Practice

Crystal Whitlow

After completing my initial EMDR training in 2008, I had an experience with a client that both surprised and frightened me. I had worked with this client for some time, and we were eager to begin EMDR to address her complex trauma. She had a history of childhood sexual abuse, neglect, physical abuse, and abandonment by both parents, compounded by a family history of substance use disorders, as well as her own struggles with addiction. After what I believed was sufficient preparation and resourcing, we began processing a childhood memory of abuse by her uncle. However, after just a few sets of eye movements, her eyes became glassy, and she entered what appeared to be a dissociative state, re-enacting the abuse on herself. Unfamiliar with the signs of dissociation, I unknowingly exacerbated the situation by saying, "Go with that," too many times. It took nearly an hour to help her reorient to the present and feel safe enough to leave my office. That session was a stark wake-up call: I needed more tools than the basic EMDR training had provided.

At my first EMDRIA conference, and many subsequent ones, I sought every workshop I could find on complex trauma and dissociation. I was fortunate to hear Jim Knipe speak at one of those early conferences, and later sought consultation for several clients. This was years before the publication of his book *EMDR Toolbox: Theory and Treatment of Complex PTSD and Dissociation* (Knipe, 2019; first published in 2014). Many of the tools referenced in this chapter are adaptations of Knipe's EMDR toolbox skills, tailored for IFS therapists working with complex trauma.

As a trainer and consultant at the Syzygy Institute specializing in IFS-Informed EMDR, I also incorporate Bruce Hersey's model into my work (see Chapter 6). Through Syzygy, I have also come to value and incorporate Coherence Therapy (Ecker et al., 2012) into my skill set and offerings. The purpose of this chapter is to offer specific advanced EMDR tools as enhancements to the IFS model. While much has been written about how IFS can elevate EMDR, less attention has been given to how EMDR can enrich IFS practice. My goal is to bridge this gap by introducing advanced EMDR concepts and tools that complement and enhance IFS.

DOI: 10.4324/9781003541554-24

A cornerstone of this integration lies in a shift of focus. In traditional EMDR, the work often begins directly with exile parts that hold trauma. However, in IFS-Informed EMDR, the emphasis is first placed on engaging protector parts (managers and firefighters) before addressing exiles. This strategy, which aligns Knipe's and Hersey's approaches, forms the foundation of the chapter presented here. Specifically, the focus on the integration of Knipe's tools and Hersey's model is most needed when blended protectors will not unblend, or will not unblend for very long, and the client has little access to Self-energy. Hersey refers to this process as Discovery (see Chapter 7), where we stay with the blended protectors as long as needed to understand and develop a connection with those parts rather than asking them to unblend.

In *EMDR Toolbox*, Jim Knipe references both the **Theory of Structural Dissociation of the Personality** (TSDP, Steele et al., 2017) and **Internal Family Systems** (IFS, Schwartz & Sweezy, 2020), using oval figures to represent internal parts. While these theories share similarities, there are two key distinctions:

1 **Categories of Parts**: TSDP classifies parts into two categories—Apparently Normal Parts (ANPs) and Emotional Parts (EPs). In contrast, IFS identifies three distinct categories: managers, firefighters, and exiles.
2 **Role of the Self**: IFS introduces the concept of the Self as the undamaged core of a person—a source of inherent wholeness and healing energy for the system. TSDP does not include an equivalent concept.

For EMDR therapists, the IFS concept of Self may feel familiar. Within IFS, the Self is the innate healing mechanism of the system, closely paralleling Shapiro's **Adaptive Information Processing (AIP)** system in the EMDR framework. These foundational ideas are central to their respective models and underscore the natural synergy between them, as explored throughout this book. See Figure 19.1 to see Knipe's ovals with IFS parts and categories added.[1]

EMDR Language: Blocking Beliefs

The term "blocking beliefs" is commonly used in the EMDR community to describe internal conflicts that hinder progress. Jim Knipe's *Blocking Beliefs Questionnaire* (Appendix 19.A; Knipe, 2019), detailed in *EMDR Toolbox*, provides specific and concrete language for identifying parts of the Self that are working against one another. In IFS, this dynamic is referred to as "polarizations," where two parts are in conflict. While IFS often addresses polarizations by inviting one part to "step back" and allowing the other to

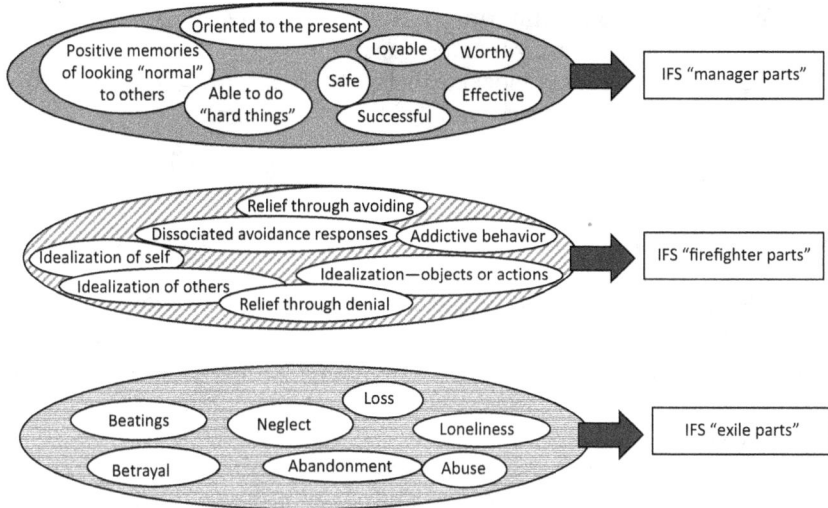

Figure 19.1 Knipe's Ovals with IFS Parts Categories Added.

become the focus, this approach can be less effective for clients with highly dissociative or fast-moving systems (due to complex trauma, neurodivergence, co-occurring concerns, etc.).

In these cases, Knipe's *Blocking Beliefs Questionnaire* offers a structured pathway to identify polarized parts (see Appendix 19.A). Clients rate their agreement with specific blocking beliefs, which not only helps them give voice to these internal conflicts but also highlights the most significant polarizations impacting their lives right now. This process is particularly useful for addressing entrenched struggles, such as addictions or compulsions, by pinpointing the biggest polarization in the system quickly. It streamlines the therapeutic work, allowing therapists to focus on the root issues more effectively.

By incorporating bilateral stimulation (BLS) during this process, therapists can deepen the dialogue with polarized manager and firefighter parts, in a way similar to the use of Robin Shapiro's "Two-Handed Interweave" technique. In the Syzygy IFS-Informed EMDR model, this approach aligns with Hersey's Discovery process, which emphasizes building a fuller understanding of protector parts. As these parts are acknowledged and heard, more Self-energy naturally arises, enabling the client to approach the polarization with greater clarity and balance.

For example, a client's manager part might state, "I want to stop eating sugary foods in front of the TV at night" or "I need to cut back on drinking." However, despite this desire, the behavior may persist, or even escalate, as firefighter parts react in opposition. In IFS, naming this as a polarization is helpful, but delving deeper into each part's intentions and protective strategies through the IFS-Informed EMDR framework using a tool like the *Blocking Beliefs Questionnaire* can be transformative.

Consider the following blocking belief from Knipe's *Blocking Beliefs Questionnaire* with a client struggling with emotional eating:

If I solve this problem, I will feel deprived.

The client rated this belief as a 7 on a scale of 1–7, indicating it felt completely true. From an IFS perspective, this belief represents two distinct parts: the manager, which sees emotional eating as a problem to solve, and the firefighter, which uses eating to avoid feelings of deprivation. Attempts to ask the manager part to step back were met with resistance, while the firefighter part's fear of deprivation led to increased eating after sessions. Neither part was willing to unblend or yield space for very long.

Using the IFS-Informed EMDR model, we identified this belief as the strongest polarization in the system and made it the focus of our work. Naming the polarization itself as the target, we added bilateral stimulation to explore both parts' positive intentions and deepen the understanding of their roles in the client's system. This approach allowed for greater insight into their protective strategies, fostering Self-energy and paving the way for meaningful resolution. The client stated, "It feels like I'm putting the weapons down on some level," and felt she could approach this entrenched pattern with more compassion, clarity, and creativity. These are all markers of Self-energy, which helped her with this problem that had felt stuck for so long.

CIPOS (Constant Installation of Present Orientation and Safety)

I am deeply grateful to Jim Knipe for his CIPOS tool, which I often describe as a pendulation technique. This approach is particularly effective for clients with strong dissociative, numbing, or phobic parts. CIPOS begins by grounding the client in the safety of the present moment, often through sensory cues like sight, sound, and smell. The client is encouraged to observe their current environment, anchoring themselves in the here and now.

From this grounded state, the therapist requests permission for the client to briefly notice a distressing memory or thought—just for a few seconds. Afterward, the therapist guides the client back to full present orientation and applies bilateral stimulation (BLS) while reinforcing their sense of safety. Over time, the duration spent noticing the disturbance can be gradually lengthened, with BLS facilitating a balanced re-engagement with the present.

In IFS terms, this technique integrates moments of Self-energy into the therapeutic process, fostering an observing stance toward parts that hold trauma burdens. These initial glimpses into the inner system build a foundation for deeper healing through IFS or EMDR processing. This EMDR strategy using pendulation can allow for parts to be seen and heard without overwhelming the system. Sometimes we can ask the parts not to overwhelm and it works, but with clients with complex trauma, dissociation, and intensely scared parts, a slower approach using CIPOS works much better.

The CIPOS skill begins by helping the client connect to their environment. For instance, I might ask them to notice features of my office or their surroundings (during telehealth sessions). This grounding step often engages manager parts, but it can also invite Self-energy as clients name comforting objects like a piece of artwork or a favorite plant. We then pendulate toward briefly noticing a part that carries trauma or a disturbing thought, often critical parts or exiles. This brief focus allows the client to observe the part without overwhelming protectors or triggering dissociation, thereby building tolerance for both parts work and trauma processing.

If the client is open to using IFS language, the CIPOS technique can be seamlessly integrated. Consider the following example:

Client: *Every time I take a shower, I hear his voice in my head, and I'll do anything to make it stop. I don't want this part anywhere near me!*

Therapist: *Can you notice where you are right now, here in my office? What do you hear, see, and smell?*

Client: *I see your plants, hear your sound machine and the traffic. It smells like … your office, I guess.*

Therapist: *Can you count the plants? Which one stands out to you? Or is there anything else in the room you like?*

Client: *There are six plants, including that ugly little cactus (laughs). Maybe the one with curly leaves. I also like the rocks over there.*

This engagement with the environment activates present awareness. From here, I invite the client to briefly shift attention toward the disturbance held by a part:

Therapist: *Would you be willing to notice, just for five seconds, the part of you that carries his voice? Afterward, I'll guide you back here.*

Client: *That sounds awful … but I'll try if you promise it's only five seconds.*

Therapist: *I promise. Right now, let's focus on the sound machine, the plants, the rocks, and your feet on the ground. Let's add a little bilateral stimulation to reinforce being here.*

The therapist initiates a short set of BLS (10–15 seconds) while reminding the client of present cues. After confirming they feel grounded, the therapist guides them to briefly notice the troubling part:

Therapist: I'll watch the clock. For just five seconds, notice the part of you that absorbed his voice.

Client: (Closes eyes tightly, takes a shallow breath.)

Therapist: (After 5 seconds) OK, open your eyes, take a deep breath, and let that part step back or move further away. Notice the sound machine, the rocks, and your feet on the ground. How here do you feel?

Client: I'm here. He feels closer, but I'm here.

Therapist: Let's ask that part to move a little further away and continue focusing on being present.

By alternating between present safety and brief contact with the part, the client builds confidence in their ability to tolerate distress. If this approach feels too intense, I offer adaptations, such as visualizing the part behind a closed door with a small window for observation.

In IFS terms, CIPOS facilitates the early stages of Self-to-part awareness, creating a safe space to approach parts holding frightening or distressing memories. This pendulation between safety and engagement allows clients to begin connecting with parts in a way that feels manageable and empowering.

Targeting Avoidance

> Sometimes the only point of entry into a dysfunctionally stored memory network is an avoidance defense, and focused targeting on the positive elements of avoidance will reduce the intensity of the avoidance, leading to the therapeutic access to, and targeting of, any remaining disturbing posttraumatic memory material.
>
> (Jim Knipe, *EMDR Toolbox*, n.p.)

"Targeting avoidance" is Knipe's EMDR term for addressing the urge to avoid directly, often using A. J. Popky's (2005) Level of Urge (LoU) scale, which measures avoidance on a scale from 0 to 10. Knipe expands on this with the **Level of Urge to Avoid (LoUA)** scale. From an IFS perspective, the urge to avoid stems from a protector part, often a manager or firefighter. For example, avoidance might show up as procrastination (e.g., scrolling social media to avoid a work task) or the client showing up to therapy each time with a "crisis of the week," diverting attention from deeper traumatic material. Knipe's method of targeting avoidance brings EMDR to the IFS process of befriending protectors and creating space for healing through witnessing the exile's disturbance underneath.

In practice, clients can identify and rate their urge to avoid. Using EMDR, the therapist asks, "How much do you want to avoid this right now, on a scale from 0 to 10?" followed by bilateral stimulation (BLS) while inviting the client to "go with that." Through this process, the therapist implicitly accesses the protective parts driving avoidance without needing to name them as such—an approach particularly useful for clients unfamiliar with or resistant to parts language. For those open to the framework, the **Level of Urge to Protect** scale, adapted by Bruce Hersey, offers a similar way to explore protector motivations.

In EMDR, targeting avoidance gently reduces barriers, allowing access to the traumatic material guarded by protective defenses. After several sets of BLS focused on the urge to avoid, memories or trauma history often begin to surface. For clients with highly protected systems, this approach offers a gradual, less overwhelming path to the exiles while befriending protectors. This creates more possibility for processing in EMDR or for witnessing, retrieval, and unburdening in IFS.

Case Example

Client: A 50-year-old Black, single, professional woman with a complex trauma history of sexual, physical, and emotional abuse by multiple family members. She reports nightmares, flashbacks, sleep disturbances, and other PTSD symptoms but often diverts therapy sessions to focus on work-related anxiety. After months of work, she acknowledges worsening nightmares and sleep difficulties.

Client: *I never sleep for more than an hour at a time. The dreams are worse. I'm exhausted all the time. This job is too much.*

Therapist: *Yes, we've been focusing on work for some time. I wonder if there's more under the surface related to the dreams and sleep issues?*

Client: *Yeah, but I just don't know if I can deal with it. My boss is a tyrant.*

Therapist: *It's a lot to consider, especially the painful parts of your past. If I remember correctly, your nightmares and flashbacks are tied to those memories, right?*

Client: Yes, but it's too much. I never want to think about it or talk about it—anywhere. But then it shows up in my dreams.

Therapist: That makes sense—it's a lot. I wonder if we could just notice how much you don't want to think about it right now?

Client: I don't want to think about it at all, ever!

Therapist: Understandable. Would you be open to trying EMDR to work with how much you don't want to think about it? Could you give that feeling a rating from 0 to 10?

Client: It's a 10. Always a 10!

Therapist: OK, let's notice that 10. Where do you feel it in your body?

Using EMDR, the therapist begins with processing sets (approximately 25 seconds each) focused on the client's urge to avoid. After a few sets:

Client: Even though I don't want to think about it, I know I need to. It's why I'm here. I can change my job, but I can't change the past. I need to deal with it to get better.

Client: These memories come up anyway—when I'm sleeping, during flashbacks, when I start dating someone new. I need to face this.

The therapist reassures her that the memories won't be addressed all at once and suggests asking the younger parts holding the memories to turn down the volume temporarily. With this agreement, they transition into deeper IFS-Informed EMDR work. Over time, her nightmares diminish, sleep improves, and flashbacks become less intrusive.

Targeting avoidance through Knipe's LoUA scale, paired with BLS, provides a structured way to approach protector parts in both EMDR and IFS frameworks. This method facilitates unblending, increases Self-energy, and creates opportunities for deeper healing. By respecting the protective intent of avoidance while gently reducing its intensity, therapists can help clients access and process underlying trauma at a manageable pace.

Targeting the Idealization Defense

Targeting idealization may feel counterintuitive for EMDR therapists, as it involves focusing on the positive affect associated with an idealized object, person, or relationship rather than the negative feelings and thoughts. This tool is particularly effective with clients who express a desire to leave unhealthy relationships but feel unable to do so. Other applications include addressing unresolved grief rooted in the idealization of a deceased partner, an unrealistic view of a peer group, or attachment to a religious organization, job, or career path the client is considering leaving.

For this intervention to be effective, it is crucial that the client acknowledges their desire to stop idealizing or remaining "stuck" in the relationship or situation. In IFS terms, this highlights internal polarization. Clients may recognize this dynamic themselves, saying, for instance, "Part of me wants to leave, but part of me feels the need to stay." Translating this from EMDR language of "Targeting the Idealization defense" to IFS-Informed EMDR, we are "befriending and (sometimes) unburdening the protective part that will not unblend."

The Level of Positive Affect (LoPA) scale is used in this intervention. The client is asked to focus on the best aspects of the person, group, or situation they are idealizing and rate their positive feelings from 0 (not at all positive) to 10 (the most positive/pleasant feelings). The therapist then uses bilateral stimulation (BLS) while the client notices those positive feelings. For this method to work, the client must have some awareness of the overly idealized nature of their attachment.

From an IFS-Informed EMDR perspective, this approach welcomes protector parts that seek to fulfill unmet needs through the idealized relationship or behavior. These parts may hold positive memories or feelings that make the relationship or situation seem appealing. The therapist engages the part, asking, "What feels so good about this person/situation?" and then applies BLS to deepen understanding and connection with the part's intentions. This process parallels Bruce Hersey's **Discovery** phase from the Syzygy Model (see Chapter 7), focusing on understanding and befriending protector parts. As the focus stays on the part that wants to keep the relationship or situation, we begin to learn its fears and positive intentions, which usually includes protecting exiles. As the protector part feels heard, underlying exile material often begins to surface, revealing deeper layers of unmet needs and pain.

Case Example

A 60-year-old white, widowed woman sought therapy for anxiety after years of intense caretaking in her family and marriage. As the oldest daughter of five children with two alcoholic parents, she had developed many parts with beliefs of "I am responsible for everything and everyone." Despite recognizing her boyfriend's emotional immaturity and manipulative tendencies, she felt "stuck" in the relationship because "the good times are so good, even though they're more and more rare." She described enjoying their physical connection and weekend outings but often felt used and exhausted afterward.

To target idealization, the client was asked to focus on a positive memory—spending Saturday night with her partner and feeling a strong sense of connection. She rated this memory a 9 on the LoPA scale. The therapist invited her to notice the memory and any good feelings it evoked while applying BLS. Over several sets, her high ratings began to lower as memories of her boyfriend's criticism, emotional demands, and dismissiveness surfaced. Eventually, connections to her childhood experiences of feeling alone and overburdened arose. She also realized that her dad, in sober moments, would frequently compliment her or praise her for being "such a good girl to take care of things and us" and how good that felt amidst the heaviness of responsibility and abuse.

From an IFS perspective, the idealization by protector parts reflected *and* protected the needs of exiles who longed for connection and validation. With increased insight into her patterns and deeper processing of childhood memories, the client was able to end the relationship. Incorporating IFS language and strategies helped her recognize unmet needs and address her feelings of aloneness. This work laid the foundation for further healing through IFS-Informed EMDR techniques, including the Loving Eyes intervention.

Loving Eyes

Jim Knipe's Loving Eyes skill naturally aligns with IFS principles but offers an EMDR enhancement for working with younger parts. While rooted in the structural dissociation model, the technique can easily be adapted for IFS-Informed EMDR.

The intervention begins by grounding the client in present awareness and connecting with the part of them currently present in the therapy office (described as the "adult" part by Knipe). Depending on client's access to Self-energy, this could be a manager "adult" part or a "Self-like" part with some access to Self-energy. The client is then invited to visualize a younger version of themselves, separate from trauma or disturbing events. If helpful, the client can bring in a photograph of themselves as a child. The therapist encourages them to "just see what you see," applying BLS to facilitate dual attention and reduce judgment. In IFS terms, this creates space between the exile and its burden, making room for healing.

Clients sometimes struggle to visualize their younger self or experience negative reactions. In these cases, Knipe suggests exploring the defense response, which aligns with IFS's approach to protector parts. Rather than asking the protector to step aside, Knipe encourages curiosity with questions like, "What's good about knowing today that you are not that child?" This reframing validates the protector's positive intent, often softening its stance. Additional interweaves, such as "Do you think that child had it rough?" or "Is there anything you know now that could help that child?" evoke curiosity, clarity, and compassion—key elements of Self-energy in IFS.

Once the younger part is visible, the next step is witnessing its feelings. In IFS, this involves slowing down and deeply attending to the exile's pain. Adding BLS allows the client to maintain present orientation while holding space for the exile's experience and a form of witnessing, supporting the memory reconsolidation necessary for healing. As compassion grows between the adult (or protector) part and the child, the therapist asks, "Now when you look at that child, how do you feel toward them?" This wording, rooted in IFS, tends to elicit Self-energy more effectively than Knipe's original phrasing of "feel about."

Conclusion

By integrating EMDR Toolbox techniques with IFS's relational, parts-oriented approach, therapists can offer clients a compassionate and comprehensive pathway to healing. Whether through targeting idealization, avoidance, or using the *Loving Eyes* intervention, these methods honor the wisdom of the client's internal system while facilitating access to deeper trauma. Knipe's tools remain invaluable in EMDR practice and, when adapted to IFS, create even greater opportunities for healing and transformation.

Note

1 This illustration is adapted with permission from Jim Knipe.

References

Ecker, B., Ticic, R., & Hulley, L. (2012). *Unlocking the emotional brain: Eliminating symptoms at their roots using memory reconsolidation*. Routledge.

Knipe, J. (2019). *EMDR toolbox: Theory and treatment of complex PTSD and dissociation* (2nd ed.). Springer.

Popky, A. J. (2005). De-TUR, an urge reduction protocol for addictions and dysfunctional behaviors. In R. Shapiro (Ed.), *EMDR solutions: Pathways to healing* (pp. 167–185). W. W. Norton & Company.

Schwartz, R. C., & Sweezy, M. (2020). *Internal family systems therapy* (2nd ed.). Guilford Press.

Steele, K., Boon, S., & van der Hart, O. (2017). *Treating trauma-related dissociation: A practical, integrative approach*. Norton.

APPENDIX 19.A: BLOCKING BELIEFS QUESTIONNAIRE (KNIPE, 2019)

PROBLEM I WANT TO SOLVE: _____

Please give a number from 1 (feels completely untrue) to 7 (feels completely true) for each statement.

_____ I am embarrassed that I have this problem.

_____ I will never get over this problem.

_____ I'm not sure I want to get over this problem.

_____ If I solve this problem, I will feel deprived.

_____ I don't have the strength or the willpower to solve this problem.

_____ If I really talk about this problem, something bad will happen.

_____This is a problem that can only be solved by someone else.

_____ If I ever solve this problem, I will lose a part of who I really am.

_____ I don't want to think about this problem anymore.

_____ I should solve this problem, but I don't always do what I should do.

_____ I like people who have this problem better than people who don't.

_____ It could be dangerous for me to get over this problem.

_____ When I try to think about this problem, I can't keep my mind on it.

_____ I say I want to solve this problem, but I never do.

_____ It could be bad for someone else for me to get over this problem.

_____ If I get over this problem, I can never go back to having it again.

_____ I don't deserve to get over this problem.

_____ This problem is bigger than I am.

_____ If I got over this problem, it would go against my values.

_____ Someone in my life hates this problem.

_____ There are some good things about having this problem.

_____ I don't have a problem.

_____ I've had this problem so long; I could never completely solve it.

_____ I have to wait to solve this problem.

_____If I solve this problem, I could lose a lot.

_____ If I solve this problem, it will mainly be for someone else.

Chapter 20

The Fire Drill Technique
Sorting Through Countertransference with IFS

Joanne H. Twombly

One of the most effective IFS strategies is the Fire Drill, which helps sort through therapists' countertransference reactions. It is an efficient way of getting organized before sessions, enabling you to start sessions from a space where you are curious, centered, and compassionate. This space is what IFS refers to as being in "Self," and during work, this is what I think of as being in my "adult-psychotherapist Self." I specify "adult-psychotherapist" to differentiate Self from child parts and Self-like parts. The Fire Drill makes it possible to locate the source(s) of the countertransference and identify whatever action is needed to deal with it. Sources of countertransference include nonverbal communications from the client, as in projections, projective identification, and reenactments. The Fire Drill also makes it possible to receive sometimes invaluable consultation from our parts, and assists with identifying trailheads that help us identify when our own issues are being brought up through work with our clients. It can be done by oneself, with a partner, or with a consultant. I regularly use it when I provide individual and group consultations, and teach it to clients when something/someone in their lives is bringing up challenging feelings and responses (see Figure 20.1).

The process of doing the Fire Drill by oneself is presented below step by step, with an example of the process I went through before one session.

Step 1. Identify that you are having or may be having a countertransference reaction.

> **Example**: Before meeting with a client, instead of planning for the session, I found myself planning what to cook for dinner, thinking about what I needed to buy at the store, and wishing I could skip the meeting. This was a big clue that I was not centered or ready to meet with this client.

Step 2. Visualize meeting with your client and "hear" the client saying or doing whatever causes you to experience countertransference reactions.

> **Example continued**: I "heard" my client talking about superficial topics.

DOI: 10.4324/9781003541554-25

The Fire Drill
1. Helps sort through countertransference.
2. Helps you get centered before sessions.
3. Often provides consultation from our parts.
4. Identifies trail heads, i.e. issues from our past that need healing.

Figure 20.1 Benefits of the Fire Drill.

Step 3. As you focus on your client, scan through your body and notice what feelings and somatic sensations are coming up. Identify where they are located. These could show up as areas of tension, extra energy, feelings, dullness, or an absence of feeling in or around your body.

> **Example continued**: I noticed I was more tired than usual and my whole body felt like it was sagging. I also felt disconnected from the client.

Feelings and sensations indicate the presence of parts. Tell the part or parts holding these feelings and sensations (or lack of feelings) that you want to get to know them and want to understand their thoughts, feelings, and reactions to the client. Then ask them to "relax back," "unblend," or ask to sit beside them. I clarify to the parts that this will help you really get to know and understand them.

- If there is more than one part, ask "Who needs to go first?"
- If the part or parts are unwilling to unblend, ask what concerns they have and address their concerns.
- If other parts have concerns, address them too.

Alternatively: If the part(s) are unable to unblend, focus on where you feel or notice the part in or around your body, and continue below. Feeling Self-energy toward the parts is another way of unblending from them (see Figure 20.2).

Step 4. Identify the parts who are present.

> **Example continued**: I identified a part who was holding the tired and sagging feelings, and a part who was disconnected.

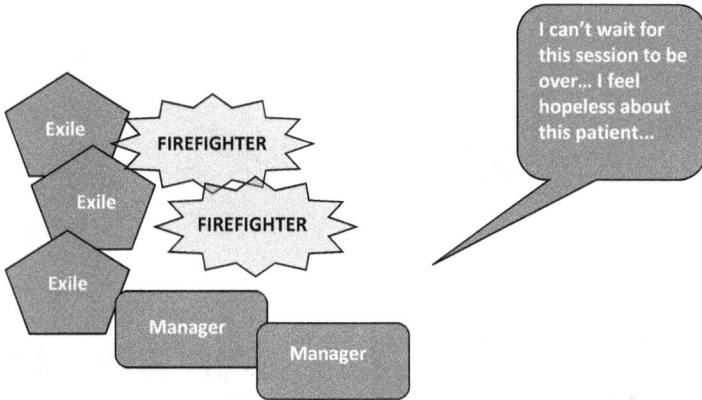

Figure 20.2 Blended Parts.

Step 5. Check for the presence of Self-energy. Ask yourself: "What am I feeling toward this part?" (or toward each part). The presence of Self-energy is ascertained by noticing that you feel one or more of the eight C's of Self-energy in relation to the part. One hundred percent Self-energy is not necessary. You just need enough Self-energy, or what IFS calls a "critical mass of Self-energy." A good place to start is checking to see if you feel some curiosity toward the part. Once you feel Self-energy toward the part, energetically send the Self-energy to the part; that is, send the part your curiosity and compassion so the part feels it and feels a sense of connection with you.

- If you don't feel one of the C's or if you feel nothing toward the part or parts, it is an indication that you are blended with another part (or parts).
- Focus on that part and ask that part to relax back or unblend. Note: You may have to ask that part what concerns or issues the part has.
- If the part agrees to relax back, continue the Fire Drill process.
- If the part does not agree, you may need to work with this part first.

The Eight C's
- Calmness
- Curiosity
- Clarity
- Compassion
- Confidence
- Courage
- Creativity
- Connectedness

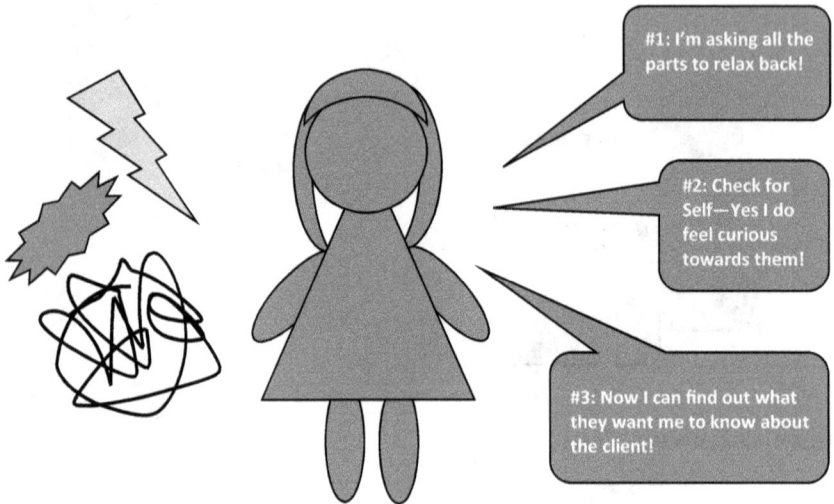

Figure 20.3 Asking Parts to Relax Back.

Example continued: As I focused my attention on the part holding the tired and sagging feelings, I asked myself, "What am I feeling toward this part?" I noticed I felt annoyed. That helped me realize I was blended with another part. I turned to that second part, checked for Self-energy toward her and, yes, I felt curious. I asked what the second part's concern was. The part said she was upset I'd agreed to work with the client in the first place. The part agreed to relax back, after I agreed that I would get back to her after finishing the Fire Drill process with the first part (see Figure 20.3).

Step 6: Once you are in Self, ask the part: "What do you want me to know about this client and about working with this client?" Continue asking the part for information until the part feels fully understood by you.

Example continued: Going back to the first part, I checked for Self-energy, felt curiosity, and sent the curiosity toward the part. Then I asked, "What do you want me to know about this client and about working with her?" Much to my surprise, the part said that she thought the client should be making more progress and that I was missing something important. She said she was tired of the client not making enough progress. I agreed that that made sense and asked if there was anything else the part wanted me to know about my client. The part said no, that was it.

Step 7: Once the part feels like you have fully heard and understood them, , ask the part: "What do you need from me to let me handle the session from my centered adult-psychotherapist Self?" Work with the part, or each identified part in turn, until these questions are fully answered.

Example continued: The part told me that I needed to address the issue with the client. I agreed to do this.

Step 8. Check back with any parts who had concerns including those who relaxed back and allowed you to work with others. See what comments, questions, and concerns they have. See if any other parts have comments, questions, and concerns.

Example continued: The part that had felt annoyed didn't feel annoyed anymore and agreed that me addressing this with the client was important. The part who held the disconnection also felt that the issue about not making progress needed to be dealt with.

Step 9. Send all parts thanks and appreciation for the process they allowed you to go through with them.
Step 10. Picture meeting with the client and check if any other difficult feelings come up and/or notice the difference.

Example continued: I did this and felt better about meeting with the client. I felt much more centered and alert, and wasn't distracted by dinner plans anymore!

When I met with the client I followed through with the part's recommendation and said, "I've been thinking about our work together, and it feels like there's something we're avoiding or are just not getting to. What do you think, do you have any ideas?" The client agreed. She said she had not wanted to come to the session that day. She wasn't in touch with why, so we used EMDR to target the not wanting to come to session. The floatback led to discovering an incident when she was punished for trying to talk to her mother about a problem. The treatment process flowed on from there (see Figure 20.4).

The Expanded Fire Drill (Twombly, 2024)

In the process of providing consultations, I began adding several other steps to the Fire Drill process, as needed. Sometimes I add these steps because the therapist appears to be experiencing a countertransference intensity about the case that appears to go beyond the case itself, or I might feel like something is off, missing, or complicated (see Box 20.1).

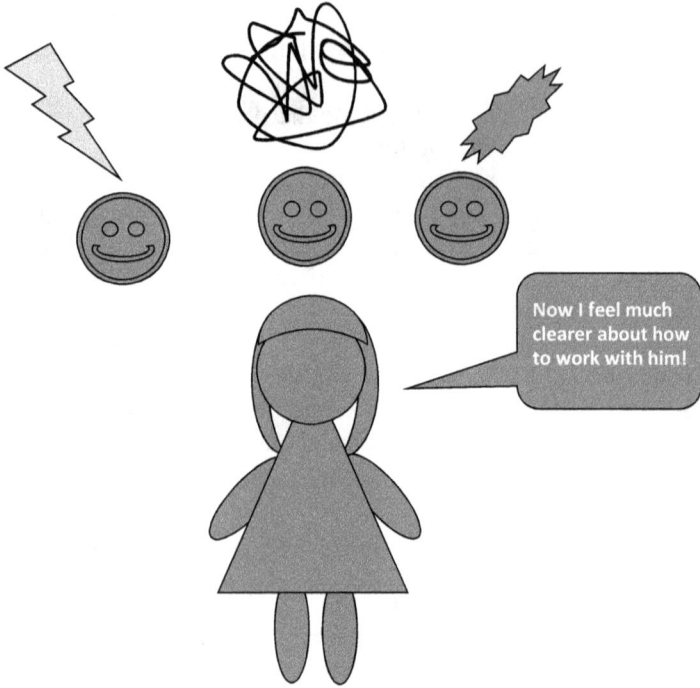

Figure 20.4 Listening to the Wisdom of Each Part.

Box 20.1 Expanded Fire Drill Questions

- How old does the part think you are?
- Is the part oriented to the present? (IFS refers to this as the part needing to be Retrieved.)
- Is the part carrying any old burdens?
- And if so, does the part need a container with a commitment built into it to work on whatever is stored in it when the time is right?
- Does the part need a Safe Space (use Twombly, 2024, or Twombly, 2000 version of SSI)?

One question I might ask is, "How old does the part think you are?"

Example: During a consultation, a therapist said he wanted to stop working with a client because the client was impossible to treat, was endlessly hopeless, and wasn't making progress. This was making him feel helpless and unskilled. Because of the complexity of the case, because the therapist had already gotten quite a bit of consultation, and because of the intensity of the therapist's feelings, I suggested we use the Fire Drill to clarify and clear out any countertransference before we discussed the case. When the therapist in his adult-therapist-Self connected with a part the part said, "She's (the client is) too hard, she's going to hurt us." Because there did not appear to be any real danger of the client hurting him, I asked the therapist to check for Self-energy in relation to the part, and then asked the therapist to "Ask the part how old does he think you are?" The part answered, "8." I said to the therapist, "Ask the part to look in your eyes as you look back into his, let him know how old you are, what skills and trainings you have, and that you have strengths and resources you didn't have when you were 8." The therapist did this, which immediately reassured the part that he, in his adult-therapist-Self could work with the client with no risk.

This process helps parts, who are often younger than the biological 1 age of the person, to update their knowledge and become more oriented to the present (see Figure 20.5).

Depending on the part's responses, another useful question can be to ask the consultee to ask the part if the part is carrying any burdens from the

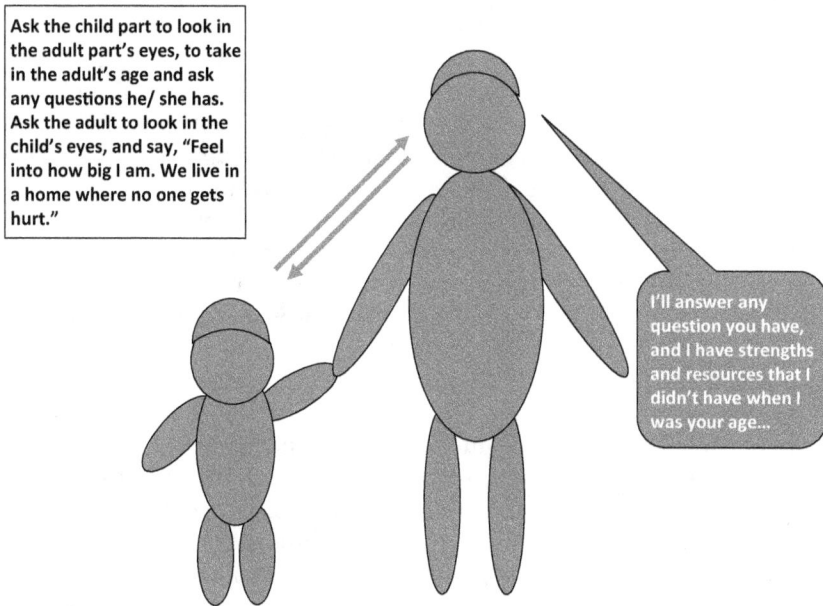

Figure 20.5 Orienting Parts to the Present.

past. Many therapists come from families with some kind of dysfunction, and in spite of having had therapy, there is always the chance that a client will trigger some aspect of the therapist's past that has not been fully worked through. If the part says "yes," then it may be helpful for the part to have a container (Kluft, 1988, Twombly, 2023) to put it in.

> **Example continued**: Checking in with himself, the therapist connected with a different part who was still worried about working with this client. When the part asked what he wanted the therapist to know, he tearfully stated, "It's my job to help the client heal and I'm a failure if I don't." I asked the therapist in his adult-therapist-Self to ask the part if he was carrying any burdens from his childhood. The part said yes. He explained that his job was to help his parents take care of his siblings. It didn't matter if he had homework, taking care of the siblings came first. I had the therapist ask him if he wanted to put that job in a container with a commitment built into it to work on everything stored inside, and he agreed.

Containers

The process of teaching container imagery builds on our normal ability to disconnect and compartmentalize. For example, if I have a fight with my husband before I leave for work, I leave it at home and focus on work. In this instance, I am using my home as a container. Another example is when a person has a history of child abuse which has been dissociated fully or partially. In this case, the information about the abuse is contained under an unconscious lid. The most effective way to help someone create a container is to point out how they're already unconsciously using containers, and then explain that evolving this unconscious ability into a container upgrades their unconscious ability into a conscious defense. In this situation, I might say, "You don't remember (or have a clear memory) of that abuse, as you unconsciously have been protecting yourself from it by putting a lid on it. Let's take that lid, and evolve it into a conscious container that gives you more control and choices … What kind of container would you like?"

> **Example continued**: I said, "When you were a kid you were given the job to take care of your siblings. That became an automatic behavior. As an adult you've worked on not automatically caretaking, learned to take better care of yourself and to consciously decide when you want to caretake and when it isn't appropriate. Your client's issues pushed that old button and this part has kicked back into that old I-have-to-caretake behavior. That old behavior had been pushed under a lid. Ask the part if he's willing to evolve that lid into a container that will give him more choices and control over when he wants to caretake. The container will have a

commitment built into it, that everything stored inside will be worked on when it's the right time." The part was willing. The next question for the part was, "What kind of container do you want?"

The part wanted a cement box with a plastic seal. I said to the therapist, "Tell the part that, as he's noticing the cement box with a plastic seal (using the exact words used by the part enhances the imagery), and focusing on the old burden of caretaking, he'll notice that the burden is going into the container in just the right way ... And as it goes in, the cement box with the plastic seal is getting stronger and stronger. The commitment to work on what's inside is built into the container and the part has the control over putting the material in (in this case an old belief/job) or taking some out if he wants ... What's it like for the part to have this old belief that he 'has to caretake' stashed in the container?" The therapist reported that the part felt lighter, and the therapist felt relief. The part was then okay with allowing the therapist to handle the therapy from his adult-therapist-Self. The therapist could now identify how that old belief/job had gotten triggered by the client's neediness and could see how it was confusing and overwhelming the treatment process. When the therapist again thought about working with the client, he felt a new sense of clarity on how to proceed. True, the client was difficult and had serious life-threatening medical issues; however the therapist could focus on what he could do therapeutically, without feeling a sense of total responsibility for the outcome of the client's life.

Safe-Space Imagery

Creating a safe space for a part can sometimes be beneficial, as in the following example.

Example: A therapist became triggered while participating in an EMDR training during the first practicum. She called me, and we did an emergency Fire Drill consultation session. Two parts identified that they held burdens of unprocessed childhood trauma. After creating containers, they still felt too at risk of becoming overwhelmed during practicums to face going back to the training. I asked her to ask the parts if they wanted safe spaces with sound- and feeling-proofing (Kluft, 1988, Twombly, 2024, p. 61) in the walls so they didn't need to hear or feel anything from the training. One said she already had one, and that she liked the idea of adding sound- and feeling-proofing. The other needed a safe space. Once this was done, the parts felt secure and protected, and agreed to allow the therapist in her adult-therapist-Self to continue the training. Note: Visualization exercises tap into innate trance ability; in trance there is increased problem-solving, so things that don't make sense consciously (feeling-proofing) make sense and work in the visualization.

In this example, the therapist had her own trauma therapist. With other therapists who don't, I've occasionally contracted with them to do a piece of short-term IFS or EMDR on the traumatic material. This shift from consultant to therapist and doing a piece of clinical work to benefit the therapist's professional work is a clinical, case-by-case decision. There are times when our clients trigger unresolved traumatic material that hasn't come up in our personal psychotherapy. The Fire Drill process is particularly useful in identifying these kinds of issues. It is important, if we're going to ask our clients to go to their deepest, darkest places, that we are willing to go to our own deepest, darkest places. Steve Frankel discussed this in his 1997 *Disruption and Repair* paper:

> Analysts who can look at themselves are experienced by their analysands as being personally accessible. They present themselves as fallible and unafraid of the same scrutiny they ask from the analysand. Issues of authority and superiority fall away. An atmosphere of safety and personal goodwill is created instead.
>
> **Example**: A therapist working with people with complex trauma disorders videoed sessions for use in consultation. As I reviewed the sessions, I noticed that she talked so fast it seemed like she wasn't giving her clients enough time to think or respond. I asked if this was a choice or something she did automatically. Because it was something she always did, we decided to use the Fire Drill. Once she got into Self in relation to the fast-talking part, the part explained that if she didn't speak fast she wouldn't be listened to. We targeted that with EMDR and the floatback went back to times when her workaholic parents ignored her. With that target cleared, the part relaxed, felt much better, and the therapist could talk with a more modulated voice. This target had not been identified in her individual treatment.

Many therapists grew up being parentified children, helpers, and/or having to manage many childhood issues on their own. These parts can easily become Self-like skilled therapist parts who do great work, but eventually become overwhelmed and burned out because they are child parts functioning in adult roles. Because these parts are so good at managing adult business, these parts can be particularly hard to detect. Identifying these parts, unblending from them, and releasing them from the burden of their old roles and traumas is important. Even if a parentified child is good at being a therapist, it is a child part and will be working harder than a therapist in their centered-adult-Self. The part can still notice things about the client and provide helpful information on the client but should not be in the therapist role.

Discussion

The Expanded Fire Drill is a fine-tuned process for identifying both non-complex and multidimensional countertransference, including projective identification and reenactments. It's useful for therapists and clients, it can be used before sessions when countertransference is noticed, and it can be used during sessions when necessary. In consultation, it provides a process that helps consultants identify and resolve complex countertransference issues as written about by Chefetz (2017):

> The task of the consultant is to protect both patient and therapist from an untoward outcome while relieving the painful burdens entailed by the treatment ... This dynamic, and others, must be understood in order to resolve impasses and create useful movement toward growth in both patient and therapist.

This chapter expands on McGoldrick's chapter in this book which describes how EMDR therapy is enhanced by using IFS (Chapter 5) by adding "a systematic approach to identifying, acknowledging and ultimately harnessing the EMDR therapist's own parts in a therapeutic process."

The Fire Drill can be very effective, although it is basically a short-term solution, or a beginning/continuation of a personal growth process. As in creating containers, committing to work on any childhood burdens or issues brought up in this experience, whether on your own, with a therapist, or in a peer group, is important.

References

Chefetz, R. A. (2017). Issues in consultation for treatments with distressed activated abuser/protector self-states in dissociative identity disorder. *Journal of Trauma & Dissociation, 18*(3), 465–475.

Frankel, S. A. (1997). The analyst's role in the disruption and repair sequence in psychoanalysis. *Contemporary Psychoanalysis, 33*(1), 71–87.

Kluft, R. P. (1988). Playing for time: Temporizing techniques in the treatment of multiple personality disorder. *American Journal of Clinical Hypnosis*, 32, 90–98. C.

Twombly, J. H. (2000). Incorporating EMDR and EMDR Adaptations into the Treatment of Clients with DID, *Journal of Trauma and Dissociation*, Vol. 1(2).

Twombly, J. H. (2024). *Trauma and dissociation informed Internal Family Systems: How to Successfully Treat Complex PTSD, and Dissociative Disorders*, 2nd edition. Self-Publishing.com.

Twombly, J. H., & Schwartz, R. (2008). The integration of the Internal Family Systems Model and EMDR. In C. Forgash & M. Copeley (Eds.), *Healing the heart of trauma and dissociation with EMDR and ego state therapy* (pp. 295–311). Springer Publishing.

Chapter 21

The Role of Therapists' Parts in Helping or Hindering Clients' Healing

Contrasting EMDR Psychotherapy with an IFS Therapy Perspective

Annabel McGoldrick

Reviewed by Laura Kosak, David Archer, and Joanne H. Twombly

EMDR Standard Protocol or a Relational Therapy

EMDR basic training in the UK and Australia is taught as a protocolised intervention where the therapist should stay out of the way and follow the standard protocol, so they do not disrupt the flow of internal processing that is going on within a client (Wachtel, 2002). My colleagues and I have argued that this leaves many therapists too scared to use EMDR (Dyson, 2024; McGoldrick, 2022; McGoldrick, 2023; McGoldrick, 2024). Others may have a different experience of EMDR basic training, but as an EMDR consultant/supervisor, having taught IFS-Informed EMDR to over 200 EMDR therapists, most participants report fears they'll harm someone with EMDR and feel ill-equipped to work with complex client presentations.

It's worth noting that: 'Within the United Kingdom and Ireland, only 10%–12% of trainees who complete EMDR basic training go on to become accredited in EMDR' (Farrell & Keenan, 2013).

Echoing such concerns, the Council of Scholars (CoS) appointed by the EMDR International Association highlighted the risk that the EMDR community is at a moment in time in which guidelines for implementing EMDR can be inconsistent and at times contradictory. There is tension between holding onto the values and standards of EMDR and at the same time remaining open to new insights and developments in the psychological field (Laliotis et al., 2021, p. 187). I believe integrating EMDR with IFS can offer a flexible, relational approach to all clients with all presentations, to make EMDR a full and dynamic psychotherapy (Laliotis et al., 2021) and not just a collection of protocols.

DOI: 10.4324/9781003541554-26

To work relationally, we must understand ourselves as therapists, and have some awareness of our own countertransference, which we bring to the therapy relationship (our feelings that we project onto the client). As we explore the intersubjective space between ourselves and our clients (see Chapter 9), we can appreciate the developing relationship, including our feelings and reactions, and any of our parts or burdens inside our system. As Joanne H. Twombly (2023, p. 35) has written, when we conceptualise countertransference, we must also consider projective identification, feeling and experiencing someone else's emotions as our own, and re-enactments, when we are unknowingly pulled into an experience in which we are recreating a past traumatic dynamic that the client has experienced before.

Since the relational aspects of EMDR were not initially emphasised, Dworkin (2005, p. xv), like many other prominent EMDR therapists, underscores the importance of integrating EMDR with other approaches as necessary, and ensuring that is driven by the needs of the client, as reflected in Shapiro's book *EMDR as an Integrative Psychotherapy Approach* (2002). But reflecting on therapists' parts is not central to EMDR therapy in the way that it is in IFS.

We learn EMDR as a technique, and yet the profound model is so much more transformational when it is used to develop us therapists as people, as humans. Many times when you speak with someone who has gone through some type of IFS training, they are quick to share how this has become incorporated into their life in a very personal way. It's been wonderful to watch colleagues evolve so much through IFS, not only as therapists but as friends, partners, and parents too.

Therapists, Know Your Parts!

This list comprises some parts EMDR therapists may not be aware they are blended with during a session. The first step is to be a parts detector! As Schwartz (2021) puts it, being blended with our parts is a form of therapy blindness. Since your protectors are reacting to the protectors of others, they can provide a significant amount of insight for the therapist, and provide us with a lot of wisdom about the client (see Chapter 20). The key is to be in Self or Self-energy, the space and energy that we access when parts relax back (Schwartz, 2021).

The following composite case examples (with details changed for confidentiality reasons) illustrate how therapist parts can stall EMDR therapy and ultimately inhibit clients' healing and access to their own Adaptive Information Processing systems (AIP), seen as the key driver of change in EMDR.

- **Worried parts**: There are so many tales of EMDR therapists with worried parts. Ask yourself,

  What am I afraid of as a therapist? Raising my fee? Experiencing angry, blaming clients? Shutdown of avoidant clients who won't share anything? Working online with clients who might destabilise? Suicidal clients? The fear that I'll make my clients worse? I won't know what to say when they are overwhelmed and very tearful?

  These are just a few of the questions we can ask ourselves that might lead to our worried parts. These behaviours in the client are what could trigger an EMDR therapist's exile parts. It is important to unblend from our own therapist parts because when we are in Self, nothing inside can harm us (Schwartz & Sweezy, 2019). John, a new EMDR therapist, provided his client with 24 sessions of EMDR therapy, yet never reached Phase 4 processing because the client was a big talker who ultimately stopped the treatment. At the other extreme, another client of John's was triggered into a dissociative episode during an extensive history-taking, when John was blended with his perfectionist part. The learning edge for John was: Worried parts can be protected by busy managers who don't want to interrupt clients, and other parts who can do too much preparation in EMDR.
- **Suicidal parts**: Melissa was afraid of doing any EMDR with clients who had a history of suicidality. She heard EMDR wasn't safe to use with them. She had to do her own therapy on her own teenage suicidal parts and further training to realise EMDR can be used safely with people in acute mental health crises (Proudlock & Peris, 2020). She also found IFS training useful, to help her unblend from her own scared parts to access sufficient Self-energy to be able to welcome and befriend suicidal protectors. With supervision, Melissa located her own Self-energy and confidence to appreciate that many suicidal parts are firefighters who usually just want peace for the client. With supervision, Melissa was very relieved to recognise that she could ask the suicidal part, 'What if we could help the exile you're protecting unburden past traumas and we could help you find other avenues to achieve peace? How does this sound to you?'
- **Doubting parts**: During supervision, Sarah was questioning the effectiveness of imagination in EMDR therapy, dismissing it as 'fluffy stuff.' Her supervisor mistook this for a cynical part, but Sarah checked inside and found that the doubting part was afraid of not being in control during a therapy session. Sarah realised that Self-energy is all about feeling comfortable with the unknown.
- **Insecure parts**: Jane felt insecure about naming that her client was stuck in the drama triangle (Karpman, 1968) of victim, perpetrator, rescuer,

and her client was blended with a victim part. Jane was scared the client would feel judged if she named this. So, after supervision, Jane said: 'I have a part who is scared to name something with you but another part who feels this could be important for your therapy, can I check it out with you?' (Twombly, 2024). After a set of BLS, the client had the insight that her victim protector found this was the only way that Jane could get attention and her needs met in her family as a child. The protector gave permission to go to the neglected exile.

- **Organised parts** and **fix-it parts**: Alison, a therapist working with a client's eating disorder (ED) firefighters, found she needed a lot of patience and flexibility. Every time Alison, feeling organised, tried the quick fix of EMDR addiction protocols, the session would go nowhere as the client's firefighter mounted a power struggle—one they were willing to go to any lengths to win. Slowly, Alison encouraged the client to stay with her parts—until they emerged as fierce native warriors protecting the client's autonomy and independence. The client was then able to unblend from her ED parts, approaching them with the respect and curiosity of an anthropologist. The sessions flowed, and her urge to restrict food began to fall significantly.

- **Dreading parts**: Many of us have those clients we dread seeing. Rose was working with an accountant she'd seen for a couple of years, and she dreaded seeing his name in the diary. He had the most enormous walls, plus an enormous expectation that she'd fix him. Rose had tried to EMDR his walls away with bilateral stimulation, but they only got bigger. In supervision, using the Extended Fire Drill (see Chapter 20), she was able to unblend from several polarised parts to see his vulnerable wounded little boy, and feel compassion for the client.

- **Bored parts**: Louise was working with a medical doctor who just wanted to complain about relationship issues. She found herself getting bored, counting the minutes until the end of the session. What was this bored part telling her about the client's inner world? During the session, Louise tuned into her bored part, who told her the client wasn't being authentic, avoiding the deep stuff, and had exiles who felt unseen, unheard, and unlovable.

- **Stuck parts**: This is one of the most common phrases I hear as an EMDR supervisor: 'I've tried everything.' This is a close relative of impatient parts and fix-it parts, with the next question being 'what's the protocol for this?',[1] often seen on EMDR group chats. For the therapist, this can quickly switch into doubting or self-critical parts, saying 'I've missed something', or 'I got it wrong.' This is usually not about the skill of the therapist but rather the therapeutic relationship, and *what is being triggered in the therapist?* is my next line of inquiry as a supervisor. After having the therapist turn inward, it's time to help an IFS-Informed EMDR therapist get curious about the client's protectors.

- **Impatient parts**: EMDR therapists often pick up the message that they must reach the target as quickly as possible, particularly an exile memory. Anna saw three clients in quick succession who were frightened by previous EMDR. They had never returned during Phase 4 of EMDR because the treatment felt too traumatising and intense. Anna had to check in with her own impatient parts to ensure she was Self-led to stay curious with each of these clients and spend lots of time in Phase 2 befriending their big protectors. When they got to Phase 4, she often needed to lay out the welcome mat to protectors again, reminding herself, 'What's in the way, is the way.'[1]
- **Judging parts**: Amanda had seen a lot of EMDR clients, and felt confident she could judge who was suitable for EMDR and who wasn't. The client, who was in her thirties, suffered from fibromyalgia. Amanda asked the client for her earliest memory, but her client couldn't remember anything. Amanda feared the client was dissociating, so tried to bring her back into the room by throwing a box of tissues back and forth. The client felt under attack, like she was getting EMDR wrong, and never returned. Later the client saw an IFS-Informed EMDR therapist, who helped her to access compassion for her exiles: They exclaimed, 'We felt that when we were with Amanda, we were being bashed by a hammer, and that Amanda believed we couldn't be fixed.'
- **Turn-away parts**: Peter was quite triggered when his client collapsed into floods of tears. He had a part who wanted to turn away, saying 'No, this is too much.' In personal therapy Peter recalled that his mother could not tolerate his tears as a baby. By exploring baby memories, Peter realised this intolerance was his mother's, not his (a legacy burden, in IFS language). Peter was able to hand this burden back to his mother (through IFS therapy), then he was able to show more Self-energy, and compassion for his baby part. Thus, being Self-led enabled Peter to access compassion for his client's vulnerable parts in the next session.
- **Angry and frustrated parts**: Chloe was feeling quite irritated with her client for not wanting to do EMDR. The client was not ready to do EMDR around never meeting her father in childhood, instead choosing to talk about numerous incidents occurring with her partner and work colleagues. The client also reflected on their desire for gender-affirming surgery. 'This is not how I work, I'm not a talking therapist' thought Chloe inside, numerous times. Although Chloe avoided voicing her frustration to the client, explaining that all of those issues could be explored deeply and effectively with EMDR and IFS, her supervisor encouraged Chloe to tune into her own angry parts to listen to them, rather than judge and dismiss them in an attempt to be a 'good therapist.' Chloe felt appreciation for her angry frustrated parts, and she realised the client was avoiding doing the work by simply talking. By hearing her angry part, Chloe

could then ask this part to step behind her with Self-energy as she invited the client, with compassion, to step into the past with IFS-Informed EMDR. This was an invitation the client was able to accept, in part because of the compassion she had felt coming from Chloe.

- **Perfectionist and getting-it-right parts**: Lucy's first EMDR client was a man who'd experienced violent abuse on his first day at a Catholic school run by nuns. The image was a towering black figure. He was four years old in the memory and his negative cognition (NC) was 'I'm going to die' (or sometimes 'I'm worthless'). Lucy had just done Part 1 of basic training and was being very perfectionist about getting the PC right, and ensuring it matched the domain of the NC. Lucy's perfectionist parts took over, so they spent two whole sessions trying to get the right positive cognition (PC). Clearly the client felt shamed, reporting, 'I'm getting it wrong'— apologising that it was his fault he couldn't do EMDR properly. Thankfully, Lucy sought IFS-Informed EMDR supervision and was able to help the client to heal early-life attachment wounds. A lot of this healing was done by witnessing and retrieving abandoned child exiles who had struggled alone through asthma attacks in the night. Once these exiles were witnessed with Self-energy, Phase 4 of EMDR desensitisation went much more smoothly. Later, Lucy returned to process the client's original school target to a subjective unit of disturbance (SUDS) of zero, install a PC of 'I'm worthwhile' with a Validity of Cognition (VoC) of seven, and a clear body scan!

- **Approval-seeking parts**: Emily wanted to please her supervisor by doing EMDR by the book. She was working with a client who had been sexually abused by her father up to the age of eight. Emily described the client as 'going everywhere.' The client would be looping in the same memory, session after session. Emily said to her supervisor, 'I'm staying out of the way, just like I was taught in my EMDR basic training.' Her supervisor, after having Emily notice her approval-seeking parts and seeing if they would relax back, shared how there must be a balance between the pros and cons of intervening. Her supervisor suggested more frequent returns to target and the use of IFS-informed interweaves. This could include having the client's Self witness the child part who was trapped in the memory, and helping the child feel safe and seen. Emily's supervisor also invited Emily to do the IFS redos with the client and ask the client, 'What did this child part need to have happen?' After this, an unburdening might be helpful in bringing the SUDs down to zero.

- **Self-disclosing parts**: some exile parts can be very open and want everyone to know about their pain. This is not to say that self-disclosure is wrong, but perhaps any therapist could first check the reason for the urge to self-disclose. If it's to get close to the client, maybe that's an exile. If it's to help the client overcome their own shame about a behaviour, perhaps that is more Self-led. Jason, who had lost his driving licence through speeding, decided to self-disclose to a client who felt shame about being arrested for being drunk and disorderly while leaving a party in her teens. The client found Jason's self-disclosure, shared briefly as an education interweave in EMDR language, central to processing the memory during Phase 4. This was the extra information the client's AIP needed. The therapist she thought so highly of was human and trusted her with such potentially embarrassing information. The client was able to install a PC that it's OK to make mistakes and learn.

- **Rescuing and caretaking parts**: Belinda found it uncomfortable when her client was upset and crying. She jumped in to rescue with resource figures (Parnell, 2013) just as the attachment story of a wounded seven-year-old was beginning to unfold. This gave the client the message that her vulnerable parts were unwelcome. During supervision, Belinda acknowledged that her rescuing caretaking parts had jumped in too quickly, and would invite them to relax back and tuck in behind her in future sessions to allow for more witnessing during Phase 4 of EMDR.

- **Trauma parts**: both rescuing and caretaking parts are trying to keep Belinda (see above) out of her own trauma parts— in other words, to protect her exiles. If Belinda was—for instance—sexually abused in childhood, and hasn't had therapy for this, Belinda's own trauma parts are likely to be activated when a client walks in who has also been sexually abused in childhood. Many therapists from both schools (IFS and EMDR) see themselves as 'wounded healers,' and are recommended to seek personal therapy to heal their own trauma to avoid its being triggered during a session.

- **Dissociative parts**: these are the parts of the EMDR therapist that block effective listening. They are firefighters trying to keep out exiled parts. Chris found himself dissociating when a client wanted to target memories of her intrusive critical mother. Chris also had an intrusive critical mother. The client felt angry that Chris wasn't listening; Chris looked blank. Through EMDR supervision, Chris was able to own his countertransference and his own parts triggered by the client, then target these parts during his own EMDR therapy. Ultimately, Chris was able to apologise for the dissociative rupture with the client. Then he targeted this moment, in Phase 3, using the dissociative rupture as a bridging point (Parnell, 2013) to the client's early attachment memory, to be desensitised in Phase 4.

- **Self-like or Self-mirroring parts**: Self-like parts in both the therapist and the client look and behave like the Self but are just another protector, because unlike the Self, they always have an agenda. In many cases they want to project to others (and ourselves) that we are good people (Schwartz, 2021). Therapists might also be in Self-like parts at times. So, how can we spot them in ourselves and clients? Firstly, the work will get stuck or will be flat and not very healing. Some of the clues include exiles not trusting Self-like parts. One EMDR therapist, Janet, feared she lacked a Self: Prior to her own therapy, some of Janet's parts insisted she had no Self-energy, that there was just a big empty void inside. Many of Janet's parts feared they wouldn't be wanted or cared for if Self turned up. Janet mistook the emptiness for a lack of Self. This was actually her childhood experience of absence, an exile. Usually, the Self has been hidden through-out childhood, to protect it—sometimes even pushed out of the body, making it hard for the therapist or client to access Self.

- **Burnt-out/tired parts**: James had recently returned from holiday, but he still found it hard not to be triggered by his clients' stories of pain, abuse, and neglect. He felt burdened by their stories, like it was happening to him. His supervisor helped him make the distinction between compassion and empathy. Although the two terms are used interchangeably, empathy is not a quality of Self for a reason. Empathy is more a merging and feel-ing for the other person ('empathetic distress'), with distress emerging from the person providing the empathy (Singer & Klimecki, 2014). In contrast, compassion is feeling *for* and not feeling *with* the other. Compassion is more a sense of being a loving, caring witness. We can still feel for the other person, and offer whatever help we can, but we are not adding our own distress and suffering into the situation. If the EMDR therapist is blended with their fix-it, rescuing, or over-empathising parts, not only are they not resonating with the client, but they risk getting over-whelmed and suffering from empathy fatigue and burnout.

Welcoming Self-Energy into Therapists' Systems

Both EMDR (Dworkin, 2005) and IFS (Twombly & Schwartz, 2008) recom-mend that therapists check in with their parts to see if they need or want to share anything before the session starts (Dworkin, 2005; Twombly & Schwartz, 2008). As Joanne H. Twombly has shared in Chapter 20, we can check in before or even during a session with our parts. We might notice some parts activated within us, and write down the feelings, such as: 'bored'; 'irritated'; 'distracted'; or 'scared'. We can check our access to Self-energy, and from Self we can ask the part, 'What do you need me to know right now? Is there any wisdom you can give me regarding my client?'

I did this with a new client who walked in looking hostile and aggressive, avoiding eye contact by looking at the wall and floor. I noticed I felt really uncomfortable as he rambled incoherently. I jotted down 'scared'. the part holding the fear felt heard; it was able to unblend enough for me to show it some compassion and curiosity, and then I realised that was what I needed to show the client. All I said was 'I notice it's really hard for you to make eye contact.' He burst into tears and said he was full of shame. My heart opened with compassion, and we had a set of seven tremendously productive sessions of EMDR. In closing he named how blended he was with a five-year-old traumatised child, for whom he now felt a great deal of compassion, and he was able to be his wise adult Self. This experience, along with many others, helped reinforce how our toughest clients can sometimes be our greatest teachers. By being our tormentors—or our tour/-mentors—(Schwartz, 2021, p. 145), they can guide us back to our own parts, who can then light the road to healing both ourselves and our clients.

Note

1 In the IFS community, this is credited to Richard Schwartz.

References

Dworkin, M. (2005). *EMDR and the relational imperative: The therapeutic relationship in EMDR treatment*. Routledge.

Dyson, N. (2024, Winter). Encouraging practising EMDR post-training. *EMDR Therapy Quarterly*. https://etq.emdrassociation.org.uk/2024/01/29/encouraging-practising-emdr-post-training/.

Farrell, D., & Keenan, P. (2013). Participants' experiences of EMDR training in the United Kingdom and Ireland. *Journal of EMDR Practice and Research*, 7(1). https://connect.springerpub.com/highwire_display/entity_view/node/69859/full.

Karpman, S. (1968). Fairy tales and script drama analysis. *Transactional Analysis Bulletin*, 7(26), 39–43.

Laliotis, D., Luber, M., Oren, U., Shapiro, E., Ichii, M., Hase, M., La Rosa, L., Alter-Reid, K., & St. Jammes, J. T. (2021). What Is EMDR Therapy? Past, Present, and Future Directions. *Journal of EMDR Practice and Research*, 15(4), 186–201. https://doi.org/10.1891/EMDR-D-21-00029.

McGoldrick, A. (2022, Summer). In reply to the Council of Scholars: How an IFS-informed approach to EMDR could help EMDR trainees on their journey to becoming fully-fledged EMDR psychotherapists. *EMDR Therapy Quarterly*.

McGoldrick, A. (2023, Winter). The flexible and relational approach of IFS enhances EMDR's eight phases: A composite case study. *EMDR Therapy Quarterly*. https://etq.emdrassociation.org.uk/case-study/the-flexible-and-relational-approach-of-ifs-enhances-emdrs-eight-phases-a-composite-case-study/.

McGoldrick, A. (2024) EMDR therapists: 'Get curious not cautious.' *EMDRIA* guest blog post (June 7).

Parnell, L. (2013). *Attachment-focused EMDR: Healing relational trauma*. New York. Norton.

Proudlock, S., & Peris, J. (2020). Using EMDR therapy with patients in an acute mental health crisis. *BMC Psychiatry*, 20(14).

Schwartz, R. C. (2021). *No bad parts: Healing trauma and restoring wholeness with the Internal Family Systems model*. Sounds True.

Schwartz, R. C., & Sweezy, M. (2019). *Internal Family Systems Therapy* (2nd ed.). Guilford Press.

Shapiro, F. (2002). *EMDR as an integrative psychotherapy approach*. American Psychological Association.

Singer, T., & Klimecki, O. M. (2014). Empathy and compassion. *Current Biology*, *24*(18), R875–R878.

Twombly, J. (2023). *Trauma and dissociation informed Internal Family Systems: How to successfully treat C-PTSD, and dissociative disorders* [Kindle Edition]. Self-Publishing.com.

Twombly, J. (2024). Trauma, dissociation, parts [Workshop]. Sydney, Sept. 3–5. Group discussion.

Twombly, J., & Schwartz, R. (2008). The integration of the Internal Family Systems model and EMDR. In C. Forgash & M. Copeley (Eds.), *Healing the heart of trauma and dissociation with EMDR and ego state therapy* (pp. 295–311). Springer.

Wachtel, P. L. (2002). Psychoanalysis and the disenfranchised: From therapy to justice. *Psychoanalytic Psychology*, *19*(1), 199–215.

Chapter 22

A Circle of Self-Energy for Memory Reprocessing

Claire van den Bosch

Mining Diamonds[1]

I used to be convinced
that if I could shrink
myself smaller than
a pin, smaller than a
mustard seed or comma,

if I could crawl inside
my head like a microbic
coal miner, the canary
would be dead within a
minute. Doesn't it feel

like that? Shine a flash-
light on this mess, and I'll
find out just how slimy,
worthless, and fundamentally
mistaken I really am.

But just the opposite is true.
The more illumination I
bring in, the more I see, the
more caved-in passageways
I excavate

The more the canary sings
In ecstasy. And the
miner, light reflecting on
wide veins of diamonds

the miner just stumbled
into paradise.

By Danna Faulds

DOI: 10.4324/9781003541554-27

Externalization and Creative Legacy Heirlooms

My beloved paternal grandmother was a toymaker. I grew up surrounded by swatches of fabric, skeins of thread, and Tupperware boxes full of buttons. Much of my soul was formed from the legacy heirlooms of cutting, sticking, and sewing, and these gifts from my grandmother began to bless me and my clients when I started rummaging in my cupboard for objects to support them in externalizing their systems in physical ways that would facilitate *unblending* (see Chapter 2).

Over the years, I've noticed that explicit invitations to go inside can paradoxically mobilize increased blending with some protectors. While this in itself will often be a rich trailhead to explore, my belief is that there is also a time and a place for finding creative ways, like with externalization, to lend our own Self-energy to the client to facilitate unblending without insight.

Using Externalization to Move from Phase 2 to Phase 3

This chapter is about an externalization ritual supported with *bilateral stimulation* that part of me created one day out of some of the treasures from my cupboard. This ritual has gone on to become almost its own treatment form and session container, with especial value for those clients of mine with parts that struggle, in various ways and for good reason, with Insight (going inside and speaking directly with their internal parts).

The ritual has as its central feature a big circle, created on the floor with thick golden thread. At some point in the treatment room, it was referred to as "Stepping into the Circle of Self-Energy" and its name was born. The language has been received by some clients with something close to reverence. Others respond to it with the deafening eye-roll of endless tolerance for my "woo-woo" experiments on them; I am ever graced by their good humor!

In truth, it's the impact on the eye-rolling clients which I treasure the most. It seems to allow their most wary or skeptical parts to step both metaphorically and literally from caution, even chaos, into compassionate connection with the rest of the client's internal system and with me.

For some clients, in some sessions, the externalization process I describe in this chapter can be understood as pure Discovery (see Chapter 7), found primarily in Phase 2 of EMDR. Externalization can support our clients in unblending from parts and thereby connecting with more Self-energy. Many IFS therapists using externalization regularly discover how this way of working particularly increases clients' clarity about, perspective on, and compassion for their different parts. This in turn often allows their parts—and their nervous systems—to experience increased calm.

Adding bilateral stimulation to this process is in line with both Shapiro's and Parnell's emphasis on the value of "tapping in" resources and enhancing the client's AIP. Over many sessions—weeks, months, and even years—my experience has been that this kind of pure Phase 2 work can eventually pave the way to more success in the later phases of EMDR (Parnell, 2008; Shapiro, 2001).

However, for other clients and in other sessions, I've found that this way of working can support—within a single session—the client's protectors with allowing access to the vulnerability being protected. When this happens, client and therapist can move, with permission, to EMDR Phases 3 and onward, to witness, desensitize, and reprocess traumatic experience. Until this can happen, this unprocessed experience continues to present as clients experiencing very little choice about the entrenched protective survival strategies that are characterizing their way of navigating life and relationships with themselves and others.

Nika (they/them) is an extended case study presented in this chapter. They have a fierce, justice-oriented protector, who they are often identified with in their day-to-day life. As with many of our very relationally traumatized clients, these protectors often double down and blend even more fiercely in reaction to invitations to go inside.

Using "Stepping into the Circle of Self-Energy," this experimental externalization process with Nika one day supported their dedicated and fierce protectors enough to unblend and allow us to be with their tender exiles, who we could then support with Phases 3–7 of EMDR to unburden and discover their true nature.

In the days and weeks that followed this session, Nika began reporting more choice and sophistication in their protective system. Their compulsion to step into conflict with both their boss and their partner reduced. They experienced increased willingness to "pick their battles," noticed a surprising emergence of "caring less" how their boss was acting, and realized their entire nervous system felt less "charged" and more energized. Consequently, they also experienced some change in how compelled they felt to use food to comfort and reward themselves. This was a big success for us, as their relationship with food and their body was also a key focus of our work, and one that seemed very stuck.

Extended Case Study: Nika and the Circle of Self Energy

I'm used to Nika arriving at our sessions furious and confused. We've worked together for seven years, and they embraced the IFS model with the same kind of enthusiasm I experienced when I discovered it. But I suspect we all know the human reality, which Nika often experiences, of really needing someone to just listen to us like the singular being that we also feel ourselves to be. This is very often the case with Nika—and me—and other humans like us, especially when we are very angry.

I noticed quickly after starting my IFS training how my "IFS-newbie-I've-got-to-*make*-them- do-Insight" part would often get into *polarization* with a part that was anxious about interrupting an angry client's need for witness (Schwartz, 1995). I've gotten to know this anxious part of me in my own work with my inner family, and of course as for so many of us on healing journeys through our own relational trauma, other people's anger (and our own) is a common trigger for young, frightened parts of us.

This kind of rich, difficult, and familiar world of *trailheads* for us as therapists is why I'm so grateful for the way the IFS model, and teachers like Joanne Twombly (see Chapter 20) and Annabel McGoldrick (see Chapter 21), emphasize the importance of tending to our own internal families when they become distressed in our client work; not just between therapy sessions, but also while we are in the middle of a therapy session.

I have come to discover that the anxiety parts of me experience, when they detect my therapist part urging me to invite a *U-turn*, serves also as a wonderful "canary" which is anticipating, often very accurately, the fears of my clients' protectors when it comes to going inside. They're the fears of many of my own protectors. In truth, it was the anxious parts of me that motivated me to try externalization with Nika.

Angry Protectors' Issues with Going Inside

It's worth mentioning that many angry protectors sometimes draw a blank in response to—or else take issue with—the classic IFS question, "What are you afraid would happen if you no longer did your job?" They might respond indignantly, "I don't feel fear!" This might even be the implicit motto of the entire angry-family. So rather than going head-to-head with that trailhead, I've learned to ask, "What is causing you to be angry? What do you feel the problem is? Why is this situation/behavior bothering you?"

Often the problem with being invited to do a U-turn, or at least to do it too soon, is that if I as therapist don't know the full story, then I won't have the information a part of my client believes I need to confirm for them that they weren't the bad guy in the situation they're describing.

Another problem is that if I as therapist am inviting clients to go inside, it's perceived as evidence that I believe (as they were often regularly told by a parent or teacher), that they "are the problem," they're "over-reacting," and that their distress is because they're triggered, not because someone else was actually being aggressive or hurtful. At the very best, what's bothersome about being invited to go inside is that it's implicitly repeating the all-too-familiar message that they're the one who must do the emotional labor while someone else "gets away with it." And I for one have a lot of sympathy with all of these perceptions. As well as the "canary" signals of anxiety already mentioned, it was understanding these triggering facets of the U-turn invitation which motivated me to try externalization with Nika.

I should state for the record that a very experienced IFS supervisor often wisely challenged my system's creativity in anticipating and avoiding activating my client's most dedicated protectors. It was important for me to understand that my creativity was sometimes being deployed avoidantly to protect vulnerable members of my inner family. At the same time, I have also been supported in celebrating the super-power of *radical resonance* that my beloved canary parts bring to my work, for the benefit of clients whose vulnerability is kept so far back that we run the risk of never making it through the barbed wire to the tender ones in such desperate need of unburdening (McConnell, 2020).

Externalization Facilitating Unblending—For Me and My Client

One day, when Nika arrived furious and confused, my own parts split like the Red Sea into their familiar *polarization*. One team wanted to witness Nika as a singular being sharing a deeply affecting story. The other team pressed me to support Nika to connect in a different way with the chain reaction of parts that was so familiar to me from our work together—but the canary-anxiety was loud.

Nika's fierce justice-oriented protector had been witnessed and validated many times, mostly using implicit direct access (I would speak directly with Nika's parts without clearly expressing that this was what I was doing). Past encouragements to go inside and get to know this protector had repeatedly inflamed the protector further.

I personally use a liberal amount of empathic conjecture (Goldman et al., 2021) during implicit direct access when clients are very blended, and never more so than when they're angry or confused. On several occasions with Nika, when their protector became more inflamed when I invited a U-turn, I empathically conjectured the variety of issues they might have with going inside. These moments had, up to this point, been exceptionally helpful for Nika's sense of being truly understood by me and for the quality of the connection between us. But this never paved the way for willingness to allow access to Nika's vulnerability.

In calmer sessions we had talked *about* the parts involved and even tried to make (ultimately fruitless) agreements that "next time" we'd try again to go inside to be with this dedicatedly fierce one. I'd tried supporting Nika's fierce protector to develop new communication skills using non-violent communication (Rosenberg, 2015). I'd tried coaching them to at least assume that a vulnerable part of them is activated when they feel fierce and to practice taking time-outs to send messages inside. Even when this wasn't met with overt scoffing, Nika's experience was clearly very often one of choiceless compulsion to fight first.

Nika's inner family has found a lot of value over the years in using strategies from *Facing the Fire* (Lee, 1993), especially at home, where a Self-like part of Nika has been able to partner with their fierce protector to go into a private room and physicalize their urge to fight for fairness. As an integrative therapist, and a pragmatist, I believe in supporting parts to develop updated strategies. But these strategies aren't so easy to practice in the workplace.

Ultimately, none of this integrative smorgasbord of approaches yielded any significant sustained change in Nika's familiar interpersonal patterns of high conflict with their boss and their partner. Time and time again, I noticed repeating sequences of Nika detecting injustice (many times accurately) and grabbing their metaphorical sword to fight, leading to inevitable interpersonal escalation, a part of Nika villainizing the other person for their response to Nika's challenges, and ultimately desperate "case-building for the prosecution." Often this would all be compounded by ostracism or rejection from the other, or else detectable appeasement. Sadly, there was regular self-recrimination, shame, hurt, and confusion for Nika.

The Importance of Getting Beyond Phase 2

My professional conviction was that these chain reactions, and Nika's compulsive fighting, could only be transformed if we could move into Phases 3–7 to reprocess the early life experiences of huge vulnerability that had forced part of Nika to become this fierce protector. But how to get permission when U-turn invitations invoked only frustration, and no amount of compassion or offering understanding changed the refusal?

Sitting with Nika's anger, I felt the familiar canary tension in my body—a frozenness, masked by a facial expression conveying attention and sympathy. Words stuck in my throat: one part trying to come up with the right words that wouldn't shame Nika, one part feeling impatient with and blaming them. The first part whispered, "this is not Nika's fault," and a third, familiar part joined in to judge my hesitation to invite a U-turn.

A therapist part reminded me of a supervisor's mantra. "Sit back. Breathe. Open your heart." I quietly used my notebook to write down the names of each of these parts of me wrestling one another so intensely, sending acknowledgment inside to them all. And then something new happened: I pulled open the door of my room cupboard, grabbed a wodge of paper, and hacked it into smaller slips before snipping a length of golden thread from its roller to demarcate a half-meter diameter circle on the floor. This was all clearly baffling Nika, and they eyed me warily.

"What are you doing?" they said.

"Making sure I'm really getting it," was what came out of my mouth without thinking.

I sat cross-legged on the floor instead of back in my chair, and, grabbing a marker, with Nika still staring at me, wary but also clearly curious, I talked about each of the reactions they'd had to the unkind, unfair thing their boss had said to them in front of the whole team. I used a different slip of paper for each "part" Nika had all but explicitly named. I added in the parts that I sensed in how Nika was showing up right now, such as the part that needed me to really understand what had happened, along with another part that was secretly afraid that Nika was in the wrong.

I set out all the slips on the floor inside the golden circle as I talked Nika through what my parts-detector part had picked up, gently positioning them in the rough shape of Cece Sykes's IFS inverted triangle (Sykes, Sweezy, & Schwartz, 2023) with firefighters at one point of the triangle, managers at another, and exiles at the third point. I checked with Nika what I'd gotten wrong and who I'd missed. There was a flicker of my old sand-tray training somewhere in my awareness (Homeyer & Sweeney, 2011), and a transpersonal perspective to do with creating an "earth-element" quality of groundedness by staying on the floor, along with the quality of containment that came with using a circle to work inside of (Edinger, 1994).

Nika was quiet for a few moments, just looking from one slip of paper to another.

"What's it like right now, Nika," I asked, "seeing all these parts of you set out like this?"

"It's never been so clear before, all the different parts, when we've talked about them," was their response.

"What effect is it having on you, being clearer like this?" I asked.

"Well, I guess I feel a bit calmer, looking at it all, seeing it down *there* rather than it all crashing around in *here*." Nika gestured to inside their head and chest in swirling movements.

"Can you feel it anywhere physically in your body, where it feels a bit better right now?" I asked.

Nika took a moment, eyes cast down toward the ground.

"Yeah, my chest and stomach are more relaxed, and my jaw," they answered.

"That's great. Would it be OK to stay for a few moments with that experience, that feeling of it being clearer, and calmer, and better in your body? Can we do some 'tapping in' while you breathe in and out of that experience?"

Nika nodded and closed their eyes while I tapped on the outsides of their knees, staying connected with them with my voice, inviting them to gently rest their attention on the positive, calmer change in their body, and the relief of a bit more mental clarity.

The words came to me: "This is your Self-energy right here, Nika. Notice how you found it, seeing each of your different parts more clearly. Remember, we don't focus on parts to make them go away or to tell them that the outside situation doesn't matter. We find ways to connect with them more clearly so we can give them the space and care they need to handle outside situations."

Nika nodded slowly, their eyes still closed, their breathing rhythmic and deeper. So was mine. I could feel my own Self-energy amplifying with theirs. I was vaguely aware that my little canary part was very calm. Even as I type this, I feel awe at the wisdom of my parts and how important it is to listen to what they're telling me in sessions. And I register yet again the importance of having access to enough of my own Self-energy in sessions. Noticing and taking my own parts seriously, externalizing Nika's system, as well as getting on the ground, and doing something physical and creative, had supported my own system to unblend.

Seeking Consent to Transition to EMDR's Phases 3–7

At this point in the session, I could feel that something new and soft was happening, and had the sense of a genuine window of opportunity opening.

"I've got another idea," I said.

I gathered up the slips of paper and invited Nika to open their palms to hold them.

"You can share the calm and the clarity with them all," I suggested. Then I asked, "Is there any one of these parts who you feel most needs extra care right now?"

Nika leafed through the slips of paper.

"The one who's scared they're being unreasonable, who can't figure out if it was OK for my boss to chew me out in front of everyone like that."

There was a slight catch in Nika's throat, and I felt my own heart ache a little. Dozens of stories tugged at the edges of my memory of Nika's controlling, critical father shaming them at the dinner table, while their mother kept her eyes down, waiting for her husband to be finished. I reached for my sunshine amulet from the sideboard.

"Would you like to stand inside the circle Nika, hold all your parts in your hands, with that part right at the top?" I ventured. I felt a part of me clench my stomach in embarrassment. "You're going WAY too far," it said. "Nika is going to think you're a total weirdo now."

Nika was grinning at me. "Are you being spooky?" they teased, using a word we'd played with together before.

"Undoubtedly!" I grinned back.

But as Nika stepped inside the golden circle, this sweet playfulness between us yielded naturally to something quiet and sincere. They looked at the paper slips in their hands. I placed the sun amulet on top and said:

"All spookiness aside, Nika, these parts of you are each so precious and deserve our care. And this one at the top, we know how much they suffer, especially with your boss, afraid that you've no right to be upset. If it's ok, I'm going to tap on your shoulders and you and me are going to spend a moment letting this part and all other parts here feel this little bit of clarity and this little bit of calm in your jaw, chest and stomach."

I started tapping on the outsides of Nika's shoulders, both of us looking gently down at the slips of paper under the sun amulet in their hands.

While I tapped, I asked:

"What do you think Nika, is this a good time to go a bit deeper with the more vulnerable parts of you who get so distressed around your boss, and see if we can help them do some processing? Have a check inside and see if that's ok with everyone."

Nika kept their eyes closed and tipped their head slightly to one side.

"I think it's a good time," they responded.

Nika moved naturally back to the sofa, and in this moment, I remember a part of me detected my therapeutic inclination—to check in again specifically with Nika's fierce protector—and that my part felt afraid that even mentioning this part would reactivate them back into outrage. I believe it's important to maintain clarity, perspective, and persistence when it comes to the necessity of supporting our clients' systems to unburden. And it's also important to be able to tell when a therapist part of us is a little overcommitted in any given moment to the agenda of moving into Phase 3 and beyond, and when there are parts fearing that they will be disappointed and frustrated for their own sake.

Writing up this session now, I can spot that at this point in the session with Nika, the fear of mentioning the fierce protector was a good readout that I was a little blended with a part with an agenda. But the truth is, I didn't spot that at the time. What I did know, somewhat blended as I was with a therapist part, was that consent from this protector was critical, and hoping to tiptoe past them wasn't right, and that was enough to get me to ask the question.

As I sat back down in my own chair, I said: "Before we create space to be with the more tender ones, Nika, let's check specifically with your fierce one? How do you feel towards them right now?"

Nika's face was soft but serious. "I totally love them. They're so courageous. Totally heroic."

"Do they know you feel like that about them Nika?" I asked.

"For sure," they responded.

"Are they OK with us creating space for the more vulnerable parts of you who get so upset by your boss?"

Nika paused. "It really feels OK. As long as they're not being asked to like him." They were half smiling at me—it was almost as if I could see a part watching me keenly—maybe the fierce one with some of their own vulnerability.

Looking them in the eye I said sincerely, "Nika. I'm fairly certain your boss is an actual maniac. I always want you—and me—to be able to stand up for ourselves with bullies and anyone else treating us unfairly. You and I both need these fierce parts of us in this life. Please let your fierce part know that from me. Being with vulnerable parts is nothing to do with stopping fighting for fairness and justice. It's important this part of you knows that. Can you check—does it feel like they know you'll always need and value them?"

Nika rifled through the slips of paper still in their hands to find the fierce part, and when they found them, they put down the other slips and hugged this one to their heart. Nika confided, "I have this sense that they've never quite been sure of that before, but that they actually feel it right now."

"Take a moment with them, before we shift our attention," I suggested.

Nika looked softly down at the slip of paper in their hands for a few beats, before looking back to me and nodding.

"Does it feel right to "sit" them somewhere?" I asked, aware of the power of having externalized parts onto pieces of paper and not wanting to treat the paper disrespectfully. "Where does this part want to be while we slow things down a bit more?"

Nika angled a cushion on the empty seat of the sofa and propped up the piece of paper as if the part were sitting apart from her but staying present to observe. Their energy still seemed calm, and simply present and open to the session unfolding, and mine felt the same.

Phase 3 Begins

"Nika, if it's OK, pull up the memory of your boss yelling at you from yesterday. Find the worst moment and tell me what you see and hear."

Their eyes closed while they responded. "I can see his wide-open mouth and can hear the *volume* of him yelling—I can feel it actually hurting my ears."

I knew I needed a way to help Nika connect even more deeply with the vulnerability that was being activated by their boss. I needed the fierce protector's help, but again I could feel the warning twinge in me urging me not to ask them the more typical "what is this part's fear" IFS-protector question. What emerged from my wordsmithing part was this:

"Nika, see if you can ask the fierce part of you sitting beside you this question. If for some reason they hadn't been able to be around when your boss was yelling that loud—with his mouth all wide open and hurting your ears with the volume of his shouting—what other feelings would you have been left with?"

First gazing quietly into their lap, then tipping back their head in the way a part of them does when tears are coming, Nika searched for the right words. "Terrified ... Frozen ... Mortified in front of everyone. Powerless ... Really confused."

"That's really good work Nika. And what's happening in your body right now that goes with all this?" I asked.

Nika's hand went spontaneously to their solar plexus. "It's that terrible knot thing. Like all my guts just twisted up."

"Well done," I said, encouragingly. "So, seeing your boss's mouth all wide open, feeling the actual pain in your ears from his yelling, and

your guts all knotted up, feeling so powerless, frozen, mortified, terrified, and confused … see if there are any words that want to come,
anything that feels true about this?"

"I'm so trapped …" Nika whispered.

I picked up my eye-movement wand from the arm of my chair
where it usually waits, patiently and hopefully. "Go with that," I said.

Note

1 Danna Faulds, "Mining Diamonds," in *One Soul: More Poems from the Heart of
   Yoga* (Peaceable Kingdom, 2003).

References

Edinger, E. (1994). *The anatomy of the psyche: Alchemical symbolism in psychotherapy.* Inner City Books.

Goldman, R. N., Vaz, A., & Rousmaniere, T. (2021). Appendix B: Distinguishing
between empathic responses. In *Deliberate practice in emotion-focused therapy* (pp.
183–184). American Psychological Association.

Homeyer, L. E., & Sweeney, D. S. (2011). *Sandtray therapy: A practical manual.*
Routledge

Lee, J. (1993). *Facing the fire: Experiencing and expressing anger appropriately.*
Bantam.

McConnell, S. (2020). *Somatic Internal Family Systems Therapy: Awareness, breath,
resonance, movement and touch in practice.* North Atlantic Books.

Parnell, L. (2008). *Tapping in: A step-by-step guide to activating your healing resources
through bilateral stimulation.* W. W. Norton & Company.

Rosenberg, M. B. (2015). *Nonviolent communication: A language of life: Life-changing
tools for healthy relationships* (3rd ed.). PuddleDancer Press.

Schwartz, R. C. (1995). *Internal family systems therapy.* Guilford Press.

Shapiro, F. (2001). *Eye movement desensitization and reprocessing: Basic principles,
protocols, and procedures* (2nd ed.). Guilford Press.

Sykes, C., Sweezy, M., & Schwartz, R. C. (2023). *Internal family systems: Therapy for
addictions.* Publishing, Inc.

Chapter 23

The Vessel Imagery

Reimagining the Container as a Resource to Support the Transformational Healing of IFS-Informed EMDR

Nancy Simons

Resourcing is a highly debated topic between the Internal Family Systems (IFS) and the Eye Movement Desensitization and Reprocessing (EMDR) community. IFS says that Self is the ultimate resource, and in EMDR, grounding and stabilization skills are the cornerstone of the Preparation Phase. The Syzygy Model (see Chapter 6) is a phase-oriented model, and many EMDR clinicians who come to learn the model often ask about resourcing. The Syzygy Model sheds light on this debated discussion and informs my reimagining of the container exercise. The Syzygy Model embodies two important concepts to consider in relation to resourcing: *Memory Reconsolidation* as the mechanism that allows for transformational healing and *Self* as the generator of adaptive knowledge. For clinicians, I believe it is important to broaden our focus from "Do we do resourcing?" to "What are we resourcing?" and "Who is doing the resourcing?" The vessel imagery introduced here resources Self-energy and supports transformational healing.

Memory Reconsolidation

As cited in Bruce Hersey's earlier Chapter 6, memory reconsolidation is the underlying mechanism that facilitates trauma healing. Memory reconsolidation is a type of neuroplasticity which, "when launched by a certain series of experiences, actually unlocks the synapses of a target emotional learning, allowing it to be not merely overridden but actually nullified and deleted by new learning" (Ecker et al., 2022, p. 4). Juxtaposing implicit emotional learning with what Ecker names as disconfirming knowledge creates the conditions for memory reconsolidation and trauma healing. Francine Shapiro's AIP model juxtaposed a dysfunctional network with an adaptive network. The EMDR Standard Protocol, based on Shapiro's AIP model, has been a powerful approach to trauma treatment. Yet, many EMDR clinicians and their clients have witnessed the process becoming stalled out, avoidance defenses becoming activated and at times, backlash occurring. Memory reconsolidation helps us understand that juxtaposing emotional learning with an

DOI: 10.4324/9781003541554-28

adaptive network that is not strong enough can cause these kinds of stalls in processing. Ecker states that, "Therapists routinely witness the extraordinary durability of original emotional learnings, which persist in their unrelenting vice grip on mood and behavior decades after they were formed." Ecker goes on to state that disconfirming knowledge "must feel decisively real to the person based on his or her own living experiences. In other words, it must be experiential learning as distinguished from conceptual, intellectual learning, though it may be accompanied by the latter" (Ecker et al., 2022).

Self and Self-energy Is the Generator of Adaptive Knowledge

In EMDR, the adaptive network is identified during the Preparation Phase. For clients whose nervous system is geared toward survival, identifying an adaptive network at this early stage of treatment can be quite difficult. Ecker would say that we are eliciting a positive belief from a conceptual, intellectual kind of knowing. Through an IFS lens, we would say that the belief is being generated by a manager who wants things to be better. In the Syzygy Model of IFS-Informed EMDR, the Preparation Phase consists of developing a Self-to-part relationship. Only when enough Self-energy emerges in the system is the client invited to identify the adaptive network (Assessment Phase) by asking the question "What do you (Self) know that the part doesn't know?"

Accessing Self-presence in relation to burdened parts opens the doorway to disconfirming knowledge. Clients experience the juxtaposition of an emotional learning with the present felt sense of Self-energy as it arises in session. The juxtaposition shifts from dysfunctional and adaptive networks to burdened parts and Self -presence. Self and Self-energy are described by Hersey as all these things: The Adaptive Network, Conscious Relational Entity, Knower of all Adaptive Knowledge, Spiritual Core, and Source of Healing Energy. IFS uses a beautiful metaphor of Self as the sun and parts as the clouds: It goes on to say that Self, like the sun, is always present; sometimes partially clouded over, sometimes fully clouded over, and sometimes fully present. Clients need as much of the sun present as possible to facilitate memory reconsolidation and trauma healing. In IFS-Informed EMDR, Self-presence is what invites and maintains the juxtaposition. Juxtaposing implicit emotional learning with disconfirming knowledge creates the conditions for memory reconsolidation.

What Is the Function of Resourcing? Transformational Change vs. Counteractive Change

From a neurobiological perspective, Ecker helps us understand that emotion regulation skills "creates brain change in the form of new neural connections; but it is only when new learning also unwires old learning that transformational change occurs, rather than counteractive change, and this is precisely what the reconsolidation process achieves" (Ecker et al., 2022, p. 33). Understanding this crucial difference between EMDR "resourcing" and IFS "connecting with Self-energy" informs the question, "Do we do resourcing when using an IFS-Informed EMDR treatment model?" As a trainer of IFS-Informed EMDR, I believe that we need to instead ask the question, "Do we want our resources to facilitate *transformational* change (deep, fundamental restructuring of information) or *counteractive* change (addressing symptoms rather than the underlying structure)?"

Following Pierre Janet's model of trauma treatment, Shapiro (2001) introduces Phase 2: Preparation Phase for grounding and stabilization. In Phase 2, resourcing is frontloaded, introducing the client to many affect management tools. When resources, such as the container, are taught at the start of treatment, an IFS-informed perspective helps us understand that protective parts, rather than Self, may be generating the resource. In Standard EMDR, the container exercise is introduced to clients as a resource to use during and at the end of an incomplete session. Clients are invited to put away any and all material that came up during the session that they would like some distance from. For many clients, it is familiar and even reflexive to put things out of mind.

The container exercise transforms the action of unconsciously resisting thinking about something to an action of consciously creating a contained placeholder. The use of the container exercise can teach clients a measure of mastery by consciously putting traumatic material in a container, with the intention of getting back to it at a later session. This is what Ecker et al. (2022) identifies as counteractive change, which (similar to transformational change) can support trauma healing. Joanne H. Twombly is a strong advocate for integrating affect management skills into treatment, including the container exercise (see Chapter 20). She is an expert on treating clients with dissociative symptoms, and in her book *Trauma and Dissociation Informed Internal Family Systems*, she discusses this in great depth. She found that "people with C-PTSD and dissociative disorders needed coping skills to help them maintain functioning while going through the painful work of healing" (Twombly, 2022, p. xviii).

Who Is Generating the Resource?

In the Syzygy Model of IFS-Informed EMDR, the Preparation Phase shifts from developing affect management skills to building a Self-to-part relationship. The model resources Self and Self-energy in order to set up the conditions for memory reconsolidation; the juxtaposition of implicit emotional learnings with disconfirming knowledge. Hersey wisely names Self and Self-energy as encompassing every imaginable resource, and the Syzygy Model of IFS-Informed EMDR beautifully demonstrates this.

Self and Self-energy generate safety, security, and stability in a client's system, and it is Self that generates safe place, safe person, and container imagery. This is a crucial shift for EMDR clinicians who are still new to the IFS model to consider. Distinguishing between whether a resource is Self-generating or not helps us understand if the resource is being used for transformational healing or if it is serving a part's agenda.

Reimagining the Container Imagery and the Importance of Using Imagery

If we are to fully consider the neurological and relational changes occurring, session to session, then it feels useful to reimagine the container exercise as a resource for the closing of a session that is relational in nature, works with the tenacity of emotional learnings, and supports the overall goal of trauma treatment: Memory reconsolidation and transformational healing. Ecker cites that "new experiences that are imagined can be effective for creating new neural circuits and new responses, because emotional centers in the subcortex hardly distinguish between perceptions arising externally versus internally" (Ecker et al., 2022, p. 31). Esther Sternberg, an immunologist and pioneer in environmental psychology and neuroimmunology, says, "Imagery and visualization are believed to access the oxytocin-opiate affective regulation system and reduce sensitivity in the amygdala" (Sternberg, 2009). This is powerful to consider. Sternberg's and Ecker's research demonstrates that imagery and visualization are powerful practices, activating neurological reactions in the brain that support care and connection, both qualities of Self. In my practice, I have been repeatedly surprised to see how clearly clients remember their container imagery, and how easily available imagery is for clients when they are offered the invitation to give up their burdens to the four elements in the IFS healing steps.

Renaming the Image: Vessel Imagery

New wording for the container exercise feels important since we are inviting the client to hold together the qualities of Self as they emerge in relation to parts. I propose using the word *vessel*. When we look at the spiritual aspect of the word vessel, it can be seen as a container for divine energy and wisdom. A vessel can also be a person or a body which is channeling love or Self-energy.

Instead of having a client imagine a container to put disturbing memories or feelings into, I invite the client to connect with their Self-energy and gently place this relationship into a vessel. This vessel is meant to support the *relationship*, while at the same time allowing movement and transformation to occur in this ever-changing connection between the part and Self. Rather than being contained, Self-qualities continue to expand within this vessel, and the relationship and healing are able to continue.

The Invitation

"I would like you to think about creating a vessel or some kind of imagery to hold together the qualities of (name qualities of Self that have emerged in session) that you are feeling now towards this part." Once they create an image, I follow this up with the IFS invitation to set an intention to connect with these parts during the week. I have found that the imagery facilitates the client's ability to tap back into the Self-to-part relationship that emerged in session. This is an important invitation. Frank Anderson, in his book *Treating the Traumatized Client*, states that disconnection between Self and parts maintains trauma, and connection heals trauma (Anderson, 2021).

When to Invite in the Vessel Imagery

The purpose of the vessel imagery is to support the Self-to-part relationship that unfolds from session to session. This can be with both protector and exile parts. Therefore, we can offer the invitation at various points in the IFS-Informed EMDR process as we are closing a session.

1 Preparation Phase—If we have identified a part and the Feel Towards Question has invited in Self-energy (see Chapter 2).
2 Discovery: When we connect with blended protectors, begin to understand their positive intention and witness protectors beginning to relax. Increasing Self-energy with any part has a positive ripple effect in the system (see Chapter 7).
3 Desensitization/Healing Steps: Incomplete session. If an exile showed up but the unburdening is incomplete, we acknowledge that the part had to previously go away because of the pain it holds, but that something different can happen now. Instead of "containing" it, we can find a safe place or vessel for the healing to continue until the next time we are able to work with this part and continue the unburdening work.

Box 23.1 shows a table that outlines the differences between the container imagery used in EMDR and the vessel imagery I am introducing for IFS-Informed EMDR.

Box 23.1 The Container vs the Vessel Imagery

	CONTAINER IMAGERY	VESSEL IMAGERY
PURPOSE	CONTAIN MEMORIES AND DISTRESS ENERGY IN THE SYSTEM	SUPPORT SELF-TO-PART CONNECTION/ALLOW FOR ONGOING TRANSFER OF SELF-ENERGY TO PARTS
WHEN IS THE RESOURCE CREATED?	PREPARATION PHASE	AFTER SELF-TO-PART RELATIONSHIP IS ESTABLISHED
IMAGE	THERAPIST PROVIDES AN OUTLINE FOR WHAT THE IMAGE SHOULD LOOK LIKE	THERAPIST OFFERS AN OPEN INVITATION FOR SELF TO CREATE THE IMAGE
	OFTENTIMES THE IMAGE REMAINS CONSTANT OR GETS STRONGER DEPENDING ON THE LEVEL OF PROTECTION NEEDED	MAY CHANGE IN RELATION TO QUALITIES OF SELF-ENERGY THAT EMERGE
WHEN IS THE RESOURCE USED?	DURING SESSION AND AT THE CLOSE OF SESSION	MOST OFTEN USED AT CLOSE OF SESSION

Case Examples

Example # 1: Needing to Attend to Present-Day Issues

Meghan[1] is a 60-year-old woman who has been seeking treatment to help her navigate a complicated relationship with her adult daughter. After many years of supporting her daughter through many rounds of rehab, the daughter lost custody of her own child due to an active addiction to opioids. My client is now the legal guardian for her grand-daughter, and her daughter has completely cut off her relationship with my client. Treatment began with a protector part that had to be responsible for everything and everyone.

This part had to work as hard as it did in order to prevent her from feeling like a failure as a mother. Alongside this belief is a very complicated grief. It has been named the "never-ending grief," and appears as an image of a nuclear core ready to explode. Her child is physically alive, but the mother–daughter relationship that she yearns for does not exist. Meghan is committed to treatment, yet focus on the part burdened by "never-ending grief" has been put on pause at various times. Meghan has an adult son who is a military veteran with PTSD and alcohol addiction, and a husband with medical issues, both currently needing her time and attention. Having the vessel imagery was immensely helpful in supporting the relational healing work (i.e., the connect between the part that was grieving and Meghan's Self-energy) to help Meghan remain focused on her parts that wanted to voice concerns around her son.

Therapist: Before we shift over to speak about the concerns about your son, notice the patience and calm that you have been extending towards these parts. I want to invite you to create a vessel or any other kind of image that helps these parts maintain this connection, even as we turn our focus elsewhere.

Meghan: I picture a big giant pillow, so the part with never-ending grief has a place to be and relax. It's like Styrofoam that is shaped to whatever it needs to hold. The shape will give the form to the pillow and still be in a comforting space. Now, with this vessel, my body feels calmer. I am less worried that the nuclear core will explode. I can nurture that too. I feel safer now. The nuclear core has morphed. It is not so scary. (Strengthened with BLS)

At the next session, as part of the re-evaluation process, I revisit the vessel imagery, curious about the Self-to-part connection burdened by "never-ending grief." Meghan was able to report that the imagery had been very helpful, that her sense of safety continued to increase, and her feelings of fear and apprehension had decreased. The imagery allowed her to connect to her part in a safer way. Witnessing this, we were able to continue to focus on her parts with present-day concerns.

Example # 2: Closing a Session Following Preparation Phase

Mare is a 61-year-old client, who came into treatment with an extensive trauma history that included relational trauma, incest, stalking, and the trauma of a chronic medical condition. Treatment was over several years and utilized both the Standard EMDR approach and an IFS-Informed EMDR approach. Recently, an event had triggered an exiled part that carried the burden of rejection. Mare had access to a lot of Self-energy, including compassion, connectedness, and presence, as a result of other trauma work we had done. In the Preparation Phase of IFS-informed EMDR we were able to explore the part that held the strong feelings of rejection. The "feel towards" question elicited her compassion, connectedness, and presence for this part.

As we heard the whole story of the part, Mare was able to connect to other experiences of rejection, including the shocking breakup of her marriage as well as feeling that her mother had never been consistently available for her (her mother had major mental illness and had to be hospitalized on many occasions when Mare was a child). BLS was introduced to draw out and strengthen the relationship between this exiled part and Self-presence as it was emerging. As we approached the end of the session, I introduced the idea of creating imagery to support the relational work occurring in the session.

Therapist: Would it be helpful to create a vessel or some kind of imagery to hold together the qualities of compassion, connectedness, and presence that you are feeling now for this part?

Mare: I am remembering my childhood swing. I loved that swing! I want that to be the vessel to hold all this together. So many bad things happened back in that house. Hurt was there; the healing should be there too. (Strengthened with BLS)

In the next session, I checked in with Mare, and asked her if she could visualize the vessel, and see how strong the Self-to-part relationship was.

Mare: The image is important to me. It helps me stay connected to her (Rejected part). We need to be together. I have this deeper understanding that I can help her heal the childhood stuff. I know that I can be in charge of this healing. When I was young, I wanted to run away. The swing lets me fly (and still be with her) without having to run away.

Example # 3: The Vessel Imagery During the Desensitization Phase

Veronica is a client in her mid-twenties who was seeking EMDR treatment for a sexual assault incident that had occurred a few years back. Subsequently, she had experienced two PTSD-induced psychotic episodes. Throughout the course of treatment, we had used the vessel imagery to support the compassion and confidence as it emerged in her system in relation to some strong protector parts. Veronica had reported that the imagery offered her a safe way to connect with these parts and was helping her access greater compassion and confidence. From there we moved into the Assessment Phase.

In the Assessment Phase, when she thought about the sexual assault, her positive cognition (PC) was, "That's over and I can trust myself again." The VOC was a 5. While processing, a different life experience was activated. From a place of compassion and confidence, Veronica was able to recognize that she wanted to stay with the part that we had first started working with. She spontaneously decided to safely place the new part into a new vessel, a jam jar with cotton balls in it since the part is, "a wooly thought." She then noticed a feeling of acceptance in her arms and chest and a sense of clarity. We added BLS to strengthen Self-energy. Veronica's decision to put the new part in her vessel was indicative of her growing ability to trust herself and the confidence to know how much she could process at a time. The vessel imagery for the wooly thought was a visual way for her to act on this trust.

A few sessions later Veronica was able to reconnect with the wooly-thought part. Her vessel of trust, compassion, and confidence had supported a strong Self-to-part connection, and when we connected with this part, it felt ready to move to the healing/unburdening steps. In this example, Self had generated the vessel and supported transformational change—which felt very different than a part constructing a container for itself (or another part) for protective/counteractive change.

Harnessing the Creative Quality of Self-Presence

As IFS-Informed EMDR clinicians we can continue to utilize imagery from a new place of understanding. I have reimagined the container exercise to support the slow, steady, and oftentimes tenuous relationship between Self and parts. For clients with C-PTSD and for systems that easily blend, allowing the Self-energy that emerges in a session to be viewed through the imagination supports the healing process. It allows the Self-to-part relationship that emerges in session to take on a form that supports the transformational healing process of IFS-Informed EMDR.

At the beginning of this chapter, I introduced the question that many EMDR clinicians ask in our Syzygy trainings: "Do we still do resourcing?" Rather than engaging in either side of the debate, I open this question to a more expansive understanding of the role of resourcing in memory reconsolidation. I have utilized Ecker's contributions on neurological change for this understanding. The vessel imagery, as the reimagined and upgraded container, strengthens the internal resource of Self-energy to support memory reconsolidation. Intuitively, I have always thought that using a container when closing a session was a useful strategy. However, when we upgrade the container to a vessel, we welcome in transformational change and allow this to become a powerful resource that clients can use in-between sessions.[2]

Notes

1 All names and identifying information have been changed to protect client confidentiality.
2 To hear about some earlier iterations of the vessel imagery, specifically the "self-compassion container" you can listen to a podcast posted on my website: www. Nancysimons.com: "Healing Through the Self-Compassion Container: The Compassion and Journey of Nancy Simons," *Empowered Through Compassion*, Mar. 16.

References

Anderson, F. (2021). *Transcending trauma: Healing complex PTSD with Internal Family Systems therapy*. PESI.

Ecker, B., Ticic, R., & Hulley, L. (2022). *Unlocking the emotional brain: Eliminating symptoms at their roots using memory reconsolidation*. Routledge.

Shapiro, F. (2001). *Eye movement desensitization and reprocessing* (2nd ed.). Guilford Press.

Sternberg, E. M. (2009). *Healing spaces: The science of place and well-being*. Belknap Press and Harvard University Press.

Twombly, J. H. (2022). *Trauma and dissociation informed internal family systems* (2nd ed.). Self-Publishing.com.

Chapter 24

The Equid-Nexus® Model
Using IFS-Informed EMDR with Equine Engagement to Heal Relational Trauma

Jenn Pagone

The Equid-Nexus® Model

Equid-Nexus® is a facilitation model with a focus on healing relational trauma. Relational trauma, defined for the purposes of this chapter, is a broad term that includes developmental and interpersonal trauma and complicated bereavement. Relational wounding severs connection with others due to fear and the belief that they will inevitably hurt the client again, resulting in feelings of isolation, loneliness, and shame. Working with the parts that became sentinels to prevent re-experiencing these feelings is an important process that is best healed within a relationship with the client's Self and within a *real relationship* with another—a horse.

Horses that partner with mental health and equine professionals in the Equid-Nexus® model are regarded for their individuality as sentient beings capable of making choices, giving consent, and bringing their unique personality and histories with them into the arena and within their interactions with clients. The best therapy horses are those who are allowed to be horses and are not coerced to perform, appease, or comply out of fear—and thereby pushed to live in a state of dissociation.

A regulated horse's Self-energy acts as a prism for clients to experience being seen and witnessed by another and as a reflection that illuminates their own sense of their core Self. Being *attuned to* and *engaged with* in silence supports the client's felt sense of connection with another and fosters awareness of the Self. Communication involves the body and all channels of sensory input, which is a bottom-up approach and a present-centered orientation.

This chapter offers a fundamental understanding of the model by providing information on the Scaffolding Steps and how IFS-Informed EMDR can be adapted to work with horses. A case study is presented to provide a snapshot into session flow. The intention is to bring equine-engaged psychotherapy to the attention of the IFS and EMDR communities with the hope that we can collectively expand the field with more Diversity, Equity, Inclusion, and Belonging, which are desperately needed.

DOI: 10.4324/9781003541554-29

The Scaffolding Steps as a Blueprint for Facilitation

The Scaffolding Steps are a blueprint to support facilitators to conceptualize and guide the process of an organic unfolding interaction both internally within the client's system and externally while fostering a relationship with the horse. The intention is for the client to hold *functional dual attention*[1] with their activated parts from Self while experiencing new relational learning and connection in the present moment that creates new neuropathways in the brain. This process supports growth and healing for the human *and* the horse.

In the therapy office, IFS-Informed EMDR therapy focuses on the client increasing Self-energy to befriend protectors and gain permission to witness and unburden exiles. EMDR's eight-phase protocol guides this process and uses bilateral stimulation (BLS) to effectively process memories and emotional material that have become embedded or stuck in the nervous system. The therapist facilitates the process by assisting the client in creating a Self-to-part relationship, which then allows the client to give their tender parts the compassion, witnessing, and connection that they did not have when the parts became burdened. The therapist extends their Self-energy and presence to the client to scaffold the client's Self-energy, with the focus being on increasing the client's connection and relationship with their own Self-energy.

The therapeutic process can be long and arduous for clients with complex trauma, who have little access to Self-energy and highly protective systems. Commonly, these internal systems do not trust the client or the therapist due to relational trauma. These clients operate from protective parts within relationships and respond from these parts' perspectives, which are frozen in time. Parts that project or have transference responses are misattuned to current interactions, leading to confusion and frustration for both people (or people and animals) when relating with one another. This reinforces feelings of stuckness and the client's negative beliefs about themselves, others, and the world, resulting in more loneliness and disconnection. Relational trauma is healed within a relationship with another *and simultaneously* within the client's own internal system with the Self at the helm. To create a juxtaposition there would need to be something that provides contradicting information, to disprove the danger of what the protector part fears the most—connecting with another person. This is where the horse trots in.

There is an inherent power differential within the therapeutic relationship, as it is transactional in nature. The client is paying the therapist for their time and expertise in the delivery of interventions to support their emotional healing and well-being. The client's relationship with the therapist can be reflective of their relationships with others. While some therapists are taught to directly work with projections, transferences, and re-enactments, the "U-turn" is used in IFS (see Chapters 20 and 21). This is an incredibly valuable technique in the therapy room but it can be difficult for clients to put into practice in their daily lives. Unlike in the therapist–client relationship, the horse will react to the client and provide instant feedback based on the parts that are showing up (which are oftentimes very similar to people in the client's life).

The therapist is present to guide the client in identifying when they are interacting from a part and to help them unblend. This provides the client the opportunity to notice parts that become activated within the present relationship, become curious about those parts, and begin to interact with the horse from an unblended state. In this way, the client receives *different feedback* and creates a new emotional learning experience. As clients interact from a Self-Led place, they accumulate evidence that relationships could be different, and are also able to practice rupture and repair in real time.

The Equid-Nexus® model uses *Eight Scaffolding Steps* to assist the client in working through unhelpful behavioral patterns that lead to fracture, disconnection, and re-enactment of past relationships. The intention is **engaged connection between the Self of the client and the "Self" of the horse.** The Self of the horse can be conceptualized by considering the regulation state of horses, and this also provides a context for what occurs when "parts" of the horse are activated (i.e., dysregulation). Regulated horses are in a state of calm awareness and Self-presence. Dysregulated horses may be operating from fear and protection. It is important to express that using parts language to describe horses' behavior is not intended to anthropomorphize them. Instead, the offering here is to provide context and IFS nomenclature to highlight the horse's uniqueness and how horses can bring their own personalities and histories into focus through their behaviors.

Horses are prey animals, and therefore have many survival and protective strategies that could be considered (defensive) parts. Horses read intention and behave in ways that have helped them in the past to survive, but which may not be adaptable in the moment with our client (or our client's parts). It is beneficial to use parts language for horses to help the client not take ownership when the horse is reacting from their own past history and trauma. This understanding and valuing of the horse as a sentient being is the hallmark of Self-Led Horsemanship™. This informs all of the ethical considerations of equines and humans interacting, in a courageous space, with the intention of co-creating a healing experience of secure attachment, mutually beneficial for both. The 12 A's of Self-Led Horsemanship™ are *Attention, Acknowledgment, Awareness, Attunement, Authenticity, Articulation, Attachment, Affirming, Accountability, Appreciation, Advocacy*, and *Alliance*.[2]

The foundation of the Scaffolding Steps is adapted from Bruce Hersey's IFS-Informed EMDR model (see Chapter 6) and integrated with equine engagement. Hersey, co-founder of the Syzygy Institute, has carefully crafted an integration of IFS, EMDR, and Coherence Therapy that combines the relational aspect of IFS, the science of EMDR and a "neuroplastic reset" from Coherence Therapy.

The Scaffolding Steps

The Eight Scaffolding Steps (see Box 24.1) have fidelity to the eight phases, with a two-prong approach of focusing on the past and present. It is important to note that some elements have been modified to focus on an alive and present relational interaction between client and horse, which is fluid and not linear. Instead of rehearsing or resourcing a future template, the client is encouraged to consider what would further support the engaged connection with the horse based upon the current state of their relationship. See Appendix 24.A for a Decision Tree which outlines this process.

Embedded in the steps is the assumption that the target part, at least initially, is a protector. There are other variables, such as blended-ness of the client and having little access to Self-energy, that may necessitate working within one step for a longer length of time, or going through the steps in a nonlinear manner. In addition, how the horses show up is another variable within an experiential practice. The intention is to understand the components of the model while practicing the art of working with what is alive in the moment, trusting the wisdom of the client's system, and being flexible. Below is a review of each step.

Step 1: Explore the Internal Landscape

Akin to EMDR **Phase 1** (history-taking and treatment planning), the therapist asks the client, "What would you like to work on? What are your hopes of how this therapy can benefit you?" As clients discuss their challenges, the

---

Box 24.1 The Eight Scaffolding Steps

1 Explore the internal landscape.
2 Increase Self-connection and differentiation of Self-energy and parts.
3 Facilitate equine engagement.
4 Identify the target part (not a target memory).
5 Guide the discovery process when working with protectors.
6 Support building relational consciousness through intersubjectivity and the Self-Led HorsemanshipTM perspective.
7 Corrective relational engagement working with exiles.
8 Reconsolidation.

therapist listens for what parts emerge connected to the different issues. The therapist and client then explore the parts that are organized around the situation, pattern, belief, energy, urge, or memory. The therapist then maps the constellation of parts to understand the protective system of the client, while building trust and rapport with the client.

Step 2: Increase Self-Connection and Differentiation of Self-energy and Parts

As with EMDR's **Phase 2** (preparation) and Phase 2 in the Hersey model of IFS-Informed EMDR (see Chapter 6), this step is aimed to draw out and strengthen the client's Self, to resource elements of Self-energy and to increase Self-presence, which is an essential ingredient for functional dual attention. Resourcing Self-energy with BLS can be done throughout the therapeutic process and is done in different ways (described later in this chapter). The therapist reflects back the Self qualities as the client explores (Curiosity, Compassion, Clarity, Creativity, Courage, Connection, Calm, Confidence). Hersey's *Presence of Self Scale* (PoS: 1–7) can be used to gauge a critical mass of Self and identify other parts that may be blended. The therapist is also listening for adaptive/positive beliefs that come from the Self rather than from parts. The intention is for the client to connect with Self-energy and start to understand that their reactions are based on beliefs, emotions, and experiences held by parts of themselves.

Step 3: Facilitate Equine Engagement

This step corresponds to the EMDR's **assessment phase (3)** and Phase 2.5, the Discovery phase in the Hersey model (see Chapter 7). At this point in the process, the mental health and equine professionals guide the horse and client interaction. It is important to note that as the horse and human become acquainted with one another, it is common for clients to be blended with some of their parts. Parts will often see and interact with the horse from the lens of their previous experiences in relationships. The therapist can begin to notice patterns, projections, transference and re-enactments with the horse. The equine professional (EP) will track the responses and parts of the horse and uphold the Self-Led Horsemanship™ Perspective. The EP is an anchor for the horse during the session and extends Self-energy to the horse before, during, and after the session. The EP expresses observations around the interactions between the horse and human, and what the client is experiencing, but there are no interpretations. The intention is to hold the space with Self-energy while gathering information on the elements of the experience such as memories, images, body sensations, negative belief(s), and/or cognitions.

Step 4: Identify the Target Part (Not a Target Memory)

It is important to note that given the organic unfolding of an equine-engaged psychotherapy session, the target part may have already been identified during the previous step(s) (such as a significantly blended protector), but often other parts may blend with the client before the part that needs the most healing is identified. When the client has a critical mass of Self-energy and can hold functional dual attention, the six F's are used with insight-oriented processing to flesh out the details of the part. The *target part is the part with the most energy*; as Hersey calls it, "the biggest part in the room." This may not be the part the client (blended with a part) says they want to work on. When the target part is identified, ask the client to check with their system to see if there are any parts, known or unknown, that have any concerns with focusing on this part. This is respectful to the system and builds trust. It also helps to identify any other parts in the constellation, to prevent backlash.

Step 5: Guide the Discovery Process When Working with Protectors

This step illuminates the aliveness and power of blending IFS-Informed EMDR with Equine Engagement. Reflective of the term used in Coherence Therapy, *discovery* in this context is the combination of the new experiences and emotional learning from being in relationship with the horse that creates the juxtaposition or mismatch in the client's past lived experience. The *negative cognition comes from the part*, and the Self holds the *disconfirming knowledge* from the present day. This helps to "rewrite" emotional learning. The protector is befriended and asked about its fears if it does not do its job, hence gathering what Hersey calls the "Protector Positive Intention (PPI)." *Implicit direct access* is used when the client is strongly blended, and shifting back to insight-oriented processing is optimal when the client achieves a critical mass of Self-energy. The client then can engage in new behaviors and experience a different outcome than in the past, since they are practicing engaging from Self, instead of from the fear of the part.

Step 6: Support Building Relational Consciousness through Intersubjectivity and the Self-Led Horsemanship™ Perspective

Intersubjectivity is a critical element in the treatment and healing of relational trauma (see Chapter 9).

The theory of intersubjectivity "is the idea of the fundamental context dependency of all psychological life," and that "a person's experience is at all times determined by and dependent upon the specific intersubjective contexts in which it takes shape and by which it is sustained (or not)" (Hagman et al., 2019, p. 7). While the Self has every imaginable *internal* resource, people live in the context of relationship with others and are interpersonal beings. Relational wounding and developmental trauma require the Self of the individual to connect with its protectors and exiles to facilitate healing and provide a redo to give the part what it needed at the time but did not receive. Building and earning secure attachment with another requires courage and confidence that emerges from Self-energy. Another essential ingredient is being able to attune to and be present with another and being curious about their internal world and the context in which they perceive things. The intention of this step is for the client and the horse to experience each other in the present instead of through parts' projections.

Building relational consciousness through intersubjectivity is achieved when the client can be aware of their own system *and* attune to the horse and understand the behavior or feedback from the horse's perspective and subjective experience. This helps with differentiation between a client's parts that are forecasting and making meaning of the interaction, and being Self-Led, to really "hear" the horse's response from their subjective context.

Step 7: Corrective Relational Engagement: Working with Exiles

This step combines EMDR's **Phase 4, desensitization** and **Phase 5, installation**. The client is witnessed by the horse, and the part is witnessed by the client's Self-presence. This results in unburdening protector and exile trauma energy, and gives new evidence to update the system on connection and building secure attachment in relationships. These corrective experiences heal relational trauma.

Body scans (Phase 6) are used throughout the steps to identify parts and Self-energy, and to increase awareness of the embodied experience of engaged connection with another.

Bilateral stimulation (BLS) can be used throughout the process, and in different ways, which are dependent upon the connection with the horse *and the horse's connection with the client*. It is facilitated with engaged connection with the horse as a *witness—not as a tool for movement while walking*. Butterfly tapping or wireless tappers can also be used throughout the process. BLS can be facilitated on the ground or mounted. The regulating and resourcing components of BLS also help us become in sync with the horse. As shared by the Natural Lifemanship Institute,[3] rhythmic, predictable, and consistent movement with the horse increases brain integration and regulation. It also increases Self-presence in the horse and the human.

Interweaves: The horse also provides valuable feedback for interweaves when the client becomes blended, loses dual attention, or is unburdening a part within their system. Often the horse will stop, speed up, slow down, or nudge the EP. These could loosely be considered BLS "sets." The EP continues to attune to the horse's responses and supports the horse if they are having difficulty with the client's emotions or maintaining connection. The EP also discerns if the horse is responding to the client or a "part" within the horse that is becoming activated. Throughout this process the EP is constantly attuning to their own systems and working with their parts as well throughout the session (see Chapters 20 and 21).

Since the intentions are to resource the system, befriend parts, or witness the exile's story, trauma material, not parts, are desensitized. Sometimes spontaneous unburdenings occur. The horse is a powerful contributor to the client's healing, as the horse can become both a "hope merchant" and a witness to the client's process (which becomes inter-relational with the horse).

Step 8: Reconsolidation

This step corresponds with EMDR's **Phase 7, closure,** and refers to the process of neuroplasticity and brain integration during and after the session. The internal system is reorganizing and recalibrating with the work done within the session and as the brain encodes new experiences. Each session begins with a **re-evaluation (Phase 8)** discussion about what the client noticed about their parts and changes in their system in between the sessions. This is explored before re-engaging with the horse.

Case Example: Dora[4]

Dora is a 30-year-old woman who experienced significant sexual and physical abuse from her father as well as neglect and emotional abuse from her mother from infancy to age nine. She had strong transference reactions to Rocky, one of my horses in the program. Dora processed that he reminded her of both of her parents. His hair reminded her of her mother, and his being male and "having male parts" reminded her of her father. At that time, Dora would freeze and dissociate when she was within 50 feet of Rocky. Even if he was not in sight, just knowing he was there or hearing him was enough to increase the fear inside parts of Dora that worried Dora would become trapped, abused, and objectified by Rocky. Although Dora cognitively knew Rocky was not her parents and would not harm her in a similar way, Dora's parts were convinced otherwise. These parts would hijack her and completely obscure her Self-energy. She also had parts that dissociated her from her body, and thus she moved arrhythmically, illustrating her dysregulated nervous system. In addition to all of this, Dora believed that all of her "Self" had been cast out by abuse, and she therefore did not possess Self-energy that could be accessed.

For all of these reasons, Dora chose to work with another horse, named Pearl. Pearl is a white miniature horse and is at my farm along with Pearl's son, Junior. Pearl reminded Dora of the horse that she had initially worked with at my farm, Casper, before Casper passed away. Casper was a very large white thoroughbred, and engaged with Dora in a way Dora had never before experienced. Casper's calmness, attunement, patience, and presence supported Dora's healing at her parts' pace. Casper was a hope merchant, a witness to her pain, and a partner for Dora, as Dora explored identifying and setting boundaries. Casper was an anchor and supported Dora with co-regulation to help move the trauma/burden energy out of her body. Casper was truly a lighthouse of Self-energy.

Pearl helped Dora's parts grieve the loss of Casper. Through their work, Dora was able to express her grief and build a new relationship that was based in the present, instead of transference from her relationship with Casper. She was able to identify that Pearl is her own unique individual and although she was drawn to Pearl by the way Pearl looked (like Casper), Dora realized that her parts were also drawn to something else. Pearl had her own grief as she had lost a newborn foal prior to Junior being born. Horses grieve in their own ways, and this can be witnessed through behavior changes, emotional distress, changes in the dynamic of the herd, eating habits, and even relationships with their humans.

Dora said that she didn't feel so alone; she had a felt sense that Pearl understood her grief. Pearl would become very still and co-regulate Dora when Dora was able to tune into her grief—Pearl even put her head on Dora's heart as if telling her she could feel the pain within her. Dora and her parts grieved for Casper, and Dora was able to connect with parts that missed Casper and had felt protected by him. Through the processing of this grief, Dora's Self-energy began to emerge again with Pearl, just as it had done initially with Casper. Dora shared, "I found a strength within me which increased when I worked with Casper. Pearl is helping me to reconnect with that strength inside me."

Dora continued her work with Pearl and gained strength and Self-energy from their attuned and connected relationship. When her parts were ready, we revisited having another session with Rocky.

Step 1: Identify the Internal Landscape

Dora and I identified the constellation of parts organized around working with Rocky. She had parts that were afraid she would freeze again, feel "icky," and be overwhelmed with terror. Dora also had a part that was worried that she would "go backwards" in her healing if she worked with Rocky again.

Step 2: Increase Self-Connection and Differentiation of Self and Parts and Discovery—2.5[5]

Before seeing Rocky during session one day, Dora worked with Pearl to help increase her Self-energy and work with nervous parts that were fearful about seeing Rocky. I asked Pearl to connect with me by walking around the arena and suggested that Dora's intention could be to focus on Pearl, while engaging in the bilateral stimulation of walking. Dora focused on her breathing (brainstem) and stepping rhythmically (diencephalon) with Pearl's pace. She was aware of Pearl and her state of being (limbic system). She also talked with Pearl (neocortex) as we walked. These pieces helped Dora integrate these different parts of her brain[6] to increase regulation.

Pearl would intuitively stop when Dora became dysregulated, blended, or lost connection with Pearl. I would increase my connection with Pearl during these moments and be curious as to what Dora was experiencing. I asked Dora how she felt toward Pearl, and with positive Self-Led responses we continued to walk. Dora was able to increase her awareness and functional dual attention with Pearl in the present, and connect with and reassure the parts of her that were fearful to see Rocky. To facilitate this process, I guided Dora's attention to Pearl (her breathing, her eyes and ears, and how she was listening to Dora) and had Dora focus on the felt sense of that awareness and presence. I asked Dora to "go with that" while walking. It took time for Dora to unblend from her fearful parts. The adaptive belief from Self was "I am an adult, and I can protect myself."

Step 3: Identify the Target Part

The "biggest part in the room" for Dora was a dissociative part that believed that Dora would be rendered helpless by the terror the exile was carrying. The *protector's positive intention* (PPI) was to freeze her in dangerous situations and to erase her memory (the protector's *solution*); otherwise, the part believed Dora would die from the shame and disgust from her abuse (the *problem—the exile's burdens*). The part's *Level of Urge to Protect* (LUP; see Chapter 6) began at 10/10 and reduced to 3/10. With BLS, this part contracted to observe instead of overwhelming Dora. Dora had a critical mass of Self-energy when she was ready to approach Rocky in his paddock. Dora was not fully unblended, but had enough Self-presence to maintain functional dual attention.

Step 4: Facilitation of Equine Engagement

As Dora and I approached Rocky, I used Hersey's *Level of Urge to Protect* (LUP 0–10) scale to gauge the protector's distress whenever I noticed Dora was becoming tense or frozen. We used the tappers to help Dora regulate and gain some internal space. It took some time, along with IFS interweaves, to support Dora while we walked toward Rocky's paddock. When we arrived in front of the gate Rocky was about 20 feet away. He turned and looked at Dora and then very slowly walked forward as he breathed softly and lowered his head. Rocky arrived at the gate, closed his eyes and breathed out deeply.

JP: What are you noticing?
D: I think he remembers me and I'm glad he moved slowly.
JP: What are you noticing in or around your body? (FIND)
D: My shoulders are tense, and I can feel the anxiety in my arms and wrists.
JP: Is it okay if we focus on that? (FOCUS)
D: Yes. It is a warning. Parts are afraid but I'm reminding them that there is a fence between us.
JP: How did they respond? (supporting the Self-to-part relationship)
D: They noticed that he is behind the fence, so they settled down a bit.

Rocky looked at me as Dora connected with her parts. I noticed the tenderness I have for him in my heart and extended that to him in support and co-regulation. I held connection with him while Dora was inside with her system.

JP: How do you feel towards Rocky right now? (FEEL TOWARDS)
D: He is a horse. (Dora unblended and was a bit surprised at this realization.)

JP: What do you notice as you hold the realization and the new per-spective that he is "just" a horse?

D: I feel relieved and another part of me can't believe it. Can't believe that I don't see him as a perpetrator. Instead, he is your horse, and he was Casper's friend.

JP: Where do you feel the relief?

D: Um, in my heart.

JP: Does it feel right to tap that in? (Asking for permission and con-sent to increase positive affect.)

D: Yes.

As Dora was tapping in the new belief (from Self) that Rocky is a horse and not a perpetrator, Rocky moved a little closer to the fence. After Dora was done with a set of BLS and resourcing in this new belief, she moved a little closer to him and gently looked him in the eyes. Rocky breathed out and looked at me and then looked back at her. Rocky then rubbed his head on his leg and yawned, releasing the pressure and energy from his body. Dora saw this and said, "he looks relieved too."

Step 5: The Discovery Process

I then guided Dora to turn her attention to Rocky while staying aware of the parts that did not yet believe that Rocky would not hurt Dora, the way Dora's parents had. I asked Dora to notice Rocky's behavior of releasing the energy from his body.

JP: What do you notice about Rocky now?

D: He seems a little relieved that I am not terrified of him. (Reduction of transference.)

JP: Can your parts look through your eyes and notice his relief? (More differentiation and connecting with her parts.)

D: Yes, they are a little afraid, but I told them I'm here and you're here, so they are okay. He seems a lot smaller than I remember ... his eyes are brown instead of black. Like the darkness I have inside of me from him [her father]. (Perspective is shifting with increased Self-presence.)

JP: What is it like to see him as a smaller horse with brown eyes?

D: I feel bad that I was so afraid of him and made him out to be a monster.

No sooner than her sentence ended, Rocky put his nose through the wooden fence and softly nickered.

D: Oh! That was cute!

I smiled and nodded. A number of my parts felt the relief and joy that Dora finally felt safe and saw Rocky the way I did: A loving horse that just wants to be connected and to feel safe. Rocky had come from a hoarding situation and had experienced his own trauma of neglect and physical abuse. It took him a long time to learn to trust and work toward having a regulated nervous system and an integrated brain. His behavior now reflects earned secure attachment within our relationship.

For the remaining minutes of this session, Dora expressed that she never thought she would be able to stand in front of Rocky and stay present. They had a few more exchanges, and then Rocky moved away from the fence and toward his herd mate. After this session, Dora journaled about her experience with Rocky and continued to connect with and update her parts.

Step 6: Building Relational Consciousness and Step 7: Corrective Relational Engagement

Over the next several sessions Dora progressed closer to Rocky, both in proximity and emotionally. At times when a protective part (freeze response) would blend with Dora, Rocky would become a little dysregulated and start to nudge me. This was his sign that he needed connection, as he couldn't feel Dora's energy when she would dissociate. Rocky's expression of dysregulation was illustrative of his anxious attachment; although this has transformed over time, his fear still became activated when he was interacting with dissociating clients. He and I continued to work on integrating his brain through our connection before, during, and after sessions. Rocky's dysregulation helped Dora to realize that he has also experienced trauma and has difficulties in relationships. This made him less threatening and increased Dora's compassion for him. It also helped Dora have more compassion for her parts that had experienced abuse from her parents, and created more space within her system. She was able to be more aware of Rocky's subjective experience as she expressed that it must have been difficult for him to lose Casper. It was very difficult for Rocky, and it was appropriate for me to share some of his reactions to his loss. Dora connected the loss of her grandfather with Rocky's loss of Casper. She was unable to get to the emotions to grieve her grandfather until this session with Rocky. Rocky witnessed Dora's pain and unburdening process with attentive reverence as he stood quietly by her side.

Step 8: Reconsolidation

Since Rocky is a sensitive horse, he attuned to Dora in a way that was pronounced, which was helpful as she had difficulty reading subtle cues. The experiences with Rocky helped her realize that she had a voice and choice, and that she was strong and could make the best decisions for herself. This resulted in Dora being more assertive at work and within relationships, upholding boundaries with others, and going out with friends more often instead of isolating. This was a real turning point for Dora in therapy, and she continues to work with Rocky and Pearl as she continues on her journey of post-traumatic recovery and growth.

A Movement Toward Healing

While the Self has *every internal resource*, humans are interactive and interpersonal beings that are wired for connection. The Equid-Nexus→ model supports Self-Led Facilitators in blending IFS-Informed EMDR with Equine Engagement to heal relational trauma and increase capacity for earned secure attachment through engaged connection between horse and human. Upholding the ethics and principles of Self-Led Horsemanship™ supports the horse as a sentient being in their work with clients. It is critical that mental health and equine professionals do their own personal work to know their systems so they can truly hold the space for the unfolding interactions between human and horse. In addition, and in the spirit of vitality and further growth and research in this field, a call to action is warranted to increase Diversity, Equity, Inclusion, and Belonging. To achieve an intersubjective perspective, therapists need to become more educated on other cultures of the clients we serve.

A Call to Action

Many chapters in this book recognize and highlight the importance of DEI and anti-racist practices (see Chapters 9 and 10) and the importance of being connected with ourselves by doing this transformative work (see Chapters 20 and 21).

This book is an invitation to join us on the journey of healing. The encouragement is to continue to dedicate and invest in yourself for ongoing growth and learning. Perhaps it might be through the Equid-Nexus→ training organization, or one of the many other incredible offerings presented in this book. The authors of this book wish you connection and inner peace as you walk beside your clients on the sacred journey of trauma healing.

Notes

1 This is a term from Bruce Hersey, Syzygy Institute (see Chapter 6; Hersey, 2022).
2 All of these are detailed in the Equid-Nexus® training manual (Pagone, 2022).
3 Found on their website: www.naturallifemanship.com.
4 I first described this case in my contribution to "Chapter 8: Blended Therapy Modalities in Equine-Assisted Psychotherapy: Integrating Equine-Engaged Internal Family Systems (EE-IFS) and Equine-Connected Eye Movement Desensitization and Reprocessing (EC-EMDR)," in the book *Integrating Horses into Healing*, ed. D. Meola (Pagone and Cho, 2023). What follows is an offering on Dora's continued post-traumatic growth and recovery journey. All names and client information has been changed to maintain confidentiality.
5 See Chapters 6 and 7.
6 Found on their website: www.naturallifemanship.com.

References

Hagman, G., Paul, H., & Zimmermann, P. B. (2019). *Intersubjective psychology: A primer*. Routledge.

Hersey, B. (2022). *Syzygy Institute: Steps 1–3 Workshops*. https://www.syzygyinstitute.com/trainingprogram.

Pagone, J., & Choe, K. (2023). Blended modalities in equine assisted psychotherapy: Integrating Equine-Engaged Internal Family Systems (EE-IFS) and Equine-Connected Eye Movement Desensitization Reprocessing (EC-EMDR) into the natural lifemanship practice of equine assisted psychotherapy (EAP). In C. Meola (Ed.), *Integrating horses into healing*. Elsevier.

Pagone, J. (2022). *Equid-Nexus® self-led facilitation training manual*. Marengo, IL: Equid-Nexus, LLC Publications.

APPENDIX 24.A: EQUID-NEXUS® SCAFFOLDING STEPS DECISION TREE

This Decision Tree (see Figure 24.1) illustrates some of the variations of the flow of the model—namely, whether the target part is a protector or an exile, and when the target part is identified. While these steps scaffold the process of the intention of the client's Self engaging with the horse's Self, there are many ways it unfolds in this experiential process.

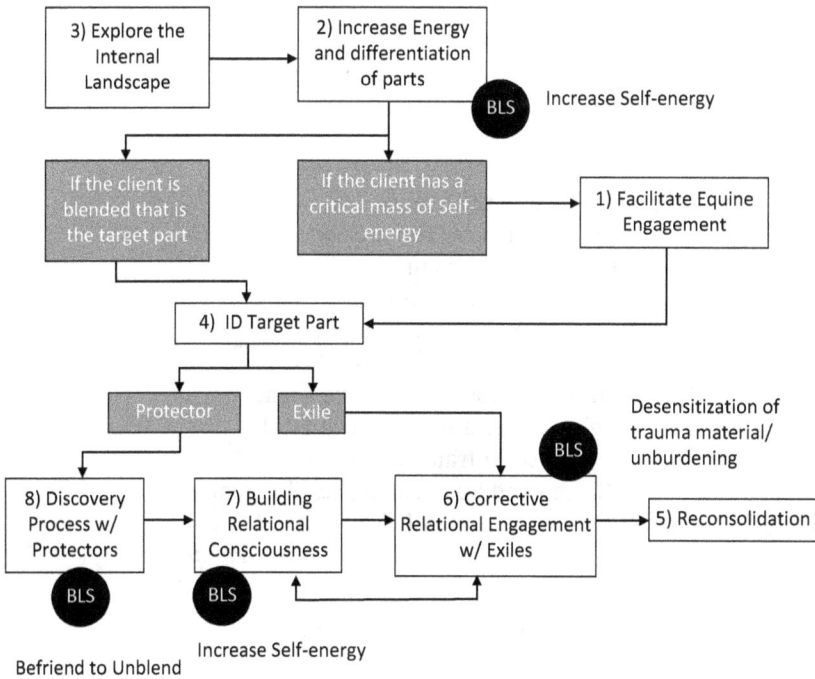

Figure 24.1 Decision Tree.

Source: Jenn Pagone.

Revolutionary Love

Please remember, you are not broken.
Everything you need, has always been
Inside. Your Value, your Worth.
Known by the Trees, the Rivers
The Sun and the Moon.
The Air whispers, You are Seen
And Loved. Your inner family
Of parts, Fellow creatures,
With Vulnerabilities, Strengths
All Longing for connection
With you. Allow your Gentle Light
To glisten. Trust that this will Heal
And transport trauma back to
A Sacred and Spiritual Space, illuminated
With Revolutionary Love.

By David Polidi

Index

For Product Safety Concerns and Information please contact our EU
representative GPSR@taylorandfrancis.com
Taylor & Francis Verlag GmbH, Kaufingerstraße 24, 80331 München, Germany